Behavior Analysis

Behavior Analysis
Foundations and Applications to Psychology

Julian C. Leslie
University of Ulster, Northern Ireland
and
Mark F. O'Reilly
University College Dublin, Ireland

harwood academic publishers
Australia • Canada • China • France • Germany • India
Japan • Luxembourg • Malaysia • The Netherlands
Russia • Singapore • Switzerland

Copyright © 1999 OPA (Overseas Publishers Association) N.V. Published by license under the Harwood Academic Publishers imprint, part of The Gordon and Breach Publishing Group.

Amsteldijk 166
1st Floor
1079 LH Amsterdam
The Netherlands

British Library Cataloguing in Publication Data
A catalogue record for this book is available from the British Library.

ISBN: 90-5702-486-1 (Softcover)

Contents

List of Figures

List of Figures

List of Tables

Preface

Behavior analysis is the natural science approach to the study of the behavior of organisms. It is an active and productive discipline within the general field of psychology. As a scientific discipline, behavior analysis is concerned with three general issues: the examination and elucidation of the theoretical underpinnings of the science; the experimental analysis of the basic principles that govern behavior; and the application of the basic principles of behavior to issues of personal and social importance. As the discipline developed, many behavioral psychologists began to focus their studies on one aspect of the discipline (e.g., applied behavior analysis) to the exclusion of other aspects (e.g., experimental analysis of basic principles). While such specialization is a healthy sign of growth within a discipline, it can lead to fragmentation, with, for example, developments in basic research going unnoticed by applied psychologists. For a scientific discipline to continue to develop, new findings from basic research must inform and fuel the development and evaluation of new applied technologies. Additionally, problems with the application of basic principles to applied settings, and the general findings of applied research, should inform and spur the development of some basic research programs. Specialization is important for a discipline but it must occur within the context of collaborative research links across subspecializations.

This book is a collaborative venture between two behavioral scientists, one who specializes in basic research (JCL) while the other focuses on applied research (MFO'R). Both of us teach behavior analysis to university students at undergraduate and postgraduate levels. For several years we lamented that while there were many excellent textbooks available for students of this discipline there was a need for a textbook that introduced students to the experimental methods, classic research findings, recent research findings, and current research questions in both the basic and applied dimensions of the discipline. We reasoned that such a textbook might foster the perception among students of the essential inherent link between basic and applied science in behavior analysis. This textbook is the culmination of our efforts to achieve this goal. We hope that it will be useful not only to psychology students, but also to all professionals, and those in training, that come to applied behavior analysis from a variety of backgrounds.

Acknowledgments

My contribution to this book was made possible by a University College Dublin Presidents Research Fellowship. Special thanks are due to Al Healy of the University of Iowa, and Terry Dolan of the University of Wisconsin, who gave me the space and facilities to complete my contribution. I want to thank Dave Wacker for his feedback while I was at the University of Iowa. I also want to thank those who taught me about behavior analysis and those who continue to contribute to my learning, including: Julian Leslie, Chris Simms, Tony Cuvo, Gina Green, Janis Chadsey-Rusch, Frank Rusch, Adelle Renzaglia, Jim Halle, Giulio Lancioni, and Jeff Sigafoos. A special thanks to my mother-in-law Eva Bernard for those hot dishes on cold Minnesota nights. Last but not least, to my wife and kids, Bonnie, Aoife, Cian, and Aisling, thanks for your patience.

Mark F. O'Reilly

My contribution to this book developed out of my earlier volume, *Principles of Behavioral Analysis* (published by Harwood Academic Publishers, in 1996), which in turn was a product of many interactions with teachers, colleagues and students since Jock Millenson first taught me about behavior analysis. I am indebted to Mark O'Reilly for his vision as to how this book should be constructed, and for teaching me a lot about applied issues as we put it together. Incidental interactions with Derek Blackman over the same period helped me focus on central issues in the experimental analysis of behavior. I am indebted to my family, Rosanne, Edward and Rowan, for their love and support.

Julian C. Leslie

We would like to thank the following for permission to reproduce copyrighted material.

American Psychological Association: Figure 6.7 from Bandura, A. (1965). Influence of model's reinforcement contingencies on the acquisition of imitative responses. *Journal of Personality and Social Psychology*, **1**, 589–595.

Academic Press: Figure 6.4 from Warren, J.M. (1965). Primate learning in comparative perspective. In A.M. Schrier, H.F. Harlow, and F. Stollnitz (Eds.) *Behavior of nonhuman primates.* New York: Academic Press, pp. 249–281.

American Association for the Advancement of Science: Figure 3.8 from Gormezano, I., Schneiderman, N., Deaux, E.B., and Fuentes, I. (1962). Nictitating membrane: Classical conditioning and extinction in the albino rabbit. *Science,* **138**, 33–34. Figure 10.1 from Neisworth, J. T. and Moore, F. (1972). Operant treatment of asthmatic responding with the parent as therapist. *Behavior Therapy,* **3**, 95–99.

J.S Bruner: Figure 6.6 from Bruner, J.S., Goodnow, J.J., and Austin, G. (1956). *A study of thinking.* New York: Wiley.

Macmillan Journals Limited (London): Figure 6.5 from Dennis, I., Hampton, J.A., and Lea, S.E.G. (1973). New problem in concept formation. *Nature* (London), **243**, 101–102.

Elsevier Science: Figure 10.8 from Peine, H. A., *et al.* (1991). The use of contingent water misting in the treatment of self-choking. *Journal of Behavior Therapy and Experimental Psychiatry,* **22**, 225–231.

B.F. Skinner Foundation: Figures 2.4, 3.1, and 3.10 from Skinner, B.F. (1938). *The behavior of organisms.* New York: Appleton-Century-Crofts. Figure 4.5 from Ferster, C.B. and Skinner, B.F. (1957). *Schedules of reinforcement.* New York: Appleton-Century-Crofts.

Society for the Experimental Analysis of Behavior: From the *Journal of the Experimental Analysis of Behavior:* Figure 3.4 from Azrin, N.H., Hutchinson, R.R., and Hake, D.F. (1966). Extinction-induced aggression. **9**, 191–204. Figure 4.8 from Hearst, E., Besley, S., and Farthing, G.W. (1970). Inhibition and the stimulus control of operant behavior. **14**, 373–409. Figure 5.2 from Dinsmoor, J.A. and Winograd, E. (1958). Shock intensity in variable interval escape schedules. **1**, 145–148. Figure 5.5 from Verhave, T. (1959). Avoidance responding as a function of simultaneous and equal changes in two temporal parameters. **2**, 185–190. Figure 5.7 from Bradshaw, C.M., Szabadi, E., and Bevan, P. (1977). Effects of punishment on human variable-interval performance. **27**, 275–280. Figure 6.8 from Baer, D.M., Peterson, R., and Sherman, J. (1967). The development of imitation by reinforcing behavioral similarity to a model. **10**, 405–416. Figure 9.5 from Ayllon, T. and Azrin, N.H. (1965). The measurement and reinforcement of behavior of psychotics. **8**, 357–383. Figure 11.9 from Kuno, H., Kitadate, T., and Iwamoto, T. (1994). Formation of transitivity in conditional matching to sample by pigeons. **62**, 399–408. Figure 11.7 from Beardsley, S.D. and McDowell, J.J. (1992). Application of Herrnstein hyperbola to time allocation of naturalistic human-behavior maintained by naturalistic social-reinforcement. **52**, 177–185.

From the *Journal of Applied Behavior Analysis*: Table 7.1 from Taylor, I. and O'Reilly, M.F. (1997). Toward a functional analysis of private verbal self-regulation. **30**, 43–58. Table 7.2 from Friman, P.C., *et al.* (1986). Testicular self-examination: Validation of a training strategy for early cancer detection. **19**, 87–92. Figure 8.6 from Tustin, D. (1995). The effects of advance notice of activity transitions on stereotypic behavior. **28**, 91–92. Figure 8.7 from Friman, P.C. and Vollmer, D. (1995). Successful use of a nocturnal urine alarm for diurnal enuresis. **28**, 89–90. Figure 8.8 from Brigham, T.A., Meier, S.M. and Goodner, V. (1995). Increasing designated driving with a program of prompts and incentives. **28**, 83–84. Figure 8.9 from Jason, L.A. and Liotta, R.F. (1982). Reduction of cigarette smoking in a university cafeteria. **15**, 573–577. Figure 8.10 from Taylor, B.A. and Harris, S.L. (1995). Teaching children with autism to seek information: Acquisition of novel information and generalization of responding. **28**, 3–14. Figure 8. 11 from Jackson, N.C. and Mathews, M.R. (1995). Using public feedback to increase contributions to a multipurpose senior center. **28**, 449–455. Figure 8.12 from Rasing, E.J. and Duker, P.C. (1992). Effects of a multifaceted training procedure on the acquisition and generalization of social behaviors in language-disabled deaf children. **25**, 723–734. Figure 8.14 from Kennedy, C.H. and Souza, G. (1995). Functional analysis and treatment of eye poking. **28**, 27–37. Figure 8.15 from Smith, R.G., Iwata, B.A. and Shore, B.A. (1995). Effects of subject-versus experimenter-selected reinforcers on the behavior of individuals with profound developmental disabilities. **28**, 61–71. Figure 9.1 from Fisher, W., *et al.* (1992). A comparison of two approaches for identifying reinforcers for persons with severe and profound disabilities. **25**, 491–498. Figure 9.2 from Foster-Johnson, L., Ferro, J. and Dunlap, G. (1994). Preferred curricular activities and reduced problem behaviors in students with intellectual disabilities. **27**, 493–504. Figure 9.4 from Vollmer, T.R. and Iwata, B.A. (1991). Establishing operations and reinforcement effects. **24**, 279–291. Figure 9.7 from Derby, K.M., Wacker, D.P., Sasso, G., Steege, M., Northup, J., Cigrand, K. and Asmus, J. (1992). Brief functional assessment techniques to evaluate aberrant behavior in an outpatient setting: A summary of 79 cases. **25**, 713–721. Figure 9.8 from Mazaleski, J. L. *et al.* (1993). Analysis of the reinforcement and extinction components in DRO contingencies with self-injury. **26**, 143–156. Figure 9.10 from Hagopian, L.P., Fisher, W., and Legacy, S.M. (1994). Schedule effects of noncontingent reinforcement on attention-maintained destructive behavior in identical quadruplets. **27**, 317–325. Figure 9.12 from Halle, J.W., Baer, D.M., and Spradlin, J.E. (1981). Teachers' generalized use of delay as a stimulus control procedure to increase language use in handicapped children. **14**, 389–409. Figure 9.16 from Wilson, P.G., Reid, D.H., Phillips, J.F., and Burgio, L.D. (1984). Normalization of institutional mealtimes for profoundly retarded persons: Effects and noneffects of teaching family-style dining. **17**, 189–201. Figure 9.17 from Lalli, J.S., Zanolli, K., and Wohn, T. (1994). Using extinction to promote response variability in toy play. **27**, 735–736. Figure 9.18 from Hughes, C. *et al.* (1995). The effects of multiple-exemplar self-instructional training on high school students' generalized conversational interactions. **28**, 201–218. Table 9.1 from Richman, G.S. *et al.* (1984). Teaching menstrual care to mentally retarded women: Acquisition, generalization, and maintenance. **17**, 441–451. Table 9.2 from Halle, J.W., Baer, D.M. and Spradlin, J.E. (1981). Teachers' generalized use of delay as a stimulus control procedure to increase language use in handicapped children. **14**, 389–409. Table 9.3 from Zencius, A.H., Davis, P.K., and Cuvo, A.J. (1990). A personalized system of instruction for teaching checking account skills to adults with mild disabilities. **23**, 245–252. Figure 10.2 from Vollmer, T. R. *et al.* (1993). The role of attention in the treatment of attention-maintained self-injurious behavior: Noncontingent reinforcement (NCR) and differential reinforcement of other behavior (DRO). **26**, 9–26. Figure 10.3 from France, K.G. and Hudson, S.M. (1990). Behavior management of infant sleep disturbance. **23**, 91–98. Figure 10.4 from Goh, H. and Iwata, B.A. (1994). Behavioral persistence and variability during extinction of self-injury maintained by escape. **27**, 173–174. Figure 10.5 from Van Houten, R. (1993). The use of wrist weights to reduce self-injury maintained by sensory reinforcement. **26**, 197–203. Figure 10.6 from Shore, B.A. *et al.* (1997). An analysis of reinforcer substitutability using object manipulation and self-injury as competing responses. **30**, 21–41. Figure 10.7 from Iwata, B.A. *et al.* (1994). What makes extinction work: An analysis of procedural form and function. **27**, 131–144. Figure 10.10 from Porterfield, J.K., Herbert-Jackson, E., and Risley, T.R. (1976). Contingent observation: An effective and acceptable procedure for reducing disruptive behavior of young children in a group setting. **9**, 55–64. Figure 10.11 from Rolider, A. and Van Houten, R. (1985). Movement suppression time-out for undesirable behavior in psychotic and severely developmentally delayed children. **18**, 275–288.

Figure 10.12 from Haring, T.G. and Kennedy, C.H. (1990). Contextual control of problem behavior in students with severe disabilities. **23**, 235–243. Figure 10.13 from Azrin, N.H. and Wesolowski, M.D. (1974). Theft reversal: An overcorrection procedure for eliminating stealing by retarded persons. **7**, 577–581. Figure 10.14 from Luce, S.C., Delquadri, J., and Hall, R.V. (1980). Contingent exercise: A mild but powerful procedure for suppressing inappropriate verbal and aggressive behavior. **13**, 583–594. Figure 11.1 from Wagner, J.L. and Winett, R.A. (1988). Promoting one low-fat, high-fiber selection in a fast-food restaurant. **21**, 179–185. Figure 11.2 from DeLuca, R.V. and Holborn, S.W. (1992). Effects of a variable-ratio reinforcement schedule with changing criteria on exercise in obese and nonobese boys. **25**, 671–679. Figure 11.3 from DeVries, J.E., Burnette, M.M., and Redmon, W.K. (1991). Aids prevention: Improving nurses' compliance with glove wearing through performance feedback. **24**, 705–711. Figure 11.4 from Derrickson, J.G., Neef, N., and Parrish, J.M. (1991). Teaching self-administration of suctioning to children with tracheotomies. **24**, 563–570. Figure 11.5 from Fox, D.K., Hopkins, B. L., and Anger, W.K. (1987). The long-term effects of a token economy on safety performance in open-pit mining. **20**, 215–224. Figure 11.8 from Mace, C. F. *et al.* (1994). Limited matching on concurrent-schedule reinforcement of academic behavior. **27**, 585–596. Table 11.1 from Fawcett, S. B. (1991). Some values guiding community research and action. **24**, 621–636. Table 11.2 from Kennedy, C.H., Itkonen, T., and Lindquist, K. (1994). Nodality effects during equivalence class formation: An extension to sight-word reading and concept development. **27**, 673–683.

Southern Universities Press: Figure 5.2B from Barry, J.J. and Harrison, J.M. (1957). Relations between stimulus intensity and strength of escape responding. *Psychological Reports, 3*, 3–8.

Prentice-Hall Inc: Figure 4.4 from Mackintosh, N.J. (1977). Stimulus control: Attention factors. In W.K. Honig and J.E.R. Staddon (Eds.), *Handbook of operant behavior.* Englewood Cliffs, N.J.: Prentice-Hall. Figure 4.7 from Catania. A.C. (1966). Concurrent operants. In W.K. Honig (Ed.), *Operant behavior: Areas of research and application.* New York: Appleton-Century-Crofts. Figure 5.6 from Azrin, N.H. and Holz, W.C. (1966). Punishment. In W. K. Honig (Ed.), *Operant behavior: Areas of research and application.* New York: Appleton-Century-Crofts.

R.M. Hull: Figure 2.6 from Hull, C.L. (1943). *Principles of behavior.* New York: Appleton-Century-Crofts.

Council for Exceptional Children: Figure 8.13 from Bates, P., Renzaglia, A., and Clees, T. (1980). Improving the work performance of severely/ profoundly retarded young adults: The use of a changing criterion procedural design. *Education and Training of the Mentally Retarded,* **15**, 95–104.

Sage Publications: Figure 9.3 from Allen, L.D. and Iwata, B.A. (1980). Reinforcing exercise maintenance: Using existing high-rate activities. *Behavior Modification,* **4**, 337–354. Figure 9.9 from Favell, J.E., McGimsey, J. F., and Jones, M.L. (1980). Rapid eating in the retarded: Reduction by nonaversive procedures. *Behavior Modification,* **4**, 481–492.

Journal of Mental Deficiency Research: Figure 9.6 from Deitz, S.M., Repp, A. C., and Deitz, D.E.D. (1976). Reducing inappropriate classroom behavior of retarded students through three procedures of differential reinforcement. **20**, 155–170.

HarperCollins Inc.: Figure 9.11 from Grant, L. and Evans, A. (1994). *Principles of behavior analysis.* New York: HarperCollins.

Education and Treatment of Children: Figure 10.9 from Rolider, A. and Van Houten, R. (1984). The effects of DRO alone and DRO plus reprimands on the undesirable behavior of three children in home settings. **7**, 17–31.

CHAPTER 1

A SCIENTIFIC APPROACH TO BEHAVIOR

We are all very interested in what other people do, and we also want to know why people act as they do. While "common-sense explanations" about these issues are plentiful, we shall be concerned here with scientific answers to the questions raised. In the last hundred years or so, many areas of human life have been transformed by scientific and technological developments. In this first chapter, we will briefly review historical progress towards a scientific account of human behavior and a possible technology for changing human behavior.

1.1 Early Attempts to Explain Human Behavior

It is never possible to identify precisely the moment at which interest in a particular subject began, but we do know that by 325 B.C., in ancient Greece, Aristotle had combined observation and interpretation into a naturalistic, if primitive, account of behavior. Aristotle sought to understand the causes of body movements, and of the discriminations made by humans and other animals. He described many *categories* of behavior, such as sense perception, sight, smell, hearing, common sense, simple and complex thinking, appetite, memory, sleep, and dreaming. His topics sound familiar to us today, as they are still to be found in some form or other in nearly every comprehensive text of psychology. Aristotle was less interested in the prediction of events than we are today, and consequently his *explanations* of behavior have a less modern flavor. Aristotle was concerned with explaining the various activities of an individual by showing them to be specific instances of general "qualities", such as appetite, passion, reason, will, and sense-ability (Toulmin and Goodfield, 1962).

The observations and classifications of Aristotle and the Greek investigators who followed him represented a substantial beginning in a naturalistic attempt to understand the causes of human and animal behavior. However, the new science declined with the demise of Hellenic civilization. In the western world, the early Christian era and the Middle Ages produced an intellectual climate poorly suited to observation and investigation: attention was turned to metaphysical matters. The Church

1

Fathers began, and the mediaeval theologians completed, a conceptual transformation of Aristotle's purely abstract "quality" of mind into a supernatural entity named the soul. In their conceptual framework the causation of human behavior was entirely attributed to the soul, but the soul was regarded as non-material, in-substantial and super-natural.

This *dualistic* (or two-system) doctrine stated that there was no direct connection between soul and body, and that each inhabited a separate realm. By locating the causes of behavior in the unobservable realm of the spirit or soul, dualism inhibited a naturalistic study of behavior, and for a very long time no interest was taken in an empirical or observational approach to behavior. We have to jump forward to the seventeenth century, the time of Galileo and the rise of modern physics, to pick up the threads that were eventually to be rewoven into a scientific fabric.

The work of René Descartes (1596–1650), the French philosopher and mathematician, represents a critical point in the development of a science of behavior. Although Descartes produced one of the clearest statements of the dualistic position, he also advanced behavioral science by suggesting that bodily movement might be the result of mechanical, rather than supernatural, causes.

Descartes was familiar with the mechanical figures in the French royal gardens at Versailles that could move and produce sounds, and observations of these probably prompted him to put forward a mechanical account of behavior. The machines in the royal gardens worked on mechanical principles. Water was pumped through concealed tubes to inflate the limbs of the figures, producing movement, or was conducted through devices that emitted words or music as the water flowed by. Descartes imagined that animals and human beings might be a kind of complex machine, perhaps constructed in a similar way. He substituted animal spirits, a sort of intangible, invisible, elastic substance, for the water of the Royal Figures and supposed the spirits to flow in the nerves in such a way as to enter the muscles, thereby causing them to expand and contract, and in turn make the limbs move.

Some of the Royal Figures were so arranged that if passers-by happened to tread on hidden tiles, hydraulic mechanisms caused the figures to approach or withdraw. Descartes took this mechanical responsiveness as a model for explaining how an external environmental *stimulus* might cause a bodily movement. An illustration in one of his works (see Figure 1.1) shows a withdrawal of a human limb from a flame. According to Descartes, the "machine of our body is so formed that the heat of the flame excites a

Figure 1.1   Descartes' model of how an external event might cause bodily movement.

nerve which conducts that excitation to the brain. From the brain, animal spirits are then passed out, or *reflected* back via that nerve to the limb, enlarging the muscle, and so causing a contraction and withdrawal" (Fearing, 1930).

Descartes' willingness to view human behavior as determined by natural forces was only partial. He confined his mechanical hypotheses to certain "involuntary" activities and supposed the rest to be governed by the soul, located in the brain. The soul guided even the mechanisms of the "involuntary" activities, much in the way an engineer might have directed the workings of the Royal Figures.

In spite of this dualism, and in spite of his choice of a hydraulic principle, Descartes' formulation represented an advance over earlier thinking about behavior. The theory of the body as a specific kind of machine was one that was *testable by observation and experiment*. This property of "testability" was conspicuously lacking in the mediaeval explanations that preceded Descartes. In re-establishing the idea that at least some of the causes of animal and human behavior might be found in the observable environment, Descartes laid the philosophical foundations that would eventually lead to an experimental approach to behavior.

1.2 REFLEX ACTION

Descartes' views symbolize the new interest in mechanism that was to lead to experimentation on "reflected" animal action. However, a century elapsed before a Scottish physiologist, Robert Whytt, experimentally rediscovered and extended Descartes' principle of the stimulus in 1750. By observing systematic contraction of the pupil of the eye to light, salivation to irritants, and various other *reflexes*, Whytt was able to state a necessary relationship between two separate events: an external stimulus (for example, a light) and a bodily *response* (for example, a pupil contraction). Moreover, Whytt's demonstration that a number of reflexes could be elicited in the frog, even when the brain had been disconnected from the spinal cord, weakened the attractiveness of the soul as an explanation of all behavior. Yet an eighteenth-century thinker was not quite able to regard the stimulus alone as a sufficient cause of behavior in an intact, living organism. The soul, thought Whytt, probably diffused itself throughout the spinal cord and the brain thereby retaining master control of reflexes.

In the following 150 years, more and more reflex relationships were discovered and elaborated, and the concept of the stimulus grew more useful in explaining animal behavior. At the same time, nerve action became understood as an electrical system and the older hydraulic or mechanical models were discarded. By the end of the nineteenth century, spiritual direction had become superfluous for "involuntary action", and Sir Charles Sherrington, the celebrated English physiologist, could summarize the principles of reflex behavior in quantitative *stimulus-response laws*. These laws relate the speed, magnitude, and probability of the reflex response to the intensity, frequency, and other measurable properties of the stimulus. The anatomy of an example of the simplest type of reflex,

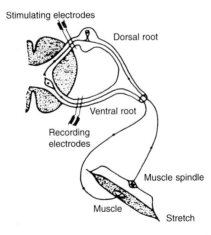

Figure 1.2   A simple reflex and its connections to the spinal cord.

consisting of two nerve cells or *neurons*, is shown in Figure 1.2. One neuron (the *afferent neuron*) transmits neural impulses resulting from the stimulus to the spinal cord and the other (the *efferent neuron*) runs from the spinal cord back to the muscle. Firing of the efferent neuron results in a motor response of the muscle.

By 1900, there could be no doubt that reflexive behavior was a suitable subject for scientific analysis and that analysis was well advanced. However, reflexes clearly accounted for only a small proportion of the behavior of human beings and so-called "higher animals", and it had yet to be established that the remainder of behavior could be subjected to the same sort of analysis.

1.3 ACQUIRED OR CONDITIONED REFLEXES

Just before the beginning of the twentieth century, Ivan Pavlov, the Russian physiologist, was carrying out experiments on the digestive secretions of dogs. He noticed that while the introduction of food or acid into the mouth resulted in a flow of saliva, the mere appearance of the experimenter bringing food would also elicit a similar flow. Pavlov was by no means the first person to make observations of this sort; but he seems to have been the first to suspect that their detailed study might provide a clue to the understanding of how animal behavior is able to adapt to circumstances. It was this insight that led him to a systematic study of these reflexes, which he called *conditional reflexes*, because they depended, or were conditional, upon some previous events in the life of the animal. The appearance of the experimenter had not originally elicited saliva. It was only after his appearance had frequently occurred along with food or acid that it had this effect. Pavlov's unique contribution was to show experimentally how *conditioned reflexes* (an early translation from the Russian rendered "conditional" as "conditioned", and this has become the normal expression) came to be acquired, how they could be removed (extinguished), and what range of stimuli was effective in their production. In time, Pavlov was to lay down a general law of conditioning: after repeated presentation of two stimuli at overlapping times, the one that occurs first comes eventually to elicit (that is, produce automatically) the response that is normally elicited by the second stimulus. A modified version of this law, or principle, is with us today.

Pavlov stated how the explanation of behavior should proceed:

The naturalist must consider only one thing: what is the relation of this or that external reaction of the animal to the phenomena of the external world? This response may be extremely complicated in comparison with the reaction of any inanimate object, but the principle involved remains the same. Strictly speaking, natural science is under obligation to determine only the precise connection which exists between a given natural phenomenon and the response of the living organism to that phenomenon... (Pavlov, 1928, p. 82).

Very often major advances in a field are the result of, or are accompanied by, methodological innovations. This is certainly true in the case of Pavlov and conditioned reflexes. Pavlov discovered that controlled *environmental conditions* were essential for successful behavioral experimentation. His dogs had to be kept in steady temperatures and in sound-proof chambers for the experiments, during which stimuli were presented in a controlled fashion and responses recorded in ways which did not interfere too much with the experimental participant. He also realized that only dogs in good general health made satisfactory participants in experiments. An illustration of the typical experimental arrangements, as used at the end of the nineteenth century, by Pavlov and his colleagues at the Institute of Experimental Medicine in Saint Petersburg appears in Figure 1.3.

The apparatus used is well described in the following passage:

First, a normal dog is familiarized with the experimental situation until he shows no disturbance when placed in harness and left alone in a room especially designed to cut off unwanted outside stimuli. A small opening or fistula is made in the dog's cheek near the duct of one of the salivary glands. When the fistula is healed, a glass funnel is carefully cemented to the

Figure 1.3   A typical arrangement for studying salivation in a conditioning experiment in Pavlov's 19th century laboratory.

outside of the cheek so that it will draw off the saliva whenever the gland is activated. From the funnel, the saliva then flows into a glass container or falls, drop by drop, upon a lightly balanced recording platform. The magnitude of responses to various stimuli can be measured by the total volume or the number of drops secreted in a given unit of time. The experimenter, who sits in an adjoining room, can make his measurements, apply what stimuli he desires (including food), and observe the dog's behavior through a window. (Keller and Schoenfeld, 1950, pp. 16–17)

The experimenter is thus in a position to measure the salivary reflex precisely. He or she is also able to control carefully the presentations of various stimulus events to the organism.

We will examine in detail an experiment by one of Pavlov's students (Anrep, 1920), as an example of the Pavlovian method and results. In this experiment by Anrep (1920), a tone was sounded in the animal's room for 5 seconds. Then, 2 or 3 seconds later, a piece of food was given to the dog. This *pairing* of tone with food presentation was repeated after intervals ranging from 5 to 35 minutes. In order to observe the effect of the tone alone, the experimenter occasionally presented it for 30 seconds, unpaired with food. Over the course of 16 days, 50 tone-food presentations and 6 tone-alone tests were made. The principal data of Anrep's experiment were obtained during the 6 tone-alone tests. During these tests, he carefully measured both the total number of drops of saliva and the time (or latency) between the onset of the 30-second test tone and the first drop of saliva. He found that, after one tone-food pairing, presentation of the tone alone produced no salivation at all. After 10 such pairings, however, 6 drops appeared in the tone-alone test, and the first of these 6 drops came 18 seconds after the onset of the test tone. After 20 such pairings, 20 drops were produced, the first drop coming now at only 9 seconds. From 30 pairings onward, approximately 60 drops of saliva were obtained during each test, and they began to appear in the first second or two after the onset of the test tone. The results of the experiment are clear-cut: salivation occurs reliably to an arbitrarily-selected stimulus, an auditory tone, after the tone is paired with food 30 times.

1.4 Classical Conditioning

Pavlov's realization that he was investigating phenomena that might be of general significance, his development of sound experimental techniques, and, above all, his careful collection of a body of systematically related experimental findings over a period of more than thirty years, mean that he was a great scientist. We now call the conditioning process he investigated *classical conditioning*, because it was the type of conditioning that was investigated earliest, and research has continued over the one hundred years since his original studies.

In the terminology we shall use here, if a *conditioned stimulus* (CS) – such as the ringing of a bell in one of Pavlov's experiments – is reliably followed by an *unconditioned stimulus* (US) – such as food in the mouth – on a number of occasions, then the CS comes to elicit (or automatically produce) a *conditioned response*. Pavlov demonstrated this process many times, and gradually varied features of his experiments to establish the generality of the effect. He also showed that there were a number of related phenomena concerned with *extinction* and *discrimination*, and we will discuss some of these in later chapters.

Pavlov, believed, and later investigators demonstrated, that he was investigating a process that enabled many species – not just dogs – to adapt to many aspects of their environments. He is thus credited with discovering the first "general learning process". It is general because it can affect many response systems, can involve many types of stimuli, and is seen in many animal species. We will see later that it is importantly involved in human behavior and the alleviation of human behavioral problems.

1.5 EVOLUTIONARY THEORY AND ADAPTIVE BEHAVIOR

Pavlov's work showed how "new" reflexes could be acquired to supplement those "built-in" reflexes that the organism possesses prior to any appreciable experience of the world. As such, it represents the culmination of Descartes' mechanistic view of reflex behavior. However, it appeared that only those responses that form part of an existing reflex (such as the salivation produced by the stimulus, dry-food-in-the-mouth) can become conditioned reflexes, and thus much non-reflexive behavior still remained to be scientifically analyzed. This behavior comes into the category traditionally described as voluntary, or under the control of the will, and it is just this category that Descartes assigned to the control of an unobservable soul. Descartes' maneuver only postponed a scientific inquiry, however, because we are now faced with the difficult problem of describing the relations between the soul which we cannot observe, and the patterns of behavior, which we do observe.

The view that voluntary human behavior was not a suitable subject for a scientific study came under attack in 1859. In that year, Charles Darwin proposed his theory of evolution, holding that human beings are members of the animal kingdom, and that differences between humans and other animals are quantitative and matters of degree. As a distinguished historian of psychology put it:

> The theory of evolution raised the problem of animal psychology because it demands continuity between different animal forms and between man and the animals. In a vague way the Cartesian [Descartes'] notion still prevailed. Man possessed a soul and the animals were believed to be soulless; and there was, moreover, little distinction then made between a soul and a mind. Opposition to the theory of evolution was based primarily upon its assumption of continuity between man and the brutes, and the obvious reply to criticism was to demonstrate the continuity. The exhibition of mind in animals and of the continuity between the animal and the human mind thus became crucial to the life of the new theory (Boring, 1929, pp. 462–463).

Darwin's theory derived support from the many careful observations that he had made of fossils and the structure of flora and fauna living in isolated areas of the earth. In addition, he had investigated the behavior by which animals adapted to their environments. Darwin's behavioral observations were so comprehensive and detailed as to mark the first systematic attempt at a comparative animal psychology (see Darwin, 1873).

Darwin's interest in behavior was, as Boring noted, based on what it could reveal about mind. Thus, the demonstration of complexity and variety in adaptive behavior of animals in relation to their changing environments seemed to prove that they, like human beings, must also think, have ideas, and feel desires. Eventually, Darwin was to be criticized for his anthropomorphism; that is, for trying to explain animal behavior in terms of mentalistic concepts generally used to account for human behavior. But few thought at the time to raise the far more radical methodological question: Do traditional mentalistic concepts (thoughts, ideas, desires) have explanatory value even for human behavior?

Darwin's friend, George John Romanes, an English writer and popularizer of science, wrote a book on animal intelligence (Romanes, 1886) in which he compared the behavior of various species of animals. Romanes gathered material from careful observation of animals, but he also took evidence from popular accounts of pets and circus animals. For this reason, his method has come to be called *anecdotal*. The anthropomorphic and anecdotal methods of Darwin and Romanes, respectively, marked the renewal of interest in adaptive animal behavior and its relationship to human behavior, and therefore represent important historical precursors of a truly scientific and experimental analysis of behavior. The crucial conceptual change had occurred: animal and human behavior was now approached from a scientific point of view and in a biological context.

1.6   SCIENTIFIC ANALYSIS OF "VOLUNTARY" BEHAVIOR

In 1898, Edward L. Thorndike, of Columbia University in the USA, published the results of a number of laboratory studies of "problem solving behavior" in kittens, dogs, and chicks. His methods departed radically from those of the casual observers who had preceded him. The behavior studied was escape from a confining enclosure, and the acts, such as pulling a string, moving a latch, pressing a lever, or prying open a lock, were chosen for their convenience and reliability of observation. A sketch of his apparatus is shown in Figure 1.4. Since any of these responses could be arranged to be instrumental in producing escape from the box, Thorndike classed them as *instrumental behavior*. A common feature of all his experiments was that, as a result of experience in the experiment, the behavior of each animal participant was systematically changed.

Four aspects of Thorndike's work on instrumental behavior gave it a modern quality not seen in earlier investigations:

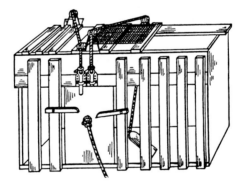

Figure 1.4   Thorndike's puzzle box for studying instrumental or operant behavior in animals. Escape from the box could be made contingent upon one of a number of responses.

1. He recognized the importance of making observations of animals whose *past histories were known* and were more or less uniform. Thus he raised his animals in the laboratory, where they would experience similar environmental conditions prior to experimentation.
2. Thorndike understood the necessity for making *repeated observations* on individual animals, and making observations on *more than one animal* in *more than one species*. In these ways, he could make it more likely that the results he obtained were applicable to animals in general.
3. Thorndike saw that unless he considered more than one particular response, his conclusions might only hold for the single piece of behavior he chose. Thus he examined *diverse* responses in several different pieces of apparatus.
4. Still another quality of Thorndike's work, and one which we recognize as a fundamental characteristic of science, was his attempt to make a *quantitative presentation* of his findings.

From his work with animals in puzzle boxes, Thorndike derived a number of principles or general laws of behavior which he believed held for many species and for many kinds of behavior. One of these, in a somewhat modified form, has come down to us today. Thorndike noticed that when animals were first put into the puzzle box, they made many diffuse struggling responses. Eventually, one of these responses would happen to operate the escape mechanism and the door would open, permitting the animal to escape from the box and to obtain a small quantity of food. Thorndike observed that the behavior which first let the animal out was only one of many that the animal made in the situation. Yet, as the animal was repeatedly exposed to the situation, it came to make fewer and fewer superfluous responses. Eventually, it made practically none apart from the successful responses.

Thorndike concluded from his experimental findings that the successful past results or *effects* of behavior must be an important influence in determining the animal's present behavioral tendencies. Consequently, Thorndike called this ability of the past effects of behavior to modify the behavior patterns of the animal the *law of effect*. It survives today as a fundamental principle in the analysis of adaptive behavior. In brief modern form, the law of effect states that if a response is reliably followed by an important consequence (such as food for a hungry organism), that response will become more frequent.

The importance of Thorndike's formulation of the law of effect for the development of behavioral analysis lies in its generality. Unlike Pavlov's laws of the conditioned reflex, the law of effect was readily applied to those responses usually regarded as voluntary. Indeed, it is more applicable to that type of behavior than to reflexive behavior, which is relatively insensitive to its consequences or effects.

1.7 THE RISE OF BEHAVIORISM

Thorndike initiated the laboratory study of behavior which is adaptive; that is, behavior which enables an organism to adapt or adjust rapidly to the prevailing environmental conditions, and comes into the category often described as "voluntary". In so doing, he discovered the law of effect and this discovery has had a profound influence on the subsequent development of behavioral analysis. However, Thorndike's own interest in behavior arose from his concern as a psychologist with mental processes, which, at the end of the nineteenth century, were seen as the key to understanding psychology.

Although psychology at that time was seen as a science of mental contents, mental processes, and mental acts, it actually involved investigations of behavior. From the results of these investigations, inferences were made about the mental processes that were presumed to be crucially involved. In some of the studies that were carried out at that time, associations of ideas were inferred from the learning of nonsense syllables, or identical sensations were inferred from observations of behavior when a human experimental participant matched two different environmental objects in different contexts (for example, two samples of gray paper under different conditions of illumination), or speed of the mental process was inferred from an individual's reaction time. Given these uses of behavioral procedures, and the influence of Darwin discussed earlier, it was perhaps not surprising that when Thorndike designed his study of problem solving he chose animals to participate in the experiments. If the behavior of human organisms could lead to inferences about mental processes, why not the behavior of animals? Furthermore, as Pavlov's and Thorndike's work revealed, the study of animal behavior may allow specific research questions to be addressed more precisely through the use of carefully controlled experiments.

Despite Thorndike's innovations, the man who did the most to clarify the relationship between behavior and psychology was John B. Watson. The earliest work of this American psychologist was concerned with the sense-modalities that the rat uses in learning to find its way through a maze. As Watson carried on his animal studies, he came to be more and more disturbed by the prevailing view that behavior possessed significance only as it shed light on mental or conscious processes. It occurred to Watson that the data of behavior were valuable in their own right and that the traditional problems of psychology, such as imagery, sensation, feeling, and association of ideas, could all be studied by strictly behavioral methods.

In 1913, Watson published a now classic paper defining psychology as the science of behavior and naming this new psychology "behaviorism". Watson argued in this paper that the study of behavior could achieve an independent status within science. The goal of such a science could be the prediction and control of the behavior of *all* animals, and no special preference need be given human beings. The *behaviorist*, claimed Watson, need relate his studies of rats and cats to human behavior no more (nor less) than the zoologist need relate his dissections on frogs and earthworms to human anatomy. By his doctrine, Watson was destroying the "homocentric" (human-centered) theory of human importance in the behavioral world just as much as Copernicus had destroyed the geocentric (earth-centered) theory of the universe, four hundred years earlier. Watson's main theme was that psychology must be objective: that is, it must have a subject matter which, like that of the other sciences, remains independent of the observer. Up until that time, psychology had attempted to take as its subject matter *self-observation* of mental processes, but this strategy lacks an independent observer located outside of the system being considered. Watson realized that this meant that conflicts about the contents of consciousness could not be resolved, *even in principle*. There were no grounds for preferring one person's report over another's. This, he argued, made that approach inherently unscientific, but the problem could be resolved if behavior itself was treated as the primary subject matter of psychology. If we take "behavior" to include only those human or animal activities that are, in principle, observable, then any statement about behavior made by one observer or experimenter can be verified by another person repeating the observations.

Watson's program for the new science of behavior was far-reaching and, for its time, remarkably sophisticated. In its insistence on behavior as an independent subject matter of a science aimed at the prediction and control of *behavior*, and in its stress on a detailed analysis of the environment and behavior into stimuli and responses as the way to eventual understanding of complex patterns of behavior, Watson's program laid the basis for modern viewpoints.

1.8　THE EXPERIMENTAL ANALYSIS OF BEHAVIOR

Thorndike's early experiments on animal behavior and Watson's definition of a science of behavior established the potential value of experimental research with animals. However, relatively little had been discovered at that early stage. In Pavlov's principle of conditioned reflexes, Watson thought he saw an explanatory mechanism for the many complex and subtle adjustments that adult organisms, including humans, make to their environments. But the attempt to force *all* behavior into the reflex mold was to prove a failure, and Watson failed to appreciate the significance of Thorndike's law of effect. Further progress was slow until another American, B.F. Skinner, made a number of innovations.

In a series of papers beginning in 1930, Skinner proposed a formulation of behavior which arose out of observations made on single organisms responding in a carefully controlled and highly standardized artificial experimental situation. Skinner's organism was the white rat, which had also been studied by Watson and others, but his apparatus consisted of an enclosure or box containing a small metal bar, or *lever*, which, if depressed by the rat, resulted in the delivery of a small pellet of food to a cup located directly under the lever. A typical version of the apparatus is shown in Figure 1.5. Under these experimental conditions, a hungry rat left alone in the box would soon come to press the lever at a sustained moderate rate until the number of food pellets delivered had begun to satiate the animal. Skinner's experimental situation and his approach to the problems of behavior were unique in many respects. Skinner saw the necessity for making available a sensitive and reliable *dependent variable*; that is, some quantitative aspect of behavior which could vary over a wide range and enter into consistent and orderly relationships with past and present environmental, or *independent*, variables. His discovery that the frequency of occurrence of the lever-press response during a given interval of time, the *response rate*, satisfied these conditions was a major step towards an analysis of how behavior is modified by many aspects of the environment.

Skinner's approach to the study of behavior differed in certain ways from those of both his predecessors and his contemporaries. As a

Figure 1.5   An experimental chamber, usually called a Skinner box, based on the one originally devised by B.F. Skinner for the study of operant conditioning.

fundamental proposition, he held that a science of behavior could be what he called descriptive or functional; that is, it could limit itself to the discovery of relationships or correlations between measurable variables. He maintained that the identification of such *functional relationships* between aspects of behavior (the dependent variables) and parameters of the environment (the independent variables) should be the goal of a science of behavior. Skinner also argued that the investigations must be systematic, in that the relationships obtained should be linked by a common thread. By confining his observations to the ways that a single dependent variable (the rate, or frequency in time, of an arbitrary piece of behavior) changed with varied environmental conditions, Skinner kept his own work highly systematic (Skinner, 1938).

Skinner's methodological contributions to the development of the experimental analysis of behavior were numerous, and we will mention only some of the more important ones here. He recognized a methodological analogy between particle emission in physics and the *emitted* character of spontaneous voluntary action. Many categories of behavior are emitted in the simple sense that they will occur from time to time. Skinner adopted the unique strategy of scientifically studying these emitted behaviors – which he called *operants*, because they generally operate upon the environment to change it – and he explored their systematic and quantitative relationship to motivational variables, and to a host of reward and punishment (or *reinforcement*) parameters. He formulated a precise vocabulary whose terms were defined by reference to the observable properties of the stimuli used and the behavior recorded, and coined the phrase, "the experimental analysis of behavior", to describe this type of research.

From the outset, Skinner emphasized the importance of detailed prediction and control of individual behavior. His own researches were invariably characterized by a great many measurements on very few organisms, with the reproducibility of the process under study as the test for reliability. Skinner's focus on the rate of a representative operant response has avoided many of the problems associated with more indirect measures of behavior. Thorndike had observed the number of errors made and the time taken to achieve success in his puzzle box, but neither of these was a property of the instrumental (that is, operant) behavior that was being acquired. If we wish to train a dog to jump through a hoop, for instance, we are less interested in the errors he makes, than in the hoop jumping itself. Errors are a measure of responses other than those we are in the process of investigating. Interesting questions about whether or not a given act will occur, or how often it will occur, can, however, be answered by Skinner's basic measure, rate of response.

The empirical basis of the experimental analysis of behavior has been gradually, but steadily, broadened. Starting from the lever-pressing of rats for food, many other responses, reinforcers and species have been examined and it has been possible to thereby show that principles derived from the original situation can be generalized to many other superficially dissimilar situations and, most importantly, to ourselves. Clearly the scope of the experimental analysis of behavior would be limited and its progress very slow if it had turned out that principles coming from one experimental situation did not apply to substantially different situations, or had no relevance to human behavior.

1.9 THE DEVELOPMENT OF APPLIED BEHAVIORAL ANALYSIS

In the last forty years of the twentieth century, the successes of the experimental analysis of behavior have led to many applications of the principles that have emerged in the laboratory in dealing with serious real-world human problems. These applications have led in turn to the development of further principles that arise primarily in real-world applications, rather than in the laboratory. In this text we seek to introduce principles of both "pure" and applied behavioral analysis.

The move to applications was initially promoted by Skinner (1953), but was taken up by a vast number of investigators. Many of these were clinical psychologists who saw in *applied behavioral analysis* the possibility of introducing techniques to their work that would be effective in bringing about *behavior change*. Some early studies involved engaging human participants in procedures that closely resembled Skinner's experimental studies with animals. For example, Lindsley (1960) examined the rate of lever press responding in psychiatric patients when this behavior was followed by presentation of money as a reinforcer. He found that the amount of lever pressing was a sensitive index of the current level of psychotic behavior, with lever pressing increasing as the frequency of psychotic behavior declined. More typically, many early studies showed that if an appropriate reinforcing stimulus was arranged to occur following socially-acceptable or personally-useful behavior, then that behavior increased in frequency while other destructive or socially unacceptable behavior declined. In making these applications to the behavior of human adults, it was often necessary to select reinforcers that were effective for particular individuals. These might include events as diverse as attendance at church services (Ayllon & Azrin, 1968) or feeding a kitten (Lindsley, 1956).

The behavioral orientation of applied behavioral analysis distinguishes it from all other approaches to ameliorating human psychological problems, most notably from those that derive from either a medical or a psychodynamic model. This behavioral orientation involves an initial behavioral assessment of the problem, the specification of behavioral objectives (that is, the changes in behavior that would be desirable), the use of an intervention strategy derived from the experimental analysis of behavior, and an assessment of whether the behavioral objectives have been achieved. As applied behavioral analysis developed, most attention was directed to the use of effective intervention strategies and demonstrations that behavioral objectives had been achieved following intervention. By 1968, there was a sufficient level of activity to support the publication of a specialist academic journal, the *Journal of Applied Behavior Analysis*, and the amount and range of work conducted has grown tremendously since then.

Some of the pioneers in this field (Baer, Wolf, & Risley, 1968) proposed some defining features of applied behavior analysis that are still useful today. It is *applied* in that the problems studied are those that are important to society rather than those crucial to theory development; it is *behavioral* in that it asks how it is possible to get an individual to do something effectively; and it involves *analysis,* and thus requires a demonstration of the events that can be responsible for the occurrence of the behavior in question. Other features are that it must be *effective,* in that substantial behavior change must be produced, and the behavior change should show *generality.* That is, it endures over time, and is also seen in a range of situations.

As noted earlier, this approach is not confined to clinical psychology and applications continue to be developed in an increasing number of areas. It can now be argued that applied behavioral analysis is capable of embracing the whole field of *applied psychology* (Goldstein and Krasner, 1987).

1.10 APPLIED AND BASIC BEHAVIOR ANALYSIS

The experimental analysis of behavior, on the one hand, and applied behavior analysis, on the other hand, can be seen as the science and technology of behavior, as the former is concerned with the elucidation of basic scientific principles while the latter is concerned with their real-world applications. However, we are describing a new science and an even newer technology, and, not surprisingly the relationship between this science and technology is still under development and a matter for continuing debate among researchers.

By 1980, there were many areas in which applied behavioral analysis had been shown to be useful in dealing with serious human behavioral problems. It had often been "the treatment of last resort" in the sense that a "case" (for example, of a child with moderate intellectual disability who showed a severe level of self-injurious behavior through gouging at his face with his hand) had been approached using applied behavioral analysis only after more conventional medical and psychological treatments had failed to be effective. When applied behavioral analysis succeeded in producing behavioral improvements in such cases, great impetus was given to its use in similar cases, and it became more likely that it would become the preferred initial approach to this type of behavioral problem.

These early successes were important for the development of applied behavior analysis, but also led to an approach which some recent commentators have seen as excessively technological (for example, Hayes, 1991), in that it is concerned solely with the meticulous implementation of well-established procedures directed at significant human problems and not at all directed at basic research questions. If this trend continues, Hayes argued, there would not be an adequate basic science to generate useful applications, These issues have resulted in calls (for example by Mace, 1994a, Wacker, 1999) for research that bridges between experimental analysis and applied analysis of behavior, The bridge should be a two-way connection, with developments in each field informing the other. Mace suggested three important strategies: (a) the development in the laboratory (with other species) of models of human behavioral problems using operations that resemble those thought to be important in human life, (b) replication (repetition) of the same experimental design with humans in a laboratory setting, and (c) tests of the generality of the model with real-world problems in natural settings. Through such strategies, applied behavior analysis is moving away from being concerned almost exclusively with the application of a simple model of operant conditioning to human problems, and towards embracing the implementation of an ever-increasing range of behavioral principles.

1.11 FUNCTIONAL ANALYSIS

In the early days of applied behavioral analysis, when practitioners were mostly concerned with the simple strategy of implementing an operant conditioning procedure, there were successes, but also a considerable "unevenness" in treatment outcomes. That is, not every person showing a particular problem, such as self-injurious behavior, was helped by the behavioral intervention methods typically used. A major breakthrough on this issue began with the work of Iwata, Dorsey, Slifer, Bauman, and Richman (1982) on self-injury. They noted that earlier work had focused on specifying behavioral objectives and implementing treatment, but had paid little attention to establishing the environmental determinants of self-injury *prior* to any intervention. That is, the question as to *why* the behavior was occurring was not being properly addressed. They remedied this by devising operant methods for assessing functional relationships between self-injury and the physical and social environment. In that study, and subsequent ones, they found that self-injury occurs for different reasons in different people. Persons that engage in self-injury may do it because it results in attention from others, because it allows them to escape from other demands (such as doing school work), because it raises the level of sensory stimulation, or for a combination of these reasons. Importantly, behavioral interventions become much more effective when the treatment strategy for each individual is directly based on a prior functional analysis of their behavior.

Methods of functional analysis have now been developed for many types of behavioral problem, and functional analysis is now seen as the key element in the behavioral assessment which should precede any behavioral intervention. We noted in Section 1.7 that Skinner (1938) stated that *functional relationships* between aspects of behavior and parameters of the environment should be the goal of a science of behavior. With the increasing prominence of functional analysis in behavioral assessment, along with the use of functionally-defined behavioral intervention, functional relationships can now be seen as the central feature of applied behavioral analysis as they are in the experimental analysis of behavior.

1.12 SUMMARY

Progress towards a scientific account of human behavior has been erratic. Although interest in it is very long standing, and dates back at least as far as Aristotle in the fourth century BC, the centuries-long domination in the Western world of religious explanations of human action made scientific progress slow. In the seventeenth century AD, Descartes provided a new dualistic framework which facilitated scientific accounts of animal behavior and even human physiology, but still impeded a scientific account of human behavior.

From the eighteenth century, developing knowledge of reflexes indicated that parts at least of the nervous system could be analyzed scientifically. I.P. Pavlov took a giant step beyond this in the late nineteenth and early twentieth century by demonstrating conditioned reflexes, or classical conditioning, in the dog. Pavlov realized that he was investigating how interaction with the environment modifies subsequent behavior in individual organisms, and he suggested that his conditioning paradigm could account for much learning and adaptation in animal behavior.

Conceptions of the relationship between human behavior and that of other animals changed radically in the late nineteenth century, following publication of Charles Darwin's theory of evolution by natural selection which implied that similar behavioral processes should be seen in humans as in other species. Also in the late 19th century, E.L. Thorndike's work on the law of effect and problem solving behavior illustrated such a behavioral process. If kittens, dogs, and chicks can "learn through experience" of the effects of their behavior, it seemed likely that this process affects humans as well as many other species.

Major shifts in the intellectual landscape usually come about through the promotional zeal of individuals, and in the early twentieth century behaviorism was fervently and brilliantly promoted as an alternative to the prevailing mentalism by J.B. Watson. Although few *scientific* data were available, Watson saw the potential of a science of behavior, which would be applicable to humans and to other species. Beginning in 1930, B.F. Skinner began to provide those scientific data by building on Thorndike's findings and establishing the branch of science known as the experimental analysis of behavior. Not only did he improve experimental techniques and thus show powerful control of animal behavior in laboratory experiments, but he also spent much of his long career suggesting how the findings of the experimental analysis of behavior could be extrapolated to explain much human behavior in real world settings.

Since 1960, those speculations about human behavior have been replaced by applied scientific data. In the developing field of applied behavior analysis, principles of behavioral analysis derived from laboratory studies are deployed in the explanation and amelioration of human behavioral problems. This applied science has progressed more rapidly in recent years, because the importance of functional analysis has been recognized. A successful functional analysis reveals the functions that a class of behavior currently has for an individual, and thus provides a sound basis for an intervention intended to change the frequency of that class of behavior.

CHAPTER **2**
OPERANT BEHAVIOR AND
OPERANT CONDITIONING

2.1 THE ANALYSIS OF PURPOSIVE BEHAVIOR

As we saw in the previous chapter, the notion that much of animal behavior consists of reflexes was well-known to the scientific community by the latter part of the nineteenth century, and Pavlov's ideas about conditioned reflexes as a model for much of learnt behavior were also rapidly and widely disseminated. However, there is much behavior that apparently occurs at the instigation of the individual, rather than being elicited by the onset of an external stimulus. This includes those actions of human beings traditionally described as voluntary, purposeful, spontaneous, or willful, and this class of behavior was thought to be beyond the scope of a scientific or experimental analysis until the turn of the twentieth century. The relationship between this sort of behavior and reflexive behavior is well illustrated by the following passage:

> . . . when a cat hears a mouse, turns towards the source of the sound, sees the mouse, runs toward it, and pounces, its posture at every stage, even to the selection of the foot which is to take the first step, is determined by reflexes which can be demonstrated one by one under experimental conditions. *All the cat has to do is to decide* whether or not to pursue the mouse; everything else is prepared for it by its postural and locomotor reflexes (Skinner, 1957, p. 343; italics added).

The cat's behavior in this situation has an essential non-reflexive ingredient, although reflexes are vital for the success of its attempt to catch the mouse. Hidden in the simple statement, "all the cat has to do is to *decide*," lies the point of departure for an analysis of *purposive behavior*, whose occurrence is not related to the presence of an eliciting (that is, immediately-producing) stimulus, either as a result of the history of the species (as in a reflex) or as a result of the history of the individual (as in a conditioned reflex).

The experimental analysis of so-called purposive behavior has proceeded in a fashion typical of the development of scientific explanation and understanding in many other disciplines. Typically, a small number of systematic relationships are established first and repeatedly investigated. As new relationships are added to those previously established, the group of principles or "laws" begins to give a partial understanding of the area. Starting with Thorndike's extensive pioneer work on learning in cats and chicks, psychologists have searched for relationships between purposive behavior and other events. Consider the problems in beginning such an analysis: how do we go about finding variables or events to which purposive behavior might be significantly related? Initially, we must proceed by intuition and crude observation. Very often, forward-looking philosophical speculation precedes scientific investigation of a problem, and in this case the British philosopher, Herbert Spencer, wrote:

> Suppose, now, that in putting out its head to seize prey scarcely within reach, a creature has repeatedly failed. Suppose that along with the group of motor actions approximately adapted to seize prey at this distance . . . a slight forward movement of the body [occurs]. Success will occur instead of failure ... On recurrence of the circumstances, these muscular movements that were followed by success are likely to be repeated: what was at first an accidental combination of motions will now be a combination having considerable probability (Spencer, 1878).

Here, a quarter of a century before Thorndike, Spencer suggests that the effect of an action is all important in determining its subsequent occurrence: "those muscular movements that were followed by success are likely to be repeated". This is the key idea that led Thorndike to the law of effect and Skinner to a thorough-going experimental analysis of behavior.

If a piece of behavior has a purpose, then that purpose can be described by the usual consequences or effect of that behavior. Indeed, we could almost say that purposive behavior is that behavior which *is defined* by its consequences. For example, we say that we tie a shoelace to keep our shoe on, but an equivalent statement is that we tie a shoelace, and on previous occasions when we tied it, it did stay on. Furthermore, we identify instances of shoelace tying by their effects: if the shoe stays on, then this counts as an example of "shoelace tying"; otherwise, it does not. Many other everyday behaviors can be subjected to a similar analysis; going to school, making a cup of coffee, playing a musical instrument, and so on.

Apparently, we have two ways in our language to account for the same behavior. These are: (1) the purposive, in which we use the term *to* (or, *in order to*) and imply the future tense; or (2) the descriptive, in which we state the present behavior and conjoin it with what happened in the past. Which is more appropriate for use in a scientific analysis of behavior? Consider the following example:

During the war the Russians used dogs to blow up tanks. A dog was trained to hide behind a tree or wall in low brush or other cover. As a tank approached and passed, the dog ran swiftly alongside it, and a small magnetic mine attached to the dog's back was sufficient to cripple the tank or set it afire. The dog, of course, had to be replaced (Skinner, 1956, p. 228).

In this example, the dog's behavior can be explained by reference to past events, as it presumably had been rewarded for running to tanks by food, petting, and the like, but not by reference to its purpose. We can immediately reject the idea that the dog ran to the tank in order to be blown up. This extreme case illustrates the general principle *that the future does not determine behavior*. When we use "purposive language", we are drawing on our knowledge of the effects of our behavior on earlier occasions; it is that "history" which determines behavior.

In brief, a very real and important class of behavior, arising out of situations that seem to involve choice or decision, is called purposive behavior. Such behavior, it should be apparent at once, falls into Descartes' category of "voluntary" and constitutes action that is often called "willful", or said to be done by "free choice". Our present analysis indicates that this behavior is in some way related to, and thus governed by, its consequences on previous occasions. For that reason we shall henceforth replace the older term, purposive, with Thorndike's term, "instrumental", or Skinner's term, "operant". Calling behavior "instrumental" or "operant" suggests that, by operating on the environment, the behavior is instrumental in obtaining consequences. Neither of these terms implies the confusing conceptual scheme that "purposive" does, yet both attempt to capture the fundamental notion that the past consequences of such behavior are one of its important determinants.

2.2   A PROTOTYPE EXPERIMENT: A RAT IN THE SKINNER BOX

If a hungry laboratory rat is put into a small enclosure, such as the one shown in Figure 2.1, and certain procedures are carried out, a number of interesting changes in the behavior of the rat may be observed. For present purposes, the significant features of the enclosure, or *Skinner box*, are: (1) a tray for delivery of a small pellet of food to the rat; and (2) a lever or bar, protruding from the front wall that, when depressed downward with a force of about 10 grams, closes a switch, permitting the automatic recording of this behavior. The significant features of the rat are as follows: (1) it is

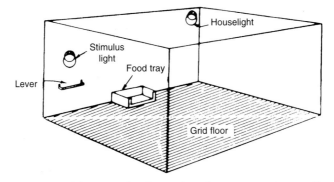

Figure 2.1   Essential features of a Skinner box for a rat, or other small rodent. The box is situated inside a sound-attenuating housing to exclude extraneous noises and other stimuli.

healthy and has been accustomed to eating one meal each day at about the same hour as it now finds itself in the box; (2) it has previously been acclimatized to this box during which time food was occasionally delivered into the tray, and it now readily approaches the food tray and eats food whenever it is available.

Consider the following simple experiment. The rat is left in the box for an observation period of 15 minutes. During this time, no food is delivered, but the rat engages in a lot of exploratory behavior. It noses the corners, noses the food tray, occasionally depresses the lever, rears up against the walls, and so forth. Other activities observed include sniffing and grooming. None of these responses is reflexive. That is, no specific eliciting stimulus can be identified for any of them. Thus, we call them *emitted responses*. Clearly, there are stimuli present that are related to the occurrence of these responses – the general construction of the box obviously determines which responses can occur, for example – but none of the stimuli elicits specific responses at specific times.

The rate and pattern of the emitted responses of an animal in an environment in which no special consequences are being provided for any response defines the *operant-level* of those responses. Operant-level recordings will provide an important *baseline* against which we shall later compare the effects of providing special consequences for one or a number of the emitted responses.

After the observation period, the following procedure is initiated. Each time the rat presses the lever, a pellet of food is delivered into the tray. As the rat has previously learned to retrieve food pellets and eat them as soon as they are delivered, each lever-pressing response is now immediately followed by the rat eating a food pellet. We have introduced a *contingency* between the lever-pressing response and the delivery of food pellets. Provided the operant-level of lever-pressing is above zero (that is, lever presses already occur from time to time), this new contingency will produce a number of behavioral changes. Soon the rat is busily engaged in lever pressing and eating pellets. These marked changes in its behavior have occurred in a relatively short period of time. In common parlance, the rat is said to have learned to press the lever to get food. Such a description adds little (except brevity) to the statement that the rat is pressing the lever frequently now and getting food, and this follows a number of occasions on which lever pressing has occurred and been followed by food.

The experiment we have described is an instance of the prototype experiments on operant behavior carried out by B. F. Skinner in the 1930s. The most striking change in behavior that occurs when food is presented to a hungry rat as a consequence of lever pressing is that lever pressing dramatically increases in rate. This is an example of *operant conditioning*, because the increase in rate is a result of the *contingency* between the lever-pressing response and the food. If there is a contingency between two events, A and B, this means that B will occur if, and only if, A occurs. We say that B is *dependent upon* A, or that A *predicts* B, because when A occurs, B occurs; but if A does not occur, B will not occur. Sequences of events in which B is contingent upon A and when B is independent of A are illustrated in Figure 2.2. In our present example, food (B) is contingent upon lever pressing (A). Another way of saying this is that food (B) is a consequence of lever pressing (A). This is a simple example of a

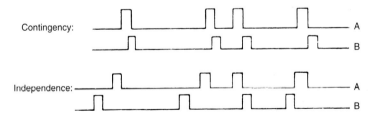

Figure 2.2   Event records, or "time lines", illustrating a contingency between, or independence of, Event A and Event B. An event occurs when the recording line shifts from the lower ("off") position to the upper ("on") position. In an operant conditioning experiment, Event A might be a lever press and Event B might be food delivery.

reinforcement contingency, a term which we will use later for more complex examples.

What we wish to do is to describe in detail, and as quantitatively as possible, the changes in behavior that result from the simple operation of providing a special consequence for only one of an individual's normal ongoing activities in a situation. To do that, we shall consider four complementary ways of viewing the changes in the rat's behavior when, as here, one of its behaviors is selected out and given a favorable consequence:

1. The increase in response frequency;
2. Changes in other behavior;
3. Sequential changes in responding;
4. Changes in response variability.

2.3 THE CHANGES IN BEHAVIOR THAT CHARACTERIZE OPERANT CONDITIONING

The increase in response frequency can clearly be seen on the ink recorder developed by Skinner: the cumulative recorder illustrated in Figure 2.3. The pen moves continuously across the paper in one direction at fixed speed, and this axis thus records elapsed time. Whenever a response occurs, the pen moves in a perpendicular direction by a small step of fixed size. The resulting *cumulative record* shows the number of responses and the time during which they occurred, and so illustrates the pattern of behavior. Examples of actual records from experimental participants exposed to a procedure like the one outlined are shown in Figure 2.4. When a contingency between lever pressing and food was established for these experimental participants, there was a relatively abrupt transition to a high rate of response. It should be noted that the time spent in the experiment before this transition varied and, in the examples in Figure 2.4, could be up to 30 minutes. Once the transition had occurred, the rate of responding was fairly constant; this is shown by the steady slopes of the graphs. The transition, because of its suddenness, resembles "one-trial" learning, rather than a gradual change. Ink recorders of the type used by Skinner in the 1930's have now been replaced by computer systems which can be programmed to draw graphs of the progress of an experiment using exactly the same dimensions as those shown in Figure 2.4.

Figure 2.3   A cumulative recorder of a type that was used extensively until replaced by computer software systems.   When operational, the paper moved continuously through the machine.   Other details are given in the text. (Courtesy of Ralph Gerbrands Co. Inc.).

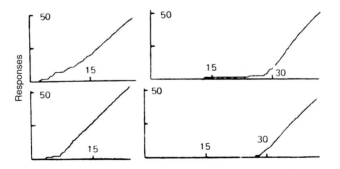

Figure 2.4   Cumulative records obtained from four hungry rats on their first session of operant conditioning.   Lever presses were reinforced with food.   Each lever press produced an incremental step of the recorder pen (Skinner, 1938).

In any case of operant conditioning, there will always be concomitant *changes in other behavior* as the operant response increases in frequency. If the experimental participant is a laboratory rat, and it begins to spend a large part of its time lever pressing, retrieving and eating food pellets, there must necessarily be a reduction in the frequency of some of the other responses (R's) that were previously occurring in the Skinner box. For example, in an undergraduate classroom demonstration of lever-press operant conditioning at Carnegie-Mellon University, the following behaviors of a hungry rat were recorded over 15 minutes of operant level, and then over a subsequent 15 minutes of conditioning the lever pressing:

R_L = lever pressing

R_S = sniffing

R_P = pulling of a small chain that dangled into the box from overhead

R_T = nosing the food tray

R_B = extending a paw to a lead block that rested in one of the far corners

R_I = remaining approximately immobile for 10 consecutive seconds.

It was found that while lever pressing and tray nosing increased, the other responses that were not associated with eating declined. Indeed, the operant conditioning process can be seen as one of *selection*. Those responses that are selected increase in relative frequency, while most of the remainder decline. Figure 2.5 illustrates with a histogram how the pattern of behavior had changed.

Sequential changes in responding also occur. When food is made contingent upon a response, other activities involved in food getting increase in frequency, but this is not the only change that takes place. A sequence of responses is rapidly established and maintained. In the lever pressing example, the sequence might be:

lever press>tray approach>tray entry>eat food>
lever approach>lever press...and so on.

This continuous loop of behavior is quite different from that seen in operant level. Two members of the established loop will serve to illustrate the point. Let us ignore, for the moment, all the other possible behavior in the situation and confine our attention to (1) pressing the lever, and (2) approaching the food tray. Prior to conditioning of the lever press, these two

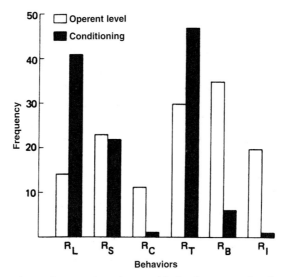

Figure 2.5   Relative frequencies of several behaviors occurring in a Skinner box before and after operant conditioning of lever pressing. Details are given in the text.

responses occur in such a way that, when the animal performs one of them, it is likely to repeat that one again rather than perform the other (Frick and Miller, 1951). Thus, a fairly typical operant-level sequence of lever press (R_L) and tray-approach responses (R_T) might be

$$R_L \ R_L \ R_T \ R_L \ R_L \ R_L \ R_T \ R_T \ R_T \ ...$$

During conditioning, this sequence quickly changes to the alternation

$$R_L \ R_T \ R_L \ R_T \ R_L \ R_T \ ...$$

with hardly any other pattern to be seen (Millenson and Hurwitz, 1961). This re-organization of behavior probably takes place as soon as rapid responding begins.

Changes in response variability always occur in operant conditioning. "The rat presses the lever" describes an effect the rat has on the environment, not a particular pattern of movements by the rat. There is a wide range of movements that could have the specified effect. Presses can be made with the right paw, with the left, with nose, shoulder, or even tail. We group all of these instances together and say that the class of responses that we call lever pressing is made up of all the possible ways of pressing a lever. However, not all members of the class are equally likely to occur in an experiment nor, on the other hand, does the same member occur repeatedly. Several processes interact to determine exactly which forms of the response are observed. First, there is a tendency for the topography of the response to become *stereotyped* under certain conditions. By "topography" we mean the pattern of muscular movements that make up the response; when this becomes stereotyped, the response looks exactly the same on each occasion that it occurs. One situation in which stereotyped behavior develops is when very little effort is required to make the response. Guthrie and Horton (1946) took photographs of cats and dogs who were required to make a pole-tilting response to get out of a box, and found that successive instances of the response made by particular individuals were strikingly similar. Relatedly, photographs of sportsman engaged in skilled performances on different occasions (for example, a tennis player serving) often look identical. A second process involved is described by Skinner's (1938) "law of least effort". This states that the form of the response made will tend to be that which requires the least effort. In the experiment described above, it is typically found that, while different participants start out by pressing the lever in various ways, as the experiment progresses, they show an increasing tendency to use an economical paw movement to press the lever. Thirdly, the biology of the species influences what can be learnt. Thorndike was the first to realize that not all behaviors can be equally easily changed by certain effects or consequences. Seligman (1970) called this the *preparedness* of certain behaviors to be modified by certain consequences, and related this phenomenon to the evolutionary history of the species.

2.4   OUTCOMES OF OPERANT CONDITIONING

In summary, when operant conditioning is implemented in a simple laboratory situation such as a Skinner Box, behavior changes in four ways:

1. The rate of the operant response increases relative to its operant- or base-level;
2. The rate of the operant response increases relative to the rate of other responses occurring in the situation;
3. The pattern or sequence of behavior changes to a loop involving the operant response and this loop is repeated again and again;

4. The form or topography of that response becomes stereotyped, while requiring a minimum effort and being influenced by the participant's preparedness to make the response for the consequence arranged for it.

Lever pressing, string pulling, and pole tilting, represent convenient acts chosen by experimenters to study the effects of environmental consequences on behavior. The suitability of these responses for studying operant conditioning depends critically upon their ability to be modified as described. Formally, responses are defined as *operants* if they can be increased in frequency and strengthened in the four stated ways by making certain consequences contingent upon them. The selection of the operant response for experiments is often said to be "arbitrary", in that the experimenter is generally not interested in lever pressing *per se*, but only as an example of a response that can be modified by its consequences. In general, lever pressing and other simple pieces of animal behavior are chosen for experiments because they are easily observed and measured by the experimenter, and can be executed at various rates and in various patterns by the organism. Throughout this book, we will continuously extend the applicability of the principles of operant conditioning and the term "operant" well beyond lever presses and rats.

2.5 OPERANTS AND REINFORCING STIMULI

Which are the consequences of behavior that will produce operant conditioning? This is a central issue that we have carefully avoided this far. In his version of the law of effect, Thorndike stressed the importance of "satisfiers". He stated that if a satisfier, or satisfying state of affairs, was the consequence of a response, then that response would be "stamped in", or increased in frequency. At first sight, Thorndike seems to have provided an answer to the question we posed, but he merely leaves us with another: which events will act as satisfiers? It seems obvious that food may be satisfying to a hungry organism, and "armchair reflection" might produce a list of events likely to prove satisfying in general, such as warmth, activity, play, contact, power, novelty, and sex. We might also notice that there are some events that become very satisfying once the organism has been appropriately *deprived*. Food comes into this category, along with water when thirsty, air when suffocating, and rest when fatigued. Interestingly, it is also evident that when we are *satiated*, these reinforcing effects are clearly removed and may even be reversed. Consider how disagreeable it is to be obliged to eat a meal immediately after completing a previous one, or to stay in bed when completely rested.

So far, we are only guessing; how can we firmly establish whether certain events are reinforcing or satisfying? One way is to see whether they have the consequence specified by the law of effect, or, more specifically, produce the four outcomes listed in the previous section. However, according to Thorndike's definition, they *must* have these properties, or these events are not satisfiers! A plausible alternative suggestion was made by Hull (1943). He claimed that all such events reduce a basic need or drive of the organism and that this *drive reduction* is crucial to their response-strengthening effect. Subsequent research has failed, however, to support Hull's suggestion, for there are many satisfiers whose ability to reduce a basic need seems questionable. These include "artificial sweeteners" that have no nutritional value but make soft drinks just as attractive as the sugar they replace.

Thorndike's term, "satisfier", carries the implication that such events will be pleasurable, or "things that we like", but this does not help us to identify them in practice. It simply changes the form of the problem again: how do I know what you like? The things we like are, in the final analysis, the things that we will work for, but this again takes us back to the law of effect, because to say that we will work for them is just another way of saying that we will do for them what our rat will do "for" food. At this point, we shall exchange Thorndike's term, "satisfier", for Skinner's less introspective term, *reinforcing stimulus,* or simply, *reinforcer.* The operation of presenting a reinforcer contingent upon a response we will denote as *reinforcement.*

A reinforcing stimulus can be defined as an event that, in conjunction with at least some behavior of an individual, produces the changes in behavior specified by the law of effect and listed in the previous section. So far, we lack an independent method of identifying reinforcers other than by their effects on behavior. Moreover, the work of Premack (1965) suggests that this represents an inherent limitation. In a series of ingenious experiments, Premack established that the property of being a reinforcer can be a relative one, and that for any pair of responses a situation can be devised in which the less probable response can be reinforced by the opportunity to carry out the more probable response, and that this relationship is reversible. He made these surprising findings by breaking some of the unwritten "rules of the game" in conditioning experiments.

In one experiment, Premack (1962) studied rats making the operant response of turning an activity wheel and being reinforced with water. To ensure that water acted as a reinforcer, the rats were made thirsty at the time of the experiment and this made water a reinforcer for wheel turning. In this very conventional part of the experiment, wheel turning duly increased in frequency. In another part of the experiment, however, Premack reversed the relationship: he allowed the rats continuous access to water, but prevented access to the activity wheel except for 1 hour/day. In this unusual situation, he found that if the opportunity to run in the wheel was made contingent upon licking water from a tube, the rats spent between three and five times as long drinking during that hour than they did when this contingency was not in effect. He thus established that it is not a "law of nature" that wheel turning by rats can be reinforced with water. Instead, this result depends on the usual practice of depriving rats of water, but not activity, prior to the experiment. If the conditions are reversed, then running in the wheel can be shown to reinforce drinking. In an earlier study (Premack, 1959) the same strategy was adopted with children and the two activities of eating candy or playing a pinball machine. When the children were hungry they would operate the machine (an operant response) in order to obtain candy (a reinforcer), but when they were not hungry they would eat candy (an operant response) in order to obtain access to the pinball machine (now a reinforcer)!

The concept of "a reinforcer" is evidently a relative one; a fact that we should especially bear in mind before uncritically calling any particular stimulus in the everyday world a reinforcer. Following the line of analysis started by Premack, other researchers (including Eisenberger, Karpman, & Trattner, 1967; Allison & Timberlake, 1974; Allison, 1993: and see Leslie, 1996, Chapter 4 for a review) have demonstrated that the amount of the operant response required and the amount of access to the reinforcer that follows must also be taken into account to specify the reinforcement relationship. Most generally, it appears that reinforcement involves a set of relationships between environmental events in which the individual is "deprived" of the currently preferred rate of access to the reinforcer unless the operant response increases above its currently preferred rate. This is called the response-deprivation principle (Allison & Timberlake, 1974, and see Leslie, 1996, Chapter 4 for a brief formal statement of the principle).

As we have now defined reinforcement with reference to the current behavioral repertoire, we should take care — in the laboratory or in real-world applications — not to presume that a stimulus will necessarily continue to be a reinforcer if the conditions are radically changed.

Conditions such as food deprivation are termed *establishing operations*, because they change the current behavioral repertoire in such a way as establish a particular event as a reinforcer. Applied researchers have recently turned their attention to establishing operations because they are not only important conditions of operant reinforcement, but may also provide a direct means of obtaining a required behavior change (see Chapters 7 and 9).

It follows form the argument developed here, that reinforcement cannot be essentially linked to biological needs or corresponding drives in the way that Hull (1943) suggested. However, it remains true that it is often possible to use the reduction of a basic drive, such as the presentation of water for a thirsty animal or food for a hungry one, as a reinforcing operation, and that for practical purposes reinforcers are often "transsituational", that is effective in many situations. This is particularly true with human behavior which is strongly affected by *conditioned reinforcement*, which will be described in Section 2.9.

2.6   THE SIMPLE OPERANT CONDITIONING PARADIGM

The matters that we have been discussing in this chapter are variously referred to in the literature of psychology as simple selective learning, trial-and-error learning, effect learning, instrumental learning, instrumental conditioning, operant learning, and operant conditioning. We prefer to use the term *simple operant conditioning* for the situation where a reinforcing stimulus is made contingent upon a response that has a nonzero frequency of occurrence prior to the introduction of reinforcement. If a reinforcing stimulus is contingent upon a response, that stimulus will be presented if and only if the required response has been made.

Formally, the simple operant conditioning paradigm is defined as follows. Each emission of a selected behavioral act or response is followed by the presentation of a particular stimulus. If this arrangement results in an increase in response frequency, relative to operant level and relative to other behavior occurring in the situation, the incorporation of the response into a behavioral loop and the narrowing of the topography of the response, then we say that the selected behavior is an operant response, that the stimulus functions as a reinforcer for that operant, and that what occurred was operant conditioning. The reinforcement contingency can be represented diagrammatically as follows:

Any instance of   Presentation

the operant   →   of the reinforcing

response   stimulus

The arrow stands for "leads to" or "produces". This diagram can, in turn, be summarized as:

$$R \rightarrow S+,$$

where R represents an operant response class and S+ the reinforcing stimulus it produces. S+ is used to denote a positive reinforcer. The distinction between *positive reinforcement,* of which simple operant conditioning is an example, and other types of operant conditioning, will be explained later.

2.7   CHANGING THE SUBJECT MATTER: VOCAL OPERANTS

This section is included partly to illustrate the breadth of application of simple operant conditioning and partly to direct our attention to some characteristically human behavior. The usual elements of all languages are sounds produced by the vibration of expelled air from the lungs, moving through and across a set of muscles in the larynx called the vocal chords. The tension of these muscles, a major determinant of the sound produced, is under the same kind of neural control as movements of the other parts of the body, and the emitted sound patterns can be considered as examples of operant behavior. The jaws, lips, and tongue act in combination with the larynx to mould the sounds and produce the more than forty different humanoid sounds known as *phonemes* that are used in various combinations in languages. Because the sounds of phonemes are directly dependent on the movements of the vocal apparatus, measurement of phoneme production constitutes an indirect measure of behavior, in the same way that measurement of the depression of a lever constitutes an indirect measure of the movements used by the rat in depressing that lever.

Human speech develops from the crude sounds emitted by infants. Surprisingly, the human infant during the first 5 months of life emits all the sounds used in every human language, including French nasals and trills, German gutturals, and so on (Osgood, 1953). This sound production is not elicited by stimuli, nor should it be confused with crying. Rather, in the early months of life, a baby exhibits a very high operant level of sound production. He or she may lie for hours producing gurgling sounds, sputterings, whistles, squeaks, and snorts. The technical term *babbling* is used to denote the spontaneous emission of these behaviors. An important advance in babbling occurs at about the sixth month, when the sequential structure of babbling is altered so that the infant tends to repeat its own vocal production (uggle-uggle, oodle-oodle, luh-luh-luh, and so forth).

The changes that occur from babbling to speaking are complex, and no single graph could describe the progress with any completeness. However, one important change that takes place is the change in relative frequency of the different sounds uttered as the baby grows older. Thus, in France, the phonemes involved in the French r and the nasal vowels are strengthened by the "reinforcing community": that is, the child's parents, its playmates, and eventually, its teachers. In English-speaking countries, a different set of phonemes is shaped into words by a different reinforcing community. Halle, De Boysonn-Bardies, and Vihman (1991) found that in four French and four Japanese 18-month-old children aspects of their vocalization, both in babbling and word utterances, already resembled the speech of adults in the two languages.

In one classic experiment, the behavior of 3-month-old babies was observed while they lay in their cribs. During two observation sessions, an adult experimenter leaned over the crib, at a distance of a little more than a foot from the child, and remained relatively motionless and expressionless. During this time, a second observer recorded the frequency of sounds produced by the infant. In two subsequent sessions, the procedure was the same, except that the first experimenter followed each non-crying sound with a "broad smile, three 'tsk' sounds, and a light touch applied to the infant's abdomen with thumb and fingers of the hand opposed" (Rheingold, Gewirtz, and Ross, 1959, p. 28). This is, of course, just:

R (babble) → S+ (smile, clucking, touch of abdomen)

The effect of this operant conditioning procedure was to raise the frequency of babbling well above its operant-level rate during these conditioning sessions.

Even more striking were the findings of Routh (1969), working with 2- to 7-month-old infants. Using the same reinforcing stimuli, he reinforced either vowel or consonant sounds rather than all vocalizations. He found that vocalizations increased under both conditions, but infants differentially increased the type of vocalization currently in the reinforced class.

Experiments of this type provide ample evidence that human vocal behavior is susceptible to control by operant conditioning.

2.8 SIMPLE OPERANT CONDITIONING OF COMPLEX OR "UNOBSERVED" HUMAN BEHAVIOR

Operant conditioning is a phenomenon which is by no means limited to the simple animal and infant behaviors we have discussed so far. We study laboratory animals because we can rigorously control their environment, past and present, but operant behavior (behavior that can be modified by its consequences) constitutes a large proportion of the everyday activities of humans. When we kick a football, sew up a hem, give a lecture, discuss the latest in fashions, bemoan the weather, and wash the dishes, we are constantly emitting operant behavior. True, our complex skills entail much more complicated sequences than the simple repetitive loop of the rat, described earlier; but surprising complexity can also be generated in the behavior of the rat, cat, pigeon, and monkey (many examples are included in Leslie, 1996).

It is not difficult to demonstrate simple operant conditioning in humans in an informal manner: we can even perform demonstrations on our friends without great difficulty. For example, with "unaware" participants, it is possible to demonstrate that reinforcing certain topics of conversation, or the use of certain classes of words, by showing approval or agreement, will rapidly change the conversational speech of the participant. (We are apt to find the demonstration more dramatic and convincing if we prevent our human participant from "becoming aware" that we are performing such an experiment, because that seems to rule out the possibility that he or she is following an implicit verbal instruction, rather than "being conditioned"; verbal behavior is discussed in Chapter 6.) Nonetheless, the direct verification of the laws of operant conditioning on human behavior is important, for it shows that despite very great apparent differences between humans and other animal species, certain functional similarities exist, and it is these similarities that, in the end, justify our frequent reliance on the study of the behavior of other organisms.

For these reasons it is important that formal experiments on simple operant conditioning with humans be conducted, and many have been carried out. For example, Hall, Lund and Jackson (1968) measured the rates of study of six 6- to 8-year old children in class, who all showed much disruptive behavior and dawdling. When attention from the teacher was made contingent upon studying, there was a sharp increase in study rates. A brief reversal of the contingency, where attention occurred after non-studying, produced low rates of studying, and reinstatement of the contingency (studying → teacher attention) once again markedly increased studying.

This example of simple operant conditioning produced conspicuous changes in a highly complex form of behavior. A very different example of a dramatic effect of operant conditioning on human behavior is provided by the classic study of Hefferline and Keenan (1963). They investigated "miniature" operant responses involving a movement so small that electronic amplification must be employed to detect it, and the participant is generally not able to report observing his or her own responses. In one experiment, small muscle-twitch potentials were recorded from the human thumb. Dummy electrodes were placed at other points on the participant's body to distract attention from the thumb response. Introduction of a reinforcement contingency, in which small sums of money could be earned by incrementing a counter, led to an increase in very small thumb twitches, even when the participant was unable to say what the required response was.

One way of categorizing the Hefferline and Keenan experiment is as "conditioning without awareness"; it showed operant conditioning occurring without the participants being able necessarily to report verbally on the contingencies that were affecting behavior. This is an exception to what appears to be the usual situation, where we can verbalize the rule describing the contingency which is in operation. Indeed, once that verbal behavior occurs it generally seems to determine what nonverbal behavior will occur. A participant in a gambling game may, for example, decide that "The coin generally comes down 'heads'". If that behavior is reinforced by chance when the coin falls that way up on the first two occasions in the game, that verbal behavior may be highly persistent — and the person may always select 'heads' — despite many subsequent disconfirming events when the coin comes down as 'tails'. We will discuss the relationship between verbal and nonverbal behavior in later chapters and will see that there are complex relationships between the two. While it is often the case that rule following occurs, and the nonverbal behavior then seems to be insensitive to its consequences because it is controlled by the verbal behavior (such as the rule "The coin generally comes down 'heads'"), it is also true that this type of verbal behavior is itself quite sensitive to its consequences. That is, if formulations of the rule are reinforced — we might follow statements that "The coin is unbiased" with social approval, for example — this verbal behavior will change quite rapidly.

2.9 CONDITIONED REINFORCEMENT

It is apparent from even a cursory examination of the world about us that some of the special consequences that we have been calling reinforcers have a more natural or biological primacy than others, and we have already noted that this led to Hull's (1943) theory that drive reduction was crucial to reinforcement. Food, water, and sex fall into a different, more "basic", category than books, money, and cars. Yet people, at one time or another, work for all of the things in the latter category. We can distinguish between these two categories by the manner in which a stimulus comes to be effective as a reinforcer. For each individual, there exists a class of reinforcers whose powers are a biological consequence of the individual's membership of a certain species. These reinforcers are as much a property of the species as are the leopard's spots, the cat's fur, the dog's tail. Possibilities of reinforcement which come built into the organism this way define the *primary* or *unconditioned reinforcers*, but there is also a second group of *conditioned reinforcers*, which appear more variable and less predictable from individual to individual than the primary set.

Money, cars, holidays, newspapers, prestige, honor, and the countless other arbitrary things that human beings work for constitute a vast source of reliable and potent reinforcers. But these objects and events have no value for us at birth. Clearly, they must have *acquired* their capacity to reinforce at some time during each individual's past history. A particular past history is a prerequisite; witness the occasional adult for whom some of the conventional reinforcers seem to hold no value. Moreover, gold has little importance for a Trappist monk, primitive man would hardly have fought for a copy of a best-selling novel, and not everybody likes Brahms. The context is also important: the business executive may enjoy a telephone call from a friend when work is slack, but be irritated by it occurring during an important meeting. Another way of putting this is that establishing operations (see Section 2.5) are important for conditioned as for unconditioned reinforcement.

While the importance of conditioned reinforcers is much more evident in human behavior than in the behavior of other species, the ways in which previously unimportant stimuli (lights, noises etc.) come to have conditioned reinforcing value have been extensively investigated in laboratory experiments with other animal species. It turns out that a relatively simple rule determines when a stimulus acquires conditioned reinforcing value: a stimulus acquires conditioned reinforcing value if it signals a reduction in the delay of (unconditioned) reinforcement (Fantino, 1977). Extrapolating this principle to human development, we would expect children to be reinforced by access to stimuli that signal forthcoming meal times, other treats, or a period of parental affection. Because the stimuli that have these functions vary from one child's experience to another's, we would anticipate that conditioned reinforcers vary in value from individual to individual.

The stimulus that seems to have most general properties as a conditioned reinforcer is, of course, money. Money has the culturally-defined property of being exchangeable for just about any other item: it therefore has the capacity to reduce the delay of many types of reinforcement. We can defined a *generalized conditioned reinforcer* as one that has acquired reinforcing value through signalling a reduction in delay (or presentation) of *many* primary reinforcers. Money fits this definition, but it is still not a perfectly generalized conditioned reinforcer, because we still tend to prefer some forms of money to others (Lea, Tarpy and Webley, 1987). Thus, we might prefer gold coins to notes, or refuse to put our money in the bank and keep the cash at home instead. These "irrational" habits presumably reflect the fact the reinforcing value of money is acquired and affected by details of the past histories of individuals. Generalized conditioned reinforcers are often used to increase adaptive behavior in applied or clinical settings (see Chapter 9).

2.10 THE DEFINITION OF RESPONSE CLASSES

Our definition of the simple operant conditioning paradigm (Section 2.6) stated that instances of an operant response class are followed by presentations of a reinforcing stimulus, but we have not yet provided a definition of response classes. One of the reasons that the science of behavior has been late in developing lies in the nature of its subject matter. Unlike kidney tissue, salt crystals or rock formations, behavior cannot easily be held still for observation. Rather, the movements and actions of organisms appear to flow in a steady stream with no clear-cut beginning or end. When a rat moves from the front to the back of its cage, when you drive 500 miles nonstop in your car, or when you read a book, it is difficult to identify points at which the continuous *behavior stream* can be broken into natural units. A further complication is that no two instances of an organism's actions are ever exactly the same, because no response is ever exactly repeated.

As a first step towards defining a response category, or *response class*, we might define a set of behaviors that meet certain requirements and fall within certain limits along specified response dimensions. This would be a *topographically-defined* response class, where topography is defined as specific patterns of bodily positions and movements. We can then check whether this response class meets the criterion of an *operant* response class by following occurrences of instances of the class with a reinforcing stimulus. If the *whole class* becomes more frequent, then we have successfully defined an operant response class.

Consider some examples. We might define the limits of a certain class of movements, such as those of the right arm, and attempt to reinforce all movements within the specified limits. If *reaching movements* then occur, are reinforced, and increase in frequency, we can conclude that reaching (with the right arm) is an operant. Words are prominent examples of the formation of culturally-determined response classes. All sounds that fall within certain acceptable limits (hence are made by muscular activity within certain limits) make up the spoken word *"please"*. When a child enunciates and pronounces the word correctly, reinforcement is provided and the class of movements that produce "please" is increased in frequency. In both these cases, the reinforced operant class is likely to be slightly different from the topography originally specified.

In nature, it seems unlikely that reinforcement is ever contingent on a response class defined by topographical limits in the way just described. In the laboratory, reinforcement could be made contingent on a restricted subset of behaviors defined in that way. But even there, units are more usually approximated by classing together all the movements that act to produce a specified *change in the environment*. We call this a *functionally-defined operant*. It is defined as consisting of all the behaviors that could produce a particular environmental change, and thus have a particular function for the organism. It contrasts with a *topographically-defined operant* which, as we have seen, would be defined as consisting of movements that fall within certain physical limits.

The use of functionally-defined operants greatly facilitates analysis, because not only do such units closely correspond to the way in which we talk about behavior ("he missed the train" or "please shut the door"), but also measurement is made easier. When a rat is placed in a conventional Skinner box, it is easy to measure how many times the lever is depressed by a certain amount; it is much more difficult to record how many paw movements of a certain type occur. Similarly, it is fairly easy to record how often a child gets up from a seat in a classroom, but hard to measure the postural changes involved.

While we can alter the specifications of an operant for our convenience, it must be remembered that *the only formal requirement of an operant is that it be a class of behaviors that is susceptible, as a class, to reinforcement.* If we specify a class that fails to be strengthened or maintained by reinforcing its members, such a class does not constitute an operant response.

2.11 RESPONSE DIFFERENTIATION AND RESPONSE SHAPING

One of the most important features of operant conditioning is that response classes, as defined in the previous section, can change. Formally, this process is called *response differentiation* and its practical application is called *response shaping.*

What we have defined as simple operant conditioning is a special case of response differentiation. Let us consider a case in which the specification of the behavioral class to be reinforced is in terms of a single behavioral dimension. In the definition of the lever press of a rat, the minimum force required to depress the lever can be specified. This minimum force is an example of a lower limit of a behavioral dimension. Hays and Woodbury (cited in Hull, 1943) conducted such an experiment, using a minimum force of 21 grams weight . That is, to "count" as a lever press, there had to be a downward pressure on the lever of 21 grams weight or more. After the conditioning process had stabilized, they examined the distribution of response force for a large number of individual responses. While many responses were close to 21 grams in force, there was a roughly symmetrical distribution with a maximum at 29 grams, or 8 grams above the minimum force required. The force requirement was then changed to a minimum of 36 grams. Over a period of time, the rat's behavior changed correspondingly, and the center of the distribution of response forces became 41 to 45 grams. Conditioning of this new class of behavior had thus been successful, but there had been a further important consequence of this conditioning. Novel emitted forces, never before seen in the animal's repertoire (those over 45 grams), were now occurring with moderate frequency. The results of the experiment are shown in Figure 2.6.

This *differentiation procedure*, where certain response variants are differentially reinforced, had resulted in the appearance and maintenance of a set of novel behaviors. This occurred through the operation of two complementary processes. At the time it was put into effect, the new requirement of 36 grams encompassed some existing forces which continued to be reinforced. Secondly, the 36-grams minimum requirement excluded many forces previously reinforced. When these responses were emitted under the 36-grams minimum procedure, they were subjected to *extinction*, which is discussed in the next chapter. Extinction is the procedure of removing reinforcement from a previously reinforced class of behavior. It has the principal effect of reducing the frequency of occurrence of that class, and it also increases response variability.

The great power of the response differentiation procedure, when used

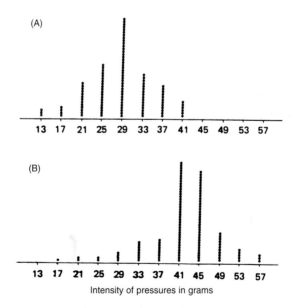

Figure 2.6 Distribution of response forces when (A, upper graph) all responses with a force of more than 21g were reinforced, and (B, lower graph) when all responses with a force of more than 36 g were reinforced (after Hays and Woodbury, cited in Hull, 1943).

with a changing series of response classes, lies in its ability to generate and then sustain behaviors hitherto unobserved in the person's or animal's repertoire. This power is extended very much further in cases in which progressive and gradual differentiations can be made to take place over time. We call this method of introducing new behavior into the repertoire *response shaping by successive approximation.* By such a process of successive approximation on the lever-force dimension, Skinner (1938) was able to train 200-gram rats to perform the Herculean feat of pressing a bar requiring a 100-grams minimal force! A better-known example from human behavior is the record time for the 100 meters race: a time that would have been the world record in 1950 is now routinely improved on by athletes in training. We can think of this as a skilled performance that has been shaped within individuals, and passed on by other means between individuals.

Response shaping by successive approximation has a straightforward and very important use in the operant-conditioning laboratory. Suppose an experimenter wishes to reinforce the pecking of a wall-mounted key or disk by pigeons with food. This response often has zero operant-level frequency (that is, prior to training it does not occur at all) and thus must be shaped. The experimenter successively approximates the desired form of the behavior, beginning with a form that may not resemble key pecking at all. For example, all movements in the vicinity of the key may first be reinforced. Once these movements have increased in relative frequency, reinforcement is made contingent on head movements directed towards the key. Once such movements are frequent, reinforcement is made contingent upon striking the key with the beak, and finally, upon depressing the key with the beak. The process of introducing a response not previously in the repertoire can be very easy or very difficult. The degree of difficulty experienced probably reflects the preparedness of the organism to associate the specified response and reinforcer as well as the stringency of the response differentiation required by the experimenter.

Response shaping is a highly important technique in the application of behavioral analysis to human problems. Many such problems can be characterized as *behavioral deficits*: the individual concerned does not succeed in making "normal" responses and thus his or her behavior is not maintained by the social consequences that influence the behavior of others. Stuttering, for example, may prevent the individual from routinely engaging in conversation with others. Howie and Woods (1982) successfully used a shaping procedure to produce and increase fluency of speech in adult stutterers. Participants were reinforced in each session of training if they met the currently required rate of stutter-free speech, if they avoided stuttering, and if they completed a target number of syllables using a continuous speech pattern. If they were successful, the required rate of stutter-free speech was increased by 5 syllables per minute for the next session, until a rate of 200 syllables per minute was achieved. Shaping adaptive responding in applied or clinical settings will discussed in greater detail in Chapter 9.

2.12 SUMMARY

We can provide a scientific account of the types of behavior described as "purposive", but the first step is to recognize that such behavior is influenced by its previous consequences. A hungry pigeon in an operant test chamber, or Skinner box, will peck at the response key because this behavior has previously been followed by food presentation.

Skinner advanced the study of such behavior by deciding to use rate of response as a measure, and by devising the Skinner box within which laboratory animals can emit responses from time to time. If a contingency, or relationship, is arranged between an emitted response and a reinforcing consequence, then a number of characteristic behavioral changes ensue and we say that operant conditioning has occurred. These changes include an increase in response frequency, the sequential organization of behavior, reduction in response variability, and reductions in other (non-reinforced) behavior.

Operant conditioning will only occur when the stimulus made contingent upon the operant response acts as a reinforcer. The property of being a reinforcer, or reinforcing stimulus, is not inherent in a stimulus. Rather, it depends upon the state of the organism and the environment at the time. Operant conditioning will occur if the organism is currently deprived of its preferred rate of access to the reinforcer and if occurrence of the operant response results in an increase in that rate of access. Food is thus a reinforcer for key pecking by a hungry pigeon because the current preferred rate of feeding is very high, and delivery of food as a reinforcer increases the actual rate of feeding towards that preferred rate. In this example, food deprivation is an establishing operation that ensures that operant conditioning will occur in the experiment.

There are many interesting demonstrations of operant conditioning with humans. These include studies of vocalization by infants and of very small movements in adults. The latter example is important because the operant response classes increased in frequency even though the participants in the experiment were unaware of the particular response required.

Human behavior is much affected by conditioned reinforcement. That is, behavior is changed when the consequence is a stimulus with a function that has been established through the previous experience of the individual. The most potent example of a generalized conditioned reinforcer is money, but other conditioned reinforcers (such as a liking for a particular type of music) will be specific to the individual and result from their own particular history.

We tend to assume that behavior, or response classes, should be described topographically, or in terms of the bodily movements involved. In fact, operant conditioning generally involves functional response classes. In a functional response class, all the members have a particular effect on the environment. Examples of this type of functional class are a pigeon pecking at a key mounted on the wall or a person writing a series of words. Operant response classes can be established through response shaping. This is necessary when the initial behavioral repertoire does not include the required response. In the shaping process, successively closer approximations to the required response are reinforced. The outcome is a change in the behavioral repertoire to include the desired response.

CHAPTER **3**

EXTINCTION AND INTERMITTENT REINFORCEMENT

"So long as life endures, a creature's behavior is a clay to be molded by circumstances, whimsical or planned. Acts added to it, and other acts which fall out, are the means by which it is shaped. Like the two hands of an artisan, busily dabbing and gouging, are the processes, reinforcement and extinction."
F.S.Keller and W.N.Schoenfeld, Principles of Psychology, 1950.

Operant conditioning results in changes in the behavioral repertoire. It provides a method by which the organism adapts to its own circumstances by selectively increasing the frequency of responses that are followed by reinforcing stimuli. It is not surprising to find that if a previously reinforced operant response is no longer followed by its usual reinforcing consequence, the frequency of the operant declines. This process is called extinction. We shall see in a later section of this chapter that operant extinction has the same overall effect as the related process of extinction following classical conditioning, first studied by I.P. Pavlov (Pavlov, 1927). This overall effect common to the two conditioning processes is the reduction in frequency of a specific response. In both cases, the process broadly reverses the effects of conditioning once the circumstances, or contingencies, that resulted in conditioning have been removed or substantially changed. However, there are also a number of associated phenomena specific to operant extinction. Not surprisingly, both operant extinction and classical extinction exert important influences on human behavior.

3.1 CHANGES IN RESPONSE RATE DURING OPERANT EXTINCTION

Extinction occurs when the reinforcement contingency that produced operant conditioning is removed, but this can be done in at least two ways. Following operant conditioning, the normal operation is to cease presenting the reinforcing stimulus at all, and most of the findings reported here are based on this procedure, but there is an alternative. If it is the particular relationship, or contingency, between operant response and reinforcer that defines operant conditioning and brings about changes in behavior, then any operation that removes the contingency will constitute extinction. Thus, a procedure in which the reinforcing stimulus continues to occur, but is no longer dependent on occurrences of the operant response, could result in extinction.

Note that the word "extinction" is used in two different ways. Extinction refers to the experimental procedure, or *operation*, of breaking the contingency between response and reinforcer. However, it is also a name for the observed resulting decline in the frequency of the response when that operation is carried out. We call this change in behavior the *extinction process*. A response is said to have been *extinguished* if the frequency has fallen close to its operant level as a result of there no longer being a contingency between that behavior and the reinforcer. There are, of course, other methods of reducing the frequency of a response (some of which will be discussed in later chapters), but these are not called extinction.

The decline in the rate of the once-reinforced response is the best documented effect of extinction. The changes in rate are clearly seen on a cumulative record, where they appear as wavelike fluctuations superimposed on a general negative acceleration of the rate of responding. In Figure 3.1 such an extinction curve appears for the lever-press response of a rat, previously accustomed to receiving a food pellet for each lever press. The response rate is highest at the start (just after reinforcement is withdrawn), and gradually diminishes over the period of an hour and a half.

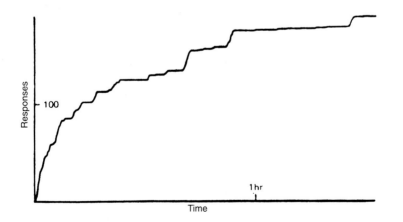

Figure 3.1   Cumulative record of responding in extinction of lever press response previously reinforced with food (from Skinner, 1938, data of F.S. Keller and A. Kent).

By the end of 90 minutes, the rat is responding at a rate only slightly higher than its operant-level rate. As Figure 3.1 shows, the extinction curve is very irregular and contains many periods of high activity interspersed with periods of low activity (the flat portions of the curve). The latter becomes more prominent towards the end of extinction. Some researchers have found that the extinction process is due principally to a gradual increase in the number of these inactive periods over time, and that when the organism responds it does so at its usual high rate.

Accompanying the overall decline in response rate in extinction, there is often seen a transitory *increase* in rate at the very beginning of extinction. This can be seen at the beginning of the cumulative record in Figure 3.1. The reason for this transient effect is suggested by the results of another procedure in which the contingency between the response (lever pressing) and the reinforcer (food pellets) is broken. Figure 3.2 shows cumulative records for two rats given food reinforcement for 100 lever presses, and then shifted to a procedure where food pellets were delivered automatically at approximately the same intervals at which they had been obtained during reinforcement.

This "free food" procedure was effective in reducing response rates, which rapidly declined to near zero, but the transient increase in rate was slight for one experimental participant and non-existent for the other. We may conclude that the transient rate increase is related to the shift to a procedure in which the reinforcer is no longer presented. Time allocation again proves a useful concept in describing this finding. During reinforcement of lever pressing, rats typically spend a great deal of time retrieving and consuming the reinforcers. This leaves comparatively little time available for making the operant response. If they are subsequently transferred to a procedure in which no reinforcing stimuli occur, the time spent on retrieval and consumption is "released" for other activities such as the operant response. The transient increase in rate described above may thus reflect the allocation of more time to lever pressing at the beginning of extinction than was available during reinforcement.

3.2 TOPOGRAPHICAL AND STRUCTURAL CHANGES OF RESPONDING IN EXTINCTION

The effects of extinction are by no means confined to frequency changes in the selected response. In particular, marked changes occur in the form of the

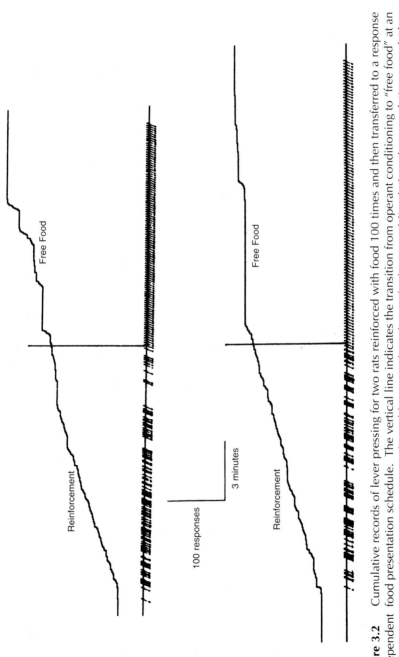

Figure 3.2   Cumulative records of lever pressing for two rats reinforced with food 100 times and then transferred to a response independent food presentation schedule. The vertical line indicates the transition from operant conditioning to "free food" at an equivalent rate. Food presentations are indicated by vertical marks on the horizontal line below the cumulative record (data collected by M. Keenan).

behavior during extinction. In a study by Antonitis (1951), in which the operant under study involved a rat poking its nose through a slot in the wall (see Figure 3.3), the effects of several sessions of extinction interspersed with reinforcement were measured. One wall of the chamber used by Antonitis contained a horizontal slot, 50 centimeters long. Whenever the rat poked its nose into the slot, a light beam was broken, causing a photograph of the rat to be made at the exact instant of the response. By reinforcing nose poking with food, the frequency of this behavior was first increased above operant level. Subsequently, nose poking was extinguished, reconditioned, re-extinguished, and reconditioned again. Antonitis found that response position and angle tended to become stereotyped during reinforcement: the animal confined its responses to a rather restricted region of the slot. Extinction, however, produced *variability* in nose poking at least as great as that observed during operant level; the animal varied its responses over the entire length of the slot. Finally, reconditioning resulted in even more stereotyped behavior (more restricted responses) than the original conditioning had produced.

The loop or chain of behavior established by reinforcement degenerates when reinforcement no longer follows the operant response. Frick and Miller (1951) gave rats 300 reinforcements over a period of five sessions in a modified Skinner box. This box had a lever on one wall and a food tray on the opposite wall. This increased the distance between lever and food tray, and made the two responses topographically and spatially distinct, and

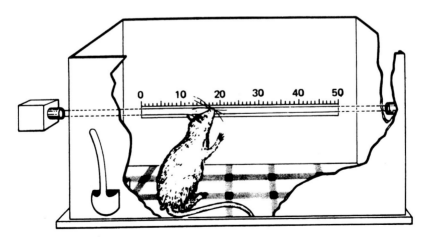

Figure 3.3   Apparatus used by Antonitis (1951) to reinforce nose poking.

thus easy to record separately. These were denoted as R_L: lever press and R_T: tray visit. During extinction, Frick and Miller observed the degeneration of the previously-established R_L-R_T-R_L-R_T... loop. As extinction progressed, lever presses began to follow lever presses (R_L-R_L-, and so on), and tray visits began to follow tray visits (R_T-R_T-, and so on). There was very little tendency for the pattern to become random during extinction. Rather, the strengthened pattern of R_L-R_T-R_L-R_T-... gradually gave way to the operant-level pattern of repeated occurrences of the same response. Notice that this result was by no means logically inevitable, for the loop of behavior could simply have declined in frequency during extinction, yet remained intact.

To summarize, the extinction procedure instigates a behavioral process whose effects include decline in frequency of the operant response, an increase in its variability, and a breakdown in the sequential structure of the behavior. These important properties of extinction indicate that while operant reinforcement acts to selectively increase certain response sequences and thus restrict the behavioral repertoire, in extinction these effects are reversed, and the variability of behavior is to some extent reinstated.

3.3   EXTINCTION-INDUCED AGGRESSION

We have described some changes in the formerly reinforced response resulting from extinction. What happens to the other behaviors that do not have a history of reinforcement in the experiment? Not surprisingly, some responses that are reduced in frequency when an operant is reinforced (in the case of a rat reinforced with food these may include grooming and investigatory behavior) increase again during extinction. More surprisingly, some "new" behavior may be seen. That is, responses occur that were not seen during reinforcement and had effectively zero operant level prior to reinforcement. The most remarkable of these is aggression. Azrin, Hutchinson and Hake (1966) trained a hungry bird to peck a disk for food. When the experimental bird had acquired key-pecking behavior, a second "target" bird, immobilized in a specially designed box, was introduced into the experimental compartment (see Figure 3.4). The box holding the target bird was mounted on an assembly that caused a switch underneath to close whenever the box was jiggled vigorously. The assembly was carefully balanced so that normal spontaneous movements of the target bird were insufficient to close the switch, whereas any forceful attacks that the

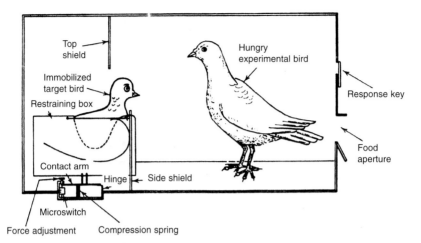

Figure 3.4 Apparatus used for measuring aggression induced by extinction in a Skinner box (Azrin, Hutchinson, & Hake, 1966).

experimental bird might direct against the exposed body of the target bird would be recorded. Attacks occurred predictably: whenever its reinforcement contingencies were abruptly changed from reinforcement of pecking to extinction, the experimental bird invariably attacked the target bird. The attacks were vicious and aggressive, lasting up to 10 minutes.

Other experiments have established a considerable degree of generality for this result by demonstrating that extinction-induced aggression can be obtained with various species and reinforcers. The important point to remember is that these attacks do not occur simply because no reinforcement is available, but because reinforcement was previously available and has now been discontinued.

3.4 RESISTANCE TO EXTINCTION

Were the extinction process allowed to go to completion, the operant-level state might eventually be reached; that is, the frequency of the operant response might return to the before-conditioning level. The time taken for this to occur could then be used as an index of the individual's persistence in the face of extinction, and thus of the strength of responding before extinction was begun. In actual experiments, a return to operant level is rarely, if ever, reached. Hence, more convenient and practical measures of persistence are based on how fast the response rate declines during extinction. For instance, the number of responses emitted, or the amount of time, up until the point at which some low rate criterion (such as a period of 5 minutes with no responses) is met, are called resistance-to-extinction measures.

Resistance to extinction provides a quantitative behavioral index which is related in an interesting way to a number of experimental operations. In everyday life, we are often interested in how persistent a person will be in the face of no reward. A person whose resistance to extinction is low is said to "give up too easily" or to lack "perseverance" at a difficult task. On the other hand, too much resistance to extinction is sometimes counterproductive. The man or woman who spends too much time fruitlessly trying to patch up a broken love affair may miss a good chance for a new and better relationship.

One of the variables that has been shown to affect resistance to extinction is the number of previous reinforcements. It seems plausible that if a large number of responses have been reinforced, resistance to extinction will be greater than if only a few have been. This general hypothesis has been confirmed by several experiments (for example, Williams, 1938; Perin, 1942; Hearst, 1961) which indicate that the resistance to extinction of an operant is low when only a few reinforcements have been given in conditioning, and then gradually increases with increasing number of reinforcements until a maximum is reached. Even bigger effects on resistance to extinction result from exposure to intermittent reinforcement, which is discussed later in this chapter.

Another variable that would seem likely to affect the persistence of a response in extinction is the effortfulness of the response. Mowrer and Jones (1943) hypothesised that responses that required great effort to make would extinguish more quickly than would responses requiring less effort. This prediction has been confirmed in a study by Capehart, Viney, and Hulicka (1958), who trained rats to press a lever for food. They varied the force necessary to depress the lever during conditioning, so that on some sessions, a heavy lever was present, and on others, it was light or intermediate. The animals were then divided into three groups, one of which was extinguished using the heavy lever, another using the light lever, and the last on the intermediate lever. Using a criterion of no responses in 5 minutes as the index of resistance to extinction, they obtained the function shown in Figure 3.5.

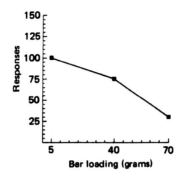

Figure 3.5 Resistance to extinction of lever pressing as a function of the weight of the lever (or bar) (after Capehart, Viney, & Hulicka, 1958).

3.5 SPONTANEOUS RECOVERY

Extinction may be extended until the rate of a previously reinforced operant response has reached a low level. If the experimental participant (for example, a rat in a Skinner box) is then removed from the situation and returned a bit later, another (smaller) extinction curve will be obtained (see Figure 3.6). Even though no reconditioning (a process which we discuss in the next section) has taken place between the two extinction sessions, a certain amount of spontaneous increase in responding has occurred.

The amount of this *spontaneous recovery* (as measured by the resistance to extinction in the second extinction session) depends on the time lapse between the end of the first extinction and the beginning of the

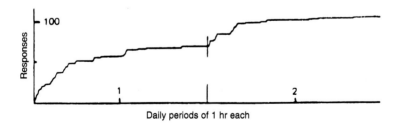

Figure 3.6 Spontaneous recovery from extinction of a rat's lever-press response. The portions of the curve to the left and right of the vertical line in the middle of the graph were separated by 47 hours away from the experiment (Skinner, 1938).

second one. With food reinforced operants, spontaneous recovery has been observed after as little as 15 minutes, and often has been found to reach a maximum after about two hours. The existence of spontaneous recovery supports a conclusion from the schedule-induced aggression findings: once a response has been extinguished, the organism is not returned to the state it was in before conditioning was started. Further support for this hypothesis will be found in the next section.

3.6 Successive Conditioning and Extinction

The first extinction after original reinforcement is a unique phenomenon. Later extinctions (after reconditioning by the reintroduction of reinforcement) differ by being more rapid and containing fewer total responses. This effect was documented by Bullock and Smith (1953). They exposed rats to 10 daily sessions of a procedure that reinforced the first 40 lever responses, followed directly by 1 hour of extinction. When the extinction curves were examined, it was found that they became progressively smaller over Sessions 1 to 10. The effect is shown in Figure 3.7. Whereas in Session 1 the average resistance to extinction in 1 hour was 50 responses, by Session 10 this had dropped to only 10 responses.

These results can be extrapolated beyond ten sessions. It would seem that only a few more sessions would be needed before the animals would

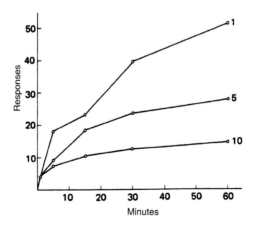

Figure 3.7   Averaged cumulative response curves for the first (1), fifth (5), and tenth (10) sessions of extinction (after Bullock & Smith, 1953).

reach what is called one-trial extinction. In one-trial extinction, only a single response is emitted following the withdrawal of reinforcement. The change in behavior has become abrupt, and it seems reasonable to conclude that the organism has come to *discriminate* the extinction procedure as such. The concept of *discrimination* is of great general importance and will be a central topic of Chapter 4. Few responses in extinction are the rule at the human level, as many of our own responses show a rapid decrement when reinforcement ceases: we do not continue to insert coins into a faulty soft drinks or candy dispenser when we fail to receive the payoff. When we open the mailbox and discover it is empty, we do not keep opening it. Like Bullock and Smith's rats, we have learned to not to respond needlessly. However, unlike those rats, we are likely to formulate verbal rules as to what is happening in the situation. As we will see later (Chapter 6), this is likely to produce particularly rapid extinction.

3.7   THE OPERANT EXTINCTION PARADIGM

The extinction procedure gives rise to the extinction process. As we have seen, the extinction process consists, in part, of a decline in response rate. However, a number of other behavioral processes (such as fatigue, habituation, satiation, and punishment) entail a similar decline, and we must be careful to distinguish them. If a decline in rate of response is all we observe, we are likely to find it difficult to say which response-reduction process is operating. As we will wish to use the extinction process to explain more complex processes, it is important that we understand both its specific procedure and the various characteristics of its resulting process. We will then be able to distinguish those instances of decline in response rate that are the result of extinction from those that reflect other processes.

Formally, the operant extinction paradigm is defined as follows. The contingency between a previously-reinforced operant response and its reinforcer is removed by either (a) ceasing to present the reinforcing stimulus, or (b) presenting that stimulus independent of the occurrence of the response. This has the following effects:

1. A gradual, somewhat irregular decline in response rate marked by progressive increases in frequency of relatively long periods of non-responding. This may be preceded by a transient increase in response rate.

2. An increase in the variability of the form and magnitude of the response.
3. A disruption of the loop or sequence of behavior that characterized the reinforced operant.

The decline in rate continues until the operant level is approached as a limiting value.

3.8   EXTINCTION OUTSIDE THE LABORATORY

We are all familiar with the power of extinction; many instances can be identified in everyday life in which the frequency or probability of certain behavior declines because it is no longer reinforced. In ordinary language, this decline in response probability may be attributed to other causes, but to the experimental psychologist the role of extinction is clear:

> An aspiring writer who has sent manuscript after manuscript to the publishers only to have them all rejected may report that "he can't write another word". He may be partially paralyzed with what is called "writer's cramp". He may still insist that he "wants to write", and we may agree with him in these terms: his extremely low probability of response is mainly due to extinction. Other variables are still operative which, if extinction had not taken place, would yield a high probability of the behavior in question (Skinner, 1953, pp. 71–72).

The task of the psychologist is easy when he or she merely provides *post* hoc analyses of everyday terms and situations, but we have already seen how, in this case, laboratory studies have already provided us with an account of the extinction process that goes well beyond that which can be extracted from casual observation.

3.9   EXTINCTION OF CLASSICALLY CONDITIONED RESPONSES

As noted in Chapter 1, not only did Pavlov (1927) carry out the initial studies of classical conditioning, but he sustained a systematic research program over many years. The investigation of extinction following conditioning was a major part of this. In parallel with operant conditioning, classical extinction occurs if the CS-US pairing is broken. This is usually achieved by repeatedly presenting the CS without the US. The result is a fairly steady diminution of the response to the CS. An example for the rabbit's nictitating membrane (blinking) response is shown in Figure 3.8. Although the data in this figure are the average performances of groups of rabbits, very similar results would be obtained from individual rabbits. In the control group, the CS and US were presented but not paired together in the "acquisition phase" and thus conditioning did not occur in that group. The experimental group showed conditioning occurring rapidly over 5 days, then reaching a steady asymptotic level. In extinction, the number of conditioned responses fell fairly steadily from day to day.

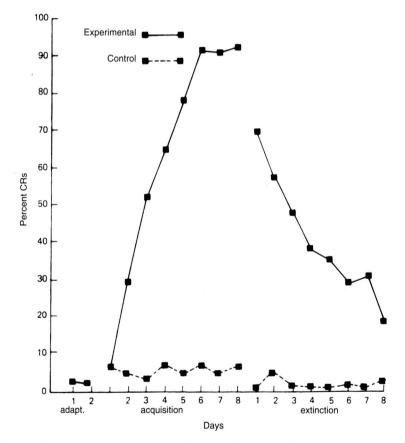

Figure 3.8 Average data for classical conditioning followed by extinction of rabbits' nictitating membrane response (Gormezano, Schneiderm-an, Deaux & Fuentes, 1962). Details are given in the text.

Various *inhibitory phenomena* were discovered in the experiments of Pavlov and his associates. This is interesting because Pavlov, being trained as a physiologist, presumed that inhibitory (response-suppressing) processes as well as excitatory (response-eliciting) processes will occur in conditioning, it is not inevitable that inhibitory concepts will be needed to explain behavior. After all, a response either occurs or fails to occur; we need not necessarily infer from its absence that it is inhibited, it might simply be that the stimulus no longer elicits a response. The need for inhibition as an explanatory concept will be made clearer by considering the related phenomenon of spontaneous recovery within classical conditioning, also demonstrated by Pavlov.

If a period of time elapses after the extinction of a classically conditioned response and then the experimental participant is returned to the experimental situation and the CS is again presented, a certain amount of *spontaneous recovery* occurs. This means that a higher level of responding is observed than at the end of the previous session. Pavlov argued that this demonstrates that inhibition had developed during the first extinction session and had dissipated, to some extent, before the next test, thus allowing the response to recover. Whatever the details of the theoretical explanation, it is interesting that the two pioneers in their respective fields, Pavlov and Skinner, both demonstrated spontaneous recovery in their conditioning paradigms. We should clearly expect to see evidence of this in real world applications. That is, when human behavior has been conditioned and then extinguished, we can anticipate some subsequent brief recovery of the behavior.

3.10 INTERMITTENT REINFORCEMENT

So far, we have restricted our discussions of operant behavior to examples of simple operant conditioning, where operant responses are *continuously reinforced* and every occurrence of the response is followed by delivery of the reinforcing stimulus, and examples of extinction, where that contingency is removed. If we change the conditions so that the reinforcing stimulus occurs only after some of the designated responses, we have defined the general procedure of *intermittent reinforcement*. Intermittent reinforcement procedures can be arranged in a number of ways, with varying rules, or schedules, determining which individual responses are followed by the reinforcing stimulus.

It has been found that intermittent reinforcement procedures have great utility for generating stable, long-term *baselines* of learned behavior, against which effects of drugs, physiological manipulations, emotional stimuli, and motivational factors can be studied. These applications of the principles of behavioral analysis are very important for the development of psychology and the neurosciences in general. These procedures have as yet been used less often outside the laboratory in applications to significant human problems, where the procedures of simple operant conditioning and extinction have traditionally been preferred, but they are currently gaining greater use there as well. Examples of these applications will be discussed in later chapters.

Early experimental studies of learned behavior were conducted by investigators who were mainly concerned with the acquisition of behavior, and these investigators took little interest in intermittent reinforcement. Although it is true that the acquisition of "new" behavior usually proceeds most smoothly when each and every response is reinforced, it turns out that intermittent reinforcement procedures produce reliable and distinctive patterns of behavior, which are extremely resistant to extinction. In intermittent reinforcement procedures, the response is still a necessary condition, but no longer a sufficient condition, for the delivery of the reinforcer. We refer to those experimental procedures that specify which instances of an operant response shall be reinforced as *schedules of reinforcement*. Thus, *continuous reinforcement* is a schedule in which every response is reinforced whenever it occurs (for reasons that will become apparent shortly, this very simple schedule is also called FR1). A host of schedules have been devised and studied in which reinforcement is noncontinuous, or *intermittent*. Each of these schedules specifies the particular condition or set of conditions that must be met before the next response is reinforced.

If we consider the relatively simple situation where only one response is to be examined and the stimulus conditions are constant, there are at least two conditions for reinforcement of an individual response that we may specify: the number of responses that must occur, and the time that must elapse. Schedules involving a required *number* of responses are called *ratio schedules* (referring to the ratio of responses to reinforcers); and schedules specifying a period of *time* are called *interval schedules* (referring to the imposed intervals of time between reinforcement). Schedules can also be either *fixed* (where every reinforcer is delivered after the same ratio or interval requirement has been fulfilled), or *variable* (where the ratios and intervals can vary within the schedule).

Here are verbal descriptions corresponding to an example of each of these four simple types of reinforcement schedules:

> *Fixed ratio 10 (FR 10)*. The tenth operant response that occurs will be reinforced, then the tenth of the subsequent operant responses will be reinforced, and so on. The *response requirement* is fixed at 10 responses.
>
> *Fixed interval 20 seconds (FI 20 seconds)*. The first operant response that occurs once 20 seconds have elapsed will be reinforced, then the first response that occurs once a further 20 seconds have elapsed will be reinforced, and so on.
>
> *Variable ratio 15 (VR 15)*. The operant response requirement varies with an average value of 15. Thus it might be that twenty-fifth response that occurs is reinforced, and then the tenth response, and then the thirtieth response, and so on. Over a long run, the average of these requirements will be 15.
>
> *Variable interval 40 seconds (VI 40 seconds)*. The inter-reinforcement interval varies, with an average value of 40 seconds. It might be that the first operant response after 20 seconds is reinforced, then the first response after a subsequent interval of 55 seconds, then the first response after a subsequent interval of 35 seconds, and so on. Over a long run, the average of these times will be 40 seconds.

Although the procedures require a complicated verbal description, each of the four schedules we have defined generates a characteristic performance, or behavioral steady state. These states can be easily identified by looking at cumulative records (see Figure 3.9). Recall from Chapter 2 that the cumulative recorder steps vertically, a small and fixed amount, each time a response occurs, while continuously moving horizontally at a fixed speed (this record can either be made during the experiment, or it can be simulated by a computer from recorded details of the session). So the slope of the record at any point reflects the rate of response; cessation of responding produces a flat record, while a very high response rate produces a steep one. Vertical marks on the record indicate the delivery of reinforcers.

Although the records in Figure 3.9 are hypothetical, they are in no sense idealized (Leslie, 1996, for example, presents many actual records that are almost indistinguishable from these). Reinforcement schedules exert such

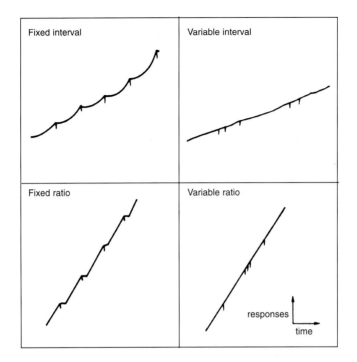

Figure 3.9   Typical cumulative records of performances maintained by four schedules of intermittent reinforcement.

powerful control over behavior that even a previously "untrained" rat, placed in a Skinner box by an "untrained" student, could generate one of these records after a few hours. Significantly, these performance patterns have been produced in many species, and with a variety of operant responses.

Here are some typical characteristics of performance generated by each schedule:

Fixed ratio (FR). A high rate of response is sustained until reinforcement occurs. This is followed by a relatively lengthy *post-reinforcement pause* before the high rate of responding is resumed. The post-reinforcement pause increases with the ratio of responses required for reinforcements, and can occupy the greater part of the experimental participant's time.

Variable ratio (VR). In common with the fixed ratio schedule, this procedure generates a high rate of response, but regular pausing for any length of time is very uncommon.

Fixed interval (FI). Like the fixed ratio schedule, this procedure also produces a post-reinforcement pause, but responding at other times occurs at a lower rate than on ratio schedules, except towards the end of the interval, where it accelerates to meet the reinforcer. The characteristic positively-accelerated curve seen on the cumulative record is called a "scallop". In general, longer fixed intervals produce lower rates of responding.

Variable interval (VI). As with the variable ratio schedule, consistent pauses of any length are rare. However, response rates are moderate to low, depending on the mean interval, with longer mean intervals producing lower response rates.

Intermittent schedule performances cannot, in general, be explained as the experimental participant adopting the most optimal strategy: experimental participants do not invariably learn to do what would benefit them most. For instance, treating operant responding as analogous to working (perhaps as a laborer), we would expect response rates on fixed interval schedules to fall until only one response per reinforcer occurred, emitted at precisely the end of the interval. Indeed, several early theorists suggested that the number of responses made on what we now call a schedule of reinforcement would be the least required to obtain all the reinforcers: this notion has not stood the test of time as many schedules generate numbers of responses that greatly exceed the minimum required. Furthermore, on fixed ratio schedules we might expect a maximum rate of operant responding to be continuously sustained for as long as possible, because that would maximize the rate of reinforcement, but long pauses occur. Leslie (1996, Chapter 4) provides a review of theoretical analyses of the behavioral processes that come together to generate the characteristic schedule performances. For our present purposes, the most important fact about schedules is that they do generate a great deal of responding, and it occurs in reliable and persistent patterns.

3.11 Differential Reinforcement Schedules

We have described four simple, or basic, schedules, FI, VI, FR, and VR. Another important class of schedules of reinforcement are those which specify a required rate of the operant response or of other behavior. An example of this is the *differential reinforcement of low rates* (DRL) schedule. In animal experimental studies, this schedule is usually programmed by reinforcement of only those responses which follow a previous response with a delay greater than a specified minimum value. On DRL 10 seconds, for example, a response is reinforced if, and only if, it occurs more than ten seconds after the previous one.

The DRL schedule can be conceptualized as a way of *reducing* the frequency of an operant response, unlike the other schedules that we have discussed so far. Consequently, it has been employed to deal with human behavioral problems where the behavior of concern occurs excessively frequently. Psychologists working with human behavioral problems are often seeking ways to reduce behavior, and a variety of other reinforcement schedules have been devised that indirectly reinforce reductions in a target behavior. These include *differential reinforcement of other behavior* (DRO), *differential reinforcement of incompatible behavior* (DRI), and *differential reinforcement of alternative behavior* (DRA). As implied by their titles, these schedules reinforce various categories of behavior other than the target behavior, but their effectiveness is measured primarily by the reduction in the target behavior that occurs. The "schedule of choice" will depend on details of the situation, but many effective interventions using these schedules have been reported. Some of these are described in Chapter 9.

Human behavioral interventions that reduce target behaviors are clearly of as much general importance as those that increase target behaviors. Another general way of eliminating unwanted behavior is through the use of *aversive contingencies.* However, as we shall see in Chapter 5, there are widespread contemporary objections to the use of aversive contingencies in modifying human behavior, and differential reinforcement schedules described here are consequently of great practical importance.

3.12 EXTINCTION FOLLOWING INTERMITTENT REINFORCEMENT

Earlier we noted that the amount of responding in extinction was affected by the number of prior reinforcers, and the effortfulness of the response during the previous period of reinforcement. An even more powerful influence on *resistance to extinction* is the schedule on which reinforcers were previously delivered. Indeed, the fact that any type of intermittent reinforcement increases resistance to extinction has generated a large research area of its own. This phenomenon, termed the *partial reinforcement extinction effect,* has been used as a baseline to study the effects of drugs and physiological manipulations believed to affect emotional processes taking place during extinction (see Gray, 1975, for a review).

From a purely behavioral standpoint, the introduction of extinction, once a schedule-controlled performance has been established, provides further evidence of the powerful control of behavior by schedules, because the pattern of behavior in extinction depends on the nature of the preceding schedule. For example, extinction following training on an FR schedule consists mostly of periods of time responding at the high "running rate" of responding that is characteristic of the schedule performance interspersed with increasingly long pauses, while extinction following training on a VI schedule consists of long periods of responding at a fairly low rate — initially similar to that maintained by the schedule — which gradually declines (Ferster and Skinner, 1957). The latter performance might be described as an "extinction curve" (similar to the one seen in Figure 3.1), but a large number of responses may be emitted. In one study (Skinner, 1950), a pigeon emitted over 3,000 responses in more than 8 hours.

In general, it is the similarity between the extinction situation and the previous conditions under which reinforcement was available that maintains behavior, and the transition from VR to extinction produces little apparent change, because the previous occasions on which responses were reinforced were unpredictable. In experiments, this can lead to high rates of behavior being maintained in extinction, at least initially. Ferster and Skinner (1957) reported that after a number sessions on VR (with the later sessions being on VR173 where an average of 173 responses was required for each reinforcement), a pigeon made around 5000 responses in extinction without a break at the high rate that had been characteristic of performance on the schedule. It is not surprising, in the light of findings such as this, that many games of chance and gaming machines provide payoffs on VR schedules. It is also clear that all these schedules give the experimental participant experience of "intermittent extinction," and thus can lead to remarkable perseveration of behavior.

It was believed for a long time that the effects of intermittent reinforcement constituted a major difference between operant and classical conditioning. This view developed because of the powerful "response-strengthening" effects of intermittent reinforcement within operant conditioning, and the apparent "response-weakening" effect seen in some classical conditioning studies. That is, use of intermittent presentation of the US following the CS can lead to a weaker conditioned response. However, it now clear that a partial reinforcement extinction effect can be obtained with a number of classical conditioning procedures; even though the conditioned response may be weaker in the intermittent reinforcement condition than with continuous, or 100%, reinforcement, when extinction is introduced there is more persistent responding from experimental participants that have previously received intermittent reinforcement (Pearce, Redhead, and Aydin,1997).

One of the most persistent problems faced by those engaged in modification of human behavioral problems is the observation that treatment gains are not maintained once the behavioral intervention has been withdrawn. The partial reinforcement extinction effect has been recognized by a number of researchers as a potential solution to this problem (Kazdin, 1994; Nation and Woods, 1980; Tierney and Smith, 1988). The way in which this effect may be used is to initially train the desired behavior on a continuous reinforcement schedule until it occurs at a high rate. At this stage, an intermittent reinforcement schedule is introduced. For example, a FR2 schedule might be used initially and the schedule value incremented gradually until the client is responding on a very "thin" reinforcement schedule (that is, one where a large number of responses are required for each reinforcer). If the program is withdrawn at this point the behavior will be highly resistant to extinction and stands a greater chance of being brought under the control of naturally occurring reinforcers in the environment. Kazdin and Polster (1973) demonstrated this effect with a group of adults with learning difficulties who were reinforced for increased levels of social interaction. In the case of highly persistent problem behaviors the opposite strategy may be adopted. Behaviors such as attention-seeking seem to be maintained on "natural" intermittent reinforcement schedules. We try to ignore them but give in occasionally, effectively reinforcing them on an intermittent basis. This makes them extremely resistant to extinction, rendering the use of extinction as a therapeutic strategy difficult. Paradoxically, deliberately reinforcing the behavior on a continuous basis can have the effect of reducing the time taken for extinction of the response to occur once the extinction phase is introduced.

3.13 Human Behavior Under Schedules of Reinforcement

It was mentioned earlier that while many species generate similar and characteristic patterns of behavior on simple reinforcement schedules, adult humans do not generally exhibit the same patterns of behavior. This is obviously an important discrepancy, because our general interest in the behavior of non-human animal species is sustained by the expectation, often borne out by empirical evidence, that their behavior resembles that of humans in similar situations.

Given very simple tasks, such as pressing a button or a key for reinforcement with small amounts of money or tokens, adult humans often produce behavior that is consistent with the "common-sense" view that they are acting in accordance with what they believe to be the *rule* determining when reinforcers are delivered. On an FI schedule, for example, the experimental participant may have come to the view that "If I wait 20 seconds, then the next button press will produce a token."

We can conceptualize this as the experimental situation leading the participant to engage in a certain sort of *verbal behavior* which generates a particular pattern of "button-pressing behavior". This may result in him or her counting to pass the appropriate length of time and then making one reinforced response. Unfortunately, the experimental participant's "common sense" may lead him or her to formulate a variety of different *verbal rules* describing the reinforcement contingencies that may be operating, and thus it is often impossible to predict how a number of experimental participants will behave under the same set of contingencies. One principle that this illustrates is that we need to know about relevant aspects of the history of the organism to predict how they will behave in a given situation. In everyday parlance, different people will bring different expectations (because of significant differences in their past lives) to the situation. Once again, this underlines the value of doing experiments on non-human animals where there is more likelihood that we can specify relevant previous experiences in such a way that they will not confound the results of an experiment. However, this does not resolve the serious problem we have encountered: a science of behavior requires us to establish how we can obtain the *same* behavior from each experimental participant under the same circumstances. We also wish to know why there are apparently differences between human behavior and that of many other species.

Fortunately, a number of different approaches have begun to resolve these problems. First of all, young children will produce the patterns of behavior typical of other species, provided they are trained before the age at which language acquisition is becoming rapid (Bentall, Lowe, and Beasty, 1985). Secondly, shaping the verbal behavior by successive approximation (by awarding tokens to "guesses" that approximate increasingly closely to the contingency in operation) changes both the verbal rule being formulated and the operant button-pressing behavior of adults (Catania, Matthews and Shimoff, 1990). Thirdly, reorganizing the situation slightly so that an alternative attractive behavior is available as well as the button-pressing activity can lead to adult humans producing the patterns of behavior characteristic of FI reinforcement schedules in other species (Barnes and Keenan, 1993).

These findings underline the importance of language, or verbal behavior, in the control of human operant non-verbal behavior, and as we shall see in Chapter 6, our developing understanding of the links between non-verbal and verbal behavior is beginning to give us an account of how humans differ from, and have greater skills than, other species. In the present context, they suggest that while other things being equal the behavior of adult humans is likely to correspond to verbal rules that they formulate, or are instructed to follow, in a situation involving a schedule of reinforcement, this rule-governed behavior is itself influenced by operant reinforcement contingencies.

3.14 SUMMARY

Conditioning changes behavior because certain relationships in the environment have been established. Once these relationships no longer exist, extinction occurs. This term refers both to the procedure of removing the conditioning relationship and to the outcome, which is that the frequency of the previously conditioned response declines.

Following operant conditioning, extinction is generally arranged by ceasing to present the reinforcing stimulus. Often there is a brief increase in response rate, followed by an erratic decline to a very low, or zero, level of responding. During extinction, response variability (which declines in operant conditioning, see Chapter 2) increases. If the operant reinforcement contingency is re-introduced, response frequency increases and response variability again declines.

The transition from operant conditioning to extinction often induces aggression in laboratory animals, if there is another animal available to be attacked. Such aggression does not occur solely because the operant is unreinforced; it only occurs when reinforcement has previously been available.

The amount of operant behavior in extinction (the resistance to extinction) is affected by a number of features of the conditioning situation, For example, both the number of reinforcements that have been received and the effort required for a response affect resistance to extinction. Following extinction, a period of time away from the conditioning situation may result in spontaneous recovery. That is, on return to the conditioning situation, the previously reinforced experimental participant emits a number of responses, even though extinction remains in effect.

Repeated cycles of operant conditioning and extinction have predictable effects. The transitions become very quick, in that as soon as operant conditioning is reinstated responding returns to its characteristic rate, and as soon as extinction is reinstated responding stops. This pattern takes a number of cycles to develop.

Classically conditioned responses are generally extinguished by repeatedly presenting the CS without presenting the US, A steady reduction in conditioned response magnitude is usually seen, with no measurable response occurring if enough CS-only trials are presented. As with operant conditioning, spontaneous recovery will occur (if the extinction session is terminated and then resumed sometime later).

In intermittent operant reinforcement, some but not all responses are followed by the reinforcing stimulus. Schedules of intermittent reinforcement, defined by a required number of responses or by the requirement for a period of time to elapse before a response is reinforced, generate large amounts of operant behavior organized into distinctive patterns. These can be used as a behavioral baseline against which the effect of motivational and other variables can be assessed. Differential operant reinforcement schedules are a further class. These are designed to either sustain a response at a low rate or to eliminate it through the intermittent reinforcement of other behavior. These are very important strategies for modifying problematic human behavior.

Perhaps the most important general consequence of intermittent reinforcement is that behavior becomes highly persistent. Following training on a schedule where many responses are required for reinforcement, for example, the experimental participant may produce hundreds of responses in extinction before response rate falls to a low level. This partial (or intermittent) reinforcement extinction effect also occurs in classical conditioning, at least in so far as conditioned responses are more persistent following intermittent reinforcement.

Although most intermittent reinforcement schedules have powerful effects on behavior, these are not always observed when adults are trained with these procedures in experiments. This is because of the role of verbal behavior and verbal rule-following in humans, and experiments with modified reinforcement schedules are providing a means of studying this complex area of human behavior.

CHAPTER 4

STIMULUS CONTROL

Ever since Pavlov (1927) extended the concept of the reflex to the study of conditioned reflexes in classical conditioning, behavioral scientists have sought to analyze the control exerted by stimuli over behavior. Many stimulus classes — that is, sets of similar or related stimuli — exert control over behavior in the sense that certain responses become much more probable (or much less probable) when a member of the stimulus class is present. As with the other phenomena that we have introduced in earlier chapters, such stimulus control is a characteristic not only of human behavior but also that of many other animal species. Consequently, we will be able to draw on the results of experimental work with various species in order to illustrate its features. However, we will begin by identifying some defining characteristics of stimuli and stimulus classes.

The environment around us has measurable physical dimensions. Thus, we talk about atmospheric pressure, ambient temperature, light energy with a given wavelength, sounds of certain frequencies, and so on. We can describe the stimuli present in the environment, or those explicitly presented during experiments, in terms of those physical dimensions. However, from our point of view, this multidimensional physical environment has some especially important aspects. The effective stimulus class, the range of events that influences the behavior of an individual in their natural environment or in an experiment, is more restricted than the whole range of events that make up the physically-defined environment for two reasons:

1. The effective stimulus class has only those properties than can be perceived by the individual organism. It makes perfectly good sense to speak of a projector displaying a field of ultraviolet radiation on a screen, but as we will be unable to see it (although a honey bee could) it is not a stimulus for us because it could not enter into a relationship with our behavior. More subtly, if your arm is jabbed by the points of two needles, you will only feel one prick if the needles are close enough together. In this case, the distance between the two is below the threshold for its detection.

2. At any given time, behavior may be influenced by some, but not all, of the stimulus properties potentially perceivable by the individual organism.

We can summarize these two restrictions on the effective stimulus class as what the organism can learn about the stimulus, and what the organism does learn about the stimulus. In terms of the classical divisions of psychology, these topics fall into the areas of perception and learning, respectively. In this chapter, as elsewhere , we are primarily concerned with learned behavior, but we will start by considering some aspects of stimulus perception

4.1   PERCEPTUAL STIMULUS CLASSES

The prevailing environment of an organism (its "psychological" environment) may be considered to be the pattern or configuration of all energies, present at any given time, that are capable of having a systematic effect on behavior. These energies are only a small subset of the energies studied by physicists. They are restricted to those that can be detected by the specialized anatomical structures, or *receptors*, that organisms have for receiving certain energies and for transforming them into electrical nerve impulses. The eye is specialized for the reception of a limited range of electromagnetic radiation, the ear for a limited range of air-pressure vibrations, the tongue and nose for certain chemical energies. Receptors in the skin detect mechanical pressure and thermal changes. There are receptors within the muscles and joints of the body that detect the movement of the muscle and joints in which they are embedded. A complete specification of the patterns of electromagnetic, mechanical, chemical, and thermal energies, impinging on an organism's receptors at any time, can rarely be undertaken. Fortunately, it is not usually necessary, as behavior can come under the selective control of only limited parts or features of the energy configurations that make up what we call the physical environment.

For purposes of simple illustration, we will only use examples in the rest of this section that relate to visual perceptual stimulus classes. A stimulus is a part of the environment and can be described in terms of its physical dimensions. In manipulating the visual environment, we frequently confine our experimental changes to one of the fundamental dimensions by which physicists describe light. For our purposes, light may be considered to be a limited range of electromagnetic disturbance, radiated at 186,000 miles/second in wave form. *Wavelength* is one important dimension of electromagnetic radiation, and part of that dimension is a stimulus dimension to which the different verbal responses we call colors have been attached. The wavelengths that we call light comprise the very small portion from about 380 to 760 nanometers of the entire electromagnetic spectrum.

Nearly all animals respond to differences in amplitude or *intensity* of light waves (we call the corresponding response dimension *brightness*), but only a limited number of species have receptors specialized for detecting changes in wavelength, and are thus said to have color vision. Pigeons, humans, snakes, and monkeys are examples of animals that do. Others, such as the rat and dog, are said to be color-blind because differences in wavelength alone cannot be learned about and thus come to control differential responding.

The wavelengths that occur in the rainbow and are perceived by us as colors (red, orange, yellow, green, blue, indigo, violet) are called *pure spectral lights* because they contain only one wavelength. They can be produced in the laboratory by a device called a monochromator. Most lights, including reflected light that reaches the eye from surfaces such as tables, chairs, blackboards, and lawns, are far from pure in this sense. Generally, even the light from a homogeneously colored surface or a lamp is made up of a large mixture of different wavelengths. Those wavelengths that are predominant usually determine the color-naming response we make. Some mixtures of light, however, are not named by their predominating wavelengths. For example, the word "purple" is never used to name a pure spectral light of one wavelength; "purple" is the color name for a mixture of red and blue. The lights we call white and the surfaces we call gray radiate heterogeneous mixtures of nearly all visible wavelengths. No single wavelength predominates in such lights, but the label "colorless" sometimes given to them seems inappropriate.

Visual stimulus dimensions are not confined to different wavelength distributions and intensities of isolated patches of light. Relevant dimensions that can control behavior may be defined to include spatial combinations of the fundamental dimensions of wavelength and intensity. For instance, the relative intensities of two adjacent light regions can be a powerful controlling stimulus dimension, determining the brightness response that an observer will make to a portion of the pattern. That is, a gray patch may be seen as bright if surrounded by a less intense surround, and as dull if surrounded by an area of higher intensity.

Note that in this discussion we use one set of terms to describe stimulus dimensions, and another set to describe corresponding behavioral responses. Although there are lawful correlations between these stimulus and response dimensions, labels for stimuli and responses should not be confused. Frequency and intensity of light energy are stimulus dimensions; color and brightness are response dimensions. Frequency and intensity of sound energy are stimulus dimensions; pitch and loudness (or volume) are response dimensions. Smell, taste, temperature, and weight are response terms associated with the stimulus dimensions of chemical structure, thermal energy, quantitative force, and so on. Recognition of the difference between the terms appropriate for describing stimuli and those for describing responses will prevent a great deal of confusion.

A perceptual stimulus class consists of stimuli that lie along a physical dimension, such as those of frequency or intensity of light or sound. Instances of a class may vary somewhat along that dimension, but still produce the same response. For example, light stimuli in the range 680 to 720 nanometers will be labeled as red, and thus fall into the same perceptual class. While perceptual stimulus classes seem to be determined in part by the evolutionary history of the species — as we have noted not all animal species have color vision, for example — we will see throughout the remainder of this chapter that animal and human behavior also comes under the control of stimulus classes that are established through the learning history of the individual.

4.2   Stimulus Control in Classical Conditioning

The first major experimental work on stimulus control was Pavlov's study of *differentiation*. As reported in Chapter 1, he carried out many experiments in which a conditioned stimulus (CS), such as the ringing of a bell was reliably followed by an unconditioned stimulus (US), such as food in the mouth, on a number of occasions, and as a result the CS came to elicit a conditioned response. Pavlov demonstrated this process many times, and carefully varied features of his experiments to establish the generality of the effect. In a straightforward elaboration of the basic experiment, differentiation was achieved by pairing one stimulus with food (this is termed the *CS+*) and, once the CS+ had begun to reliably elicit conditioned salivation, another stimulus (*CS–*) was introduced which was not followed by food. The CS– and the CS+ were presented alternately, in a random sequence. The results of two of Pavlov's experiments are as follows. In the first, CS+ was a rotating disk and CS– was the same object, rotating in the other direction. In the second, the two stimuli were a tone and its semitone. In both experiments, before the differentiation phase began CS+ had been established as an eliciting stimulus for salivation. When CS– was introduced, salivation to it was, at first, slight. With continued presentations of both CS+, followed by food, and of CS–, not followed by food, salivation to CS– *increased* until it approached that to CS+. Following this rise, there was a decline in salivation to CS– until it reached zero. The ability of CS+ to elicit salivation continued undiminished, and a *discrimination* was established between the two stimuli. The results of these two experiments are illustrated graphically in Figure 4.1. According to Pavlov, the process of what he called differentiation, and we shall call discrimination, involves inhibition because of the time course of its development. The idea is that the similarity of CS+ and CS– induces a response to CS–, but subsequently the fact that the US does not follow the CS– results in inhibition of responding developing to that stimulus.

Many classical conditioning experiments show that the strength of the conditioned response increases rapidly over early trials, but with additional trials these increases become smaller and finally stop (we say that the strength of the conditioned response has reached an asymptote). However, Kamin (1968) was the first to demonstrate that not every CS paired with a US will result in a conditioned response that increases in this fashion. He showed that one can obtain a *blocking effect* in the following manner. If CS1 (for example, a light) is paired with a US over number of trials there will be an increase in the conditioned response strength to a high asymptotic value, but if CS2 (for example, a tone) is then introduced and presented for a number of trials *at the same time as CS1* and paired with the same US, not much conditioning to CS2 will occur. That is, on subsequent trials presentation of CS1 alone will elicit a substantial conditioned response, but presentation of CS2 alone will not.

One further stimulus-control phenomenon in classical conditioning is related to the biological significance of conditioning. Pavlov discovered that if CS1 is a stimulus of high intensity and CS2 is a weaker stimulus, and the two are presented together and followed by a US, then only CS1 will come to elicit a strong conditioned response. We say that conditioning to CS2 has been overshadowed by conditioning to CS1, and this phenomenon is called *overshadowing*. An interesting type of overshadowing can occur if CS1 and CS2 are from different sensory modalities. Then the overshadowing that occurs depends on the nature of the US. For example, Garcia and Koelling (1966) found that in an experiment with rats, if CS1 was lights and noise and CS2 was the taste of a liquid, then conditioning would occur to CS1 (but not CS2) if the US was a painful electric shock, and conditioning would occur

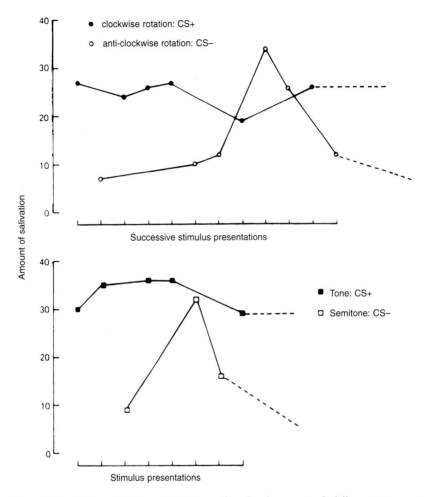

Figure 4.1 Data of Pavlov (1927) on the development of differentiation, or discrimination, by two individual dogs in salivary conditioning experiments. Details are given in the text.

to CS2 (but not CS1) if the US was a treatment that caused a stomach upset. There are clearly "rules" — further aspects of what Seligman (1970) called *preparedness* (see Chapter 2) — determining which potential CS comes to elicit a conditioned response

The phenomena of discrimination, blocking and overshadowing indicate that classical conditioning provides a sophisticated set of processes whereby relevant classes of stimuli gain control over behavior, while irrelevant stimuli do not. This is very much what Pavlov (1927) believed when he presented his original findings and contradicts the contemporary media notion that "Pavlovian reactions" are somehow not part of intelligent behavior (see also Rescorla, 1988). We will present other information relevant to this issue later in this chapter.

4.3 THE THREE-TERM RELATIONSHIP OF OPERANT CONDITIONING

Recall that in Chapter 2 we provided a preliminary formal account of simple operant conditioning that consisted of only two terms, the operant response and the reinforcing stimulus. However this relationship is established, either implicitly or explicitly under certain stimulus conditions, there is a restricted set of stimuli that specify the occasions on which the response can be reinforced. In an experiment, these may be simply the stimuli arising from being in the apparatus and having the opportunity to make the response. Our general account of operant conditioning should thus include this feature. We will, therefore extend our formal account of operant conditioning to a *three-term relationship* by including the *discriminative stimulus*.

Consider the example of the lever-pressing response of a hungry rat in a Skinner box being reinforced with food. The complex of stimuli arising from "being in the Skinner box" stand in an obvious relationship to reinforced lever pressing; after all, this is the only location the rat has the opportunity to lever press. The experimenter may also arrange that a *discriminative stimulus* (S^D) is provided that explicitly signals when lever pressing is reinforced. This may simply be the houselight in the ceiling of the Skinner box, or it may be an additional auditory or visual signal. In either case, the situation is one in which *the S^D sets the occasion for reinforcement*. The S^D is thus a stimulus that does not elicit responding, but in its presence responses are emitted and reinforced (either continuously or intermittently). When the S^D is effective, and response rates are higher in its presence than in its absence, we say that it exerts *stimulus control*.

The three-term relationship between the discriminative stimulus, operant response, and reinforcing stimulus, is written thus:

$$S^D: R \rightarrow S+$$

For our present example:

S^D is the houselight
R is the lever-press
S+ is delivery of a food-pellet

The use of an S^D implies that at times during the experiment this stimulus is not present. It may simply be absent (for example, houselight switched off), or may be replaced with a different one (for example, a steadily illuminated houselight might be replaced with a flashing one). In either case, we refer to the alternate stimulus situation, which generally signals extinction, as S^Δ ("S-delta"). S^D and S^Δ are often referred to as positive and negative discriminative stimuli. Both an S^D in operant conditioning procedures and a CS in classical conditioning exert stimulus control. The differences between the two lie in the nature of the behavioral control — an S^D sets the occasion for a higher frequency of a reinforced response while a CS elicits a response — and the type of conditioning history — operant or classical — that led to that stimulus gaining control over the behavior.

4.4 STIMULUS GENERALIZATION

This behavioral phenomenon is seen in crude form when a child learning to speak refers to all furry objects as "cats", and calls all male adults "Daddy". It is exemplified in our own behavior when we hail a stranger mistakenly because he appears to resemble a friend. The phenomenon of generalization is obviously very important, and the conditioning processes provide a useful way of studying it. It would be highly maladaptive if operant or classical conditioning produced responses that were so specifically linked to the training stimulus (S^D or CS) that the response disappeared if some small "irrelevant" feature of the stimulus changed. Conversely, it would be equally inappropriate if huge changes in the stimulus produced no change in the response. That would represent an absence of stimulus control; stimulus control being defined as the presentation of the stimulus reliably increasing (or decreasing) the probability of the behavior.

The method of studying stimulus generalization is simple in principle. In the case of operant conditioning, once a response has been conditioned, variations are made in some well-controlled aspect of the environment and the rate or amount of responding at various stimulus values is measured. This is called *generalization testing* along a particular stimulus dimension. Let us consider a specific example. The apparatus shown in Figure 4.2 is a modified Skinner box in which pure light from a monochromator illuminates the pecking key. The monochromator permits the precise selection and presentation of any one of a very large number of visible wavelengths. The apparatus also includes provision for rapidly changing from one wavelength to another. In an experiment performed by Guttman and Kalish (1956), birds were shaped to peck the disk which was transilluminated by a yellow-green light of wavelength 550 nm. Following some continuous-reinforcement training, the birds were transferred to a variable-interval schedule (VI 1-minute). When behavior had stabilized under VI, tests were made to determine to what extent the 550 nm light on the disk was specifically controlling behavior. This test consisted of an extinction procedure in which the birds were exposed to a randomized series of successive 30-second presentations of different wavelengths, only one of which was the 550 nm actually used in training. No other changes were made in the bird's environment.

When the numbers of extinction responses emitted under each of the different stimuli were calculated, they formed the curve in Figure 4.3. This indicates that the pigeons gave the maximum number of extinction responses only at their training stimulus, and gave progressively fewer responses at the test stimuli located progressively farther away from the training stimulus along the wavelength dimension. This gradation of responding, seen when response strength is assessed in environments somewhat different from the environment in which original conditioning took place, is known as the *generalization gradient*.

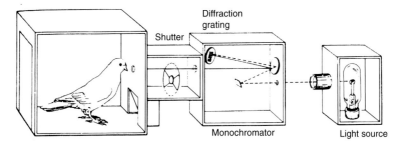

Figure 4.2　A pigeon Skinner box fitted with an optical system to project pure light on to the pecking key (after Guttman, 1956).

Behavior Analysis

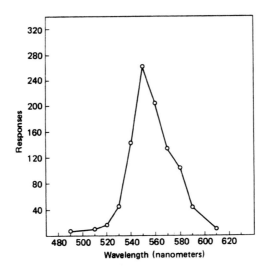

Figure 4.3   Numbers of key pecking responses emitted by pigeons in the presence of 11 different wavelengths of light, projected one at a time on to the pecking key. Previous reinforced training took place only at 550nm, and during these tests no responses were reinforced (Guttman & Kalish, 1956).

Generalization is a pervasive and often useful property of behavior. For instance, skills learned in one environmental situation can be used in new situations. Having learned to catch a ball thrown from a distance of 5 feet, we will catch it pretty well at 10, 20, and maybe even 40 feet. Parents who teach their children to say "thank you" at home are implicitly relying on generalization to see to it that "thank you" will be emitted outside the home. Our educational system is predicated on the assumption that the skills acquired in school will spread to environments outside the school. Nonetheless, the generalization gradient is there to remind and caution educators that the more closely a training situation resembles the situation in which the behavior will later be needed, the more effective will be the training. Schools and other agencies use this principle when they make the teaching situation as near to "real life" as possible.

4.5 STIMULUS SALIENCE

Various factors determine whether a particular stimulus dimension will acquire control over behavior. Among these are discrimination training, which is discussed later in this chapter, and the *salience* of that stimulus dimension. By salience, we mean roughly, "likelihood of being noticed and responded to". Even within one stimulus dimension, certain stimulus values may be more likely to be responded to. Hailman (1969) was able to demonstrate the adaptive value of this phenomenon. He measured the unconditioned pecking behavior of newly-hatched gull chicks elicited by various monochromatic stimuli (or "colors"). He obtained a function that peaks sharply and resembles a generalization gradient. There is clearly a stimulus class of a fairly narrow range of wavelengths of light which is effective in producing pecking; the peak corresponds to the color of the adult gull's beak and reflects the newly-hatched chicks' tendency to peck at their parents' beaks, rather than anything else, and thus enhance their chance of being fed in the first few crucial hours of life.

The phenomenon of overshadowing, discussed in Section 4.2, suggests that if a stimulus dimension is not the most salient of those present, it will not acquire control over responding. Pavlov (1927) demonstrated that if a compound CS, consisting of one intense and one weak component, was used in classical conditioning with dogs, very often no conditioned response was seen to the weaker component of the CS when it was presented by itself. He thus described it as overshadowed by the intense CS. Van Houten and Rudolph (1972, and reported in Mackintosh, 1977) have demonstrated this effect in two operant conditioning experiments with pigeons. In the first experiment, one group of pigeons was reinforced for pecking a key illuminated with white light and in the presence of a 30-mph flow of air, while another group had the same conditions, except that the key was unilluminated and the box was dark. Subsequent tests showed that air-flow speed controlled responding in the second group, but not the first. The second experiment was similar, but now a 1,000-Hz tone was presented to both groups while key pecking for food. Again, one group had a white illuminated key, while the other had an unilluminated key in a dark box. The results are shown in Figure 4.4. As in their earlier experiment, the presence of the visual stimulus prevented control being acquired by the other modality. The other stimulus did acquire control, however, when no visual stimulus was presented.

Very often, human behavior does come under the control of several features (or dimensions) of a complex stimulus. A child may learn that buses in his or her hometown are red, have six wheels, two decks, and a rear door, that they are very noisy, and smell of diesel oil. Visiting another town and seeing rather different vehicles, the child may still correctly identify them as

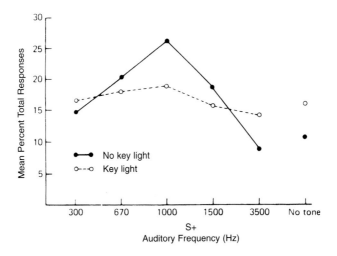

Figure 4.4   Van Houten and Rudolph's data showing generalization gradients for pigeons that had been trained in the presence of 1000 Hz auditory frequency, either in the dark (no key light) or with an illuminated key (Mackintosh, 1977).

buses. His or her response "bus" is not attached to only one (or very few) of the stimulus features. With children that show autistic behavior, on the other hand, a phenomenon has been demonstrated that resembles over-shadowing. Lovaas and Schreibman (1971) trained autistic and other, non-autistic, children to pull a lever on an FR4 reinforcement schedule for candy, with a compound auditory and visual discriminative stimulus. After acquisition (which took longer for the autistic children), the children were tested with the auditory and visual components of the S^D, separately. Most of the other children responded on 100 per cent of trials of both types, while the autistic children tended to respond differentially, some responding on 100 per cent of one type of trial and none of the other. This abnormal acquisition of stimulus control may underlie various aspects of autistic behavior, which has often been described in terms of over-selectivity.

4.6   THE STIMULUS DISCRIMINATION PARADIGM

We noted earlier, that the phenomenon of generalization is of great importance. Similarly, the capacity to learn to discriminate appropriately is vital. If we are exposed to conditions where appropriate behavior is signaled by the presence or absence of specific stimuli, we need to be able to learn to respond at the "right times". The behavioral process of discrimination has this outcome, and in this section we provide a brief formal account of it.

The three-term relationship of operant conditioning, between S^D, R and S+, specifies that the response, R, will become more frequent in the presence of S^D. If S^D is sometimes present and sometimes absent, a discrimination learning procedure has been set up. The simplest type of stimulus discrimination in operant conditioning involves one response (R) class and two stimulus conditions. The response is reinforced in one of the stimulus conditions (S^D) and is extinguished in the other stimulus condition (S^Δ, or S-delta). The result is that the probability of responding in S^D comes to exceed that in S^Δ. Eventually, the probability of responding in S^Δ may fall to operant level or below. The term S^Δ is also used to denote conditions of less reinforcement, as well as zero reinforcement (or extinction).

Note that although we here define discrimination as an operant paradigm, there is a closely related classical conditioning paradigm. Earlier, in Section 4.2, we described the *differentiation paradigm*, in which one CS (CS+) is followed by food (or another US) while another is also presented but never followed by the US. With this procedure, after a number of CS+ and CS– presentations, a greater response is elicited by CS+ than CS–. In parallel with the operant procedure, the response to CS– often tends towards zero with extended training. These related operant and classical procedures turn out to have very similar behavioral consequences.

Like reinforcement and extinction, discrimination is both a procedure and a behavioral process with a specified outcome. This interdependence between procedures and outcomes reflects the fact that behavioral phenomena are neither pieces of behavior nor sets of environmental conditions, but interactions between the two.

Our formal definition of discrimination corresponds quite closely to our everyday use of the term. Discriminations are demonstrated at the human level by the ability to "tell two or more things apart". Some of us, for instance, discriminate the paintings of Monet from those of Manet, butter from margarine, or two sets of similar finger-prints. In "telling these things apart," we are showing differential responding to them. Human discriminations vary considerably in the number of stimulus situations and response alternatives involved, as the following examples show. In every case, the necessary condition of differential reinforcement (and behavior) associated with different environments is met:

1. The discriminating moviegoer does not go to every film that arrives at his or her neighbourhood cinema. He or she goes to some , and does not go to others.
2. We say that some groups of people are discriminated against when they are treated differently from the way that other people are treated. That is, the discriminated group is treated one way and other people are treated another way.
3. The professional wine-taster can discriminate a variety of wines that all taste the same to the novice. The professional's discrimination is evidenced by his or her ability to give a unique name (R1, R2, R3, ... R1000) to each one of a thousand different wines (S1, S2, S3, ... S1000).

4.7 MULTIPLE AND CONCURRENT SCHEDULES OF REINFORCEMENT

In our discussion of operant reinforcement schedules in Chapter 3, we used examples in which only one schedule was in effect in any one session of an experiment. Now that we have introduced the three-term relationship between S^D, response and reinforcer, we can consider more complex schedules, where two or more schedules are programmed within the same session. Thus, we might alternate two different schedules for the same operant response which is a *multiple schedule*; or we might simultaneously have two different schedules programmed, one for each of two different operant responses, which is a *concurrent schedule*. Multiple and concurrent schedules represent examples of the control of behavior by more complex schedules, and provide information about the ways in which schedules interact. An important feature of a multiple schedule is that each component schedule has an associated discriminative stimulus. For example, in a multiple FI FR schedule, a tone might signal the FI component, while white noise would be presented during the FR (in each case, the same response would be reinforced). Once stable performance is established, we say that behavior is under stimulus control, and each stimulus produces the distinctive performance characteristic of the corresponding schedule when presented. An example of the development and maintenance of rat behavior on a multiple FI 5-minute FR 20 schedule is shown in Figure 4.5. The lever pressing had previously been trained on simple FR and evidence of this is seen in the first session (Record A), but by the end of this session (B), control by both components of the schedule is evident and becomes clearer by 11 hours of training (C). After 38 hours, behavior is fairly stable (D), although bursts of FR-type responding occur occasionally during FI (at d and e). The lower panel of Figure 4.5 shows performance after much more training, when the ratio has been changed to 40. This example shows how multiple-schedule performance develops from the previous performance and how, as training proceeds, control by both components becomes stronger and inappropriate behavior less common. It is a very important general feature of schedule-controlled performance that its acquisition, and sometimes the actual nature of the performance, is strongly influenced by the experimental participant's previous experience. Where the previous experience is known, we can see how it affects performance.

On a multiple schedule, discriminative stimuli signal different

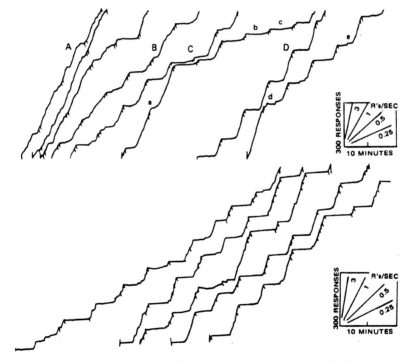

Figure 4.5   Cumulative records of lever pressing by a rat on a multiple FI 5-minute FR20 schedule (upper panel), and on a multiple FI 5-minute FR 40 schedule (lower panel) (Ferster & Skinner, 1957). In both cases, periods of time on the FR schedule are characterized by continuous responding at a high rate with a high rate of reinforcement. Other details are given in the text.

schedules for one response at different times. This makes it an example of a *successive discrimination procedure*. Alternatively, in a concurrent schedule, two or more independent reinforcement schedules are applied to two response classes at the same time. Concurrent schedules are thus a type of *simultaneous discrimination procedure*. Unlike a multiple schedule, the experimental participant in a concurrent schedule determines when to switch from one schedule to the other. A typical concurrent responding situation is illustrated in Figure 4.6. In this example of a pigeon Skinner box, the two keys are equally accessible, although only one can be contacted at a time, and both are available all the time. Each key has an independent reinforcement schedule associated with it; this means that responding on key B has no effect on the programming or delivery of reinforcements for responding on key A.

After adequate training on a concurrent schedule, the experimental participant divides its time between the two schedules and produces appropriate behavior on each. An example of stable performance on a concurrent FR 100 FI 5-minute schedule of a hungry pigeon, key pecking for grain, is shown in Figure 4.7. Characteristic FI and FR performances are seen alternating with each other. The only new feature seen is a "staircase" effect, from time to time, in the FI component. This is produced by the

Figure 4.6   A two-key pigeon Skinner box, which allows concurrent schedules of reinforcement to be investigated.

89

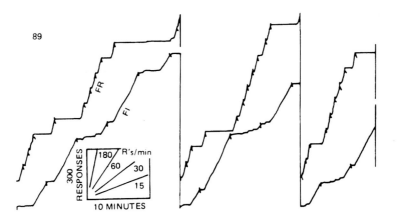

Figure 4.7 Cumulative records of key pecking by a pigeon a concurrent FR100 FI 50minute schedule of reinforcement. Two records are created simultaneously and the FR record has been placed above the FI record (Catania, 1966).

experimental participant responding on the FI key during postreinforcement pauses on the FR key.

As well as enabling the study of behavior under two different reinforcement schedules, concurrent schedules have been extensively used to investigate choice between two schedules that may offer different rates or amounts of reinforcement. In such concurrent schedules, the relative rate of the two responses turns out to be a sensitive index of choice between alternatives. These studies, and their applications to human behavior, are discussed in Chapter 11.

4.8 THE EFFECTS OF DISCRIMINATION TRAINING

The discrimination procedures we have described have been used many times to successfully establish differential responding to two or more stimulus situations. Consequently, we know that they specify sufficient conditions for a discrimination to develop. But given that an experimental participant successfully discriminates between two stimulus conditions, it does not follow that every difference between the two conditions controls responding. Mackintosh (1997) points out that in many human experiments that formally resemble the studies with other species that show differential responding and generalization gradients, humans do not show the same patterns of behavior. Rather, and as discussed in Chapter 3, the behavior of human experimental participants often appears to be under the control of verbal rules. So, for example in an experiment involving visual stimuli of different wavelengths, responding might occur in correspondence with a rule "Only respond when the stimulus is bright red", and generalization along the dimension of wavelength of light might not be observed. We will discuss the general difference between contingency-shaped and rule-governed behavior in more detail in Chapter 6, but Wills and Mackintosh (reported in Mackintosh, 1997) were able to demonstrate that if a human experimental task was made very difficult, then responding did generalize along the dimension of physical similarity which distinguished the stimuli in their experiment and the overall pattern of behavior was as would be predicted from studies of other, non-verbal, animals.

Recall from Section 4.5 that more salient stimuli gain control of responding at the expense of others, even when both are equally associated with reinforcement. In the experiments of Rudolph and Van Houten described there, we saw that pitch or air-flow did not gain control over responding (that is, variations in those stimulus dimensions did not produce a generalization gradient peaked at the training stimulus value) when a visual stimulus was also present, but *dimensional control* did develop when the visual stimulus was removed. Other studies have shown that discrimination training, with presence and absence of tone or air flow as S^D and S^Δ, is sufficient to establish control by these dimensions. We may therefore conclude that differential reinforcement along a stimulus dimension results in dimensional control when that dimension is the only one that distinguishes S^D from S^Δ. If S^D and S^Δ differ along several dimensions, control may be established by the most salient dimension.

Discrimination training procedures can be classified as *intradimensional* or *interdimensional*. In intradimensional training, S^D and S^Δ lie on the same stimulus dimension (for example, two different wavelengths of light). This technique provides us with information about the effects of the interaction of reinforcement at S^D with extinction at S^Δ on values along that stimulus dimension. In interdimensional training, S^D and S^Δ are located on independent stimulus dimensions. For example, in an experiment with pigeons reinforced for key pecking, S^D could be green key illumination, while S^Δ is an oblique white line on a dark key. This technique enables us to obtain separate generalization gradients about S^D and S^Δ along the corresponding dimension, and can result in *inhibitory stimulus control*.

4.9 INHIBITORY STIMULUS CONTROL

We have described instances of stimulus control where the maximum point on the generalization gradient occurs at S^D, but stimulus control also exists when the minimum of the gradient occurs at S^Δ. Only when S^D or S^Δ lie on independent dimensions, is it possible to sort out the excitatory (response-facilitating) effects of S^D from the inhibitory (response-suppressing) effects of S^Δ. If we vary a stimulus dimension on which S^Δ lies and which is independent of S^D (in the sense that all stimuli on that dimension are equally unlike S^D), and find an inverted generalization gradient with a minimum at S^Δ, then we can say that S^Δ exerts *inhibitory stimulus control*.

Hearst, Besley, and Farthing (1970) trained hungry pigeons to peck a blank white key (S^D) for VI food reinforcement, and alternated periods with the white key with periods of extinction, with a thin black line bisecting the white key (S^Δ). When the number of responses to S^Δ was less than 4 per cent of the number to S^D, a generalization procedure was introduced. Various line tilts were presented for 30 seconds at a time, and the VI reinforcement schedule was always in effect. The results for five successive sessions of this procedure for two groups, trained with different angled lines at S^Δ, are shown in Figure 4.8.

For both groups of pigeons, a U-shaped gradient, with a minimum at the training S^Δ value, is seen on the first two sessions. By the fifth session, the curve has flattened out. This is not surprising, because the birds are now being trained *not* to discriminate on this dimension as reinforcement is available at every value presented. Note that in the first session, all values of the line tilt stimulus suppress responding below the S^D value (shown as B). This shows that the overall effect of the line stimulus is inhibitory. This effect has also dissipated by the fifth test session.

Such demonstrations of a gradient with a minimum at S^Δ confirm the predictions made by accounts of discrimination, which assume that a stimulus associated with extinction acquires inhibitory properties. Similar predictions are made by theories of classical conditioning, from Pavlov's (1927) to more recent ones (for example, Rescorla and Wagner, 1972). These assume that a CS associated with the absence of the US comes to actively inhibit the conditioned response, rather than merely failing to elicit the conditioned response. It seems that stimuli associated with operant extinction acquire similar properties.

Behavior Analysis

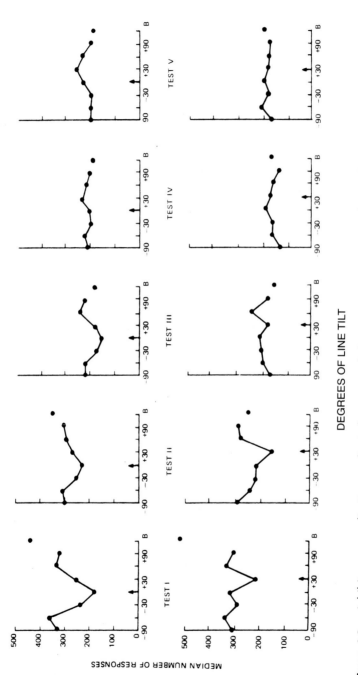

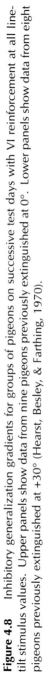

DEGREES OF LINE TILT

MEDIAN NUMBER OF RESPONSES

Figure 4.8 Inhibitory generalization gradients for groups of pigeons on successive test days with VI reinforcement at all line-tilt stimulus values. Upper panels show data from nine pigeons previously extinguished at 0°. Lower panels show data from eight pigeons previously extinguished at +30° (Hearst, Besley, & Farthing, 1970).

4.10 STIMULUS EQUIVALENCE

Thus far we have discussed stimulus control in terms of the physical properties of stimulus classes. We have seen that human and non-human experimental participants can emit a response in the presence of a stimulus they have never encountered, as long as it is physically similar to an S^D used during training. Furthermore, the more dissimilar a test stimulus is from the S^D the weaker, or less frequent, is the emitted response. We have suggested that generalization and discrimination could account for aspects of complex human behavior. However, if we examine more closely the stimulus classes that control complex aspects of our behavior, such as social interaction, we quickly come to realize that the types of stimulus control discussed thus far are only part of the story.

Consider the following example. You are driving a car and you encounter a red traffic light: the red light acts as an S^D for applying the brakes of the car and stopping. However, many other stimuli could serve the same function. Here are some examples:

- a policeman stepping onto the road with a raised hand,
- a passenger shouting "Stop the car!",
- an elderly person trying to cross the road.

In this context, all four stimuli are *functionally equivalent*; that is, they control the same behavior. Even in the case of this very simple example it is apparent that the basis of this functional equivalence is not physical similarity and it is necessary to consider alternative explanations. We might argue that each stimulus acquired control through direct training: in other words, stopping the car has been reinforced in the presence of each of these stimuli. However, this seems a laborious method, and, in the case considered here, a dangerous method, for stimuli to acquire control over behavior.

There have been some recent developments in behavioral analysis that provide an account of how *functional stimulus classes* may be formed efficiently. These developments have arisen from research on *stimulus equivalence*, or *equivalence classes*.

Before describing equivalence classes, we must describe the discrimination training procedure most commonly employed to study them, which is *matching-to-sample training*. The experiments have usually been carried out on human experimental participants and, for convenience, computer-generated images are often used as stimuli. Stimuli are usually nonsense syllables or random shapes and thus have no meaning for the experimental participants prior to the experiment. The procedure involves presenting a stimulus, referred to as the *sample*, centrally near the top of a computer display screen (see Figure 4.9). Several (usually three) *comparison* stimuli are presented simultaneously at the bottom of the screen. The experimental participant's task is to learn through trial and error which comparison goes with the sample. Choices are made by striking an appropriate key, and feedback on correct choices is given automatically by the computer. It is important to note that the "correct" response is defined by the experimenter and that there is no logical connection or physical similarity between the sample stimulus and any of the comparison stimuli.

Given sufficient training, human and nonhuman experimental participants can readily learn to match stimuli in this manner, and select the correct comparison to go with each sample that is being used on all, or a very large percentage, of trials. (In the example given, there will be a total of three different sample stimuli and three corresponding comparison stimuli.) However, it is when human experimental participants are trained on a number of related matching-to-sample tasks that some interesting *emergent relationships* are observed which have not been explicitly trained. These are observed in the case of *verbally-competent* human experimental participants (those who are able to speak and use language) and they give rise to equivalence classes.

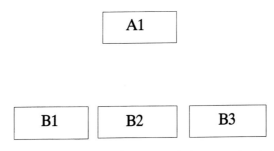

Figure 4.9   Schematic diagram of a typical layout of stimuli presented simultaneously (or with onset of A1 slightly before the other stimuli) on a computer screen for matching-to sample training of the A-B relationship. The sample stimulus A1 must be matched to correct comparison stimulus, B1, by selecting a corresponding response key. On other trials for this task, B1, B2 and B3 will presented in different sequences, and A1 will be replaced by A2 or A3 as the sample stimulus.

The simplest experiment of this type involves two related matching responses. Experimental participants are initially trained to match several (typically, three) comparison stimuli (B1, B2, B3) to the same number of sample stimuli (A1, A2, A3). On a trial, either A1, A2, or A3 is presented as a sample and B1, B2, and B3 are all presented simultaneously as comparisons, as in Figure 4.10. Feedback is given for correct choices (which will be B1 given A1, B2 given A2, and B3 given A3) and for incorrect choices. (A difference between "feedback" and "reinforcement" is that we use feedback to describe a procedure in which information is provided to the participant on *each* occasion on which they make a response. They are told whether this is "correct" or "incorrect", and this feedback is usually presumed to act as reinforcement for the correct responses.) Once criterion performance is achieved on the matching-to-sample task, which typically involves making correct responses on more than 90% of a batch of trials, a second phase of training begins. In this phase either B1, B2, or B3 appears as a sample and three new comparisons C1, C2, and C3 appear. Correct choices will now be C1 given B1, C2 given B2, and C3 given B3. Once again, there is generally no physical resemblance or logical relationship between the B sample stimuli and the C comparison stimuli that must now be selected to go with them, just as there was no such A-to-B relationship in the earlier phase. Again, training continues until a criterion level of correct responding is achieved.

If tested at this stage on certain untrained matching responses, verbally-competent human experimental participants may respond correctly. For example, they will correctly match the appropriate A stimuli with the B stimuli, if the B stimuli appear as samples and the A stimuli appear as comparisons. This emergent matching response is referred to as *symmetry*, because it is the reverse of the relationship which had previously been trained. Similarly, they will correctly match the appropriate B stimuli to C stimuli, another type of symmetry response. If the A stimuli are presented as both sample and comparisons, they correctly match each A stimulus with itself. This is referred to as *reflexivity*, and will be observed in the case of B and C stimuli also. As reflexivity essentially involves successfully matching something to itself, it seems most unsurprising but, as we shall see later, it is not normally a consequence of matching-to-sample training in nonhuman species. If the A stimuli appear as samples and the C stimuli as comparisons, verbally-competent human participants will correctly match C stimuli to the appropriate A stimuli. This is called *transitivity*. They will also show *combined symmetry and transitivity*, which is observed when the C stimuli are presented as samples and the A stimuli as comparisons. When all these matching responses are observed, a *stimulus equivalence class* (involving A, B, and C) is said to have been formed, because each member of the class is treated equivalently (Sidman, 1971, 1986). Figure 4.10 is schematic representation of the three-member equivalence classes described above.

The notion that physically unrelated stimuli are treated as equivalent when they are members of the same class is a formal statement of something that is very familiar to us. For example, the written word "shoe", the spoken word "shoe" and a picture of a shoe are all said to refer to the same thing, and a child could be taught to treat them as equivalent through matching-to-sample training (Sidman, 1990). However, this may be a uniquely human capacity. While A-to-B and B-to-C training is sufficient to produce equivalence classes in verbally-competent humans, animals of other species (including chimpanzees, see Dugdale & Lowe, 1990) may succeed in reaching criterion performances on the matching-to-sample tasks but not show any emergent relationships. They may not, for example, even match stimuli to themselves (such as A1 to A1) without explicit training.

A striking feature of equivalence classes is that as the number of members (stimuli) increases, the number of emergent matching responses increases dramatically. For example, training two relationships (A to B and B to C) produces a three member class with a further seven matching relationships emerging (A to A, B to B, C to C, B to A, C to B, A to C, C to A, a total of $3^2 - 2 = 7$) but training four relationships (A to B, B to C, C to D, D to E produces a five member class with a further 21 matching relationships emerging ($5^2 - 4 = 21$) (Fields and Verhave,1987). "Natural" stimulus equivalence classes (that is, those that enter into relationships with

CLASS 1	CLASS 2	CLASS 3
A1	A2	A3
B1	B2	B3
C1	C2	C3
etc	etc	etc

Figure 4.10 Outcome of stimulus equivalence class training. The arbitrary and physically dissimilar stimuli A1, B1, and C1 are now in Class1 and will be treated as equivalent. Subsequent training could add further elements, D1, E1, etc., to this class and they would also be treated as equivalent to A1, B1, and C1. The same properties apply to Classes 2 and 3.

human behavior in real-life settings) may have very many members with a huge number of emerging matching responses. This fact, along with the account of generalization between physically similar stimuli we gave earlier in this chapter, gives us a way of dealing with some long-standing philosophical problems. Philosophers have posed questions such as "What is the essential feature of a chair? How do we decide what is, and what is not, an example of a chair?" We now have the elements of a general answer to this question, and many like it. A chair is a class of stimuli which are functionally equivalent in allowing us to make the response of sitting down. Some members of the class have physical similarities, but a new design of chair (which does not have those physical features) can be added to the class and subsequently be seen to be as "chair-like" as the more conventional members of the class. It is worth noting that every individual will have their own "class of chairs": someone who has never encountered a particular new design of chair may not identify it as a chair. This type of example suggests that some of the traditional philosophical questions may be misconceived, and that there are no absolute or essential features of "being a chair".

As noted above, a key feature of equivalence classes is that under certain circumstances behaviors controlled by one member of a class may be controlled by other members of the class without explicit training. It is this characteristic of equivalence that provides an account of how physically dissimilar stimuli may control the same behavior without the need for explicit training, and thus be *functionally equivalent*. That is, a pattern of behavior under the control of an S^D may be transferred "automatically" to other stimuli that are in an equivalence class with that stimulus. For example, if you typically talk in a certain way with same-sex friends, you may start to talk in this way to any new same-sex friend that you make, without a history of reinforcement for talking to that person in that way. Clearly, this is a powerful method of extending a person's behavioral repertoire. It may also contribute to less desirable outcomes by providing a rapid method of attaching fear and anxious behavior to specific situations that were not previously feared.

This could happen in a number of ways. Most straightforwardly, if we suppose that a young child has a stimulus class of "places where frightening things happen", then he or she may go to some lengths to avoid being in those places, may show extreme fear if encountering one of them by accident, and so on. Any stimulus that is added to the class will then control the whole range of fear-related behaviors, and it may be very easy to introduce a new member to the class. For example, the child may go into a strange room and be somewhat frightened by a sudden noise, and this may be sufficient for this place to become a new member of that stimulus class and thus control the whole range of fear-related responses. Alternatively, saying to the child "You are frightened of monsters, aren't you? Well, there are monsters in the wood-shed!", may be sufficient to produce an aversion to *all* wood-sheds. Finally, a frightening experience in one particular store might produce a fear of all public places because, for that child, they are all members of the same stimulus class.

4.11 SUMMARY

Behavior comes under the control of many aspects of the environment, in that the probability of a response class changes markedly when certain stimuli are presented. These stimuli cannot be any aspect of the physical environment, because only some aspects of the physical environment can be perceived. A further limitation is that at any particular time only some of those aspects of the environment that could influence behavior are actually effective in so doing.

Perceptual stimulus classes are classes of events that differ only in terms of a physical stimulus dimension, such as wavelength of light or amplitude of sound, and thus lie along that physical stimulus dimension. Pavlov showed that if two stimuli that varied in one dimension were used as CS+, which was followed by the US, and CS−, which was not, then the important phenomena of generalization and discrimination could both be demonstrated. Generalization occurred after only a few trials when the conditioned response acquired to CS+ was also shown to the physically similar CS−, but after many trials discrimination occurred and there was now no response to CS− because it had not been followed by the US. Classical conditioning procedures have also been used to demonstrate other stimulus control phenomena such as blocking and overshadowing.

Operant conditioning can only be fully defined in terms of a three-term relationship that includes the discriminative stimulus, or S^D, that sets the occasion on which the operant response, R, can be followed by the reinforcing stimulus, S+. When an explicit S^D is used in an experiment, such as the houselight in a Skinner box, it can be shown that the S^D exerts stimulus control and the operant response is much more frequent in its presence than in its absence. As in classical conditioning, stimulus generalization can be demonstrated following operant conditioning. If various stimuli are presented that differ from the S^D along a salient dimension (such as the wavelength of light), then a generalization gradient may be obtained with higher response rates being emitted to stimuli that more closely resemble the training S^D. Generalization is an important aspect of behavior, because it results in behavior persisting — to an extent — as the environment changes slightly. Generalization does not occur along every dimension of an S^D, and less salient (or "unimportant") stimulus dimensions may not turn out to control the operant response.

Operant discrimination training occurs when a negative discriminative stimulus, S^Δ, is provided as well as S^D. In the presence of S^Δ, which may alternate with S^D, there is a lower or zero rate of reinforcement for the response. Like reinforcement and extinction, discrimination is both a procedure and a behavioral process with a characteristic outcome, as the S^D comes to control a high rate of responding, while S^Δ maintains a low rate and may inhibit responding. Discrimination is an important behavioral process which results in selective responding to relevant environmental cues.

The three-term relationship for operant conditioning enables us to define more complex schedules of reinforcement. These include multiple schedules where different discriminative stimuli signal different schedules of reinforcement for a single operant response class, and concurrent reinforcement schedules where two independent reinforcement schedules are simultaneously available for two operant responses. These procedures maintain more complex patterns of behavior, but the patterns are made up of the patterns characteristic of the simpler component reinforcement schedules.

Human behavior is not only controlled by perceptual stimulus classes. Often it is affected by stimulus classes with physically dissimilar members that are determined by the individual's learning history. These stimulus equivalence classes are pervasive in everyday life (for example, the class consisting of the written word "chair", the spoken word "chair", a picture of a chair, etc.), and they can be investigated experimentally using matching-to-sample procedures. With verbally competent participants, a limited amount of training with these procedures (such as, given A1 pick B1, given B1 pick C1) can result in the emergence of many relationships between stimuli that have not been explicitly trained (such as, given A1, pick A1, given A1 pick C1, given B1 pick A1, given B1 pick A1, given B1 pick B1, given C1 pick A1, given C1 pick B1, given C1 pick C1). These stimuli are thus treated as equivalent, and appear to have the same functions as each other . That is, a function acquired by one member of the class transfers to all other class members. This finding has enormous potential for explain rapid changes in human behavior, including undesirable ones such as fear of many situations that have never been directly experienced (see Friman, Hayes, & Wilson, 1998).

CHAPTER 5

AVERSIVE CONTINGENCIES

The first step in our systematic account of operant behavior was the definition of simple operant conditioning. It was defined as the presentation of a response-contingent stimulus, which produced a number of characteristic response changes that included an increase in response frequency. We called the stimulus in that paradigm a positive reinforcer and, to this point, have generally restricted the account of operant behavior to those situations involving such positive reinforcement.

Only casual observation is needed, however, to detect the operation of another kind of reinforcement, defined by the operant conditioning that occurs through the response-contingent removal of certain environmental events. We see that birds find shelter during rainstorms, dogs move to shady spots when the summer sun beats down upon them, and people close windows when the roar of traffic is loud. In these instances behavior is emitted that removes or terminates some environmental event: rain, heat or light, and noise, in the examples given. These observations suggest the existence of a distinctive class of reinforcing events. Because the operation that defines these events as reinforcing is their removal, and is opposite in character to that of positive reinforcers (defined by their presentation), they are known as negative reinforcers (S–). In general, negative reinforcers constitute those events whose removal, termination, or reduction in intensity, will increase or maintain the frequency of operant behavior.

In this chapter, we shall describe two important experimental paradigms, escape and avoidance, as procedures with a characteristic outcome. In these procedures, negative reinforcers (aversive stimuli) operate as the special response-contingent stimuli that are used in characteristic ways to produce the outcome characteristic of each procedure. A third procedure which also involves aversive stimuli and has a characteristic outcome, is punishment. This involves the response-contingent presentation of an aversive event, and has the characteristic outcome that the frequency of the operant response is reduced by this contingency. Finally, we shall consider classical conditioning procedures where the US has aversive properties. In parallel with what we have found in our consideration of positive operant reinforcement and classical conditioning with appetitive US's, there are similarities in the outcomes of operant conditioning procedures involving aversive stimuli and aversive classical conditioning.

Throughout this chapter, we shall, as in earlier chapters, seek to identify basic processes of operant and classical conditioning, to describe their action and interaction in particular situations. Here and in later chapters we seek to demonstrate the applicability of these behavioral processes isolated in the laboratory to significant issues in human life. Unlike positive reinforcement, the use of aversive contingencies is strongly linked to ethical concerns. Some of these will be introduced in this chapter, and we will return to them when considering the management of human behavioral problems in detail in later chapters.

5.1   ESCAPE FROM AVERSIVE STIMULI

In the laboratory, aversive stimuli have typically taken the form of electric shocks, prolonged immersion in water, and high intensities of light, sound, or temperature. These are the events that, in common parlance, we call "annoying", "uncomfortable", "painful", "unpleasant", "noxious", and "aversive". Of these terms, we shall use the word "aversive" as a technical synonym for negative reinforcement.

Aversiveness suggests the key notion of "averting", "moving away from", or "escaping from" a situation. We may reasonably expect to find that the acquisition of behavior that leads to escape from (or termination of) an aversive stimulus is a fundamental behavioral process. After all, if an organism is not equipped to escape from potentially physically damaging stimuli, its survival is endangered. It is thus likely that evolution will have equipped most species with the capacity to learn through escape contingencies.

We need a clear definition of escape in order to distinguish it from other aversive procedures that will be introduced later. In the *escape procedure*, a stimulus is presented and termination of that stimulus is contingent upon the occurrence of a specified operant response. If this contingency results in an increase in frequency of the response, and in the other associated behavioral changes described for positive reinforcement in Chapter 2, then *escape learning* has occurred. We can also conclude that the stimulus presented is an *aversive stimulus*, which is acting as a *negative reinforcer* for the response specified because its *termination* is the crucial event.

We can represent the escape procedure symbolically by the following three-term relationship:

$$S-: R1 \rightarrow S^o$$

where   S– = aversive stimulus
         R1 = specified operant response
         S° = absence of aversive stimulus

Note the following important points:

1. Escape learning, as defined here, is a form of operant conditioning.
2. The stimulus is designated as aversive, and its termination as negatively reinforcing, on the basis of the results of the experiment. The experiment can, therefore, be seen as a *test* of the aversiveness of the stimulus.
3. The aversive stimulus also has other properties, because it sets the occasion on which the escape response is reinforced by its termination (we will discuss this aspect further later in this section).

Typically, an experiment involves a number of *escape trials*, each terminating after a correct response or a fixed period of exposure to the aversive stimulus, separated by intertrial intervals in which no stimuli are presented.

Various simple procedures have been used for experimental studies of escape training. In an early study by Muenzinger and Fletcher (1936), a rat was placed in a T-shaped maze that contained an electrically charged grid floor. The floor was wired so that as long as the animal remained on the grid, a continuous shock was administered to its paws. A cover over the maze prevented the rat from escaping the shock by jumping out of the apparatus. One escape route remained; the animal could find safety by running consistently to a designated arm of the T.

Behavior in the T-maze is usually measured on each trial by timing the rat from start to safe, or by counting the "incorrect" turns ("errors") into the unsafe arm of the T. On early trials, the rat is equally likely to run right or left, but as acquisition of the response of turning to the safe side proceeds, responses to the "incorrect" side decrease.

More recent studies of escape have generally used apparatus in which a long series of trials (S– presentations) can be presented at appropriate intervals without the participant having to be removed. In the Skinner box, for example, lever presses can be arranged to terminate electric shocks coming from the grid floor. But the most common apparatus for the study of escape conditioning has been the shuttle box of Figure 5.1. This box is simply a two-compartment chamber, where the measured operant response is movement from one chamber to the other (usually movement in either direction counts as a response). Movement is detected by spring switches under the floor, or by photocells. The aversive stimulus (S–) is usually pulsed

Figure 5.1   A shuttle box designed to study avesive contingencies with rats. When the shutte raised, the rat can jump the hurdle and get into the other half of the apparatus.

electric shock delivered through the grid floor. Escape behavior is rapidly acquired in this apparatus, possibly because the required operant response (running) is closely related to the unconditioned behavior elicited by the shock.

Many experimental studies have employed rats as participants and electric shock as the S–. These choices were made because it is relatively easy to deliver a controlled shock to a rat through the grid on which it is standing. Other stimuli (for example, noise or blasts of air) are less easy to control, and other species present a variety of methodological problems. These biases of experimenters towards using methods that are convenient are understandable, but have not been based on much knowledge as to how representative the situation studied is of escape learning in general, so we must be ready to expect some surprises when the escape paradigm is used with other species and other stimuli.

However, it has been possible to demonstrate some generality of the effects of various different procedures for escape training. Results for rats which learned to press a lever which turned off electric shocks intermittently delivered through the grid floor appear in Figure 5.2A, while Figures 5.2B and 5.2C document the results of similar experiments with other aversive agents. Figure 5.2B illustrates the effects of increasing the intensity of a sound on VI lever-pressing escape rate of cats. The results of

Figure 5.2C were obtained from a group of rats whose pushing of a panel on FI contingencies terminated lights of various intensities. Both the (B) and (C) panels of Figure 5.2 demonstrate that escape behavior may reach a maximum rate and then decline if the aversive-stimulus intensity is made very great. The decline in responding associated with very intense aversive events is not well understood, but is thought to be due to a general suppressive (emotional) effect of strong aversive stimuli. This "side-effect" will be discussed later.

Since we are interested in possible parallels between negative and positive reinforcement, we may ask to what variable in the field of positive reinforcement does aversive stimulus intensity correspond? Superficially, the intensity of a negative reinforcer seems analogous to the magnitude of a positive reinforcer. Intensity of S– and magnitude of S+ are both stimulus properties of the reinforcer, and increases in both variables can generate increases in responding in some procedures. However, closer analysis of the functional role that these two variables play in negative and positive reinforcement, respectively, suggests that the analogy is only superficial. The principal effect of raising the intensity of a light, or a sound, or a shock, from a low to a high value, is that the reinforcement of behavior is made possible through termination of the new intensity. Increasing the intensity of an S– has, therefore, the effect of a *reinforcement-establishing operation*. Thus, in the presence of a weak intensity of light, or noise, a rat will not show conditioning of a response that terminates the light or noise. Similarly, with a small value of food deprivation, a response that produces food will not be strengthened. Conversely, high values of both shock intensity and

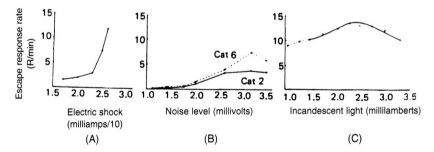

Figure 5.2   Escape response rates as function of the intensity of three different aversive stimuli. A Dinsmoor and Winograd, 1958; B Barry and Harrison, 1957 C Kaplan, 1952.

food deprivation make it possible to use shock termination and food presentation as reinforcers for operant behavior. Thus, shock intensity is better described as a *motivational* variable, than as a reinforcement magnitude variable.

Ethical concerns have limited the number of experiments on escape behavior with human participants (but see Chapter 7 for some examples of where assessment of escape-motivated behavior requires repeated presentation of aversive stimuli). That is, we are reluctant to carry out, or sanction others carrying out, experiments which necessarily involve people being presented with aversive events. Our concern is perfectly reasonable — as is concern with the ethics of carrying out experiments with nonhuman animals that involve aversive stimuli — but it can be argued that it is misplaced because escape behavior is very important in humans as in other species. Consequently, our general scientific curiosity should be aroused, and, more importantly, a better knowledge of how it occurs in humans would enable us to devise *intervention strategies* for significant human problems. Let us consider the example of self-injurious behavior. This is a very distressing problem that greatly reduces the quality of life of a large number of people with learning difficulties. One way of conceptualizing this phenomenon would be as a failure of escape learning that normally occurs. For most of us, the pain of striking our head on a wall, for example, rapidly leads to a change in behavior and this is a form of escape learning. It may be that some people lack the capacity to readily learn in this way, or, more likely, that other escape contingencies (perhaps escape from social pressures) have a greater influence on their behavior. As with all forms of conditioning, we need basic research on escape procedures with human behavior, and comparative studies with other species, in order to understand the behavioral processes and to design effective interventions for serious behavioral problems.

5.2 AVOIDANCE BEHAVIOR

Consider the escape paradigm applied to the example of someone walking in the rain:

S– :	R	→	S°
rain	put up		rain
falling	umbrella		escaped

This seems to be a clear case of escape behavior; putting up the umbrella is reinforced by escape from the rain. Consider, however, another behavioral element of this incident; the fact that the person was carrying an umbrella. Can we explain the "umbrella carrying response" in terms of an operant reinforcement contingency? It seems likely that umbrella-carrying on a showery day is reinforced by the avoidance of getting wet that would otherwise occur. We can thus state:

$$\text{S}^D: \qquad \text{R} \qquad \rightarrow \qquad \text{S}^o$$

showery	carry an	rain
day	umbrella	avoided

Note the differences between this three-term relationship and the one for escape. The discriminative stimulus (S^D) for making the response is not now an aversive stimulus as well: it need not actually be raining when we leave the house for us to take an umbrella. Furthermore, the consequence of making the response is rather different. In the escape paradigm, S– offset occurs as soon as the response is made. In the avoidance paradigm, S– *is prevented from occurring* by the response.

In an avoidance procedure, a stimulus is programmed to occur unless a specified operant response occurs. Occurrence of that response cancels or postpones these stimulus presentations. If this contingency results in an increase in frequency of that response, then *avoidance learning* has occurred, and the stimulus has *negative reinforcement properties* for that response. Notice that the avoidance procedure supplements the escape paradigm in giving us a second, independent, way of discovering negative reinforcers, and thus defining *aversive stimuli*.

Representing avoidance diagrammatically is awkward, because the crucial element is the postponement or cancellation of an event which has not yet occurred. Figure 5.3 illustrates "timelines" for two types of *avoidance schedule* which have often been used in experimental studies. (The aversive stimuli are assumed to be electric shocks.) In *free operant avoidance* (Figure 5.3A), shocks occur at regular intervals, the shock (S-S) interval, unless an operant response occurs. If it does, the next shock is postponed for a period of time, the response-shock (R-S) interval. On this schedule, no shocks will ever be delivered if each response follows the preceding one within the response-shock interval. In *discriminated avoidance* (Figure 5.3B), a discriminative stimulus (S^D) precedes each shock delivery. A response during the "warning signal" S^D cancels the shock

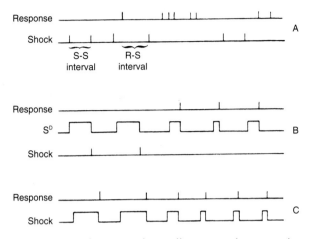

Figure 5.3   Event records or timelines illustrating the procedures of (A) free operant avoidance; (b) discriminated avoidance; and (c) escape.

delivery and (usually) terminates the S^D. Responses during the intertrial interval have no effect. Every shock will be avoided if one response occurs during each S^D.

Some data on the acquisition by rats of a lever-press response to avoid an aversive stimulus of foot shock are shown in Figure 5.4. After an intertrial interval which averaged 10 minutes, a 1,000 Hz tone S^D was presented. If the lever was pressed during the S^D, it was terminated and shock was avoided. This study also involved an escape contingency. If the rat failed to make the avoidance response within 60 seconds, shock was delivered continuously until a response occurred (Hoffman and Fleshler, 1962). Figure 5.4 shows that the average response latency for the group of rats declined steadily across sessions, while the number (percentage) of avoidance responses increased. Both latency and number of responses reached an *asymptote* in the seventh session and showed little further change. The third measure shown is the number (percentage) of intertrial intervals (S^Δ periods) in which a response occurred. Comparison of the avoidance curve with the intertrial interval responding curve gives a classic example of the development of a discrimination: S^D responding increases first, then S^Δ responding increases. Then, as S^D responding continues to increase, S^Δ responding reaches a peak, thereafter declining towards zero. The acquisition of avoidance behavior and its discriminative control thus proceeds in the fashion familiar to us from many types of positively reinforced behavior, as discussed in Chapter 4.

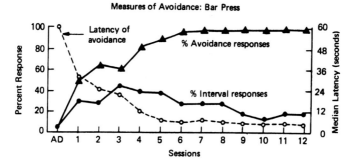

Figure 5.4 Three measures of behavior during acquisition of a discriminated lever-press avoidance response. Data are from a group of 12 rats (Hoffman & Fleshler, 1962).

In discriminated avoidance, the response generally has *two* consequences: S^D termination, and shock avoidance. What happens when only one of these consequences is provided for the response? Kamin (1957) found that while shock avoidance *per se* produces a certain level of responding, the S^D-termination contingency also enhances responding. So the removal or absence of the S^D for the avoidance response appears to be a reinforcing event, an idea to which we shall return shortly.

Free operant avoidance is, as its name implies, a procedure in which a response occurring at any time serves to postpone or eliminate programmed aversive events. No signals are ever presented to warn the participant of impending aversive stimuli. This schedule, first devised by Sidman (1953) and illustrated in the time-lines of Figure 5.3A, leaves the animal free to respond at any time, and without any external cues, or signals, as to when to make that response.

An example of the acquisition of a lever-pressing response by a rat on Sidman's free-operant avoidance schedule is shown in Figure 5.5. In this case, both the R-S and S-S intervals were 30 seconds. After an initial period where many of the shocks used as aversive stimuli were delivered, the rat developed fairly rapidly a sustained moderate rate of responding, which resulted in shocks being delivered only occasionally (Verhave, 1959). This means that only rarely did the rat pause for more than 30 seconds (the R-S interval) or fail to respond within 30 seconds of receiving a shock (the S-S interval).

This is a remarkable performance when you consider that when the rat is successful, nothing happens. That is, since no external stimulus

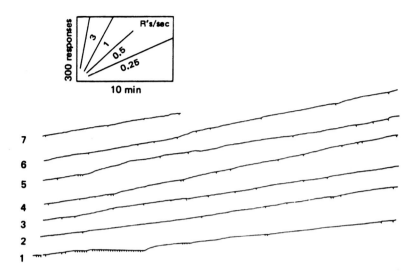

Figure 5.5   Cumulative records of lever press avoidance during training of a rat on free operant avoidance. Shock deliveries are indicated by small vertical marks. The first record is at the bottom of the figure. From the second record onwards, very few shocks were delivered (Verhave, 1959).

consequences are presented, the only feedback from making a response constitute so-called kinesthetic aftereffects (that is, sensations produced within the body by the movements involved in pressing the lever) and whatever small noise the lever makes. Compare this situation with the discriminated-avoidance schedule, where an explicit S^D signals the time to respond, and S^D termination usually follows completion of the response.

As discussed in Chapter 2, everyday descriptions of avoidance behavior are couched in purposive terms. In the case of avoidance, we say that we turn the wheel of a skidding car away from the direction of the skid *to* avoid a crash, that one builds a bridge in a certain way *to* avoid its collapsing, that a deer flees *in order to* avoid a pursuing wolf. The term "to", or "in order to", imputes a certain purposive quality to the behavior. Purposive or teleological explanations are generally rejected by scientists on the grounds that such explanations purport to let a future (and, therefore, nonexistent) event be the cause of a present (existing) event; and because purposive explanations add nothing to the bare facts. Consequently, behavior theorists persistently sought to explain the facts of avoidance by a mechanism that was clearly non-teleological. However, in attempting to frame an account of avoidance behavior that was analogous to simple operant conditioning or escape behavior, they struck a serious problem. In both simple operant conditioning and escape learning, behavior is reinforced by making a stimulus change consequent upon that behavior (even with intermittent reinforcement, *some* responses are immediately followed by the reinforcing stimulus). In avoidance learning, however, the aversive stimulus is present neither after the response nor before it. Rather, it occurs intermittently in the absence of responding.

There are at least two routes to a solution of this problem. Either some stimulus, or stimulus change, must be identified which is a consequence of responding and acquires the power to reinforce avoidance responses; or we accept the facts of avoidance behavior as a basic, and irreducible, process in which behavior changes because that change produces a reduced frequency of aversive events over a period of time. A review of the extensive experimental research literature shows that, in various nonhuman species, negatively-reinforced behavior can be maintained by conditioned aversive stimulus termination, safety signal presentation, aversive stimulus density reduction, and delay of the aversive stimulus. This suggests that while short-term consequences (for example, the onset of a safety signal) may have big effects, consequences over a longer period (for example, the occurrence of a period of time with a lower frequency of aversive events) may also be effective. However, avoidance behavior sometimes fails to develop where one or more of these inducing factors are present.

The main reason for "failures" is that every avoidance procedure involves not only a negative reinforcement contingency, but also the necessary ingredients for aversive classical conditioning, which is discussed in Section 5.4. Aversive stimuli are repeatedly paired with either apparatus cues or S^D's, and we often find that *species-typical aversive behaviors* are elicited by avoidance situations (Bolles, 1970). Species-typical aversive behaviors represent those unconditioned behaviors that occur naturally in response to attack. In rats — most often used in experimental studies — the most readily identifiable ones comprise freezing, flight, and attack, and these behaviors are sometimes incompatible with the required operant response. When factors relating to the evolutionary history of the species start to "interfere" with the outcome of conditioning experiments, the choice of operant response class is no longer arbitrary, in the sense defined in Section 2.4, and, relatedly, the findings may not generalise to other species and to human behavior. Fortunately, with avoidance, as with the other behavioral processes we have introduced, most of the findings are not restricted in this way.

5.3 PUNISHMENT

Punishment is a procedure in which aversive stimuli are made contingent upon behavior. The modification of behavior by contingent presentation of aversive stimuli is an extremely controversial subject. Punishment is an emotive word, and much progressive thinking in education, psychotherapy, child rearing, penal reform, relationship-improvement programs, and even radical social change, is based on the premise that our first step must be to eliminate punishment. The validity of this claim depends on what is meant by punishment, the effects (direct and indirect) that punishment has, and ethical considerations. These issues are discussed in Chapter 10.

We define punishment, similarly to other behavioral processes, as a procedure with a characteristic outcome. In the punishment procedure, a stimulus is made contingent upon a specified response. If a variety of characteristic effects occur, particularly a *reduction in frequency* or suppression of that response, then we say that punishment has occurred, and that the contingent stimulus is a punisher, a punishing stimulus, or an aversive stimulus. We can represent the procedure as:

$$R \rightarrow S-$$

where   R is the specified response, and
         S– is an aversive stimulus.

Clearly, the punishment paradigm supplements escape and avoidance procedures as an independent way of assessing the aversiveness of contingent stimuli. However, note that, in parallel with all other operant procedures, the effect of the contingent stimulus depends on the particular situation, the particular response selected for study, and other contextual variables. We cannot assume, for example, that the verbal command, "Sssh!", which effectively silences a child talking in church, will also have this effect in a schoolroom. Neither can we assume that a stimulus identified as an effective punisher for one operant will necessarily effectively punish another operant behavior, or that a stimulus found aversive from escape or avoidance procedures will necessarily act as a punisher. In practice, the ubiquitous punishers in laboratory experiments with nonhuman participants have been, almost exclusively, electric shocks, as has also been the case in studies of escape and avoidance. Occasional studies with humans have also used shocks, but, as we shall see later, aversive stimuli that do not cause pain are more ethically acceptable. All the issues concerned with the application of punishment procedures with human behavioral problems are discussed in Chapter 10.

In ordinary language, the word "punishment" is used ambiguously. It can either mean the delivery of an aversive stimulus contingent upon a response, as here, or simply the delivery of an aversive stimulus in no particular relation to behavior. We have removed this ambiguity, and we shall see later in this chapter that there are important behavioral differences between the two procedures. We also depart from ordinary language in specifying that punishment has only occurred when a particular behavioral *effect* is seen.

Early laboratory work on punishment appeared to support the conclusion that punishment yields only a transient effect on operant behavior (Estes, 1944; Skinner, 1938), and this conclusion is still occasionally quoted. However, as long ago as 1966, an authoritative review was produced by Azrin and Holz of later findings where reliable punishment effects were obtained. They pointed out that a number of methodological requirements must be met to enable punishment phenomena to be investigated successfully, and these were not always achieved in the early studies. There must be a reliable methodology for maintaining operant behavior in the absence of punishment, which is supplied by the use of schedules of intermittent positive reinforcement, and there must be a punishing stimulus which can be defined in terms of physical measurements (so that it can be reliably reproduced), delivered in a consistent manner to the experimental participant, and which cannot be escaped from (for example, by leaving the experimental situation). The punishing stimulus should also be one that does not elicit strong behavioral responses itself, and which can be varied in intensity over a large range. From the 1960s, use of intermittently reinforced operant behavior in Skinner boxes with electric shock delivered as the punishing stimulus, met all these requirements. The main conclusions of Azrin and Holz (1966) were consistent with the hypothesis that punishment can have effects that are broadly opposite to those of positive reinforcement: within limits, more intense and more frequent punishment produces greater response suppression, provided that the punishing stimulus is reliable and immediately follows the response. Interestingly, if the punisher is itself delivered on an intermittent schedule, then the effects are analogous to those seen with positive reinforcement. Thus, response suppression tends to increase towards the end of the ratio requirement if the punisher is delivered on a fixed ratio schedule, and towards the end of the time interval if the punisher is delivered on a fixed interval schedule. Other factors they identified as contributing to punishment effectiveness were that long periods of punishment should be avoided, that punishment should be correlated with extinction but not with delivery of a positive reinforcer, and that punishment effectiveness increases when an alternative (reinforced) response is available. Not all the data they reviewed was from nonhuman studies, and Figure 5.6 shows a clear effect of punishment (by "an annoying buzzer sound") on human operant behavior, which was greatly enhanced when an alternative reinforced response was also available.

Inhibitory stimulus control (as described in Section 4.9) can also be demonstrated with punishment procedures. Using pigeons pecking at an illuminated plastic key located on the wall for food reinforcement, Honig and Slivka (1964) punished key-pecking in the presence of one wavelength of the light used to illuminate the key. They found that response rates were suppressed in the presence of that wavelength, and response suppression generalized to other wavelengths with suppression declining as the wavelengths become more different from the punished wavelength. This effect is directly analogous to that seen when responding is extinguished in the presence of one visual stimulus (S^Δ) while being reinforced in the presence of others (S^D).

Punishment can be shown to modify human behavior under laboratory

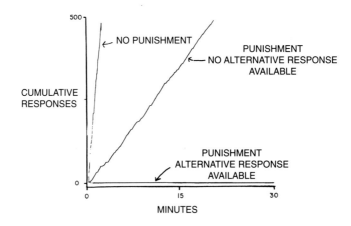

Figure 5.6   Cumulative records of the punished responding of human participants on a VI schedule of reinforcement under three conditions. When an alternative response was available, punishment totally suppressed responding (Azrin & Holz, 1966, based on data from Herman & Azrin, 1964).

conditions. We need not employ painful aversive stimuli, since we can rely on the aversiveness of loss of potential reinforcements. Bradshaw, Szabadi, and Bevan (1977) examined the effects of a punishment contingency on the performance of humans pressing buttons for points on a variable-interval (VI) schedule. The points could be exchanged for money at the end of the experiment. After initial training, multiple VI schedules were used, in which different reinforcement rates were obtained in different components, and a variable-ratio (VR34) punishment contingency was superimposed on alternate sessions. Reinforcement on the VI schedules were always signaled by a very brief green light flash and the addition of one point to the score on a counter in front of the participant. When punishment occurred, a red light flashed on briefly and one point was subtracted from the counter.

The results from their three participants are shown in Figure 5.7. Without punishment, response rate was a negatively accelerated function of reinforcement rate in each component of the multiple schedule, and the data are a good fit to an equation describing Herrnstein's (1961) matching law. The matching law, which is discussed further in Chapter 11, is a quantitative formula which relates rate of responding for an operant to

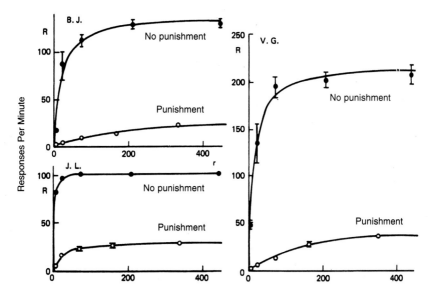

Figure 5.7 Response rate, with and without a punishment contingency for three human experimental participants as a function of reinforcement rate in the components of a multiple VI schedule. The bars give standard errors (Bradshaw, Szabadi, & Bevan, 1977).

obtained rate of reinforcement for that response. As can be seen, the response rate increases towards an asymptote. This function has been shown to fit data for a very large number of experimental studies with nonhuman participants, and is here shown to fit human data. During punishment, the maximum (asymptotic) response rate was greatly reduced for all participants, but the data were still a good fit to the curve predicted by the matching law. This shows a consistent and extremely orderly effect of punishment on human operant performance.

It is also important that the effectiveness of punishment is evaluated in significant non-laboratory situations and a number of such studies are described in Chapter 10. Given that, within laboratory settings and applied settings, punishment can be an effective contingency, many questions still remain. One of the most interesting is the question as to what behavior *increases* if a punishment contingency is successful in greatly reducing one category of behavior. Not much research has been done on this, but Dunham (1971) suggested, based on experiments with gerbils in which several different behaviors were recorded while one was punished, that it was the most frequent unpunished behavior that increased in probability, and thus filled the time made available by suppression of the punished behavior. However, Crosbie (1993) in a formally similar study with human participants found that when one of four operant responses was punished with monetary loss, in a similar fashion to the Bradshaw et al. (1977) study, the punished response was reduced in frequency but no rule of the type suggested by Dunham predicted which responses would increase in frequency.

5.4 AVERSIVE CLASSICAL CONDITIONING

Escape, avoidance, and punishment procedures all involve programmed relationships between responses and aversive stimuli. The other general class of aversive contingencies involves relationships between neutral (conditioned) stimuli and aversive stimuli, and are varieties of *classical conditioning*. Classical conditioning can occur in procedures that were designed to demonstrate the operant conditioning phenomena of escape, or avoidance or punishment. These findings can be seen as a "nuisance" (given that the classical conditioning was not the main focus of study), but are better taken as illustrations of how operant and classical conditioning interact in laboratory settings as well as in natural settings.

Aversive classical conditioning is studied directly when contingencies are arranged between CS's and aversive US's. Many aspects of the resultant process parallel appetitive classical conditioning. Indeed, many Pavlovian phenomena were originally demonstrated with aversive conditioning. The responses most often studied were salivation and leg flexion in dogs, and eyeblinks and heart rate in humans and other species. However, all these paradigms involve *restrained* organisms. If freely-moving participants are used, some effects are seen in aversive classical conditioning that distinguish it from appetitive classical conditioning.

These effects are twofold: species-typical aversive behaviors and suppression or disruption of ongoing behavior can be elicited by the aversive CS. In some situations, these are two sides of the same coin, because the elicited aversive behaviors interfere with the ongoing behavior; but in others disruption occurs during an aversive CS that cannot be attributed to species-typical aversive behaviors. The latter case is called *conditioned suppression* and is discussed later.

Although species-typical aversive behavioral repertoires vary from species to species (as the term implies), there are some common behaviors in these repertoires. Zener (1937) carried out an early investigation of classical conditioning in which, following initial training, he removed the restraints from the dogs and then observed the effects of presenting various CS's. Where a localized CS (such as a light coming from a lamp) had previously been followed by an appetitive US, the dogs approached it (and licked it!), but where the CS had previously been followed by an aversive US, the dogs simply ran away from it once given that opportunity. Withdrawal of this type has, not surprisingly, been found to be a common classically conditioned species-typical aversive behavior, in situations which allow it to occur. A fair amount of other information is available about the laboratory rat, which at one time was the experimental psychologist's favorite experimental participant, and piecemeal data on other species have been recorded. It is widely agreed that freezing, defecation, flight (running away), and aggression are components of the rat's aversive repertoire. Of these, defecation and freezing can be conditioned to a CS associated with aversive stimulus (Hunt & Otis, 1953), and components of aggressive behavior are seen if a pair of rats receive a CS that has been paired with aversive stimulus (Ulrich, 1967).

Our lack of detailed information about the human behavioral repertoire makes it difficult to assess the role of species-typical behavior. However, the pioneer behaviorist, J. B. Watson, suggested that our emotional responses are acquired through classical conditioning of species-typical behavior, and similarly many contemporary accounts of the effects of "stress" on human behavior state that these species-typical emotional responses commonly occur in complex social situations where they are not appropriate or useful. One such response is the pronounced change in heart rate which occurs in fear and stress, and this has often been shown to be influenced by classical conditioning.

A typical study of *conditioned suppression* was carried out by Hunt and Brady (1951). They trained liquid-deprived rats to press a lever for water reinforcement on a VI schedule. When response rate on this schedule had become stable, a clicker CS was presented periodically for 5 minutes, and immediately followed by a brief electric shock US to the rat's feet. Some of the typical behavioral changes that ensued are shown in the cumulative lever-pressing records in Figure 5.8. The first CS presentation had little discernible effect, but the accompanying US (denoted by S in panel B) temporarily slowed the response rate. After a number of CS-US pairings, the CS suppressed responding almost totally, but responding recovered as soon as the US had been delivered. Because suppression of responding during the CS is dependent on a conditioning history, it is called conditioned suppression.

The conditioned-suppression procedure, first developed by Estes and Skinner (1941), has proved to be a very sensitive behavioral technique. The effect of the CS is usually described in terms of the degree of suppression of the positively-reinforced operant behavior relative to the rate of the operant response during the non-CS periods. Measured in this way, conditioned suppression increases with magnitude of the US, decreases with length of the CS, and is in general, such a sensitive indicator of classical-conditioning parameters that it has often been treated as the best method of studying classical-conditioning effects (for example, Rescorla, 1968), although it actually measures the reduction in, or disruption of, operant responding.

The sensitivity of the conditioned-suppression technique has led to its widespread use in evaluation of drug effects (Millenson & Leslie, 1974). The drugs tested have mostly been those known clinically to reduce anxiety, because conditioned suppression has often been treated as a model of fear or anxiety. Recent studies have demonstrated that conditioned suppression can be used to disentangle neuropharmacological mechanisms. For example, the conditioned-suppression reducing effects of some anxiolytic (anxiety-reducing) drugs can be selectively reversed by another drug with a

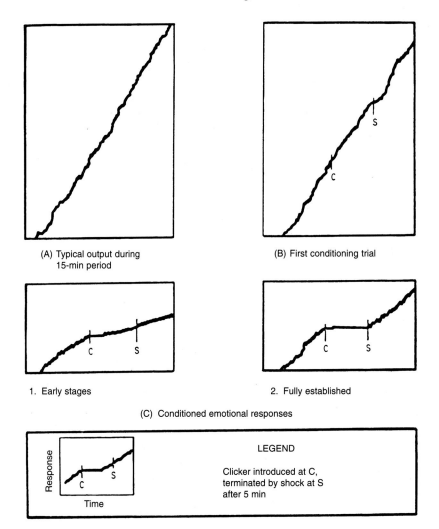

(A) Typical output during 15-min period

(B) First conditioning trial

1. Early stages

2. Fully established

(C) Conditioned emotional responses

LEGEND

Clicker introduced at C, terminated by shock at S after 5 min

Figure 5.8 Cumulative records showing development of conditional suppression in a rat lever pressing for water reinforcement on a variable-interval schedule (Hunt and Brady, 1951).

known effect in the brain. From this evidence we can deduce much about the pharmacological action of the anxiolytic agent.

5.5   THE ETHICS OF AVERSIVE CONTINGENCIES

Laboratory demonstrations, along with our everyday experience, suggest that punishment is a pervasive and important behavioral process. Like positive reinforcement, negative reinforcement, and classical conditioning, the sufficient conditions for its occurrence are frequently met in the natural environments of humans as well as of other organisms. As Azrin and Holz (1966) point out, to "eliminate punishment from the world" would involve elimination of *all* contact between the individual and the physical world, because there are so many naturally occurring punishment contingencies. We learn *not* to do a great many things, such as touching hot surfaces, falling out of bed, shutting our fingers in doors, and all the other ways in which we avoid natural aversive consequences.

If we agree that the contingencies of punishment specified by the physical world are not eradicable, can we and should we nevertheless minimize the number of punishment contingencies operated by individuals and institutions upon individuals? We can distinguish between those that involve painful stimuli and those that involve response cost or time out. "Time-out" refers to all procedures which involve temporary prevention of access to positive reinforcers. In everyday life, these include removal of attention (being ignored), withdrawal of privileges, and levying fines. Many experimental studies with nonhuman animals have shown that painful stimuli elicit aggressive behaviors and these can become predominant. Clearly, this is highly undesirable and would seem to be sufficient reason to reject the use of punishment contingencies that involve painful stimuli, if alternatives can be found. Time-out has been used effectively to modify behavior in a number of procedures, and unsurprisingly works best when there is a high rate of reinforcement prior to time out (Kazdin, 1994). We will provide a detailed account of its application in Chapter 10.

There is a more subtle problem that applies to *all* types of punishment contingency that are administered by another individual or an institution. Through classical conditioning, the agent may itself become aversive, or the aversive properties of the situation may result in avoidance learning. The punishment contingency will then be ineffective, because it will no longer make contact with the individual's behavior. Instead, the individual will refuse to have anything to do with the other individual or the institution.

Against the drawbacks of punishment, must be set any advantages it may have over alternatives. Its chief advantage is undoubtedly the rapidity with which response suppression can be produced. It is often pointed out that an equivalent change can be produced by positive reinforcement without undesirable side-effects, but reinforcing an alternative response may not have as specific or rapid effects on the behavior to be eliminated. If a child persists in running off the sidewalk into the path of vehicles, socially administered punishment may be the only way of preventing the "natural" punishment contingency from having more drastic effects. Again, in Chapter 10 we will review recent studies that have successfully used punishment to eliminate an otherwise life-threatening behavior.

It might be objected that the issues raised in this section so far concern the "pragmatics" rather than the "ethics" of using punishment. From the point of view of behavioral analysis, however, these two topics cannot be dissociated. An ethical precept, such as "hitting people is wrong", can only be evaluated by defining the terms involved, assessing the consequences of implementing the procedure so defined, and comparing these with the consequences of alternative procedures, or of doing nothing. As indicated by the choice of example of ethical precept given above, a major contemporary concern is whether procedures that involve inflicting pain should be used, particularly in child rearing or with other vulnerable individuals. The discussion in this section, and indeed in the whole of this chapter, indicates that rather than trying to answer apparently simple questions of this sort directly it will be more productive to go through the steps of defining terms, specifying procedures, and then assessing outcomes, or consequences, of such interventions and their alternatives.

It is perfectly possible, at least in principle, to carry out such analyses for specific cases, perhaps of a child who is highly disruptive in classroom settings or of a person with learning difficulties who engages in self-injurious behavior, but we should note that throughout this volume two major themes have been the importance of context, or control by discriminative stimuli, and of personal history. Thus we can anticipate that any judgment that is arrived at as to the appropriateness of punishment or another non-aversive intervention will apply to that specific case in the context where the behavior of concern occurs and in the light of the relevant history of reinforcement of the person. A case of disruptive classroom behavior might, for example, be successfully eliminated by the threat that all the children in the class will miss a break period if it continues (this a *group punishment contingency*); while self-injurious behavior might decline if social interaction were to be provided as an alternative activity. Such examples show how behavioral analysis uses general principles to explain how people are different from each other and require individualised assessment and treatment if their behavior is to change. They also suggest that general ethical precepts, such as "hitting people is wrong", cannot be shown to be true or false. In Chapter 11, we will review how human rights of individuals in treatment should be protected. Amongst the guidelines presented there is "an individual has a right to the most effective treatment procedures available". This is a key idea in evaluating the appropriate use of aversive contingencies.

Although completely general conclusions on these issues cannot be drawn, it is possible to discover whether there is a broad consensus as to how to proceed. Wolf (1978) argued that it was appropriate to establish the *social validity* of applied behavioral analysis by assessing public opinion as to the social significance of its goals, the appropriateness of its procedures and the importance of its effects. Relatedly, Kazdin (1980) devised the "treatment evaluation inventory", which presents people with a written (but hypothetical) case description along with a description of a number procedures and asks them to rate acceptability of each of the procedures for the behavioral problem described. Blampied and Kahan (1992) used this inventory with 200 people recruited from a cross-section of the general public and asked them to rate the acceptability of response cost, social reprimands, time out, overcorrection and physical punishment (the actual use of all these procedures is reviewed in Chapter 10) for a 10-year-old boy or a girl, at home or at school. They found that response cost procedures (where a "fine" or other penalty is imposed) were rated the most acceptable, with physical punishment being markedly less acceptable than any of the others.

This discussion has dealt with the general implications of aversive contingencies in human behavior. Chapter 10 includes an extended discussion of the use of behavioral techniques designed to decrease human behavior in problem cases, and there we will see that, as suggested here, many of the difficult issues can be resolved in specific cases. It will also be clear, however, that value judgments are inevitably involved and we will return explicitly to those in a review of human rights issues in Chapter 11.

5.6 SUMMARY

Behavior is affected not only by positive reinforcement contingencies but also by operant and classical conditioning processes involving aversive contingencies. Consequently, this chapter presents a review of the operation and effects of aversive contingencies.

Escape learning, a form of operant conditioning, is perhaps the simplest and most basic type. A variety of experimental procedures have been used in studies of nonhuman animals to show how conditioning proceeds when the operant response results in termination of an aversive stimulus. In such procedures, the presentation of the aversive stimulus acts as an establishing operation, because it motivates the animal to remove it. While few studies have involved human participants for ethical reasons, it is important that we understand escape because it is just as important for humans as for other species.

In avoidance learning, an aversive stimulus is programmed to occur unless the operant response occurs. Again, a variety of different procedures have shown this contingency to be effective in modifying the behavior of nonhuman animals. The success of other species on this apparently more complex task suggests that the same set of behavioral processes is involved as in other tasks. More complex experiments have shown this to indeed be the case. However, there are some instances where the avoidance contingency fails to produce the expected change in operant behavior. In these instances, the occurrence of other unconditioned or classically conditioned behavior is responsible for the "failure". This illustrates the importance of understanding all the effects that aversive stimuli may have.

Punishment is a procedure in which aversive stimuli are made contingent upon the operant response and thereby reduce its frequency. This also has reliable effects in experiments with nonhuman animals, provided various methodological concerns are addressed. A small number of experimental studies with humans have also produced consistent effects. The general pattern is that punishment has effects that are broadly opposite to those of positive reinforcement. It is important to realize that "punishment" is here used as a technical term that does not have all the meanings it has in everyday language.

Classical conditioning has often been demonstrated in experiments with aversive unconditioned stimuli, and the outcome is similar to that when positive, or appetitive, unconditioned stimuli are used. However, the form of the conditioned response often involves behaviors associated with fear and escape when aversive stimuli are used. This means that these behaviors may "interfere" with operant behavior in any procedures where aversive stimuli are being used. These issues are addressed directly with the conditioned suppression procedure, where aversive classical conditioning is superimposed on positively reinforced operant behavior. This procedure has provided a useful baseline for investigation of many variables, including anxiety-reducing drugs.

Discussion of aversive contingencies invariably raises ethical issues. It is important to remember that aversive contingencies exist in the physical as well as the social environment of everyone, and we should therefore make efforts to understand their operation. We will see in later chapters that there is good evidence to prefer the use of positive reinforcement contingencies to change behavior wherever possible, but that this is not possible in every case. This further underlines the need to know how aversive contingencies affect behavior. Later chapters will provide a detailed account of the appropriate use of contingencies designed to reduce unwanted problematic behavior, and relate this to the human rights of individuals in treatment. The use of aversive contingencies is a major issue in the assessment of the social validity of behavior analysis, and techniques for this assessment have been developed in recent years.

CHAPTER 6

COMPLEX BEHAVIOR: CONCEPT ACQUISITION, MODELING, AND VERBAL BEHAVIOR

The principles elaborated in the preceding chapters permit us to describe and analyze a large fraction of the learned behavior of people and other animals. But were we to terminate our account of behavior with the phenomena of operant conditioning, classical conditioning, stimulus control, and aversive contingencies, we would still be forced to admit that the bulk of complex human behavior had either been left untouched or at best dealt with rather indirectly. The activities that might be classified as complex human behaviors are, of course, extremely diverse, and in this chapter we will examine concept acquisition and modeling, and then turn to verbal behavior itself which seems so intimately associated with many forms of complex human behavior.

For each category of complex human behavior, we will set out to define it carefully in behavioral terms, and examine the extent to which we can relate it to the principles of behavior outlined in earlier chapters. In so doing, we will be using the comparative perspective that is prevalent throughout this book. That is, we will be seeking to identify those behavioral processes that contribute to complex human behavior that are shared with other species. Because behavioral science is a biological science our initial strategy should always be to seek to establish these commonalties. We will also extend this strategy to verbal behavior, which has often been seen by philosophers, linguists, and psychologists of other orientations, as not being susceptible to this approach.

6.1 CONCEPT ACQUISITION: THE EXAMPLE OF LEARNING SETS

To "acquire a concept" or "form a concept" sounds like an abstract mental process, with no obvious behavioral connotations. Consideration of what it means to "have a concept", however, suggests that concept acquisition is closely related to the behavioral process of *discrimination*.

If a child has the concept of "school", he or she will apply this name to educational establishments, but not to other large public buildings, as he or she may have done when younger. We may say that the response "school" is under the *discriminative control* of a particular stimulus class. This class might be defined as those buildings having features common to schools and not found in other buildings, or it might be a class established through the process of *stimulus equivalence class formation* described in Chapter 4. In either case, an experimental investigation would be necessary to find out which features are important in the control of this child's behavior. It is an important general point that each person's stimulus classes, or concepts, are their own. That is, two people might both use the phrase "new car", for example, but it may mean something slightly different to each of them. This difference will have come about through the different experiences of the two individuals.

We begin with a consideration of a simple animal discrimination learning paradigm, which shares certain important properties with human concept acquisition. This will enable us to identify the term *concept* with certain precise features of behavior.

One class of discriminations involves two situations and two responses (this is slightly more complicated than the examples used in Chapter 4), and has been studied using the Wisconsin General Test Apparatus (WGTA), shown in Figure 6.1. Seated in front of the WGTA, a monkey or other primate, may be presented with several objects on a movable tray, one object concealing a peanut in a well beneath it. Suppose two objects to be in use, a solid wooden cross and a solid wooden U-shaped object. The peanut is always to be found under the cross figure, whether the latter appears on the left or on the right. The two possible contingencies may be diagrammed as

$$S_{+u}: R_L \rightarrow S+ \text{ and } S_{u+}: R_R \rightarrow S+$$

where S_{+u} means that the cross is on the left, S_{u+} means that the objects are reversed, R_L means that the monkey lifts the object on the left, and R_R means that the monkey lifts the object on the right. Any "incorrect" responses have no consequences except the removal of the tray, while "correct" responses (those specified above) produce the peanut (S+). A learning trial consists of presentation of one of the two possible contingencies. Either a correct or an incorrect response terminates the trial, and the next trial follows after a short intertrial interval.

Over a number of such trials, a discrimination will develop favoring reaching for the "cross". Since this process is a gradual one, tens to

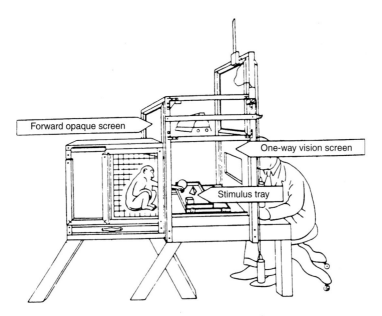

Figure 6.1 The Wisconsin General Test Apparatus. The experimenter can retract the tray, re-arrange the objects, place food under some of them, and then present the tray again to the monkey (Harlow, 1949).

hundreds of trials, depending on species and individual differences, may be necessary to reach an asymptotic value of near or at 100 per cent "correct" responses.

Each single set of these contingencies is called a *discrimination problem*. Suppose, once the discrimination process has reached its asymptote, or steady maximum value, we present a new set of contingencies, differing from the old contingencies only in the objects used as the two stimuli, for example, a solid wooden sphere and an inverted wooden cone. This time, the discrimination process will be slightly more rapid. We can then continue to present new problems, one after the other, using different objects, and the discrimination processes will become appreciably more rapid: perhaps less than a half-dozen trials are necessary for errorless performance by the time 100 discriminations have been learned. Eventually, after several hundred problems, the monkey is able to solve any new problem of this sort immediately. If, by chance, it chooses the correct object on Trial 1, it thereafter continues to choose the correct object. If, by chance, it chooses the wrong object on Trial 1, it reverses its response pattern immediately and chooses the correct object from Trial 2 on. In both cases, the monkey's performance is nearly always perfect by Trial 2. In effect, presentation of a long series of similar problems has eradicated the gradual discrimination process. We are left with an animal that solves new discriminations immediately.

Figure 6.2 shows results of this *learning set* (L-set) procedure obtained from a typical experiment with rhesus monkeys. Each curve is the average of a number of discrimination processes resulting from different discrimination problems, shown for Trials 1 to 6 only. "Discrimination process 1 to 8" is gradual, and it is clear that its maximum value would occur well beyond the 6 acquisition trials shown. The average process for problems 9 to 16 is less gradual; the curve is steeper and will reach its asymptote more quickly. Subsequent processes are still steeper, until, after 232 problems, there is no "process" as such. There is only the result: on Trial 2, the monkey is nearly always correct. Performance on Trial 2 can be used to track the development of this skill, known as a learning set (L-set).

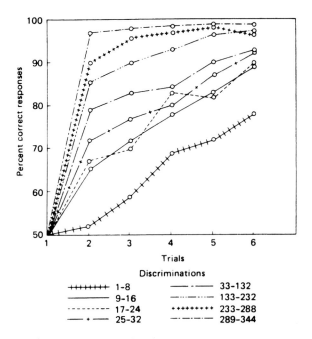

Figure 6.2   Changes in rate of acquisition of acquisition of discrimination processes. The curves are average scores of eight monkeys (after Harlow, 1949). Details are given in the text.

Figure 6.3 shows the performance level on Trial 2 as a function of the number of problems previously presented. The figure is, then, a convenient description of the L-set acquisition process, and an important feature of the process shown is its gradual and continuous character: the ability to solve a discrimination problem in one trial is itself acquired by a gradual process.

L-set performance varies with the species tested. Children tested in L-set procedures typically surpass chimpanzees and monkeys in overall performance, but they, too, exhibit a continuous L-set acquisition process. Primates lower on the phylogenetic scale than rhesus monkeys, such as squirrel monkeys and marmosets, show a more gradual L-set acquisition process than Figure 6.3 depicts. Even after 1,000 or more problems, the asymptote of their L-set process is significantly lower than perfect L-set performance. Other animals, like rats and cats, show some steepening in successive discrimination processes, but they never reach sophisticated L-set results within the limits of the experiments that have been performed. A summary from five species is shown in Figure 6.4.

These data suggest that "true" L-sets are a privileged ability of primates. Such a conclusion would have to be treated with great caution, in view of the many methodological difficulties in establishing comparable problems for different species, but has in any case turned out to be wrong. Herman and Arbeit (1973) have shown that a bottle-nosed dolphin is capable of performing from 86 to 100 per cent correct on Trial 2 of each problem of an auditory L-set task. The experimental study of learning continues both to erode the number of behaviors attributable only to humans and to "upgrade" many species not previously suspected of "higher" learning abilities.

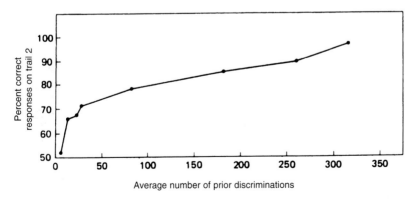

Figure 6.3 Development of a learning set. Data are derived from Figure 6.2, based on performance on Trial 2.

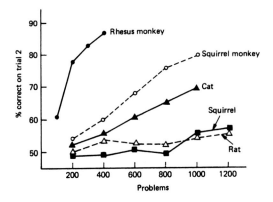

Figure 6.4   Performance of five species on a series of visual discrimination problems (from Mackintosh, 1974; after Warren, 1965).

6.2   CONCEPTUAL BEHAVIOR AND DISCRIMINATIONS

We have avoided using the term "concept" in the preceding discussions, but it seems natural to wonder whether an organism possessing an L-set for the larger of two objects, or for the green one of two objects might reasonably be said to exhibit the concept "larger of two", or "green one of two". Perhaps the "concept" acquired in the example with the WGTA is "the object of the two presented which had the peanut under it on the previous trial". Such behavioral control in humans is often the basis upon which we assign the word "concept". For instance, we agree that a child has the concept of ownership when he or she can discriminate his or her own possessions from those of anyone else. We say that a child has the concept of a noun phrase when he or she can pick out the noun phrases from unfamiliar sentences. Similarly, we credit the child with the concept of equality of number when he or she can identify equal quantities in unfamiliar settings, as when he or she can match the number of beads in one jar to the number of apples on a table. However, we require a more rigorous definition of a "concept" if we wish to examine in detail the relation between L-sets and concepts.

Put more formally, an organism is said to exhibit a concept when it can identify any member of a set of related situations. Additionally, the organism can acquire that ability via an explicit reinforcement history, or instructions relying on a previous reinforcement history, in the presence of a subset of the situations.

This definition enables us to link the L-set paradigm to concept formation. The L-set procedure is a systematic way of ordering a reinforcement history that leads to conceptual behavior. Though the monkeys do not speak, the behavior they acquire from L-set procedures seems analogous to what humans in concept-formation experiments do, using verbal responses. The word "concept" denotes the behavioral fact that a given response is under the control of a class of related S^D's. An interesting corollary of this definition is that it does not separate a concept from a discrimination, which is the behavioral fact that an S^D has come to control an operant response. Our word usage in a particular case will be determined merely by the broadness of the class of controlling S^D's. If the class of S^D's seems relatively narrow, we call the behavior a discrimination, if it seems relatively wide or broad, we are more likely to call the behavior a concept. We may also use the term concept where it is clear that the stimulus class that controls the behavior has been established through a process of stimulus equivalence class formation and contains elements that are physically unrelated. We will further discuss this category in the next section.

6.3 ARBITRARY STIMULUS CLASSES: DISJUNCTIVE CONCEPTS AND EQUIVALENCE CLASSES

In the previous sections, we have claimed that when the behavior of organisms comes under the discriminative control of the members of a broad class of S^D's, these organisms are demonstrating conceptual behavior. In the concepts discussed, the controlling SD classes may be described as a set of stimuli bound together by a common relationship of spatial arrangement or structure. In other concepts, such as "bigger than", "comes from", "to the right of", "is a member of", "leads to", and "threeness", the common relationships binding all the elements of the class are not spatial structure, but other types of relationships that are named by the verbal responses they produce. Thus, "bigger than" is a verbal response that names *the relationship* shared by the members of the controlling S^D class.

While *relational concepts* are very common, behavior is also frequently observed to come under the control of broad classes of stimuli whose members seem to lack common relationships. An obvious physical stimulus relationship, for instance, is absent in the S^D's for "food". A carrot, a pea, a leaf of spinach, and a glass of milk appear as extremely diverse objects. From its visual characteristics alone, a pea is more like a marble than it is like a leaf; a carrot is more like a stick than it is like a glass of milk.

Evidently, dissimilarity in the members of a broad S^D class is no deterrent to their ability to control a similar response. Such stimulus classes are known as *disjunctive concepts*. The members of the S^D class "food" are *either* carrots, *or* peas, *or* spinach, *or* milk, … . The response is under the control of a broad class of S^D's, and therefore, meets one of the important criteria of conceptual behavior; nevertheless, the lack of a single common relationship, a thread linking all the members of the class, prevents the generalization to new members that is typical of other concepts. These disjunctive concepts are very important. That is, there are many stimulus classes where all the elements control the same response but where the members of the class are very physically diverse, such as the concepts "my friends", or "famous writers".

The key point is that an individual who has such a concept has *learnt* to treat the elements as *equivalent*. We have already described this process in Chapter 4 as *stimulus equivalence class formation*. Verbally-competent humans appear to be different from other animals in that they can develop large classes of functionally-equivalent stimuli, even though those stimuli, the elements of the class, are physically dissimilar from each other. Once a new member is added to the class it is treated the same as the others. Thus, if a person acquires a new friend, he or she may then invite them to a party along with other friends. Similarly, if a person learns that Thackeray is a famous writer he or she may then buy Thackeray's books when they appear in the store without further encouragement. In each case, the new member of the stimulus class is being treated as if it is the same as other class elements that have been encountered previously and reinforced under certain circumstances.

6.4 POLYMORPHOUS CONCEPTS AND NATURAL CONCEPTS

Formally, in an *m-out-of-n* polymorphous rule, there are *n* relevant conditions of which *m* must be satisfied. An example is given in Figure 6.5 from a study by Dennis, Hampton, and Lea (1973) who used a card-sorting task to examine *polymorphous concepts*. The rule here is: "A member of Class A possesses at least two of the properties symmetric, black, and circular (all other stimuli are members of Class B)." While the card-sorting task is highly artificial, it is arguable that most of our "real world" or natural concepts are of this type. For example, a person will have many features common to people in general, but no one feature is necessary.

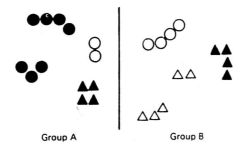

Group A   Group B

Figure 6.5   Patterns of geometric symbols grouped according to a two-out-of-three polymorphous rule (Dennis, Hampton, & Lea, 1973).

In the first experiment of Dennis et al. (1973), college students were asked to sort packs of cards showing either rows of shapes (as in Figure 6.5), typewritten letters, or random shapes into two piles (A and B). After each response, the experimenter told them whether their allocation of a card to a pile was "right" or "wrong". On different trials, the participants were required to sort the cards by a conjunctive rule (for example, "A's are black AND composed of circles"), or disjunctive rule (for example, "A's are black OR composed of triangles"), or a polymorphous rule such as the one previously described. They sorted a pack of 48 cards and the response measured was the number of cards sorted before the last error, where an error is putting a card in the wrong pile. Dennis et al. (1973) found that the median number of cards sorted was 9, 28, and 40 for the conjunctive, disjunctive, and polymorphous rules, respectively. This shows that the polymorphous concept was the most difficult to acquire, then the disjunctive, then the conjunctive.

In a second experiment, each participant was given four examples in each category (A and B) and asked to state the rule. Again, each participant was tested with cards divided according to a conjunctive, disjunctive, and polymorphous rule. They were given a maximum of 10 minutes to solve the problems. The median solution times were 34 seconds, 2 minutes 35 seconds, and 10 minutes, respectively. This means that typically the participants failed to state the polymorphous rule within 10 minutes, although the disjunctive rule was produced fairly quickly and the conjunctive rule very quickly. Comparison between their first and second experiments suggests that polymorphous conceptual behavior in response to reinforcement contingencies is acquired only slightly more slowly than conjunctive and disjunctive conceptual behavior, but polymorphous *rules* take a great deal longer to acquire than the other types. This points out that contingency-shaped behavior does not depend on prior acquisition of the corresponding verbal behavior, or rules.

This view is supported by experiments with pigeons. Using food reinforcement for key pecking, pigeons have been trained to successfully discriminate between color slides with and without people in them, although the people were at all sorts of positions, angles, distances, and so forth (Herrnstein & Loveland, 1964). "Person" is clearly a polymorphous concept as previously defined. Furthermore, Lea and Harrison (1978) trained pigeons in a similar procedure to discriminate on the basis of a 2-out-of-3 polymorphous concept, similar to the ones used by Dennis et al. (1973). If pigeons can acquire polymorphous concepts, but humans have great difficulty in stating polymorphous rules, we can only conclude that acquisition of the verbal rule is not a necessary condition for solving this sort of problem. Further research has provided extensive evidence of pigeons' ability to discriminate both *natural concepts*, such as people, fish, trees, etc., and artificial concepts, such as Lea and Harrison's polymorphous concepts (for example, Bhatt, Wasserman, Reynolds, & Krauss, 1988).

The studies of conceptual behavior discussed in this chapter illustrate both the continuity between psychological processes in humans and other species, and also the differences. While many species need, and can be shown through experiments to have, the capacity to make subtle discriminations and to identify natural concepts, human beings show greater facility and have the additional capacity to form stimulus equivalence classes. This in turn is related to our use of verbal behavior, which will be further discussed later in this chapter.

6.5   RULES AS SOLUTIONS TO PROBLEMS

A standard combination lock presents a problem, which can only be solved by trial and error. Thus a lock with 50 numbers, which opens when the correct sequence of three numbers is dialed, will require an average of $50^3/2$ or 62,500 sequences to be tried before it will open. Supposing each sequence took 6 seconds to complete, this would take about four days and thus makes such a lock an effective form of protection. The statement "try every possible combination" is a *rule* guaranteeing its eventual (but not rapid) solution. In other situations we may use search strategies, or "rules of thumb", designed to save time in reaching a solution. If an individual can solve problems of a particular type, he or she is said to *know the rules* for their solution.

"Knowing the rules" is clearly related to "having the concept". Correctly identifying dogs, is like being able to state a rule specifying what will count as a dog. However, there are important differences. First, accurate use of concepts does not imply that the user will be able to produce a verbal rule. Second, once a rule has been stated, it may exert control over behavior directly. This is an interesting phenomenon, because from a behavior analysis perspective "stating a verbal rule" is itself a type of behavior, albeit verbal behavior. We are here noting a very important and complex aspect of human psychology: our accounts of some psychological processes involve *behavior-behavior* relationships, as well as the environment-behavior relationships which have been frequently encountered in this volume. *Rule-governed behavior*, discussed further in Section 6.8, is the general name for those occasions where verbal behavior, in the form of a rule, is acquired either through verbal instruction or through direct experience of some reinforcement contingencies, and then determines other behavior.

If a three-number sequence is required to open a combination lock, and the sequence is always such that the third number is twice the second number, which is the same as the first, then once this rule is acquired, it will be used. The rule provides for very efficient problem solution (and thus reinforcement of the appropriate behavior). However, as we saw in the previous section, *learning the rule is not the same as responding to the reinforcement contingencies*. There are many types of human behavior that are influenced by reinforcement contingencies without the individual knowing rules or even thinking them relevant. The baseball pitcher pitches with great accuracy without being able to articulate the rules governing his or her own movements or the flight of the ball in the air.

With human participants, it is possible to carry out concept formation experiments, and concurrently ask them to verbalize the rule that defines the concept. They are asked to specify which features of a stimulus determine its allocation to a particular category. These procedures are called *concept identification*. Bruner, Goodnow, and Austin (1956) presented human participants in experiments with the 81 cards shown in Figure 6.6. These cards varied in four ways: (1) the number of figures (1, 2, or 3), (2) the color of the figures (red, green, or black), (3) the shape of the figures (cross, circle, or square), and (4) the number of borders (1, 2, or 3). The participants were

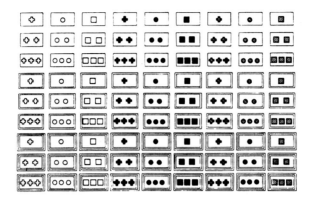

Figure 6.6   A set of cards used to study concept identification. The forms vary in number, shape, color, and number of borders (Bruner, Goodnow, & Austin, 1956).

first shown a given card (for example, the one with three red circles and two borders, which can be written as "3R-o-2b") and told that this was a positive instance of a concept that they were to identify. The participants were then advised that they could choose additional cards from the 80 remaining to obtain more information. After each choice, they were advised whether the particular card they chose was or was not an instance of the concept When the task consisted of identifying conjunctive concepts (red circles, two green figures and so on), the majority of participants adopted a strategy which consisted of choosing cards that varied in one, and only one, dimension from the known initial positive card. In this way, each selection eliminated one or more concepts. Bruner, Goodnow, and Austin were able to show that a number of variables, such as whether the concept was conjunctive or disjunctive, the manner in which the 81 cards were displayed, and the number of examples the participants were permitted to choose, affected the type of systematic strategy employed. In such a situation, the participant is prompted to devise rules which are in turn highly effective strategies for arriving at correct responses.

6.6 MODELING

The experimental analysis of behavior has been mostly concerned with the factors that govern the *performance* of a behavior, and less concerned about how that behavior is *acquired*. For this reason, operants selected for study have usually been simple acts which can be completed in a very short space of time (lever pressing, key pecking, button pressing, and so on). Similarly, although it is acknowledged that classical conditioning can simultaneously produce diverse effects on behavior, investigators have normally looked in detail at a single, relatively simple, aspect of behavior (salivation, eyeblinks, heart-rate, and so forth). Thus, neither operant nor classical-conditioning techniques are oriented to the analysis of the *acquisition of complex behavioral sequences*. However, it is a compelling fact that humans readily acquire such sequences, and often do so very rapidly. Moreover, in applied behavior analysis, acquisition of behavior sequences is often the primary objective. In Chapter 9, we will discuss a range of techniques for enhancing such acquisition. These involve combinations of techniques that have already been introduced, along with *modeling*, which will be introduced here.

Many everyday examples of acquisition of complex behavior sequences seem to depend on *observation*. For example, the new factory worker may be shown how the machine works by the supervisor, and then he or she can operate it himself or herself *immediately* with reasonable efficiency. His or her subsequent improvement towards being a skilled operator depends on feedback (reinforcement) from the machine and from co-workers, but the rapid initial acquisition is hard to explain by operant principles. We might crudely conceptualise it thus:

S^D:	R	$\rightarrow$ S+
operation of machine by supervisor	copying supervisor's behavior	successful operation of machine

While this might suffice to explain why "copying supervisor's behavior" is *performed*, it does not provide a mechanism for its *acquisition*. How does the worker manage to execute a long and complex behavior sequence that he or she has not produced previously or been reinforced for?

The only operant principle that might provide an explanation is *chaining*, which will be one of the techniques discussed in detail in Chapter 9. Behavior chains are sequences that are reinforced when completed. They can be long and complex, but they are established through a relatively lengthy piecing-together process of shaping — also discussed at length in Chapter 9 — and this involves *explicit reinforcement*. In our present example, however, there is only a single demonstration (trial) and no explicit reinforcement for either worker or supervisor.

If an *observer* acquires a new response pattern or behavior sequence by observation of another individual, this is an instance of *modeling*. There are three types of modeling influence. The first, and most striking, is the one we have described. This can be called the *response acquisition effect* of modeling. Observation of a *model* (another person) may also lead to the inhibition or facilitation of already learned behavior. For example, observing someone else making jokes about a taboo subject and gaining approval may lead to the observer telling similar jokes. We will call this the *response modulation effect*. The third modeling effect occurs when the behavior of others functions as a discriminative stimulus for the same type of behavior by the observer. If the person walking along the street in front of you suddenly stops and gazes up into the sky, it is very likely that you will do the same when you reach that point in the street. This is the *response facilitation effect*. It differs from the response modulation effect in that the *consequences* of the model's behavior are important in response modulation, but not in response facilitation. If your companion makes a joke about religion which is followed by an embarrassed silence, this will tend to inhibit similar behavior on your part. Response facilitation, on the other hand, can occur without the observer seeing the consequences of the model's behavior. The response facilitation effect differs from the response acquisition effect because response facilitation does not involve any "new" behavior. Rather, the observer produces behavior already in his or her repertoire. In both cases, however the model's behavior functions as a *discriminative stimulus* for the same behavior by the observer.

The response facilitation effect is well known to ethologists (scientists concerned with the observation of animal behavior in natural settings). The coordinated behavior of flocks or herds of animals is controlled in this fashion. Psychologists, on the other hand, have been primarily concerned with the response acquisition and response modulation effects. These differ in that the former is an effect on *learning* (the acquisition of behavior or change in the behavioral repertoire), while the latter is an effect on *performance* (the probability of the behavior occurring in a particular situation).

Bandura and associates carried out a classic series of studies showing the powerful effects on children of short periods of observing adults or children modeling specific behaviors. In a typical study (Bandura, 1965), children (aged 42 to 71 months) watched film of an adult who produced several novel, physical and verbal aggressive behaviors. The film lasted 5 minutes and involved an adult approaching an adult-sized plastic doll and ordering it out of the way. Then the model (the adult) laid the doll on its side, sat on it, and punched it on the nose. This was followed by hitting it on the head with a mallet and then kicking it round the room. Finally, the model threw rubber balls at the doll. Each act of physical aggression was accompanied by a particular verbal aggressive response. Following this performance, the children observing the film saw one of three closing scenes. Either another adult appeared with candies and soft drinks and congratulated the model, giving the model food and drink (model-rewarded group), or the second adult came in and reprimanded the model, while spanking the model with a rolled-up magazine (model-punished group). For a third group of children, the film ended before the second adult arrived (no-consequences group). Immediately after watching the film, each child was taken to a room containing a similar large doll, a mallet, balls, and a number of other toys not seen in the film. The child spent 10 minutes in this room, where they could be observed through a one-way mirror. The experimenter then entered, carrying soft drinks and pictures. These were offered to the child as rewards if he or she could imitate what the model had done in the film. Each modeled behavior that the child produced was reinforced with a drink or a picture.

The results from both parts of the experiment are shown separately for boys and girls in Figure 6.7. There were 11 participants in each of the six groups. The most notable feature of the data is the generally high level of modeling behavior. After watching a short film, a number of conditions produced mean levels of between 3 and 4 different modeled behaviors out of a possible maximum of 8 (4 physical acts and 4 verbal behaviors). Apart from this, the sex of the children, the consequences for the model, and the consequences for the children all influenced behavior. Figure 6.7 shows that in the first observation period, when no reinforcement was provided, the boys reproduced more of the model's aggressive acts than the girls. In the second period, however, when modeling was reinforced, all groups considerably increased modeling behavior and the differences between the sexes were largely eliminated. These two phases demonstrate: (1) that some modeling occurs without reinforcement for the participants (this is the *response acquisition* effect); (2) some modeled responses are acquired that may not be performed unless explicitly reinforced; and (3) the sex difference in aggressive behavior diminishes when aggression is reinforced. In the first observation period, the amount of modeled behavior was also influenced by the observed consequences of the behavior for the model. If the model had been seen to be punished for the aggressive behavior, the children showed less aggression. The effect was particularly dramatic for the girls in the model-punished group. They modeled an average of less than 0.5

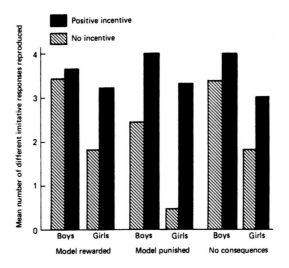

Figure 6.7   Average number of aggressive acts modeled by children as a function of consequences for the model, sex of child, and whether the child was reinforced for modeling (Bandura, 1965).

aggressive acts in the first period, but increased this to more than 3.0 when subsequently reinforced for aggressive acts. This exemplifies a powerful *response modulation* effect: performance of aggressive behavior was jointly influenced by the observed consequences for the model and the available consequences for the participant.

In Bandura's (1965) study, observation of the adult model for a short period of time was a sufficient condition for the children to imitate some of the model's behavior without reinforcement or explicit instructions. This is a remarkable finding and suggests that modeling may be responsible for the acquisition of many social and complex behaviors. After all, we spend a great deal of time observing the behavior of others. However, we obviously do not acquire *all* the behavior we observe, and some models must be more likely to be imitated than others. It turns out that models with demonstrated high competence, who are experts or celebrities, are more likely to be imitated. The age, sex, social power, and ethnic status of the model also influence its effectiveness (Bandura, 1969).

Bandura (1969) describes modeling as "no-trial learning" because response acquisition can occur without the observer being reinforced. As modeling effects cannot be described as classical conditioning either,

Bandura concludes that there is a *modeling process* that can be distin-guished from both operant and classical conditioning processes. However, it is possible that modeling is maintained by *conditioned reinforcement*. We all have a history of being reinforced for behavioral similarity, or matching the behavior of a model. During language acquisition by a young child, for example, parents often spend long periods of time coaxing the child to repeat a particular word or phrase. When the child finally produces the appropriate utterance, this *behavioral similarity* is immediately reinforced.

As behavioral similarity is often paired with reinforcement in this way, it could become a conditioned reinforcer. If behavioral similarity does have conditioned reinforcing properties, this might explain how modeling behavior can occur in experimental and clinical studies, even though it is not apparently reinforced. The paradigm would be:

$$S^D: \qquad R \qquad \rightarrow \qquad S+$$

S^D:	R	$\rightarrow$	S+
model's	imitate		behavioral
behavior	model		similarity

where the last term, S+, is a conditioned reinforcer. Behavioral similarity would only acquire and retain conditioned reinforcing properties if it was explicitly reinforced in a variety of situations. Nonreinforced modeling in the test situation can then be described as generalized imitation, because modeling behavior is generalizing from reinforced to nonreinforced situations. Gladstone and Cooley (1975) were able to demonstrate conditioned reinforcing effects of behavioral similarity. Children were given the opportunity to model a behavior sequence (that is, act as models) and then operate a bell, a horn, or a clicker. If the appropriate one of these responses was made, the experimenter (acting as the observer) immediately imitated the behavior the child had modeled. If behavioral similarity has reinforcing properties, the child-model should select the response that resulted in imitation by the experimenter-observer, and this did indeed happen. This study demonstrates reinforcing effects of behavioral similarity, and raises the possibility that these effects are involved in all modeling situations.

Even if conditioned reinforcement contributed to modeling effects, however, we still have to explain how behavioral similarity is achieved by the observer. As we pointed out earlier, the sudden production of integrated behavior sequences is one of the most striking features of response acquisition through modeling, and this cannot be accounted for by operant reinforcement principles alone. Operant conditioning principles, as outlined so far, are concerned mainly with processes of *selection*, because a reinforcement contingency operates to increase or decrease the frequency of an existing category of behavior relative to other categories of behavior. However, as we have noted from time to time, we need also to investigate those processes of behavioral variation that provide the "raw material" on which contingencies operate. In Chapters 2 and 3 we discussed extinction and shaping which are examples of these, and this aspect of modeling may be another source of behavioral variation.

6.7   REINFORCEMENT OF MODELING

Given that operant reinforcement and modeling can both modify the behavioral repertoire, the joint operation of both should be a highly effective method of altering behavior, and so it has proved. It is particularly suitable for conditions of *behavioral deficit*. A behavioral deficit means that an individual simply lacks a class of behavior common in other individuals. We will present much information on the use of modeling with reinforcement to resolve human behavioral problems in Chapter 9; the discussion here is to address theoretical issues.

Behavioral deficits have a peculiar influence on the relationship between the individual's behavior and the contingencies of reinforcement provided by the society in which he or she lives. Normally, the incidence of a class of behavior, for example, talking, is continuously modified by the social environment. Someone who never speaks, however, *fails to make contact with these contingencies*. Their situation is quite different from that of a low-frequency talker, whose talking may have been suppressed by verbal punishment, or may subsequently increase as a result of reinforcement. The non-talker will be neither reinforced nor punished.

Behavioral deficits, then, represent a severe type of behavior problem. Baer, Peterson, and Sherman (1967) attempted to alleviate this problem in three children with learning difficulties (aged 9 to 12 years) with very large deficits that included failure to imitate any behavior. The children were taught a series of discriminated operants of this form:

S^D :	R	$\rightarrow$	S+
"Do this" followed by demonstration by model	behavioral similarity by child		food

As no imitative behavior occurred initially, shaping was used. This involved assisting the participant, physically, to make the appropriate sequence of actions, and then delivering food reinforcement. Sessions were always conducted at meal times, and the amount of assistance was gradually reduced.

After initial training, imitation of some of the model's demonstrated responses were never reinforced and these responses thus formed an S^Δ class. Following $S^D - S^\Delta$ training, all imitation was extinguished, and reinforcement was now delivered if *no* imitation occurred for a specified period after the model's demonstration. (This is a DRO schedule, the differential reinforcement of other behavior than the previously reinforced response.) The results for a representative participant are shown in Figure 6.8. Reinforcement maintained a high level of S^D responding, but also a high level of S^Δ responding. When the DRO schedule was introduced, both rates declined gradually to zero. Responding to S^D and S^Δ recovered when reinforcement for S^D was reintroduced.

Baer, Peterson, and Sherman's procedure had powerful effects: responding to S^D was maintained at a high level by reinforcement and suppressed by the DRO contingency. Modeling was undoubtedly critical, as

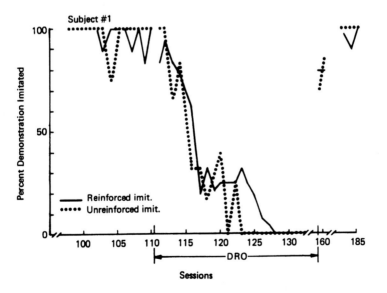

Figure 6.8   Reinforced imitative and nonreinforced imitative responding by a single child during a sequence of different reinforcement conditions (Baer, Peterson, & Sherman, 1967). Details are given in text.

well, because reinforcement alone could not account for the high levels of responding shown by these participants. Remember that prior to the experiment, they had a *very* limited behavioral repertoire. The procedure also generated a high level of S^D responding, and extended $S^D - S^\Delta$ training failed to suppress responding to S^Δ.

The S^Δ responding represents a "failure to discriminate" in operant terminology, which might have resulted from the discrimination being difficult because both S^D and S^Δ classes were demonstrated by the same model. Bandura and Barab (1973) replicated this result with a single model, but found that S^Δ responding was suppressed if there was one model for S^D and a different model for S^Δ. The fact of "discrimination failure" when a single model is used is important, because it is a further demonstration of the response acquisition effect; under appropriate conditions observers will imitate the behavior of a model, even when there is no explicit reinforcement for imitation.

There has been much debate as to the role of reinforcement and modeling in language acquisition by children; it has even been claimed that these strategies of "training by parents", which all parents engage in at a high level, are not very relevant to children's acquisition of these crucial verbal behavioral skills (Chomsky, 1959). However, Halliday and Leslie (1986) provided extensive evidence from a longitudinal study of mother-child interaction that there are strong, but complex, relationships between modeling of verbal behavior by mothers and the development of verbal competence in children. For example, from early on (perhaps when the child is 18 months old), the child imitates labels (names given to objects by the mother), and the mother may then selectively imitate the child's utterance by expanding it into a sentence. After weeks or months where this pattern of interaction is typical, the child develops the capacity to produce complete descriptive statements (we will see in the next section that these are called *tacts*). As throughout this developmental sequence the mother will be engaging in many other behaviors designed to interact with the child (praising, smiling, maintaining eye contact etc.), there is every reason to believe that modeling and reinforcement are key processes in this, as in other, aspects of the child's development.

6.8   VERBAL BEHAVIOR

Chomsky's (1959) scepticism about a behavioral analysis approach to language was expressed in a review of B.F. Skinner's (1957) book, *Verbal behavior*. In that volume, Skinner set out a general approach that was so radical that it took several decades before the scientific community was able to take it seriously, and only recently has research from this perspective begun to gain momentum.

We will only mention some of Skinner's key concepts here. The one that linguists and others have found most surprising is that he provides a *functional*, and not a structural, account of language. Talking is the most obvious and important type of verbal behavior and it should be seen as the emission of various types of operants which have different functions. For example, a person might emit a *mand* (this term is derived from "demand") which is reinforced by the removal of a cold draught from a door. That is its function, its *form* might be to say "Shut the door!", or "It is draughty in here", or even to gesture at the person standing nearest the door that they should close it. Skinner saw this as strictly analogous to the various response topographies that might occur when a rat presses a lever: a paw, the nose or even the tail might be used, but these members of the operant response class all have the common effect on the environment of depressing the lever. Another type of verbal operant is the *tact* (a descriptive act) where a person might say "What a beautiful day", or "It has turned out nice again", or the person may simply smile with pleasure as they emerge from a building into the sunshine. Sources of reinforcement for this type are not specified by the operant itself, as they are with mands, but usually involve eliciting social approval or conversation from other people.

Dialogue or conversation is crucial to Skinner's general conception of verbal behavior, which he actually defined as behavior reinforced by the behavior of other people. Key concepts here are *the speaker and the listener*, who are both part of a *verbal community*. In a normal conversation, two people repeatedly swap the roles of speaker and listener, or "take turns" and a hypothetical example is given in Figure 6.9. As conversation progresses, an utterance (an element of verbal behavior) by one person may act as the discriminative stimulus for the next utterance by the other person, which may in turn act both as a reinforcer for the previous utterance and a discriminative stimulus for the next utterance by the first person. This analysis is complex, but it is entirely consistent with the treatment of other behavioral processes within behavioral analysis in that the *function* of a feature of behavior or of the environment is not fixed, but depends on the context in which it occurs.

Verbal behavior takes place within a verbal community. Being members of a verbal community simply means being part of a group of people who routinely talk to each and reinforce each others' verbal behavior. Most of us are extremely sensitive to how our verbal behavior is reacted to by the verbal community: our enjoyment of many social occasions, for example, is critically dependent on the occurrence of "good" conversation. The social practice of shunning, or "being sent to Coventry", where at school or work no-one speaks or replies to the victim, is rightly seen as a severe and cruel punishment.

What is the relationship between verbal behavior and language? Baum (1994) suggests that while verbal behavior is actual human activity (and thus an appropriate subject matter for psychology), language is an abstraction: "The English language, as set of words and grammatical rules for combining them, is a rough description of verbal behavior. It summarizes the way a lot of people talk. It is rough because people often use poor English. Neither the explanations in a dictionary nor the rules in a book of grammar exactly coincide with the utterances of English speakers." (p. 111).

Throughout, we have said that processes of both *variation* and *selection* are essential for a complete account of behavior. In the case of verbal behavior, we have outlined some of the important selection processes, but

Figure 6.9   The behavior analytic account of dialog is like a tennis match with each person taking turns as speaker and listener. In this example, Fred and Barney are discussing a tennis match. Responses (verbal utterances) are in boxes, and each response acts as a stimulus for the other person. These are labeled as discriminative stimuli (S^D's), but they also have reinforcing properties. Note that the first S^D for Fred is a visual one. Barney's second response will act as further S^D for Fred who is about to say something else.

we have not said very much about "where verbal behavior comes from" (although modeling is clearly an important source), and it is this question, together with the fact that it appears to be a uniquely human activity, that has often preoccupied the attention of psychologists.

Recent work on *stimulus equivalence class formation*, outlined in Chapter 4, has led Hayes and Hayes (1992) to suggest that this process underpins our verbal skills. Their argument is best understood as applied to *verbal labelling*, which itself can be seen as a basic aspect of verbal behavior. A key event in their view is *bidirectional training*. This occurs when a child is encouraged to say a name for an object, and is also reinforced for selecting the object when hearing the name. A simple example will be when the child is reinforced on some occasions for saying "dog" when the family pet appears, and on other occasions for pointing to the same animal when asked "Where is the dog?". This training, which is a conspicuous feature of child rearing, may result in the dog and the spoken word "dog" becoming members of the same stimulus equivalence class. As we saw in Chapter 4, this means that, in a particular context, they are treated as being the same even though they may be physically dissimilar. With our hypothetical child who has undergone bidirectional training, someone may subsequently shout "Dog!" and elicit the same behavior as if a real dog was leaping towards the child. If the child then learns some French, a shout of "Chien!" when heard in Paris may also produce exactly the same behavior.

It is not yet clear whether stimulus equivalence underpins verbal labelling or *vice versa*, but it is revealing that humans do appear to be normally able to do both, while extensive research has provided only unconvincing evidence of either phenomenon in other species. Ever since the late-nineteenth century origins of modern psychology, clear evidence for differences in learning capacity between species has been sought but not found. However, this recent work does appear to suggest a clear disconti-nuity between humans and other species, even chimpanzees (Dugdale & Lowe, 1990; see Leslie, 1993, for a discussion of some related issues).

In Section 6.5, we provided a definition of rule-governed behavior as follows: it is the general name for those occasions where verbal behavior, in the form of a rule, is acquired either through verbal instruction or through direct experience of some reinforcement contingencies, and then determines other behavior. We later noted that while "having a concept" and "following a verbal rule" are related they are not the same thing, because animals that do not appear to have verbal abilities, such as pigeons, can show some evidence of conceptual behavior, and humans can solve complex problems even on occasions when they prove unable to verbalize the correct rule.

These complexities can be clarified by distinguishing between *following the rule*, and *stating the rule*. Skinner (1969) defined a rule as a *verbal discriminative stimulus* that points to a contingency, and for any contingency it is possible to state a verbal rule but, as we have seen with various types of examples, observation that behavior consistent with the verbal rule is occurring does not prove that it is *rule-governed*; it may be *contingency-shaped*. With verbally-competent humans, these two types of influence on behavior interact in complex ways. A vehicle driver, for example, cannot provide verbal statements about the adjustments he or she makes to the controls of the car in response to changes in the road surface, but he or she will be able to describe what they decided to do once they realized that they had taken the wrong turning.

A further feature of human behavior is that verbal rules, or instructions, exert powerful effects on behavior that may preclude the operation of contingencies that would otherwise be effective. The presentation of a verbal rule may restrict behavioral variation that would otherwise occur and result in certain behavior being reinforced. Many older people in urban areas, for example, have been given messages such as "You will be attacked if you go out at night", or "Your home will be robbed". Under these influences, but without suffering any crime themselves, they may then lead very restricted lives with much time spent barricaded into their homes. Their behavior may or may not be appropriate, depending on the local level of crime, but it has not been shaped directly by the contingencies.

A general feature of human behavior is that it is more influenced by *short-term* rather than *long-term* consequences or contingencies. Many everyday phenomena fit in with this "rule of thumb": we eat sweets (followed by short-term positive consequences) and fail to clean our teeth adequately (avoiding short-term negative consequences) and thus incur the long-term negative consequences of tooth decay and aversive dental treatment, we stay up late having a good time at the party and are unable to complete our work requirements the following day, and so on. Our tendency to follow rules, rather than allowing contingencies to shape our behavior can be seen as a further instance. Rule following is generally itself followed by immediate positive social consequences, while the contingency pointed by the rule may be very far off. An example of the two contingencies, the "real" contingency and the contingency involving following the corresponding rule, is shown in Figure 6.10. Although it may not always be possible to identify reinforcing consequences for a particular instance of rule following, we also engage in a great many social practices that offer generalized support for rule-following behavior. These range from children's games that reward rule following *per se*, to using negative labels (such as "psychopath") for adults who fail to obey rules.

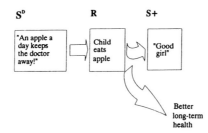

Figure 6.10   An example of rule following. The response receives short-term social reinforcement, and also results in long-term benefit for the child.

6.9 SUMMARY

This chapter examines a number of types of complex behavior, using the same strategy of relating human behavior to that of other species, and seeking to use the minimum number of behavioral processes, that characterizes the previous five chapters.

Concept formation is a form of discrimination learning, and studies with a number of species of the development of learning sets provide an illustration of species similarities and differences in complex behavior. If "having a concept" describes the situation where a given response is under the control of a class of discriminative stimuli, then it is clear that stimulus equivalence classes are also examples of concepts. Use of stimulus equivalence classes by verbally-competent humans is an extremely powerful strategy for modifying the behavioral repertoire, because the acquisition of a new function for one member of the class transfers to all the other, physically dissimilar, class members.

Experimental studies have shown that both humans and other species (including pigeons) can establish complex polymorphous concepts, where a positive exemplar has *m* out of *n* characteristics. These studies are important because polymorphous concepts are formally very similar to natural concepts (such as trees, or houses), and the studies show that verbal rule-following is not necessary — even in humans — to acquire these concepts.

With human participants, it is possible to carry out concept formation experiments and ask them to verbalize the concepts as they go through the experiment. Rule-formation and rule-following is a highly effective problem solving strategy for humans, and these studies illustrate the tactics adopted.

Modeling is an important behavioral process not discussed in previous chapters, but crucial to the account of acquisition of behavior sequences that will be given in later chapters. It provides a rapid mechanism for acquisition of complex behavior. Experimental studies have shown that robust effects can be obtained on children's behavior, particularly when aggressive behavior is learnt by observing an adult model. It is possible that such modeled behavior is maintained by conditioned reinforcement, but the modeling procedure seems in any case to be an important source of "new" behavior.

A common feature of people with developmental delay or learning difficulties is that they do not imitate behavior readily. However, positive reinforcement of showing behavioral similarity leads to enhanced modeling in such individuals. It is also possible to show that reinforcement of modeling occurs frequently in everyday mother-child interactions.

Recently, researchers in behavior analysis have developed Skinner's (1957) suggestion as to how a functional account of language, or verbal behavior, might proceed. This approach is radically different from the structural approach characteristic of linguistics, but it is readily linked to the functional account of behavior in general that is provided by behavior analysis. One example of this is that the very common human behavior of rule following (such as is specified by the rule "stop at the red light", for example) is maintained by frequent social reinforcement which occurs in close proximity to the rule following behavior, while the contingency described by the rule (such as the possibility of a road crash when vehicles do not stop) often operates only over long periods of time with occasional reinforcement. The rule-following behavior is thus much more useful than direct interaction with the environment.

It is striking that while the conditioning processes reviewed in earlier chapters seem applicable to many species, including humans, both the use of language and ability to form stimulus equivalence classes seem almost exclusively human attributes. It may be that this is where a degree of "discontinuity" between humans and other species is located.

CHAPTER 7

ASSESSING BEHAVIOR IN APPLIED SETTINGS

The next four chapters will describe how the research findings from the experimental analysis of behavior can be translated into applied assessment and intervention techniques. The first step in the process of conducting an applied behavioral intervention is to clearly identify the behaviors that need to be changed. These behaviors must be described in ways that can be systematically observed and measured on a more or less continuous basis. Additionally, the relationship between these behaviors and their environmental determinants must be detailed. In this chapter the assessment techniques used to identify a behavior and its environmental determinants will be described.

Identifying the behavior to be changed is only the first step. The behavior must also be measured over time in such a manner that the impact of the intervention on the behavior can be causally evaluated. Applied behavior analysts have designed a number of experimental methods that can be used to examine the effectiveness of behavioral interventions on selected behaviors. These research methods will be described in Chapter 8.

Following this, in Chapters 9 and 10 a series of applied behavioral intervention techniques will be described that are derived from the operant principles of reinforcement and punishment. These techniques can be used to increase appropriate behavior or decrease inappropriate behavior. Applied interventions often involve combinations of these intervention techniques to decrease maladaptive behaviors while concurrently increasing adaptive behaviors. Issues related to the selection of interventions based on prior assessment of the target behavior will be discussed in these chapters.

7.1   A MODEL FOR UNDERSTANDING AND GUIDING BEHAVIORAL ASSESSMENT IN APPLIED SETTINGS

Behavioral assessment involves selecting and defining the behavior to be changed. This behavior is typically referred to as the *target behavior*. Additionally, the context or environment in which the behavior occurs must also be clearly identified. Environmental conditions may be operationalized as establishing operations (sometimes called setting events), antecedent stimuli, and consequences or reinforcing stimuli. The relationship between these environmental conditions and the behavior of interest is presented in Figure 7.1. Information from assessment is essential prior to selecting intervention strategies that may increase adaptive behavior or decrease maladaptive behavior.

In Chapter 2, we described a two-term relationship between an operant response class and the consequent or reinforcing stimulus as a step towards a definition of operant conditioning. In Chapter 4, we recognized the limitations of that simple formula by adding in the antecedent or discriminative stimulus to make the well-known three-term relationship, of S^D, R and S+, our definition. In Figure 7.1, there are *four* terms with the addition of *establishing operations*. For reasons that are explained below, this does not really make a "four-term relationship", but establishing operations are none the less necessary conditions for operant conditioning to occur. Establishing operations are social or biological conditions of satiation or deprivation that may affect the evocative power of a discriminative stimulus and/or the reinforcing power of a consequence (Carr & Smith, 1995; Michael, 1982; 1993). For example, candies may be powerful reinforcers for increasing appropriate behavior (such as cleaning up the toy room) with some children, but the effectiveness of such a reinforcer may be related to the level of food deprivation at any given point in time. Hence, contingent candy (that is, presentations of candy made contingent upon appropriate behavior) may produce high levels of room cleaning prior to dinner but low levels following dinner. O'Reilly (1995) investigated a day-care situation where a person with severe intellectual disabilities sometimes showed a great deal of aggression. He demonstrated that this occurred on days following loss of sleep during the previous night, and that sleep deprivation was correlated with high levels of escape-

Establishing Operations:	**Antecedent Stimuli :**	**Behavior** $\longrightarrow$	**Consequence Stimuli**
Or EO:	**A:**	**B** $\longrightarrow$	**C**

Figure 7.1 A model of the behavior and environmental conditions to be assessed. Note that here the terms "Antecedent stimuli", "Behavior", and "Consequence stimuli" are used in ways that are exactly equivalent to the terms "discriminative stimulus" or S^D, "response" or R, and reinforcing stimulus or S+, in Chapter 4. The terms used here give us the "ABC of behavior analysis".

maintained aggression during demanding tasks. Sleep deprivation acted as an establishing operation to enhance the aversiveness of demanding tasks and increase the power of escape as a reinforcer. Establishing operations include *all* the social and biological conditions necessary for the three-term relationship of S^D, R and S+ to be effective, and thus while of great importance, should not be construed as a specific fourth term with respect to the other three.

Antecedent stimuli are those environmental conditions that occur prior to the performance of a behavior and predict specific consequences. In other words, behavior has been reinforced in the presence of these stimuli and therefore these stimuli acquire a discriminative function. Chapter 4 gave a detailed description of stimulus control and Chapter 9 will describe applied interventions with this technology. Much of our everyday behavior is under stimulus control. A knock at the door or a telephone ring predicts that opening the door or answering the phone will reveal a person or a voice at the other end. In our earlier example, the presence of a parent may predict that cleaning the room will result in candy for the child. Cleaning the toy room in the presence of the babysitter will not result in a candy reward and therefore the room remains untidy. The presence of a parent is therefore a discriminative stimulus for room cleaning.

Behavior refers to the responses of an individual or group. These responses must be observable by at least one individual. Behaviors in our previous examples include, picking up toys and placing them in appropriate containers, hitting and pinching staff, picking up the phone, and answering the door.

Consequence stimuli are those events that follow the performance of the behavior. They are also contingent upon the performance of the behavior. In other words, these consequences are only available to the person following the performance of that behavior and are otherwise not available. Contingent consequences can either increase (reinforce) or decrease (punish) the probability of a behavior. Chapter 2 provided a detailed description of the functional properties of positive reinforcement, and Chapter 5 described negative reinforcement and punishment, Chapters 9 and 10 will describe corresponding applied interventions with these processes.

In summary, a comprehensive behavioral assessment must provide unambiguous and measurable information about the behavior to be decreased or increased and the context in which the behavior occurs. The context is operationalized in terms of how establishing operations, antecedent stimuli, and consequence stimuli enter into a functional relationship with the behavior of interest.

7.2 SELECTING TARGET BEHAVIORS

Prior to beginning an assessment it is important that the behavior identified as in need of change is of social relevance for the client. It is usually self-evident that the desired change in the target behavior will increase positive reinforcement and minimize punishment for that person. On occasions, however, the reasons for selecting a specific target behavior may not be entirely clear or appropriate. For example, Taylor, O'Reilly, and Lancioni (1996) assessed a child with autism who exhibited severe aggressive behavior in the classroom. His teacher requested a behavioral program to decrease the aggression. Following further observation it was noted that the child's aggression only occurred when he was not engaged in academic activities. The behavioral program eventually focused on teaching the teacher to engage the student continuously in academic activities which resulted in significant reductions in classroom aggression. This revised target behavior eliminated the need for the use of punishment procedures with the child.

There are no hard and fast rules for selecting appropriate target behaviors. It may be helpful for the behavior analyst to ask a number of questions about the proposed target behaviors prior to a formal assessment. These questions, coupled with a rationale for each, are presented below.

Will increasing and/or decreasing this behavior result in positive outcomes for the person? It is important that a behavior program results in a positive outcome for the individual. Developing a list of these potential outcomes often helps to clarify and justify the development of a behavioral program.

Who will be the primary beneficiary of this program? This is especially relevant when the referring agent is somebody other than the potential client. In such cases it may be important to do an ecological assessment of the client's environment (for example, the family home or the classroom). Such ecological assessments may reveal that the primary motive for the behavioral program may be to maximize reinforcers for the carers and not for the client. In these cases alternative target behaviors should be selected. *Is the behavior appropriate or typical for somebody of that age?* This is an important consideration when selecting behaviors to decrease and increase. For example, head-banging (i.e., rhythmic hitting of head against solid stationary objects) is a behavior that is seen in approximately 15% of infants up to 24 months of age (deLissovoy, 1964). The vast majority of these children do not continue to head-bang into early childhood and do not require intervention (Oliver, 1995). Extensive behavioral interventions are typically warranted for those cases that do persist into later childhood. Occasionally, teachers may choose rehabilitation goals for persons with developmental disabilities based on developmental age and not on chronological age. For example, toy-play with infant materials may be the planned outcome for adults with developmental disabilities. Such goals are not appropriate, because if they are achieved they will only serve to exclude these people from activities with same-age non-handicapped peers in normal life settings.

7.3   DEFINING THE TARGET BEHAVIOR

Once there is agreement regarding the need for a behavioral intervention the target behavior must be carefully defined. Initially, the presenting behavior is typically defined in general terms such as personality characteristics, and summary labels in the form of statements such as "I want to lose weight", "My child is too aggressive", or "This student is withdrawn". These global terms must be translated into operational definitions. *An operational definition is a description of the subject matter in terms of how it will be measured.* In applied behavioral analysis an operational definition is a description of overt, observable behavior.

This is an essential step in any behavioral program for several reasons. First, it clarifies to all stakeholders (that is, the client, their family, teachers etc.) the precise nature of the behavior to be changed. If stakeholders disagree with the focus of treatment, then new target behaviors may be selected and unnecessary interventions may therefore be forestalled. Second, it allows for ongoing evaluation of the target behavior throughout the intervention process. If desired change is not occurring then the intervention can be altered. Third, it allows for dissemination and replication of findings within the scientific community.

Hawkins and Dobes (1975) provide three guidelines for developing operational definitions of target behaviors:

1. The definition should be objective, referring only to observable characteristics of the behavior (and environment) and translating any inferential terms (such as "expressing hostile feelings", "intended to help", or "showing interest in") into more objective ones.
2. The definition should be clear in that it should be readable and unambiguous so those experienced observers could read it and readily paraphrase it accurately.
3. The definition should be complete, delineating the "boundaries" of what is to be included as an instance of the response and what is to be excluded, thereby directing the observers in all situations that are likely to occur and leaving little to their judgement.

Thus, the operational definition should be objective, referring to observable behaviors and environmental events. It should also be clear or unambiguous to the extent that other observers could accurately paraphrase it. Finally, the definition should be complete and identify what should and should not be included as an instance of the target behavior.

An example of an operational definition of behavior arising from the statement "My child is too aggressive" might be, "Striking siblings in a forceful manner with an open hand or closed fist but excluding touching siblings with tips of fingers or with an open hand in a nonforceful manner." This operational definition identifies the problematic behaviors in objective terms and delineates examples of behavior to be included and excluded from the definition. In the case of the withdrawn student in the examples cited at the beginning of this section, it is most probable that the target of the intervention will be to increase appropriate social interactions in the school setting. One potential target behavior might be to increase verbal interactions and might be defined as, "A verbal statement that begins a conversation, changes a topic, or provides instruction to take some action".

Defining Complex Target Behaviors: Task Analysis

It is often the case that the focus of a behavioral intervention will be with individual and discrete target behaviors such as those described in the last section. In other instances, an intervention may be designed to develop a complex sequence of behaviors. In such cases it is not possible to produce a simple operational definition. Such complex behaviors must be broken down into their component parts. Each component behavior must be discrete and essential for completing the task sequence. The process by which a complex sequence of behaviors is broken down and the outcome of such a process (that is, the set of behaviors) is called a *task analysis.*

Developing a task analysis can be a complex affair. The first step consists of identifying the essential behaviors involved in performing the task sequence. This can be achieved by observing and recording the behaviors of individuals who are skilled in performing that task. For example, Cuvo, Leaf, and Borakove (1978) taught janitorial skills (sweep and mop the floor, clean the stool, clean the mirror, etc.) to persons with intellectual disabilities. The task analyses for these skills were developed by observing janitors perform these tasks.

Alternatively, task analyses can be developed by consulting individuals with expertise in a given area. These people can identify the important behaviors and how they are to be performed. For example, O'Reilly and Cuvo (1989) taught self-treatment of cold symptoms (identify symptoms and over-the-counter medication to treat symptoms; recognize when to consult a physician) to a woman who had suffered a severe brain injury due to cardiac arrest. The task analysis was developed with input from a group of physicians.

Finally, specialist texts may be consulted. For example, O'Reilly, Green, and Braunling-McMorrow (1990) taught adolescents who suffered brain injuries from vehicle accidents to amend potential hazards in their daily living arrangements. Common home hazards that often led to injury were identified from publications available from the American National Safety Council. Task analyses were developed for each of these situations by observing non-disabled adults dealing with these situations.

Once the essential behaviors of a task are identified they must be broken down into a series of discrete and trainable behaviors. The size or number of behaviors in each step of the task analysis must be determined by the skill level of the person to be taught. Individuals with low levels of functioning will require a task to be broken into small component behaviors. A summarized series of generic behaviors may be required for individuals with higher levels of functioning. Once the task has been tailored to the person then training is initiated to teach each individual component behavior until the entire task sequence is performed correctly.

An example of a task analysis to teach grocery shopping skills to adults with mild intellectual disabilities is illustrated below (Taylor & O'Reilly, 1997). The purpose of the intervention was to enhance independence for these individuals in ordinary life settings. The task analysis was developed by observing non-disabled individuals engaged in grocery shopping in local community stores. The level of difficulty of each step of the task analysis was determined by consulting staff who worked on a daily basis with these individuals. These skills were then successfully trained in local grocery stores through repeated practice, prompts and reinforcement. This example clearly illustrates how a behavior that will enhance the quality of life for an individual (through increasing independence), can be operationalized into a series of objective behaviors (task analysis), and successfully taught to individuals using applied behavioral techniques.

In another example of a task analysis, Friman, Finney, Glasscock, Weigel, and Christophersen (1986) taught a group of adult males to examine themselves for testicular cancer. Testicular cancer is one of the leading causes of death in males between the ages of 15 to 40. Early identification

Table 7.1 *Steps of the Supermarket Shopping Task Analysis (Taylor & O'Reilly, 1997)*

Step	Description
1.	Walks from car to supermarket
2.	Enters the supermarket through the correct door
3.	Lifts a basket
4.	Looks at shopping list
5.	Looks on shelves for item
6.	Puts item in basket or picks up item
7.	Looks at list for next item
8.	Looks on shelves for item
9.	Puts item in basket or picks up item
10.	Checks list to see that both items are in the basket
11.	Goes to correct checkout (i.e., express checkout)
12.	Takes place in line
13.	Behaves appropriately in line (i.e. moves forward when line moves)
14.	Puts contents of basket on counter
15.	Replaces basket
16.	Pays for items using next dollar strategy
17.	Waits for change
18.	Packs sack
19.	Picks up sack
20.	Exits store through correct door
21.	Returns to car

and medical treatment of this disease can lead to recovery. The behaviors required for correct self-examination were identified through consultation with urologists and various professional materials on testicular cancer. The task analysis of testicular self-examination behaviors is presented in Table 7.2. The participants were then successfully taught to perform these behaviors.

The development of a successful behavioral intervention rests initially on the selection of an appropriate target behavior and the correct operationalization of this behavior. The importance of this assessment process cannot be overstated. Interventions are tailored to the type of behavior to be changed. Also, the success of the intervention is measured by continuous assessment of changes in the target behavior. These issues will be discussed again in Chapters 8, 9 and 10.

7.4 MEASURING AND RECORDING BEHAVIORS

Once the target behavior has been identified and operationalized the next step is to select an appropriate measurement strategy for that behavior. The measurement strategies used in applied behavior analysis provide a direct assessment of the target behavior in the criterion or real-life setting before, during, and after the implementation of treatment procedures. The measurement procedures used in applied behavior analysis usually consist of an assessment of discrete occurrences of the target response or the amount of time the response occurs. It is important that the measurement procedure selected be both sensitive and practical. A sensitive measurement system is one that produces an accurate and complete picture of the target

Table 7.2 *Task Analysis for Testicular Self-Examination (Friman, Finney, Glasscock, Weigel, & Christopherson, 1986)*

---

1. Gently pulls scrotum so that it hangs freely.
2. Uses fingers and thumbs of both hands to isolate and examine one testicle.
3. Locates the soft tender mass (the epididymis and spermatic cord) on top of and extending behind the testicle.
4. Rotates the entire surface areas of the testicle between fingers and thumbs.
5. Uses fingers and thumbs to isolate and examine the other testicle.
6. Locates the soft tender mass on top of and extending behind the testicle.
7. Rotates the entire surface area of the testicle between fingers and thumbs.

---

behavior. For example, if the interest lies in increasing or decreasing the duration of a behavior it is important that a measurement of duration of the target response is used. Similarly, if the frequency of the behavior is of interest then a frequency measurement system should be adopted. A practical measurement system is one that is usable from the point of view of the observer. Often, the applied behavior analyst must balance sensitivity with practicality when choosing a measurement procedure. Whether a measurement system is usable depends on the applied context. For example, it would be difficult for a teacher with a normal classroom responsibility of some 30 students to conduct duration measurements of "out-of-seat behavior" (that is, time spent away from the seat the student should be occupying) for an individual student. Such a context may require less time consuming assessment protocol that may not be as sensitive to the behavior of interest (such as momentary time sampling, discussed below). Some of the most common measurement protocols used include frequency or event recording, duration and latency, and time sampling methods.

Frequency or Event Recording

Frequency or event recording requires a tally or count of the number of times that the target behavior occurs during a given period of time. Frequency recording is most often used with discrete behaviors of a constant duration. A discrete response is one that has a clear beginning and end. Discrete responses allow the observer to separate each instance or occurrence of the behavior. Each instance of the behavior should take a similar amount of time to perform. If different instances of the behavior are of different durations then an alternative measurement strategy that is sensitive to the temporal dimension of the target behavior should be used. For example, certain ongoing behaviors such as conversing with others might not be suitable for assessment using frequency measures. If a student plays with one peer for 10 seconds and another peer for 5 minutes then these would be counted as two instances of talking. The temporal dimension of these two instances of playing would be lost if a frequency count was used.

Frequency measures have been used to assess a variety of behaviors in applied settings. For example, Stark, Knapp, Bowen, Powers, Jelalian, Evans, Passero, Mulvihill, and Hovell (1993) successfully taught parents to implement a behavioral program to increase caloric intake for three malnourished children with cystic fibrosis. One of the measures of the programs effectiveness was the number of bites of food each child ate at dinner. Other examples of behaviors measured using frequency protocol include social skills (such as initiating conversations), aggression (verbal and physical abuse), attendance (such as appointment keeping at pediatric outpatient clinics).

Frequency measures can be expressed as the number of times a target behavior occurred (for example, number of families that attended outpatient clinic). Number should not be used as an expression if the observation times themselves differ from session to session. In such instances rate of behavior is a more appropriate expression. Rate of response can be calculated by dividing the total frequency of the target response by the number of minutes for that particular observation. Response rate per minute is therefore comparable across observation sessions of different durations.

Frequency or event recording has a number of obvious advantages. First, it is an easy recording system to use. It merely requires a tally of ongoing behavior. Various recording devices such as wrist counters and hand-tally digital counters are available that can facilitate recording. Second, because they are a direct measure of the amount of behavior, frequency or event measures are sensitive to changes in behavior resulting from contingency manipulation (Kazdin, 1994).

Duration and Latency Recording

Duration and latency are time-based methods of measurement. These measurement systems are used when the temporal dimension of the response is of interest. Measures of duration are particularly useful with continuous behaviors or with discrete behaviors of such high rate that it would be difficult to measure each response accurately using frequency or event recording. Continuous behaviors such as free play or conversations are behaviors that can occur for extended periods of time and usually happen for different lengths of time during each occurrence. Some individuals with severe behavior disorders emit high rates of discrete behaviors such as head hitting, and eye poking. Counting each occurrence of such behavior would be difficult and unreliable. One alternative approach is to count the amount of time or duration the individual engages in such behavior.

Duration measures can be conducted using either a duration per occurrence or a total duration procedure. For duration per occurrence, the observer measures the duration of each instance of the behavior during an observation session. A total duration procedure measures the total duration of responding during an observation session. Duration per occurrence provides a temporal and numerical assessment of behavior. For example, Gaylord-Ross, Haring, Breen, and Pitts-Conway (1984) measured the duration and number of social interactions between students in a school setting. Such a protocol provides a measure of how many interactions each student engaged in and how long these interactions were. As the purpose of the intervention was to increase the quality and quantity of interactions between students a duration per occurrence measure was more sensitive to the goals of the program than frequency or total duration measures. De Luca and Holborn (1992) used a total duration measure to examine the impact of a variable-ratio reinforcement schedule with changing criteria on amount of time spent pedaling stationary exercise bicycles with obese and non-obese boys. The total amount of time spent pedaling during observation sessions was of interest in this intervention. The use of a duration per occurrence protocol would have provided additional and unnecessary information for the purposes of this study. It is therefore important to consider the purpose of the planned intervention (that is, which dimensions of the behavior are to be increased or decreased) in addition to the nature of the target behavior when selecting a measurement system.

Latency is an additional measure based on the time dimension of responding. Instead of measuring the duration of a response when it occurs, latency is a measure of the length of time between the presentation of an initiating stimulus and the occurrence of the target response. Latency should be used when the major issue is the length of time between an opportunity to perform a behavior and the initiation of that behavior. For example, latency can be used when an individual is too slow at following directions (for example, beginning a classroom exercise, or complying with parental requests). The main purpose of an intervention in such cases may be to decrease the latency between the request and performance of the task. Latency to responding may also be used as a measure when performing the behavior can be dangerous to the individual concerned. For example, O'Donoghue and O'Reilly (1996) examined the function of serious self-destructive behavior for an adult with autism and developmental disabilities. Self-injury was so severe (including tearing eyelids, and banging head on hard surfaces) that the individual was physically restrained throughout the day. During assessment procedures a latency protocol (amount of time from the initiation of a task to engagement in the first episode of self-injury) was used as it was dangerous and unethical to allow the individual to engage in the problematic behavior for an extended period of time.

Typically, a stopwatch is used to record duration or latency during observation sessions. For total duration the stopwatch is activated as the behavior begins and is stopped as the behavior ends. This is repeated during the observation session without resetting the stopwatch. A total duration is then available at the end of the observation session. For latency, the stopwatch is activated once the stimulus is presented and is stopped as the target behavior occurs. Duration is usually expressed as the cumulative duration the person engaged in the behavior during a session. If observation session times differ across days then total duration should be reported as percentage of time ([duration of target behavior/total time of observation session] × 100 = %). Percentage of time allows for the direct comparison of the target behavior across observation sessions of different durations. Reporting practices are similar for latency measures. Duration per occurrence is not affected by observation session length and is simply reported or expressed as the duration for each occurrence of the behavior.

Interval Recording

Interval recording procedures are the most frequently used measurement protocol in applied behavior analysis. Interval measures can be used with discrete, continuous, and high rate behaviors. These procedures are used to record the number of time intervals within an observation session that the target behavior occurred. Each observation session is divided into brief time intervals of equal size. The target behavior is recorded as occurring or not occurring during each interval. Multiple occurrences of the target behavior within each interval are not scored separately. However, multiple target behaviors can be scored within each interval. Interval recording therefore does not provide an estimate of frequency but of occurrence per interval. Additionally, target behaviors for multiple individuals can be recorded during an observation session. For example, if an observation session is 10 minutes long and each observation interval is 15 seconds, the session is divided into forty 15 second units. The specific interval size should provide enough time for the observer to accurately observe and record the behavior. To facilitate accurate recording a data sheet is usually developed with a box for each interval (see Figure 7.2). During the observation each box (interval) is filled with a symbol to indicate whether the target behavior occurred or did not occur. Data are subsequently reported as percentage of intervals in which the target behavior occurred during each observation session (number of intervals in which behavior occurred divided by total number of intervals multiplied by 100). The data for Figure 7.2 show that the target behavior occurred for 50% of the intervals ([8/16] × 100 = 50%).

Figure 7.3 presents a data sheet to record multiple behaviors for an individual. In this case a symbol for each behavior is included in each interval box. The observer circles each behavior that occurs during an interval. This data sheet indicates that the student spent the majority of the time out of his seat and talking with other students during the observation. Each behavior (i.e., out of seat, talking to other students, talking to teacher) is presented separately as percentage of intervals. A data sheet for recording the behavior of multiple individuals is presented in Figure 7.4. When collecting interval observations with multiple individuals an observer usually focuses on one individual for each interval. For example, the first individual is observed for the first 15 second interval followed by the second person for the second interval. This sequence is continued until each person is observed for one interval. The sequence is then repeated across individuals.

There are two types of interval recording protocol. The most frequently used procedure is called *partial-interval recording*. This protocol requires

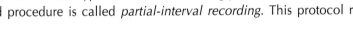

Intervals

		15 Sec.	15 Sec.	15 Sec.	15 Sec.
	1	X	X	O	X
Minutes	2	O	X	O	O
	3	O	X	X	X
	4	O	X	O	O

X = Behavior occurred

O = Behavior did not occur

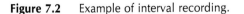

Figure 7.2   Example of interval recording.

Intervals

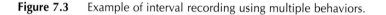

		15 Sec.	15 Sec.	15 Sec.	15 Sec.
	1	⊗ Y z	⊗⊗ z	⊗Ⓨ z	x Ⓨ z
Minutes	2	⊗ Y z	⊗Ⓨ z	x Ⓨ z	x Y z
	3	⊗ Y z	x Ⓨ z	⊗ Y z	⊗ Y z
	4	⊗ Y z	⊗Ⓨ z	x Y Ⓩ	x Y Ⓩ

X = Out of seat
Y = Talking to students
Z = Talking to teacher

Figure 7.3   Example of interval recording using multiple behaviors.

Intervals

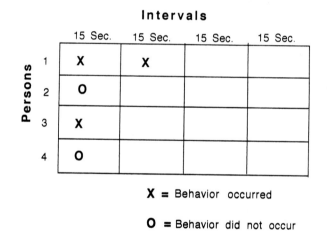

		15 Sec.	15 Sec.	15 Sec.	15 Sec.
	1	X	X		
Persons	2	O			
	3	X			
	4	O			

X = Behavior occurred

O = Behavior did not occur

Figure 7.4   Example of interval recording with multiple persons.

the observer to record the target behavior as present if it occurs at any time during an observation interval. Alternatively, a *whole-interval recording* procedure can be used. Whole-interval recording requires that the behavior be present throughout the entire interval for it to be recorded as occurring. The whole-interval measurement protocol is therefore more sensitive to the duration of occurrence of the target behavior during an observation session. Partial-interval procedures tend to overestimate the occurrence of the behavior whereas whole-interval protocol tend to underestimate behavior. Again, the type of interval protocol chosen will be determined by the nature of the target behavior and the goals of the proposed intervention program. For example, Allen, Loiben, Allen, and Stanley (1992) evaluated the effectiveness of a dentist-implemented intervention (escape contingent on brief periods of cooperative behavior) on levels of disruptive behavior for 4 children who were receiving restorative dental treatment. Body movement, crying, moaning, and complaining were recorded for the children using a 15 second partial interval recording protocol. Lagomarcino, Reid, Ivancic, and Faw (1984) evaluated the effectiveness of an intervention procedure including stimulus prompts and contingent positive consequences to teach dance skills to persons with severe developmental disabilities. Observation protocol consisted of observing each of two dancers individually for one-minute sessions. Appropriate dancing was measured using a 10-second whole-interval procedure during the 1-minute observations.

An alternative interval measurement procedure is called *momentary time sampling*. Momentary time sampling differs from the other interval protocol in that target behaviors are recorded as occurring or not occurring immediately after the specified time intervals. Recording devices (i.e., data sheets) and protocol (i.e., observation sessions are divided into specified time intervals) are similar to the other interval measurement systems. Momentary time sampling is easy to use especially when and observer is also involved in concurrent tasks. For example, teachers often use a momentary time sampling procedure as it does not interfere with the teaching routine. The end of an interval can be signaled by a device such as a tape recorder. At that point the teacher observes the target student and records whether or not the behavior of interest was occurring. The teacher can then continue with their teaching duties until the end of the next interval.

In summary, once a target behavior is operationalized it is necessary to select an appropriate measurement system for that behavior. The target behavior must be measured over time in order to provide an evaluation of the behavior before, during, and after the intervention. Selecting a measurement system for a target behavior requires consideration of a number of factors. In particular, the measurement system must be sensitive and practical. Measurement systems are typically based on the number of occurrences or duration of the target behavior. The most frequently used measurement systems have been outlined here (these are frequency, duration, and interval recording). Specific variations of these measurement procedures can be found in the behavioral literature (e.g., physiological measures such as heart rate; permanent products of behavior such as amount of weight lost) but all address either a frequency or duration dimension of the target behavior.

7.5   Conducting Observations

The purpose of assessment is to identify the extent to which the target behavior is performed before, during, and after the intervention. In addition to operationally defining the target behavior and selecting an appropriate measurement strategy, it is important to clarify when observations of the behavior in the applied setting will be conducted. Observation sessions must be conducted in a manner that will produce a representative sample of the target behavior. Behavior typically fluctuates over time. Observations should be conducted in a manner that will account for these fluctuations and produce an accurate picture of the overall rate of the behavior. Additionally, the strategy for conducting observations will also be influenced by the overall goal of the proposed intervention. A number of factors should be considered when deciding to conduct observations. First, the number of times that observations are to be conducted should be considered. It is preferable to conduct observations each day and during those periods of the day when the target behavior is most probable. This is typically not feasible because of time constraints on observers. Generally, the more observations the better with at least one observation daily. Second, the length of time for which each observation is to be conducted must be decided. It is preferable to observe behavior for a period of time that will produce data that is representative of performance for the period of interest. For example, if a child is engaged in problem behavior throughout the school day it would be preferable to observe for an extended period of time during the day rather than conduct a brief observation at the beginning of the day. Finally, it is important to consider when the observations should be conducted. Often the behavior of interest will occur during a particular time period (for example, bedtime tantrums, or aggression during lunch period at school). Observations should therefore be conducted during these critical time periods. If behavior occurs throughout the day then multiple observations during each day are preferable.

7.6 RELIABILITY OF ASSESSMENT

Another essential criterion of an applied behavioral investigation is that the target behavior be reliably assessed. Reliability generally means that two observers can concurrently but independently observe the target behavior and agree on its occurrence and nonoccurrence. Reliability or interobserver agreement is therefore an assessment of the consistency and accuracy with which the target behavior is measured before, during, and after the intervention. High levels of interobserver agreement allow the therapist to conclude that patterns of responding (e.g., percentage of intervals that the target behavior occurs across days) reflect actual client performance. Low levels of interobserver agreement may imply that patterns of client responding reflect observation biases and not actual performance. Observer bias typically occurs when an observers' definition of the target behavior changes over time. For example, an observer may see improvements in the target behavior during an intervention phase because he or she expects this to occur. Interobserver reliability is therefore a check or control for observer bias. There is no single rule about how often interobserver reliability should be conducted during an applied behavioral intervention. It is generally accepted that observations of the target behavior by another independent observer should be conducted during baseline (or prior to intervention), intervention, and follow-up phases (or after intervention). Interobserver agreement measurement is typically required for a minimum of 20 percent of all observations in research studies. An acceptable level of agreement between observers typically ranges between 80 to 100 percent. An agreement of less than 80 percent indicates that there is an unacceptable level of error occurring with the recording protocol. Such low agreement can indicate that the target behavior is not clearly defined or that observers are not adequately trained to record the behavior. These potential biases should be identified and remedied prior to conducting baseline observations of the target behavior. This can be accomplished by conducting reliability observations and checking agreement levels on the target behavior prior to formal baseline observations.

The protocols for estimating agreement differ depending on the measurement procedure used to assess the target behavior. Methods for estimating frequency and interval reliability will be discussed as these protocols can be adapted for all other measurement systems (e.g., duration). If frequency of the target behavior is the measurement system used then interobserver agreement is assessed using a percentage frequency agreement between observers. This percentage agreement measures the degree to which both observers agree regarding the occurrence of the target behavior. Interobserver agreement is calculated by dividing the smaller frequency by the larger frequency and multiplying by 100. For example, the number of times a student hits other students may be a target for intervention in a classroom. Two observers independently count the number of times the student hits others during an observation session in the school. By the end of the observation period one observer has counted 10 hits while the other observer has counted 8 hits. Percentage agreement for this observation was therefore 80 percent ([8/10] × 100). It is important to note that this form of reliability reflects agreement on the total number of responses and not on any specific response. It is impossible to determine whether observers agree on each specific response. Such agreement estimates must therefore be treated with caution as they may conceal disagreement on individual target responses.

Interobserver agreement with interval recording methods is usually calculated on the basis of the percentage of intervals in which two observers agree on the occurrence of the target behavior. An agreement is scored if both observers agree on the occurrence of the target behavior during the same interval. A disagreement is scored if one observer records the behavior as occurring during an interval and the other observer does not. Interobserver agreement is calculated by dividing the number of intervals which both observers agreed the behavior occurred (agreements) by the number of intervals that they did not agree the behavior occurred (disagreements) plus the number of agreements and multiplying by 100. For example, if two observers recorded behavior for 20 10-second intervals and agreed on the occurrence of the behavior for 15 intervals and disagreed on 5 intervals, overall agreement would be [15/(5 + 15)] × 100 = 75%. While this is the generally accepted method for calculating interval agreement, some investigators have questioned whether agreement should be confined to intervals where both observers record an occurrence of the behavior. Agreement can also be extended to intervals where both observers record a nonoccurrence of the behavior. The inclusion of nonoccurrences as well as occurrences in the calculation of interval reliability percentages inflates reliability estimates beyond the level obtained when occurrences alone are calculated. The more conservative estimate of interobserver agreement is to use occurrence agreement percentages only.

7.7 FUNCTIONAL ASSESSMENT AND ANALYSIS OF ABERRANT BEHAVIOR

At the beginning of this chapter a model was presented that identified the important parameters to be considered when conducting an assessment of behavior. In addition to operationalizing the target behavior, this model emphasized an assessment of the environmental stimuli (both antecedent and consequent stimuli) that entered into functional relationships with that behavior. It is no accident that the majority of this chapter focuses on the strategies used to develop a clear identification of the target behavior. Until recently, applied behavior analysts have primarily been interested in isolating target behaviors and selecting interventions to increase or decrease the frequency of these behaviors. The behavior of applied behavior analysts themselves (in terms of the interventions they have selected) seems to have been controlled by the structure or topography of the target behaviors rather than by the operant function of these behaviors. For example, the target behavior might be "eye gouging", without reference to its function for the individual. This approach contradicts a fundamental premise of behavioral analysis which describes behavior primarily in terms of its function (see Chapter 1). These points do not detract from the importance of systematically identifying and operationalizing target behaviors. However, an analysis of the environmental determinants of target behaviors from a functional perspective has often been missing from the practice of behavioral assessment. The assessment of severe aberrant behavior is one notable exception to this. Over the last decade the majority of published studies that have examined aberrant behavior have conducted a functional assessment or analysis of the environmental determinants of target behaviors and subsequently matched a treatment to maintaining contingencies. It is therefore instructive to examine the assessment strategies developed in this particular area of applied behavior analysis.

The term *functional assessment* has been used to describe a variety of systematic procedures to determine antecedent and consequent variables which occasion and maintain aberrant behaviors. Functional assessment typically involves a process whereby target behaviors are defined by interviewing significant others and are subsequently observed in naturalistic contexts (in those contexts where the behavior has been described as being problematic). This form of assessment reveals correlational information regarding establishing/discriminative conditions and consequences for the target behavior. Assessment procedures may also involve the systematic manipulation of hypothesized controlling variables to empirically demonstrate causal relationships. This latter assessment technique is typically referred to as a *functional analysis* (Axelrod, 1987; Iwata, Dorsey, Slifer, Bauman, & Richman, 1982).

A knowledge of controlling variables derived from such assessment protocol assists in the development of effective treatment procedures in at least three ways (Lennox & Miltenburger, 1989). First, assessment may identify reinforcing consequences (positive or negative) contingent on target behavior performance which can subsequently be eliminated or prevented (Carr, Newsom, & Binkoff, 1980). This means that instead of the planned intervention "inventing" new contingencies to modify problem target behavior, it can change those that already control it. Second, an assessment may identify motivational (Michael, 1982; 1993) and/or discriminative (Skinner, 1935) conditions that evoke the target behavior, and by removing or altering these conditions the behavior may be prevented (Dunlap, Kern-Dunlap, Clarke, & Robbins, 1991). For example, if sleep deprivation leads to inappropriate aggression, the aggression can be eliminated by ensuring that suffcient sleep takes place (O'Reilly, 1995). Finally, such pre-intervention assessments may allow the practitioner to identify more efficient and socially appropriate responses to access similar consequences as the problematic behaviors (Carr & Durand, 1985). That is, if the client engages in the problem target behavior because it is their only way of obtaining attention from caregivers, for example, that attention may be provided contingent upon other, more acceptable, behavior.

The remainder of this chapter will outline specific examples of functional assessment and functional analysis strategies, and examine their strengths and weaknesses.

7.8 FUNCTIONAL ASSESSMENT

The major functional assessment protocols include behavioral interviews and direct observation methods such as scatterplots and ABC assessments.

Behavioral Interview

Behavioral interviews rely on subjective verbal reports to identify the nature of the aberrant behavior and the environmental conditions that are controlling it (Cone, 1987). Those who are interviewed (such as parents, teachers, and others) should be in daily contact with the client and therefore be in a position to describe events as they have witnessed them in the past and to draw conclusions about the causes of an individual's behavior. There are three main objectives of a behavioral interview: 1) operationalization of the behavior(s) – *what is it?*; 2) identification of those physical and environmental factor(s) predictive of the aberrant behavior(s) – *when does it occur?*; 3) identification of the potential functions of behavior(s) in terms of their maintaining consequences– *what reinforces it?*

To achieve these outcomes a complete interview should include questions which probe the informant about the topography of the behavior, the situations in which it does and does not occur, and the typical reactions of others in response to the aberrant behavior. In essence, the behavioral interview attempts to review a large number of potential variables and narrow the focus to those that appear to be of some importance in generating and maintaining the undesirable behavior. A number of behavioral rating scales, checklists, and questionnaires are commercially available and can be used to guide the interview process. For example, one of the most frequently used instruments is the *Motivation Assessment Scale* (Durand, 1990) which provides a specific description of the targeted problem behavior and attempts to isolate one of four possible reasons for this behavior: positive reinforcement in the form of attention, positive reinforcement through access to materials, negative reinforcement through escape, or sensory reinforcement. Some examples of questions used in the Motivation Assessment Scale are presented in Table 7.3. These questions assess whether the aberrant behavior serves a sensory function (i.e., automatic positive or negative reinforcement); a negative reinforcement function (i.e., escape from tasks); and a positive reinforcement function (i.e., access to attention) respectively.

Table 7.3 *Examples of Questions Used in the Motivation Assessment Scale (Durand, 1990)*

1. Would the behavior occur continuously, over and over, if this person was left alone for long periods of time? (For example, several hours).
14. Does the behavior stop occurring shortly after (one to five minutes) you stop working or making demands on this person?
15. Does this person seem to do the behavior to get you to spend some time with him or her?

There are a number of advantages to the interview approach, including ease of application, cost and efficiency (administration takes only a brief period). On the reverse side of the coin, there are a number of inherent difficulties. Such methods do not allow for direct access to the relevant behaviors and their controlling variables and are therefore subject to a variety of difficulties including faulty recollection of events, observer bias, observer expectation etc. (Kazdin, 1994). As such, information gained through these methods may provide unreliable estimates of behavior and lead to invalid conclusions about its controlling variables.

Direct Observation Procedures

A more objective and systematic approach to assessment involves first hand observation of an individual's behavior in environmental contexts that are relevant to the problem. The individual is observed in their typical daily routine in as many settings and across as much time per day as is possible for a minimum period of 3–5 days (O'Neill, Horner, Albin, Storey, & Sprague, 1990). Notably, there is little, if any, control exerted over the environmental conditions during assessment. Such direct observations should be based upon information gleaned from the interview process (i.e., behaviors and situations that have been identified as problematic are observed). The process is usually carried out by those parents, teachers, and support staff who already work with the individual and is conducted in a manner that does not require extensive training on their part. Two general classes of descriptive analyses have been forwarded in the literature and each will be discussed.

The Antecedent – Behavior – Consequence (ABC) Assessment

This observation method attempts to evaluate the immediate antecedent and consequent events surrounding the target behavior and assess the extent to which these specific events may be related to the occurrence of behavior. This assessment usually entails a narrative account of directly observed behavior and temporally related environmental events (Bijou, Peterson, & Ault, 1968).

Those working with the individual exhibiting the aberrant behavior write brief descriptors of what occurs immediately prior to and following the target behavior. Such accounts are usually recorded on an ABC or sequence analysis chart (Sulzer-Azaroff & Meyer, 1977). Although the procedure is relatively easy to learn, it requires extensive effort to implement (Pyles & Bailey, 1990). Further, such a procedure often leads to subjective interpretation of events rather than objective descriptions (Lerman & Iwata, 1993).

To overcome such difficulties a number of approaches have been recommended. It is essential that observers are aware of the temporal parameters involved in an ABC assessment to combat the temptation to record global environmental events that are far removed from the target behavior. In a practical measure to overcome this difficulty of subjective interpretation, Pyles and Bailey (1990) developed the "inappropriate record form" which lists already-specified preceding and consequential events coupled with the problem behavior. Observers are therefore cued to record certain antecedent and consequent events upon the occurrence of the target behavior. A less formal measure is simply to train observers not to infer motivation from an observation but to describe events clearly and accurately (Lennox & Miltenburger, 1989).

Scatterplot Assessment

The most recently-developed and simplest direct observation method is the scatterplot assessment which records temporal distributions of behavior (Touchette, MacDonald, & Langer, 1985). Observers are trained to record the time of day of the occurrence of each instance of the target behavior on a grid that identifies time of day on the ordinate (usually in 30 min segments) and consecutive days on the abscissa. As the behaviors are repeatedly observed and plotted, correlations between particular times of day and differential rates of behavior can become evident. This data allows for more detailed observational analyses (such as ABC assessments) during those time periods in which the behavior has been identified as most probable. An example of a scatterplot data sheet used by staff to identify the temporal distribution of "scratching other clients" by an adult with severe mental disabilities in a group home is presented in Figure 7.5. This scatterplot shows that the target behavior clusters around certain time periods during the day when the client was required to engage in task related activities. These results would imply that the aggressive scratching behavior might be maintained by negative reinforcement contingencies (i.e., escape from demanding activities).

Direct observation methods have a number of advantages. They allow direct access to problem behavior in the natural environment and therefore are more objective in that they reflect current behavior and not recall of past observations. Like most procedures, direct observations have a number of limitations. Relative to indirect methods such procedures are time consuming. More important perhaps is that these procedures do not necessarily reveal functional relationships (Iwata, Vollmer, & Zarcone, 1990). For example, it may be difficult to identify the consequences of behavior maintained by intermittent reinforcement schedules (Lerman & Iwata, 1993).

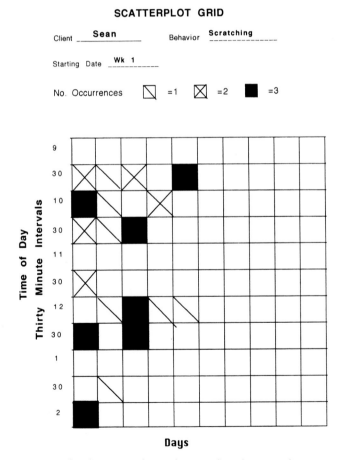

Figure 7.5   Example of a scatterplot grid over a five-day period.

7.9 FUNCTIONAL ANALYSIS

Experimental analyses of behavior constitute the final means of conducting an assessment of aberrant behavior. The most distinguishing feature of this method of analysis lies in its direct and systematic manipulation of variables that potentially maintain the aberrant behavior (Iwata et al., 1990). Of the many assessment techniques to evolve from the literature in recent years, functional or experimental analyses have perhaps been used most frequently. This approach has been used successfully in the analysis and treatment of such behavior problems as stereotypic behavior (Durand & Carr, 1987; Sturmey, Carlsen, Crisp, & Newton, 1988), disruption (Carr & Durand, 1985), aggression (Slifer, Ivancic, Parrish, Page, & Burgio, 1986), pica (Mace & Knight, 1986), and self-injurious behavior (O'Reilly, 1996).

This form of analysis is important for many reasons. First, it emphasizes the importance of gaining information about the contingencies maintaining behavior rather than merely describing the topographical features (e.g., biting or hitting). It also explains how topographically similar behaviors can serve different functions for a given individual. For example, one individual may engage in self-injurious behavior to gain access to attention and their behavior may be maintained by attention functioning as positive reinforcement. On the other hand, another individual's self-injury may be negatively reinforced and serve to escape from an aversive situation. It is through a realization of these different functions of topographically similar behaviors that researchers have recognized the need to develop highly individualized treatment programs that are tailored to the specific function of aberrant behavior.

Methods of conducting such an in-depth analysis of the functions of behavior are a relatively recent advance, with the degree of rigor and sophistication of the different methods varying. The control necessary to adequately demonstrate functional relationships in an experimental analysis is often difficult to obtain in the natural environment. Functional relationships are therefore often verified in an analogue setting which approximates the natural environment. Once the conditions that control the behavior are identified, these contingencies can then be manipulated in the natural environment. Iwata et al., (1990) describe this model as involving at least one condition (experimental) in which the variable of interest is present and another condition (control) in which the variable is absent. These conditions are then alternated in a multielement or reversal design while the behavior of interest is observed. A complete description of these experimental designs is found in Chapter 8.

There are two variations of this model that can be found in the literature. One approach involves demonstration of the effects of a single hypothetical controlling variable (such as attention from a care-giver) on a particular behavior. An early example of this method was conducted by Lovaas and Simmons (1969) in which a client who exhibited self-injury was exposed to several conditions differing on the variable of attention (social deprivation, non-contingent delivery of attention, and social attention contingent on occurrences of self-injurious behavior), and demonstrated that self-injury was higher during the contingent attention condition.

More recent research has shown that aberrant behavior may be multiply controlled (that is, simultaneously influenced by a number of reinforcers) and therefore a second model has developed in which several variables are compared to determine behavioral function. Iwata et al., (1994) presented an epidemiological analysis of 152 cases that used a multielement design format to compare four analogue conditions to assess the function of self-injury. These analogue conditions assessed the impact of positive reinforcement (attention contingent on self-injury), negative reinforcement (escape from demands contingent on self-injury), automatic reinforcement (placement in a barren environment with no access to either attention or toys), and a control (no attention for self-injury, no demands, play materials available and attention contingent on the absence of self-injury). Their results showed specific functions of these various sources of reinforcement for 145 of the cases. Two hypothetical examples of analogue analyses for self-injury using multielement designs are presented in Figure 7.6. For Graph 1 in the figure there are higher levels of self-injury in the attention condition relative to the other conditions. These results imply that self-injury for this individual is maintained by social positive reinforcement. In Graph 2 we see higher levels of self-injury in the demand condition relative to the other conditions. The results in graph 2 imply that self-injury for this person is maintained by escape from task demands or social negative reinforcement.

Among the strengths of an experimental functional analysis are its objectivity and quantitative precision and its ability to analyze the effects of several variables. It has also been noted that the control condition included in an experimental analysis may indicate some temporary intervention strategies that can be implemented until the treatment program is designed and put into effect. Procedures to reduce aberrant behaviors will be discussed in detail in Chapter 10.

Although providing more conclusive data, one potential disadvantage with conducting such an assessment is that it may be difficult or impractical

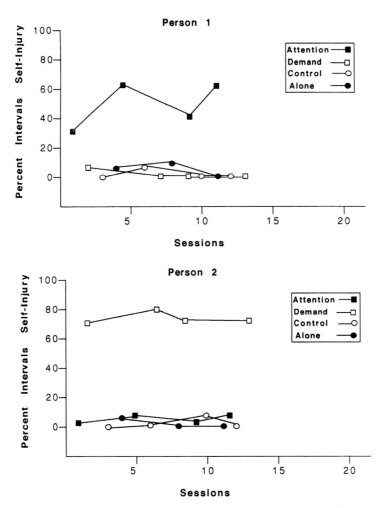

Figure 7.6 Functional analysis results of self-injury for two individuals.

for use in many applied settings due to the stringent control necessary and also the limitations of staff, time, and facilities (Lennox & Miltenburger, 1989). However, Iwata, et al., (1990) point out that "this criticism is unwarranted because precisely the same requirements must be met in order to implement most treatment programs with any degree of consistency" (p. 310). In recent years, Wacker and colleagues (see, for example, Northup, Wacker, Sasso, Cigrand, Cook, & DeRaad, 1991) have shown how such analyses of aberrant behavior may be successfully carried out during one

90-minute outpatient clinic session. O'Reilly, O'Kane, Byrne, and Lancioni (1996) used a mini-reversal design during a 60-minute therapy session to establish the antecedent variables of challenging behavior for a person with severe brain injuries. This research overcomes the potential problem of an extended experimental analysis delaying implementation of an effective treatment.

Another potential disadvantage, which has been suggested by LaVigna and Donnellan (1986), is that the analogue analysis may not be ecologically valid (that is, it may not mirror exactly the variables operating in the natural environment). This is a potentially serious problem, but it has been overcome in studies where experimental analyses have been successfully conducted in natural settings such as classrooms (Sasso & Reimers, 1988) and outpatient clinics with parents present (Northup et al., 1991). Additionally, Iwata et al., (1990) point out that a functional analysis does not reveal the functional variables involved but merely tests those variables that have been proposed through prior functional assessments. Hypothesized contingencies must be systematically identified prior to an experimental analysis. Therefore, all functional analyses must encompass additional information from background sources to facilitate how best to construct the analysis (i.e., to identify which variables to manipulate).

Research on the functional assessment and analysis of aberrant behavior has made a unique contribution to the behavioral assessment literature. These assessment technologies emphasize an examination of the environmental determinants of target behaviors. Interventions can therefore be selected based on the function of the behavior. Traditionally, applied behavior analysis assessment has focused on a detailed analysis of the target behaviors at the expense of examining functional variables. This traditional assessment approach results in the selection of intervention techniques that must override current maintaining contingencies in order to produce successful behavior change (Mace, 1994b). Implications for using such assessment techniques on the selection of intervention strategies will be discussed in detail in Chapters 9 and 10.

7.10 SUMMARY

Applied behavioral assessment involves selecting and defining the behavior to be changed. Additionally, it is important for behavior analysts to identify the environmental conditions that influence the probability of the behavior targeted for change. These environmental variables can occur prior to and following the target behavior. A detailed knowledge of these contextual influences on the target behavior will help the behavior analyst to select interventions that may increase adaptive behavior or decrease maladaptive behavior.

Behavioral assessment is a rigorous process involving a number of steps. First, a socially relevant target behavior must be identified. Behaviors selected for change must be of primary importance to the individual client. Changes in the selected behaviors should maximize positive outcomes and minimize negative outcomes for the client. Target behaviors must then be operationalized to reveal a clear, complete, and objective description of the behavior to be changed. This clarifies to all involved (for example, client, family, therapist) the nature of the behavior to be changed. It also allows for an ongoing evaluation of changes in the behavior throughout the treatment process. Complex target behaviors can be broken down into a series of discrete behaviors known as a task analysis.

Second, a measurement system is selected to provide a continuous assessment of the target behavior before, during, and after the intervention. The measurement system should be sensitive to the relevant dimensions of the target behavior. It must also be possible to use the selected measurement system in an unobtrusive manner within an applied context. Common measures used include frequency, duration, latency, and interval protocol.

Third, observations must be conducted in such a manner as to yield a representative sample of the target behavior. It is important to consider when to observe, where to observe, and the length of time for each observation. Additionally, interobserver reliability should be conducted throughout the behavioral program. Agreement estimates provide an assessment of the consistency and accuracy with which the target behavior is measured.

Recent developments in the assessment and analysis of aberrant behavior were discussed in the final sections of this chapter. Functional assessment and functional analysis protocol examine the relationship between behavior and its environmental determinants. Prior to using any of these assessment techniques the target behavior must be systematically identified and operationalized according to the criteria outlined earlier in the chapter. Functional assessment protocols describe a set of techniques which include interview and observational methods to identify environmental events that evoke and maintain the aberrant responding. These functional assessment techniques produce correlational information regarding the controlling variables. Functional analysis protocols involve the systematic manipulation of hypothesized causal variables and therefore make a causal analysis possible. Whenever feasible, functional analyzes should be conducted in natural settings, or using materials from natural settings, in order to produce results that are externally valid. Interventions can then be tailored to the function of the behavior identified through these assessments.

CHAPTER **8**

SINGLE-CASE EXPERIMENTAL DESIGNS

In Chapter 7 we outlined the protocols used to identify, operationalize, and assess target behaviors over time. Applied behavior analysis is also characterized by a series of experimental techniques known as *single-case designs*. These experimental techniques are used to determine if changes in the dependent variable or target behavior can be attributed to the independent variable or treatment. Single-case research designs are therefore used to examine whether treatment applications actually cause the desired change in the target behavior. In other words, these experimental techniques examine the *functional relationships* between changes in the environment and changes in the target behavior. Single-case designs are also unique in their ability to examine causally such functional relations with individual cases (i.e., one person) in addition to groups of individuals. Applied behavior analysts use several different types of single-case designs. These designs can also be combined to tease out complex maintaining variables (Higgins-Hains & Baer, 1989). Despite the variety of single-case designs, they are all based on the same set of fundamental premises and techniques.

8.1 INTERNAL AND EXTERNAL VALIDITY

All single-case methods are designed to eliminate threats to *internal validity*. Internal validity refers to the extent to which a research method can rule out alternative explanations for changes in the target behavior. The application of a treatment does not occur in a vacuum. There are other dynamic environmental conditions that are constantly changing and influencing a person's behavior. These other environmental influences may pose as alternative explanations for changes in the target behavior above and beyond the treatment application, and are thus described as threats to internal validity. Several categories of threats to internal validity have been described in the literature (see Kazdin, 1982). History and maturation are two such threats. History refers to any environmental event that occurs concurrently with the experiment or intervention and could account for similar results as those attributed to the intervention. History encapsulates a myriad of possible idiosyncratic environmental influences for a given case (for example, negative interactions with individuals, adverse environmental conditions etc.). Maturation refers to any changes in the target behavior over time that may result from processes within the person. These personal processes may include the health of the individual, boredom, or aging. For example, allergy symptoms have been shown to have a significant influence on treatment applications (Kennedy & Meyer, 1996). Single-case research methods are designed to rule out these and other threats to internal validity. The process by which each design accomplishes this will be discussed in later sections of this chapter.

External validity refers to the ability to extend the findings of an experiment to other persons, settings, and clinical syndromes with confidence. Some applied researchers have proposed that external validity should take precedence over internal validity when designing applied research studies (Kazdin, 1982). While such a proposition is probably incorrect, because demonstrating internal validity is a necessary prerequisite for demonstrating external validity, it emphasizes the importance of external validity in applied research.

Aspects of the experimental preparation that may limit the generality of findings are referred to as threats to external validity. There are numerous threats to the external validity of an experiment (see Cook & Campbell, 1979; Kazdin, 1982). Two of these threats include generality across settings, responses and time; and multiple treatment interference. This former threat to external validity proposes that, for any experimental manipulation, the results may be restricted to the particular target behaviors within the immediate context of the intervention and during the time of intervention only. Such threats to external validity can be minimized by using particular research design options (such as multiple baseline designs, discussed below) that can systematically examine these issues of generalization within the context of a given experimental preparation. Multiple treatment interference occurs when two or more treatments are evaluated with a given target behavior. When treatments are compared there is always the possibility that the effects of one treatment are confounded by experience with a previous treatment. In other words, the sequence of treatment administration may influence the performance of the individual. Strong conclusions about the influence of any one treatment cannot be made from such an experimental preparation. Extended single-case experimental preparations can be used to tease the relative effects of two or more treatments (see Barlow & Hersen, 1984) but such research designs may be impractical in most applied settings (Higgins-Hains & Baer, 1989).

8.2 Graphic Display

Single-case research designs typically use graphic display to present an ongoing visual representation of each assessment session. Graphic display is a simple visual method for organizing, interpreting, and communicating findings in the field of applied behavior analysis. While many forms of graphic display can be used the majority of applied research results are presented in simple line graphs or frequency polygons. A line graph is a two-dimensional plane formed by the intersection of two perpendicular lines. Each data point plotted on a line graph represents a relationship between the two properties described by the intersecting lines. In applied behavior analysis the line graph represents changes in the dependent variable (e.g., frequency, rate, or percentage of the target behavior per session) relative to a specific point in time and/or treatment (independent) variable.

An example of a line graph is presented in Figure 8.1. The major features of this graph include the horizontal and vertical axes, condition change lines, condition labels, data points and data paths. The horizontal axis represents the passage of time (consecutive sessions) and the different levels of the independent variable (baseline and intervention). The vertical axis represents values of the dependent variable. The condition change lines represent that point in time when the levels of the independent variable were systematically changed. Condition labels are brief descriptions of the experimental conditions in effect during each phase of the study. Each data point represents the occurrence of the target behavior during a session under a given experimental condition. Connecting the data points with a straight line under a given experimental condition creates a data path. A data path represents the relationship between the independent and dependent variables and is of primary interest when interpreting graphed data (see below).

The use of graphic display to examine functional relations has a number of inherent benefits. First, as a judgmental aid, it is easy to use and easy to learn (Michael, 1974). Second, it allows the therapist to have an ongoing access to a complete record of the participant's behavior. Behavior change can therefore be evaluated continuously. If the treatment is not proving effective then the therapist can alter the treatment protocol and

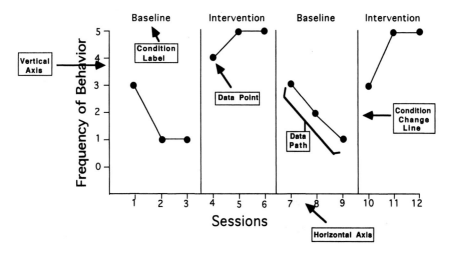

Figure 8.1   Hypothetical example of a single-case design graph depicting the major features of graphic display.

subsequently evaluate these changes on an ongoing basis. Third, visual analysis provides a stringent method for evaluating the effectiveness of behavior change programs (Baer, 1977). Finally, graphic display provides an objective assessment of the effectiveness of the independent variable. These displays allow for independent judgements on the meaning and significance of behavior change strategies.

Interpreting Graphic Displays

The primary method of analysis with all single-case research designs is a visual interpretation of graphic displays. There are several properties of graphic displays that are important to consider when making a determination of the effects of the treatment variable on the target behavior or when deciding to change from one condition (e.g., baseline) to another (e.g., treatment) during an applied behavioral intervention. These properties include number of data points, overall stability of the data, data levels, and data trends.

It is important to collect a sufficient number of data points in order to provide a believable estimate of the performance of the target behavior under a given experimental condition. There are no hard and fast rules about the number of data points that should be collected under a given experimental condition. Sidman (1960) suggests that at least three measures of the target behavior should be collected per experimental condition. This is an optimal suggestion if the data path is stable (see below) and the nature of the target behavior allows for multiple assessments under baseline and intervention conditions. For example, if the target behavior is dangerous to the client or others (for example, when it involves aggression) it may be unethical to conduct extended assessments under baseline conditions (that is, when the treatment variable is not present).

Stability refers to a lack of variability in the data under a given experimental condition. In Figure 8.2 it is clear that Graph A presents a stable data path whereas the data in Graph B are variable. It is unusual in applied research to achieve prefect stability of data as illustrated in Graph A. Tawney and Gast (1984) provide a general rule for determining stability of data within experimental conditions. We may concluded that there is stability if 80–90% of the data points within a condition fall within a 15% range of the mean level of all data points for that particular experimental condition. It is unusual for applied researchers to use such mathematical

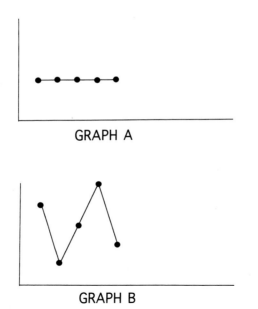

GRAPH A

GRAPH B

Figure 8.2 Hypothetical example of a stable data path (Graph A) and variable data points (Graph B).

formulae. If stability is not obvious from a visual examination of the data then it may be prudent to identify those environmental stimuli that are causing such variability in the data set. This further analysis may yield additional functional variables that may need to be manipulated to achieve successful intervention results.

Stability of data within a given experimental condition is also important because the data path serves a predictive function for interpreting data within the subsequent experimental condition. A stable data path within a given experimental condition allows the therapist to infer that if that experimental condition was continued over time, a similar data pattern would emerge (see Figure 8.3). The effects of the subsequent condition are determined by comparing the observed data (i.e., the actual data obtained when the experimental conditions were changed) with the predicted data from the previous condition. Stability of predicted data therefore allows for a clearer interpretation of the effect of subsequent experimental conditions

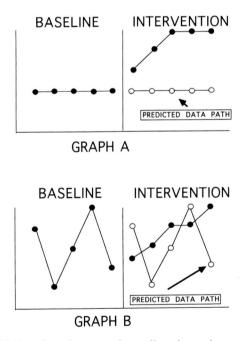

Figure 8.3   Stable baseline data (Graph A) allow for a clear interpretation of the effectiveness of treatment in the intervention phase. When baseline data are variable (Graph B) it becomes difficult to evaluate the effects of the treatment in the intervention phase.

on the target behavior. In Figure 8.3 the predicted data paths for a stable data set (Graph A) and variable data set (Graph B) are plotted. It is obvious that the effects of the intervention can be more clearly interpreted by comparing predicted with observed data for Graph A than for Graph B.

Level can be defined as the value of a behavioral measure or group of measures on the vertical axis of a line graph. Level can be used to describe overall performance within an experimental condition or between experimental conditions. Typically, the levels of performance within and between conditions are analyzed visually by the therapist. However, a mean level can also be calculated for each condition. Stability and level are inextricably linked in the visual analysis of data. If extreme variability exists in the data paths then a visual examination of level within and between conditions may be impossible. Level is also used to examine the difference

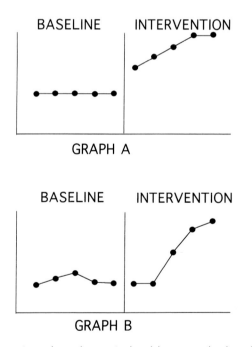

Figure 8.4 There is a clear change in level between the last data point of the baseline phase and the first data point of the intervention phase in Graph A. There is no change in level between the baseline and intervention in Graph B until the third data point of the intervention phase. This delayed change in level when treatment is applied may mean that something other than the treatment caused a change in the target behavior.

between the last data point of a condition and the first data point of the following experimental condition. If there is an obvious level change in behavior at that point in time when the new experimental condition is implemented then the therapist can more confidently infer that the change in behavior is due to a change in the experimental condition. In Figure 8.4 (Graph A) there is an obvious level change between conditions when the intervention is implemented. In Graph B the level change during the intervention phase does not occur until the third data point. It may be the case for Graph B that something other than or in addition to the intervention causes a level change in behavior from the third data point onwards.

Trend can be defined as the overall direction taken by a data path. Trends can be described as increasing, decreasing, or zero. A stable data path represents a zero trend. Increasing and decreasing trends can be problematic for interpreting data. If, for example, a therapist wants to increase responding, an increasing trend in the baseline data path may make interpretation of the effects of the intervention difficult (see Figure 8.5, Graph A). This logic also holds for decreasing trends (see Figure 8.5, Graph B). It is advisable in such cases to withhold the intervention until the data path stabilizes under baseline conditions or until the behavior reaches the desired goal. In some applied situations it may be impractical (the presence of the therapist may be time-limited) or unethical (the behavior may be dangerous to self or others) to withhold treatment for extended periods. In these situations experimental control may need to be sacrificed in order to achieve the desired behavioral outcomes. Under some circumstances a trend in data may not interfere with the interpretation of the subsequent experimental condition. This is true for situations where the trend under a given experimental condition is going in the opposite direction that would be predicted when the subsequent experimental condition is implemented (see Figure 8.5, Graph C).

8.3   WITHDRAWAL OR ABAB DESIGNS

Withdrawal or ABAB designs represent a series of experimental arrangements whereby selected conditions are systematically presented and withdrawn over time. This design typically consists of two phases, a baseline or A phase and an intervention or B phase that are replicated (hence the ABAB notation). The design begins with an assessment of behavior under baseline conditions. Once the target behavior stabilizes

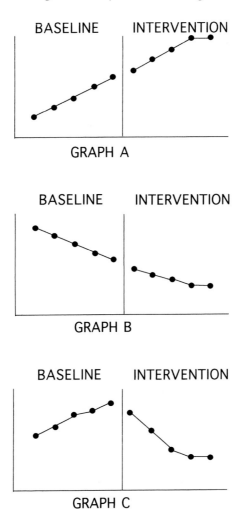

Figure 8.5 An increasing or decreasing trend in baseline data paths can be problematic if the subsequent intervention is designed to increase (Graph A) or decrease (Graph B) the target behavior respectively. A trend in the baseline data path may not interfere with an interpretation of an intervention effect if the treatment is designed to change the trend in the opposite direction (Graph C).

under baseline conditions the intervention condition is implemented. The intervention condition is continued until the target behavior reaches a stable level or diverges from the level predicted from the baseline data. At this point the intervention is withdrawn and the baseline condition is replicated until stability is achieved. Finally the intervention condition is once again implemented. Experimental control is achieved when there is a visible difference between the data paths in the A and B phases *and* this difference is again achieved in the A and B phase replications.

Examples of the use of ABAB designs abound in the applied literature. In a recent study, Tustin (1995) used a withdrawal design to compare the effects of two methods of requesting activity change on the stereotypic behavior of an adult with autism. Persons with autism tend to engage in stereotypic behavior (e.g., body rocking, hand flapping) when asked to change from one activity to another. An immediate request for change involved the work supervisor presenting new materials, removing present materials, and instructing the new task. An advanced notice request involved much the same behavior by the work supervisor with the exception that the activities for the new task were placed in view of the participant 2 minutes prior to the request to change tasks. Stereotypy was measured using a partial interval recording procedure, and the influence of the two requesting conditions was examined over a 20-day period. The results of the investigation are presented in Figure 8.6. The immediate request condition produced a relatively stable pattern of responding during the first five days of the assessment. The advanced notice request condition produced an immediate reduction in stereotypy and stable responding over the next five days. These results were again replicated in an immediate and advanced notice condition. The results of the ABAB design clearly show the

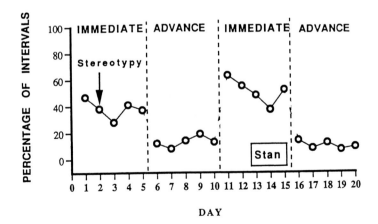

Figure 8.6   Percentage of intervals of stereotypy during transition between work activities for a man with autism. This ABAB design compared immediate requests with an advanced notice procedure to change work tasks (Tustin, 1995).

effectiveness of the advanced notice requesting technique in reducing stereotypy when transitioning between tasks for this participant.

In another example, Friman and Vollmer (1995) examined the effectiveness of a urine alarm to treat chronic diurnal enuresis for a young female diagnosed with depression and attention deficit hyperactivity disorder. Wetness was examined twice a day under baseline conditions (i.e., no intervention in place) for a 5-week period. The participant was then fitted with a moisture sensitive alarm for 4 weeks. The baseline and alarm conditions were then replicated. The results of this study are presented in Figure 8.7. During the initial baseline assessment the participant had wetting accidents each day. Once the alarm intervention was implemented the wetting accidents decreased dramatically to zero levels. When the alarm was removed (second baseline condition) the number of wetting accidents increased again but did not return to the same level observed during the initial baseline condition. Once the alarm was reinstated the number of accidents decreased to zero with maintenance of these results for up to 6 months.

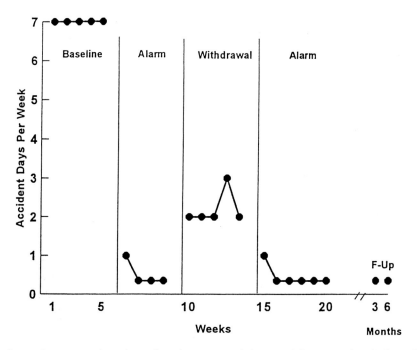

Figure 8.7 Number of accident days per week for an adolescent girl with diurnal enuresis (Friman & Vollmer, 1995).

Finally, Brigham, Meier, and Goodner (1995) examined the influence of a prompts-with-incentives program to increase designated drivers in a local bar (that is, people who would not drink alcohol that night, and thus be fit to drive). The intervention consisted of a series of posters displayed around the bar that indicated the availability of free non-alcoholic beverages (beer, wine, coffee, juice etc.) for those patrons who identified themselves as designated drivers. These posters were not displayed during baseline conditions. The dependent measure consisted of those bar patrons who identified themselves as designated drivers to the bar staff (and received free beverages) and subsequently drove a vehicle away from the bar. The intervention was conducted on Friday and Saturday nights and used an ABAB design to evaluate its effectiveness (see Figure 8.8). Overall, the results of this study indicate that there is an increase in designated drivers under the intervention conditions. However, these results are not as clear as those of the other two studies described. For example, there is not a clear visual differentiation or separation between the data paths under baseline and intervention conditions. Additionally, there is no immediate level change between the last data point of the second baseline phase and the first data point of the second intervention phase. Data paths during both

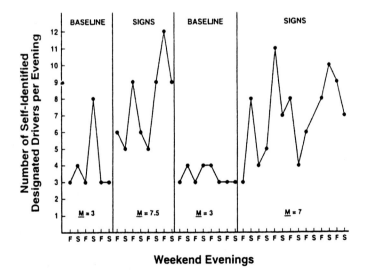

Figure 8.8   The number of self-identified designated drivers per evening during weekend evenings in a college campus bar. The mean number of self-identified designated drivers in each phase for the design is also included in the graph (Brigham, Meier, & Goodner, 1995).

intervention conditions did not achieve stability, however there is a data trend in the direction expected by the intervention (the intervention is expected to increase designated drivers). Based on these visual analyses of the data, the positive effects of the intervention must be interpreted with caution.

Variations of the Withdrawal Design

Withdrawal designs can be adapted to answer additional research questions (other than the comparative effect of a baseline and an intervention on a dependent variable) and to examine causality where the traditional design strategy would be inappropriate. For example, the ABAB design has been used to examine the influence of a baseline and intervention condition on multiple and simultaneous data paths. Kern, Wacker, Mace, Falk, Dunlap, and Kromrey (1995) evaluated the effects of a self-evaluation program to improve peer interactions of students with emotional and behavior disorders. The experimental protocol used by Kern et al., (1995) included a withdrawal design that simultaneously measured appropriate and inappropriate interactions of the targeted students with their peers during observation sessions.

Withdrawal designs can also be used to examine the effectiveness of more than one treatment. Occasionally the initial treatment (in the B phase) may fail to achieve sufficient change in the target behavior. In such situations an alternative treatment may be examined. This type of design is typically described as an ABABCBC design. Such a design incorporates a systematic comparison of the first treatment with baseline (ABAB) and the first treatment with the second treatment (BCBC). The results of such treatment comparisons must be interpreted with caution as they do not rule out sequence effects (that is, the effectiveness of C may be influenced by the fact that it was preceded by B). Jason and Liotta (1982) used an ABABCBC design to compare the effects of sign prompting alone and sign prompting plus verbal prompting on the reduction of smoking at a university cafeteria. Figure 8.9 shows the results of this study. The sign prompting alone did not produce a significant change in the number of smokers or the number of minutes smoked during observation sessions. When sign prompting was combined with verbal prompting there was a significant reduction in the target behaviors.

The sequence of A and B conditions in a withdrawal design can also be reversed, to BABA, without compromising the experimental validity of this

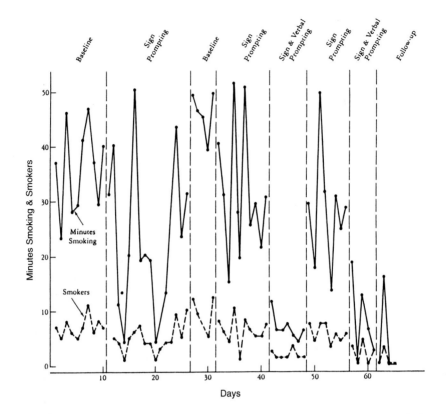

Figure 8.9   An example of an ABABCBC design. This research examined the influence of two interventions (sign prompting and sign plus verbal prompting) on minutes smoking and number of smokers in a university cafeteria. The first intervention (sign prompting alone) was not successful (see ABAB phases of the design). Sign prompting was then compared with sign plus verbal prompting (see BCBC phases of the design) (Jason & Liotta, 1982).

design option. In other words, once the target behavior is clearly identified the intervention can be implemented immediately. Once the data path achieves stability in the B phase the intervention can then be withdrawn. These phases can then be replicated. For applied intervention purposes the design can be completed with a third replication of the intervention phase (i.e., BABAB). Several authors have suggested such a design option for behavior that is in need of immediate intervention (behavior that is of danger to self or others) (Cooper, Heron, & Heward, 1987; Tawney & Gast, 1984). However, this research protocol would be inappropriate in such cases as it continues to require a return to pre-intervention conditions.

Alternative design strategies that do not require extended baseline assessments (such as multielement designs) would be more efficient and ethically appropriate in such cases.

Considerations when Selecting Withdrawal Designs

Withdrawal designs have been described as the most rigorous of the single-case research options for ruling out threats to internal validity (Kazdin, 1994). The withdrawal design is a very effective means of examining the effects of a treatment on selected target behaviors. There are several issues that must be considered however, before selecting to use the withdrawal design above one of the other design options. This design option demonstrates experimental control by systematically applying and removing the treatment variables. The purposeful withdrawal of treatment is seldom a preferable option in clinical practice. There may therefore be ethical reasons (as in the example of behavior that is dangerous to self or others) for not using such a design option. Certain types of behaviors (e.g., social skills) might be expected to maintain or at least to continue to be performed above initial baseline levels after the intervention is withdrawn. If the target behavior does not revert to the initial baseline levels with the withdrawal of treatment (i.e., second A phase) then experimental control is lost. It is therefore important to consider whether the target behavior would be sensitive to the changing contingencies of an ABAB design. Again, alternative designs can be chosen if this is a potential issue.

8.4 MULTIPLE BASELINE DESIGNS

The multiple baseline design is an experimental preparation whereby the independent variable is sequentially applied to a minimum of two levels of a dependent variable. There are three types of multiple baseline design described in the literature. The *multiple baseline across behaviors design* examines behavior change across two or more behaviors of a particular individual. The *multiple baseline across settings design* examines changes in the same behavior of the same individual across two or more different settings. Finally, the *multiple baseline across subjects design* examines changes in the same behavior across two or more individuals. The multiple baseline design can therefore examine the effects of a treatment variable across multiple behaviors for an individual, across multiple settings for a given behavior of an individual, and across multiple individuals for a given behavior. It is essential that only one component of the dependent variable (i.e., behaviors, settings, or persons) be systematically changed within the context of an experiment. If, for example, the effects of an independent variable were examined across different behaviors of different persons then it would be unclear whether changes in the dependent variable were a function of different individuals, different behaviors, or a combination of both.

Experimental control is demonstrated by sequentially applying the treatment variable across behaviors, settings, or persons. In a multiple baseline across persons design, baseline data on a target behavior are collected across two or more individuals. Once baseline reaches stability for all individuals then the intervention is implemented with the first individual. Baseline assessment is continued with the other individuals while the intervention is implemented with the first individual. The behavior of the first individual is expected to change while the other individuals should continue to show stable baseline responding. The intervention is continued with the first individual until the target behavior reaches a stable level or diverges from the level predicted from the baseline data. At this point the intervention is implemented with the second individual while the third individual continues to remain under baseline conditions. This procedure is continued until all individuals are exposed to the treatment protocol. Experimental control is demonstrated if baseline responding changes at that point in time when the treatment variable is applied to each person. A minimum of two behaviors, persons, or settings are required to demonstrate experimental control. Typically, three or more behaviors, persons, or settings are used in a multiple baseline design.

A multiple baseline across persons design was used to examine the effects of an instructional strategy to teach three children with autism to ask the question "What's that?" when presented with novel stimuli during an instructional task (Taylor & Harris, 1995). A time delay instructional protocol was used to teach the response to the children when they were presented with photographs of novel items. Photographs of novel items were presented randomly during teaching sessions in which the children were asked to name pictures of familiar items. The results of this investigation are presented in Figure 8.10. During baseline conditions the children, for the most part, did not ask the question when presented with novel photographs. With the introduction of the instructional program the children rapidly acquired the question asking skill. Each child did not begin to acquire the question asking skill until the intervention was introduced.

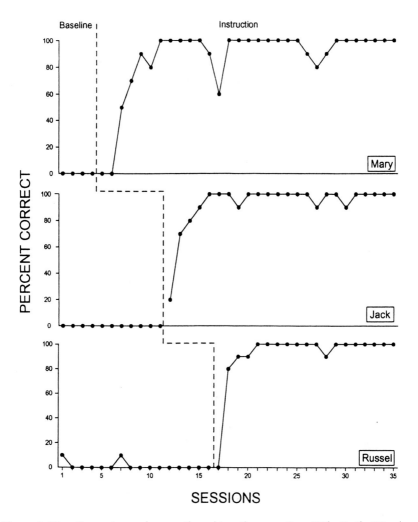

Figure 8.10   Percentage of correctly asking the question "What's that?" when pointing to a novel stimulus across baseline and instruction phases of a multiple baseline design for three students with autism (Taylor & Harris, 1995).

This example of a multiple baseline design provides a clear demonstration of the effects of the intervention on the acquisition of the skills by the students.

Jackson and Mathews (1995) used a multiple baseline design across settings (that is, various grocery stores) to examine the effectiveness of a public posting program on contributions to a senior citizens center. Grocery store customers were given the opportunity to redeem coupons or to donate the worth of the coupon to the senior center. The experimental condition consisted of posting signs around the store that included visual and written instructions and feedback on the value of coupons donated by customers the previous week in that particular store. Figure 8.11 demonstrates the effects of the public posting condition over baseline conditions across three stores. The percentage and value of coupons donated are plotted separately. The results of this public posting intervention are unclear. Baseline data did not achieve stability prior to the intervention in any of the three stores. As a result it would be difficult to predict what performance would be like if baseline assessment had continued and the intervention had not been implemented. Additionally, there are no clear level changes between baseline and intervention conditions across the three stores. These results seem to implicate that the intervention had little effect on shoppers behavior above and beyond baseline conditions. This study also demonstrates an interesting variation of the multiple baseline across settings design. There is no control exerted over the number or identity of the individuals who purchase items in each store during any given assessment period. This variation of a multiple baseline across settings design is frequently used in community behavior analysis applications (Greene, Winett, Van Houten, Geller, & Iwata, 1987).

In an example of a multiple baseline design across behaviors, Rasing and Duker (1992) examined the effects of a teaching protocol to train social skills to children with severe and profound hearing loss. The intervention was implemented across two classrooms (consisting of 4 and 5 children respectively). Experimental control was demonstrated using a multiple baseline design across social skills for each classroom. The teaching strategy consisted of modeling, role-play, corrective feedback for incorrect responding, and positive reinforcement for correct responding. The social skills taught included turn waiting during conversations, initiating interactions with others, and interacting with others. The mean percentage of intervals of appropriate and inappropriate instances of the target behaviors for each class was recorded during observation sessions. The results of the intervention for Class 2 are presented in Figure 8.12. These results indicate a reduction of inappropriate instances of all three target behaviors with the introduction of the intervention. The effects of the intervention for appropriate instances of the behaviors are less definitive. For turn waiting, the intervention produced a clear level change in responding for the class, however, differences between baseline and

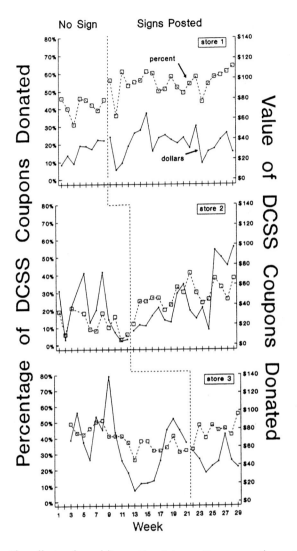

Figure 8.11 The effects of a public posting intervention across three stores on the percentage of coupons (designated by the open squares in the graphs) and value of coupons (designated by the closed dots in the graphs) per week that were donated to a local senior citizens center (Jackson & Mathews, 1995).

intervention for the other two target behaviors are less dramatic. Overall, the results of this intervention must be viewed with caution. Stable baselines were not established for appropriate instances of initiating interactions and

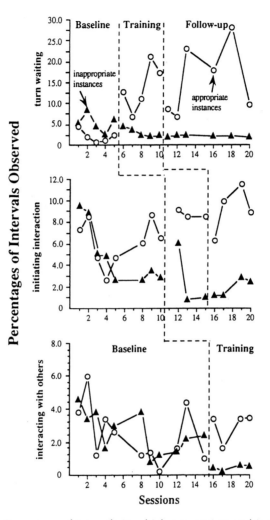

Figure 8.12   Percentage of intervals in which appropriate and inappropriate turn waiting, initiating interactions, and interacting with others was observed for a class of students with severe/profound hearing loss (Rasing & Duker, 1992).

interacting with others prior to introducing the intervention with the class. This violates one of the fundamental properties of single-case research design logic, as mentioned previously.

Considerations when Selecting Multiple Baseline Designs

This design demonstrates experimental control by sequentially applying the independent variable across multiple baselines (persons, behaviors, or settings). A confident interpretation of the effects of the independent variable can be obtained if there are visible changes in the data paths when and only when the independent variable is applied across the separate baselines. The multiple baseline design therefore does not require a withdrawal of treatment in order to demonstrate experimental control. This design option should be considered when it is expected that a withdrawal of treatment might not result in a return of behavior to previous baseline levels. Multiple baseline designs are often employed to examine the effectiveness of teaching strategies on the acquisition of skills as such skills are expected to maintain once instruction is withdrawn (Cuvo, 1979). The multiple baseline design would not be an appropriate option for behaviors that are in need of rapid elimination (such as behaviors that are dangerous to self or others) as measurement of responding prior to intervention is required.

8.5 CHANGING CRITERION DESIGNS

The changing criterion design is used to increase or decrease the rate of responding of a behavior that is already in the repertoire of the individual. As the design has such a specific application it is seldom reported in the literature. This design demonstrates experimental control by showing that the target behavior achieves and stabilizes at a series of predetermined criteria of responding.

A baseline level of responding is initially established for the target behavior. Once behavior has stabilized under baseline conditions the experimenter establishes a criterion of responding that is more stringent than baseline levels of responding. The participant must achieve this criterion in order to access reinforcement. Once behavior stabilizes at this criterion an alternative criterion for responding is set and so on. The nature of the behavior must be of such that it requires multiple changes in criteria to be made before the desired rate of responding is achieved. There are no strict rules for calculating the magnitude of criterion change from one phase to the next. A general rule of thumb is that the criterion change should be small enough to be achievable but not so small that it will be exceeded. If responding exceeds or does not achieve the criterion level then experimental control is lost. Experimental control can also be enhanced if criteria are made less stringent from time to time during the intervention phase and the target behavior reverses to these criteria. A withdrawal design logic can therefore be incorporated within a changing criterion design without the need for the behavior to return to original baseline levels.

Bates, Renzaglia and Clees (1980) used a changing criterion design to examine the effectiveness of reinforcement contingencies to increase the work productivity of three adults with severe and profound developmental disabilities. One participant was taught to self-administer a penny following completion of two work units. The number of pennies needed to access a snack during break period were identified for the participant prior to each work period. The rate of work units per minute was measured for each work period. The criteria of work units per minute was systematically increased across fourteen phases during the intervention (i.e., the participant needed to earn more pennies in order to access a snack item). The results for this participant are illustrated in Figure 8.13. Overall, the patterns of participant responding stabilized around the criteria established by the experimenter. Interestingly, responding began to exceed the established criteria, particularly in the last three phases of the design. These data in the final phases of the design seem to indicate that a more stringent criterion for reinforcement should have been established at that point in order to regain experimental control.

Considerations when Selecting Changing Criterion Designs

The changing criterion design has a very specific application. The behaviors selected for change must already be in the repertoire of the individual. It must also be possible and appropriate to increase or decrease these behaviors in incremental steps. Cooper, Heron, and Heward (1987) note that this design is often mistakenly recommended for use when shaping new behaviors. A shaping program focuses on gradually changing the topography of behavior over time whereas the changing criterion design is suitable for examining changes in the level of responding of an already established behavior. It can be difficult to determine responding criteria for future phases of the design. If responding exceeds or does not reach the criterion within a phase then experimental control is lost for that phase of the design. In such instances it may be prudent to reverse the criterion to a level that had previously established stable responding. Experimental control can thus be re-established and a more sensitive criterion can be calculated for the following phase.

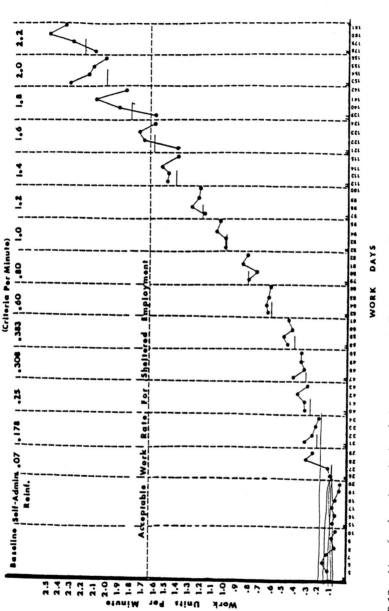

Figure 8.13 Use of a changing criterion design to systematically increase work units per minute for workers with developmental disabilities (Bates, Renzaglia, & Clees, 1980).

8.6 ALTERNATING TREATMENT DESIGNS

The alternating treatment design is used to compare the effects of two or more contingencies or treatments on a target behavior. All treatment comparisons are implemented during a single phase of the design. Treatments are rapidly implemented in a random or semi-random order. Other potential extraneous variables such as time of day or therapist are held constant across the treatments in order to control their influence. Experimental control is demonstrated if there is a clear visible differentiation between treatments. If there is no clear difference between treatments it may be that each selected treatment is equally successful or that there is some extraneous factor influencing the results (e.g., carryover effects). Baseline levels of responding are sometimes assessed prior to the alternating treatment phase of the design. A prior baseline phase is not necessary in order to establish experimental control. On some occasions a baseline condition is implemented as part of the alternating treatments phase of the design in order to examine rate of responding without treatment. Alternating treatment designs are frequently used to assess the contingencies that maintain responding and to examine the comparative effectiveness of various treatment options.

Kennedy and Souza (1995) used an alternating treatment design to examine the contingencies that maintained severe eye poking for a young man with profound developmental disabilities. The duration of eye poking was measured across four conditions. Each condition was implemented during 10-minute sessions in a random order across days. In the no-attention condition the participant was seated at a table and received no social interactions. During the attention condition the therapist sat next to the participant and provided 10 seconds of social comments contingent on eye poking. During the demand condition the participant was taught to perform a domestic task. If the participant engaged in eye poking the task was removed for 15 seconds (negative reinforcement). In the recreation condition various magazines were provided and the participant was praised every 15 seconds in the absence of eye poking. The results of this analysis are presented in Figure 8.14. Eye poking only occurred during the no attention condition. The results of this intervention imply that eye poking served an automatic or self-stimulatory function for the participant.

In another example, Smith, Iwata, and Shore (1995) combined an alternating treatments design with a multiple baseline design to compare the effectiveness of participant-selected versus experimenter-selected

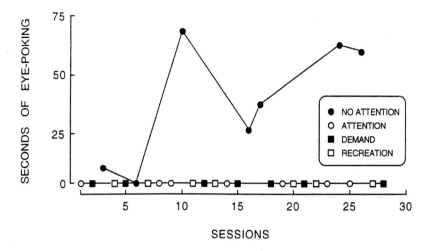

Figure 8.14 Total seconds of eye poking during four assessment conditions presented in an alternating treatments design (Kennedy & Souza, 1995).

reinforcers on the performance of four individuals with profound disabilities. A series of items were initially identified as reinforcing for the participants (e.g., mirror, light, music etc.). Participants were required to perform a free operant task (closing a microswitch or placing small blocks in a plastic bucket) during trials. Task performance under baseline conditions (in multiple baseline across participants format) was measured prior to the comparison phase of the design. In the experimenter selected reinforcer condition the therapist delivered a reinforcing item on a fixed-ratio (FR) 5 schedule. In the subject selected reinforcer condition the participant was allowed to choose from an array of reinforcing items on an FR 5 schedule. The experimenter and subject selected reinforcer conditions were compared in the alternating treatments phase of the design. The results of this experiment are shown in Figure 8.15. The results of the multiple baseline design show stable responding or decreasing trends prior to the reinforcement conditions. There is an increase in responding with the implementation of the reinforcement contingencies for the first three participants. Variability in responding under baseline conditions for participant 4 make data difficult to interpret for that participant. The results of the alternating treatments design phase demonstrates that there is little difference in responding across the two reinforcement conditions for all four participants.

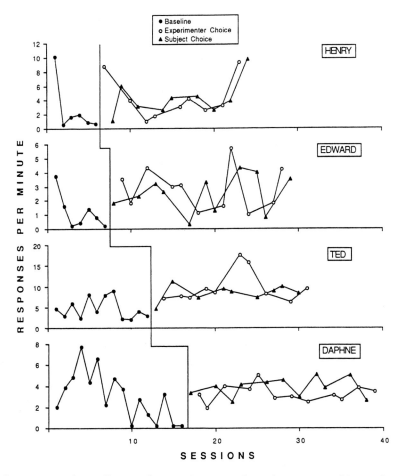

Figure 8.15 The effects of experimenter-selected versus subject-selected reinforcers on responses per minute for four individuals with developmental disabilities (Smith, Iwata, & Shore, 1995).

Considerations when Selecting Alternating Treatment Designs

Alternating treatment designs allow for the comparative assessment of various treatments or contingencies within one experimental phase. It is therefore more efficient than reversal or multiple baseline designs for examining the effectiveness of one or more treatments as it does not require multiple phases or withdrawals of treatment. Additionally, the alternating treatment design does not require a baseline assessment prior to intervention nor a reversal to baseline levels during the evaluation of treatment. If responding under baseline is of interest to the therapist then a baseline condition can be included and assessed as a treatment within the alternating treatments phase of the design. This design can be a useful protocol for examining the comparative effectiveness of different treatments to reduce dangerous behaviors. The alternating treatment design produces relatively rapid results and does not invoke ethical concerns regarding extended baseline assessments for behaviors such as self-injury or aggression.

8.7 Summary

The experimental methods used by applied behavior analysts to evaluate the effects of interventions on target behaviors have been described in this chapter. These experimental designs can clarify the effects of the intervention by ruling out alternative explanations for changes in the target behavior. In other words, single-case experimental designs are used to identify the functional relationship between the intervention and the target behavior. Additionally, single-case designs can be used to examine the generalizability of interventions across persons, settings, and behaviors.

Single-case research designs typically use graphic display to present an ongoing visual presentation of the target behavior over time. The effectiveness of the intervention is evaluated by visually comparing the target behavior when the intervention is not available (baseline phase) and when it is applied (intervention phase). The target behavior should be fairly stable prior to implementing or removing the intervention. This allows for a clearer prediction of what the behavior would be like if these experimental conditions remained in place. It also allows for a clearer comparison between predicted and actual performance under the subsequent experimental phase. Variability or trends in data paths can temper any firm conclusions about the effectiveness of the intervention.

Several of the most frequently used design options were presented. The withdrawal or ABAB design consists of an A phase (baseline) and B phase (intervention) that are replicated. Experimental control is demonstrated if there is a visible difference in the data paths of the A and B phases and this difference is again demonstrated in the A and B phase replications. The multiple baseline design can examine the effects of an intervention across multiple persons, settings, or behaviors. The intervention is applied sequentially across multiple baselines, and experimental control is demonstrated if baseline responding changes at that point in time when the treatment variable is applied to each baseline. The changing criterion design is specifically used to examine incremental changes in the level of the target behavior over time. Experimental control is demonstrated if the level of responding matches the established criteria for responding during each phase of the design. Finally, the alternating treatments design is used to compare the effects of multiple interventions on the target behavior. Treatments are rapidly implemented in a random or semi-random order. Experimental control is demonstrated if there is a visible differentiation between treatments.

Selection of a research design is determined by the applied question of interest, constraints of the applied setting, nature of the target behavior and so on. The applied behavior analyst must find an appropriate balance between the need for experimental control and the constraints of the applied setting. For example, the ABAB design demonstrates the most powerful experimental control. However, this design may be difficult to implement in many instances for therapists or parents may be unwilling to withdraw or withhold treatments for extended periods of time. In such cases a multiple baseline design or alternating treatment design should be selected.

CHAPTER 9

INCREASING ADAPTIVE BEHAVIOR IN APPLIED SETTINGS

Many behavioral interventions are designed to increase adaptive responding in clients. In such cases, individuals may possess appropriate behavioral repertoires but not perform them frequently. For example, an individual who is described as being socially withdrawn may possess the appropriate social skills for initiating interactions with others but may not perform these skills when in the presence of other people. In a similar vein, community behavioral interventions often seek to increase adaptive community behaviors, such as healthy lifestyles, use of safe working and leisure environments etc. In other instances, individuals may not possess the targeted skills. For example, people with developmental disabilities sometimes exhibit deficits in various social, daily-living, and academic skills. In these cases behavioral techniques can be used to establish or teach these new skills. This chapter will examine a variety of behavioral strategies, based on the principles of reinforcement, that can be used to increase adaptive responding in applied settings. Shaping and chaining techniques that can be used to establish new behaviors or complex sets of behaviors will also be examined. In addition to increasing the frequency of behaviors or establishing new behaviors, it is equally important that these gains are maintained over time, and, in many cases, can be demonstrated across different settings other than the treatment setting. The power or validity of a behavioral intervention is not only measured by its ability to increase behaviors; a behavioral intervention must produce behaviors that can generalize across persons, settings, and time. Strategies that can be used to program generalized responding will be discussed. Finally, the use of negative reinforcement, which produces increases in behavior to avoid or escape stimuli, in applied settings will be examined.

9.1 Increasing Adaptive Behavior Using Positive Reinforcement

The functional properties of operant reinforcement have been described in Chapters 2, 3, and 4. The use of positive reinforcement strategies in applied settings will be described in this section, with negative reinforcement strategies described in a subsequent section.

Positive reinforcement is the most frequently used intervention by applied behavior analysts. To recap, it can be defined as the contingent application of consequences that increase the probability of behaviors. The process of positive reinforcement requires several necessary conditions. First, a consequence must be contingent on responding. Second, the response must increase in probability when the consequence is made contingent on responding. Finally, the application of the consequence must be a necessary and sufficient condition to explain the increase in probability of responding. The reinforcing effectiveness of particular consequences may be idiosyncratic across individuals. Reinforcers may also vary in effectiveness for a particular individual over time. These variations in the effectiveness of consequences to act as reinforcers can be explained by factors including the learning history of the individual and establishing operations, such as the level of deprivation that an individual experiences for a particular consequence at any given point in time. Crucial steps prior to implementing an intervention based on the principles of positive reinforcement are to identify consequences that will act as reinforcers, and the conditions under which these consequences will be effective.

9.2   SELECTING REINFORCERS

There are several assessment approaches that can be used when selecting a reinforcing consequence to increase a target behavior. Reinforcer assessment procedures, or *protocols*, differ in terms of their empirical rigor. The easiest, and least rigorous, procedure is simply to ask the clients what they prefer. For example, students may state that they prefer free time in class, recess, group work etc. However, reflections on the reliability of what people say about themselves suggests that such statements of preference may not predict that such stimuli or activities will act as reinforcers, and this is supported by empirical studies (see Cooper, Heron, & Heward, 1987). A more systematic approach to reinforcer selection is to observe the individual in their natural environment over a period of time. Such observations can produce information on activities or events that might subsequently be used as reinforcing consequences. As with the functional assessment techniques detailed in Chapter 7, this approach to identifying possible reinforcers provides only indirect or correlational information regarding reinforcing consequences.

Empirical methods to assess the reinforcing effectiveness of various stimuli and activities have also been devised. For example, Pace, Ivancic, Edwards, Iwata, and Page (1985) developed a two-step process to identify reinforcers for persons with profound disabilities. Clients were systematically exposed to several stimuli (such as a vibrator, a fan, or a rocking chair). Approach behaviors such as orienting towards the item and manipulating the item were used to measure preference for particular items. This *preference protocol* was validated by demonstrating that those stimuli that were frequently approached acted as more powerful reinforcers than the stimuli that were not frequently approached. In an interesting extension of the Pace et al. (1985), study Fisher, Piazza, Bowman, Hagopian, Owens, and Slevin (1992) compared the preference protocol mentioned above with a forced-choice assessment protocol for individuals with profound developmental disabilities. In the later study, participants were initially exposed to 16 stimuli and approach behavior was measured. Subsequently, during the forced-choice assessment, each of the same 16 stimuli were presented in pairs (with each stimulus paired with every other stimulus), and participants were given access to the first stimulus approached. Results of the forced-choice assessment indicated fewer items as highly preferred. Finally, participants were given the opportunity to choose between stimuli that were identified by the preference protocol and forced-choice assessments as highly preferred and stimuli that were identified as highly preferred by the preference protocol only. (Incidentally, all stimuli that were identified as highly preferred in the forced-choice assessment were also identified as highly preferred by the preference protocol.) The results of this concurrent operants assessment with four participants are presented in Figure 9.1. These results indicate that the forced-choice assessment protocol better predicted stimuli that resulted in higher levels of responding when presented in a concurrent operants paradigm.

Allowing participants to choose between alternative stimuli seems to produce a more sensitive assessment of the potential reinforcing effectiveness of stimuli above and beyond merely observing approach and manipulation of stimuli. These results have been further supported by more recent research (Paclawskyj & Vollmer, 1995).

Applied researchers have also developed systematic protocols to examine the reinforcing effectiveness of various activities. Foster-Johnson, Ferro, and Dunlap (1994) examined the use of a systematic protocol to identify reinforcing classroom activities for students with emotional and behavioral disorders. The experimenters presented a series of regular classroom activities (including coin and number identification). Student

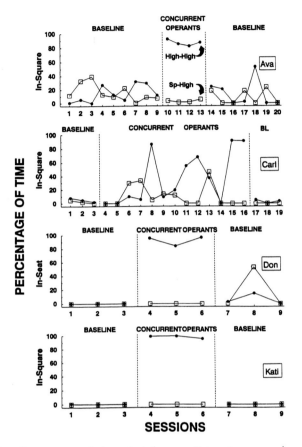

Figure 9.1 Percentage of time that four participants engaged or manipulated items that were identified as preferred in the forced-choice assessment and preference assessment (identified as high-high data set in the graph) versus stimuli that were identified as highly preferred in the preference assessment only (identified as Sp-high data set in the graph). This comparative assessment is presented in the middle phase (described as Concurrent Operants phase in the graph) for each participant (Fisher, Piazza, Bowman, Hagopian, Owens, & Slevin, 1992).

preference for each classroom activity was evaluated in terms of: (a) the extent to which the student manipulated the classroom activities without instructor prompting, (b) the degree of student resistance when the materials were removed and, (c) student initiations towards the materials when they were moved a short distance away. Results of this assessment for three students demonstrated a variety of definite preferences for particular classroom activities. Following this preference assessment the experimenters presented preferred and nonpreferred activities in an ABAB design for the three students. Desirable (e.g., following instructions, appropriate vocalizations) and problem (e.g., off task, noncompliance) behaviors were measured across the phases of the design. The results of this experiment are presented in Figure 9.2. Overall, the results show that the students engaged

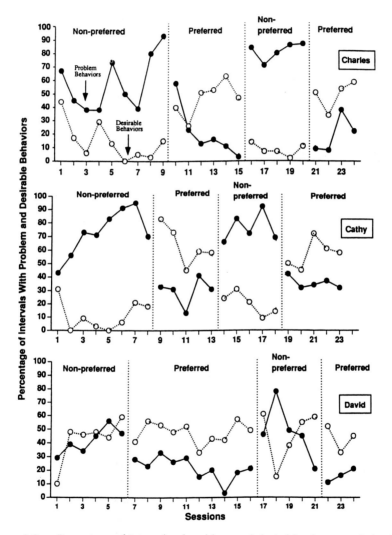

Figure 9.2   Percentage of intervals of problem and desirable classroom behavior for three students with emotional and behavioral problems under preferred and non-preferred curricular activities (Foster-Johnson, Ferro, & Dunlap, 1994).

in low levels of problem behavior and high levels of desirable behavior during preferred classroom activities relative to non-preferred classroom activities. While this experiment does not demonstrate that preferred activities acted as reinforcers, it does provide an interesting applied extension — that engagement in preferred curricular activities can produce increases in appropriate and decreases of inappropriate responding with such students. The systematic presentation of preferred activities has also been shown to reduce self-injurious behavior for individuals with developmental disabilities (Ringdahl, Vollmer, Marcus, & Roane, 1997).

Allen and Iwata (1980) adopted the Premack Principle, explained in Chapter 2, to examine the reinforcing effectiveness of a high probability activity (game participation) when made contingent on performance of a low probability activity (exercise performance) for 10 individuals with mental retardation. Participants were required to perform 5 physical exercises before they could participate in game activity. Figure 9.3 shows the mean percentage of participation in exercise, game activities, and length of exercise sessions. These data suggest increases in the low probability behavior and little change in the high probability behavior when the

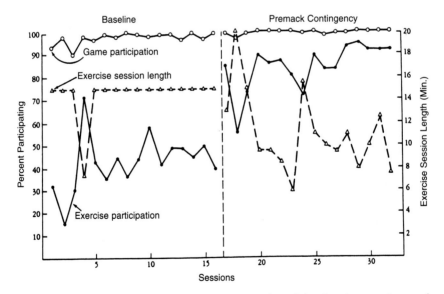

Figure 9.3   Daily mean percentage (N = 10) of participation in exercises and games and the exercise session length during baseline and group contingency phases. Participation is scaled on the left ordinate, and exercise session length on the right ordinate (Allen & Iwata, 1980).

Premack contingency was in effect. This example demonstrates how the Premack Principle may be used to identify the reinforcing effectiveness of activities in applied settings (but note the restrictions on the Premack principle, also outlined in Chapter 2) .

The first essential step in any reinforcement-based program is to identify consequences that are reinforcing for a particular individual. Many of the methods used to identify reinforcing consequences have been outlined in this section. Interview and observation techniques provide general or correlational information regarding reinforcing consequences. If possible, it is preferable to verify empirically the reinforcing effectiveness of consequences prior to implementing an intervention. Various preference and forced-choice assessment protocols have been described which are designed to assess the reinforcing value of stimuli or events. Ultimately, the reinforcing effectiveness of a contingent consequence can only be determined by causally examining its influence on the probability of the target behavior.

9.3   Optimizing Reinforcer Effectiveness

Aside from the application of a contingent consequence of known reinforcing value there are several other factors that should be considered when implementing a reinforcement program. These factors include: delay of reinforcement, schedules of reinforcement, establishing operations, amount of reinforcer, and the use of generalized conditioned reinforcers.

Delay of Reinforcement

The power of a reinforcing consequence can be influenced by the delay between performance of the target behavior and access to the reinforcer. In general, the greater the delay between behavior and consequence the less effective the reinforcer will be (Mazur, 1997). In applications, reinforcement should therefore be delivered immediately following the target behavior. This rule is particularly true when introducing a new reinforcement-based program or, relatedly, when attempting to establish a new behavior for an individual. If there is a delay between the target behavior and delivery of the reinforcer then a different behavior which is performed after the target behavior may be reinforced. For example, verbal praise is often used to increase appropriate play activities such as sharing with children. A child may engage in sharing and then return to playing alone. If verbal praise is delayed following an instance of sharing then the more immediate behavior to the verbal praise (e.g., playing alone) may actually be reinforced. Once the contingency between the target behavior and reinforcing consequence has been established then the delay may be systematically lengthened.

Schedules of Reinforcement

The wealth of experimental research demonstrating the various patterns of responding under different schedules of reinforcement was briefly described in Chapter 3. Although some differences are found between humans and other species in laboratory studies (see Section 3.15), other aspects of these experimental findings are of particular significance when implementing positive reinforcement programs in applied settings. Schedules of reinforcement detail which instance of the response will be reinforced. When beginning a program each occurrence of a target behavior should be reinforced. This continuous reinforcement schedule (FR1) is recommended in the initial stages as it produces the most rapid increase in responding. Once the behavior has reached desired levels then the schedule of reinforcement should be made more intermittent. Programming behavior on an intermittent schedule of reinforcement is one tactic for guarding against rapid extinction of the target behavior once the behavior change program is removed. As discussed in Section 3.14, this strategy has been successfully adopted in a number of applied studies (Kazdin & Polster, 1973; Kazdin, 1994; Nation & Woods, 1980; Tierney & Smith, 1988).

Establishing Operations

Responding is influenced by the level of satiation or deprivation that the person experiences with regard to a reinforcer. It is not unusual to observe fluctuations in response strength, even when discriminative and reinforcing conditions are held constant (Carr, 1994). In other words, the behavior analyst may identify an effective reinforcer, but such consequences may produce desired levels of responding on some occasions and not on others. Such variations in responding can be attributed to various third variables such as establishing operations (see Chapters 2, 5, and 7). Behavior analysts have typically attempted to deal with fluctuations in the power of reinforcers by programming consequences that produce high and persistent levels of responding. Such strategies as incorporating generalized conditioned reinforcers into a reinforcement program (discussed in next section) and establishing intermittent schedules of reinforcement are recommended in these instances. More recently, applied behavior analysts have begun to examine the functional properties of environmental variables that produce fluctuation in response strength when discriminative and reinforcement stimuli are held constant. This research is important in that it identifies environmental conditions under which a given reinforcing consequence may be more or less effective. Through an understanding of these contextual influences on the power of reinforcement the behavior analyst may be able to identify optimal times and conditions to conduct training.

Vollmer and Iwata (1991) examined the influence of satiation and deprivation conditions on primary, conditioned, and sensory reinforcing stimuli for five individuals with profound developmental disabilities. The behavior assessed consisted of the simple task of placing blocks in a container. Food was used as a primary reinforcer, and the effects of satiation and deprivation were assessed with three of the participants. This was achieved by presenting the task 30 minutes prior to lunch (deprivation) and 15 minutes following lunch (satiation). The satiation condition was also preceded with 10 minutes of free access to food. Food items were presented on a fixed-ratio schedule during sessions. No food was presented during baseline conditions. The effects of the satiation and deprivation conditions for the three participants are presented in Figure 9.4. Rates of responding were higher under conditions of deprivation. These results were replicated with music and social contact as reinforcers under satiation and deprivation conditions, showing that these "non-biological" reinforcers are affected by establishing operations in a similar manner.

The results of Vollmer and Iwata (1991) clearly demonstrate the influence of satiation and deprivation on effectiveness of a range of reinforcers. Behavior analysts should take advantage of natural levels of deprivation for reinforcers when implementing reinforcement-based programs.

Amount of Reinforcer

The amount of a reinforcer that an individual receives over the course of a given training session can also affect performance. While it is generally

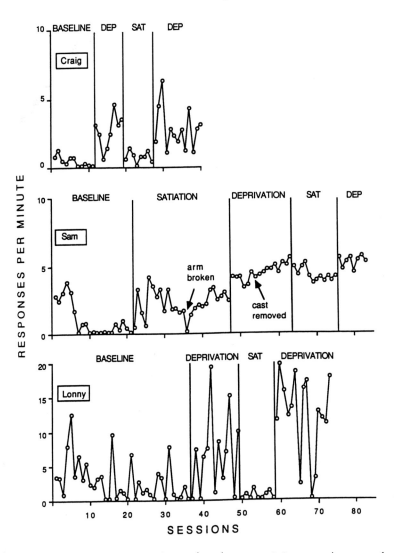

Figure 9.4   Responses per minute for three participants when no food (reinforcement) was presented (baseline conditions in the graph) and when food was presented contingent on responding under satiation and deprivation conditions (Vollmer & Iwata, 1991).

believed that the greater the amount of reinforcement the more probable the target response will be, this is contradicted by the response-deprivation principle introduced in Chapter 2 (Allison & Timberlake, 1974, and see

Leslie, 1996, Chapter 4 for a brief formal statement of the principle). For a reinforcer to be effective, the individual must remain deprived of it during the session, and if the amount delivered is too great the deprivation will be reduced too much. This is an example of the influence of establishing operations within training sessions. This form of satiation may be more pronounced for primary reinforcers such as food. Secondary reinforcers such as social attention and generalized conditioned reinforcers such as money may be more resistant to satiation within training sessions. If responding wanes during a training session and this phenomenon is evident for many training sessions the behavior analyst may want to reduce the amount of reinforcement available for responding. This may introduce a mild level of deprivation throughout training and thereby enhance the reinforcing effectiveness of the consequence.

9.4 TOKEN ECONOMIES

The token economy is an applied example of the use of a generalized conditioned reinforcer to control behavior (See Chapter 2 for a description of conditioned reinforcement). Tokens typically consist of coins, check marks, stars, or "smiley faces". In and of themselves these tokens have no inherent reinforcing value, but within the token economy system they can be used to purchase back-up reinforcers. Back-up reinforcers are consequences of known reinforcing value to those participating in the token system. Back-up reinforcers can consist of anything from food and other consumables to activities and outings. Each back-up reinforcer can be purchased by a specific number of tokens. Because tokens can allow the participant to access various reinforcers they are defined as generalized conditioned reinforcers.

The participant is required to perform certain target behaviors at predefined levels in order to receive a particular number of tokens. The target behaviors and the number of tokens associated with each target behavior are clearly identified prior to the implementation of the program. Additionally, the participant must be capable of earning the number of tokens to access each one of the back-up reinforcers. Certain inappropriate behaviors can also be associated with the removal of a predefined number of tokens. It is important however, not to create a situation where the participant ends up with a negative number of tokens. Under these conditions, the tokens may lose their reinforcing value as they are not paired with access to back-up reinforcers.

When beginning a token system it is important to clarify to participants the contingencies that will operate. This can be done by explaining to participants the target behaviors required, the number of tokens that can be earned for each target behavior, and the token cost of each back-up reinforcer. These conditions may have to be modeled for participants who do not understand such verbal descriptions.

Token economy systems have proved successful in increasing appropriate behavior for many populations (developmentally disabled, psychiatric, children etc.) and across many settings (hospitals, institutions, the home etc.). In one of the seminal evaluations of the token economy system, Allyon and Azrin (1965) developed such a system to increase appropriate responding in hospitalized psychiatric patients. High frequency activities such as going for walks, privacy, and religious services were identified as back-up reinforcers for participants. Participants earned tokens from ward staff for engaging in a number of targeted work activities around the hospital. The findings of this intervention are presented in Figure 9.5. In this study, the token system was implemented for an entire ward of 44 clients. The effectiveness of the token system was evaluated using a BAB design. In the reversal or A phase, access to tokens and reinforcers was noncontingent on the target work activities. When the token system was made contingent on performance there was a dramatic increase in work activity in both B phases.

As illustrated above, the token economy system is a powerful procedure for increasing appropriate responding in individuals. The use of tokens as a generalized conditioned reinforcer has a number of inherent advantages over using single conditioned or primary reinforcers within a reinforcement program. First, because the participant has access to a set of back-up reinforcers the problem of satiation on any one reinforcer is reduced. Also, additional back-up reinforcers can be identified and added to the token economy during the intervention. Second, because of the nature of tokens themselves they can be presented immediately following the performance of the target behavior. This overcomes the potential problem of delaying access to reinforcers. Third, token delivery does not interfere with ongoing activities. Some reinforcers such as food and preferred activities may be difficult to deliver as they may interfere with responding in the current context. Tokens can be exchanged at a later and more appropriate time in order to access such consequences as activities and food etc. It is important to guard against theft of tokens by other participants.

Those who administer the system should keep an ongoing account of

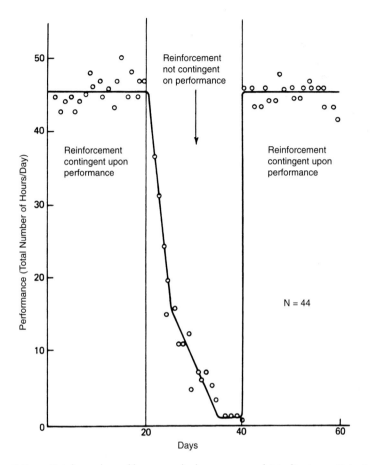

Figure 9.5   Total number of hours each day a group of 44 clients participated in rehabilitative activities under conditions of reinforcement with tokens (first phase), independent or non-contingent presentations of tokens (second phase), and reinstatement of reinforcement with tokens (third phase) (Ayllon & Azrin, 1965).

the number of tokens that each participant possesses. Staff must also be trained to administer the token system consistently. In fact, a token system can be seen as an intervention to change the behavior of those who work with the participants, as well as that of the "participants". For example, a token system can be used to establish positive interactions between parents and their children. The use of a token system in such instances can help parents focus on positive behaviors of children and to systematically reinforce those positive behaviors. Similarly in psychiatric contexts, staff must be aware they should attend to positive behavior and not selectively respond to disruptive behavior by clients.

In any case, a token system should be monitored periodically to ensure that the system is administered consistently and correctly. In some instances it may be appropriate to remove the token system eventually. This can be difficult to achieve and might result in a return of behavior to baseline levels. Suggestions that have been made for removing a token system include pairing the tokens with a more natural reinforcer, such as verbal praise, while gradually fading the number of back-up reinforcers, and reducing the number of tokens required to access the remaining back-up reinforcers.

9.5 INTERIM SUMMARY: SELECTING REINFORCERS AND IMPLEMENTING A REINFORCEMENT PROGRAM

Behavior change programs based on the principles of positive reinforcement are the most frequently used intervention strategies by applied behavior analysts. These programs are used to increase adaptive responding for clients. At the simplest level, such interventions require the contingent application of a consequence of known reinforcing value. However, several other factors need to be considered in order to maximize the effectiveness of such programs.

Before beginning a behavior change program, it is important to identify a reinforcer that will be effective in the context in which it will be applied. Rather than relying on previous practice, or simply asking the participants for their preferred reinforcers (and neither of these options may be practicable in some cases), it is better to use an empirical method of reinforcer assessment. Various preference and forced-choice assessment protocols have been developed which are designed to assess the reinforcing value of stimuli. Ultimately, the reinforcing effectiveness of a contingent consequence can only be determined by its influence on the probability of the target behavior.

When beginning a reinforcement program it is important to provide a rich schedule of reinforcement and to immediately reinforce responding when it occurs. This enhances the discriminability of the contingencies that are in effect which can result in a rapid increase in the target behavior. These guidelines may rule out certain types of reinforcers such as activities or food as it may not be possible to deliver such consequences immediately.

The relationship between behavior and its consequences is not a static one. The power of reinforcing consequences can be affected by the momentary levels of satiation and deprivation that the client experiences with regard to a particular consequence. Behavior analysts should, where possible, structure intervention sessions to take advantage of mild deprivation states (for example, using food as a reinforcer immediately prior to lunch and not immediately after lunch, and using smaller rather than larger portions of food) in order to maximize the power of reinforcers. Once the target behavior achieves a stable level of responding, the schedule of reinforcement should be thinned in order to enhance maintenance of responding in the natural environment when the intervention is withdrawn. Other strategies that can be used to promote maintenance and generalization of target behaviors will be discussed later in this chapter. One of the most effective strategies used to increase behavior is the token economy system. In this tokens, which have been established as generalized conditioned reinforcers, are made contingent upon target behaviors. Such systems, when appropriately implemented, are typically resistant to satiation and overcome the problems with delayed administration of certain types of reinforcers.

9.6 USING REINFORCEMENT TO DECREASE MALADAPTIVE BEHAVIOR

One of the major purposes of many reinforcement-based techniques is to decrease maladaptive behavior. These techniques could well be described in Chapter 10 (as techniques to decrease behavior) but because they are based on the principles of positive reinforcement they are included here. There are at least five positive reinforcement strategies that can be used to decrease maladaptive behavior. All these strategies are based on the fundamental premise that if behavior other than maladaptive responding is reinforced there should be a decrease in maladaptive behavior. These techniques are therefore described as *differential reinforcement* strategies because selected responses or levels of responding are reinforced while other responses are not. Before describing these particular strategies it is vital to realize that many of the techniques discussed previously in this chapter and in Chapter 7 are an essential part of these differential reinforcement techniques.

First, it is essential to identify the reinforcers that are maintaining the maladaptive behavior. Differential reinforcement is based on two principles of learning — extinction and reinforcement (the applied uses of extinction are discussed in detail in Chapter 10). The reinforcers that maintain the aberrant behavior must therefore be withheld from that behavior, and can be delivered contingent on other more appropriate responses (or contingent on lower levels of maladaptive responding after a predetermined period of time). The behavior analyst should therefore conduct a functional analysis of the maladaptive behavior prior to developing the intervention. Second, reinforcing stimuli must be selected and applied contingent on appropriate responding. These reinforcing consequences should be systematically identified through preference assessments. Alternatively, the reinforcers that previously maintained aberrant responding can be used to increase adaptive responding. Additionally, the behavior analyst should incorporate the techniques described earlier in the chapter for maximizing reinforcer effectiveness (including immediate reinforcement, use of an initially rich schedule of reinforcement etc.).

Differential Reinforcement of Incompatible and Alternative Behavior

Differential reinforcement of incompatible behavior (DRI) is a technique whereby reinforcement is delivered contingent on the occurrence of a behavior that is topographically incompatible with the targeted maladaptive behavior. The increase in frequency of the incompatible behavior results in a decrease in the frequency of the maladaptive behavior as both behaviors cannot be performed simultaneously. Deitz, Repp, & Deitz (1976) used a DRI intervention to decrease episodes of in-class sleeping for a student with mild disabilities. The intervention consisted of teacher-delivered praise for appropriate academic activity approximately every 5 minutes. Academic performance is directly incompatible with sleeping. The effectiveness of the intervention was evaluated using an ABAB design. The results of this intervention are presented in Figure 9.6 and demonstrate the effectiveness of the DRI intervention.

Differential reinforcement of alternative behavior (DRA) is a similar protocol to DRI. In this case however the behavior chosen for reinforcement is not topographically incompatible with the maladaptive behavior. The DRA protocol is based on the premise that increasing the frequency of alternative behaviors will decrease the frequency of the undesired behavior.

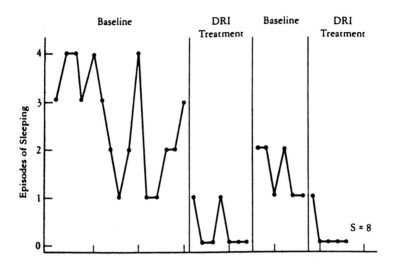

Figure 9.6   Episodes of sleeping in class under baseline and DRI (differential reinforcement of academic performance) contingencies (Deitz, Repp, & Deitz, 1976).

For example, reinforcing academic activity may decrease maladaptive behavior in the classroom such as talking out, leaving ones seat etc. DRA is a frequently used protocol in applied practice.

Differential Reinforcement of Functionally Equivalent Behavior

As discussed in Chapter 7, functional analysis technologies have equipped applied behavior analysts with methodologies to examine the operant function of challenging behavior. A functional analysis is an important prerequisite for any differential reinforcement program. Functional analysis identifies the reinforcing stimuli for the maladaptive behavior which need to be withheld. Additionally, a functional analysis can allow the behavior analyst to tailor an intervention to the function of the behavior. For example, a functional analysis may demonstrate that a person engages in hand biting to access attention from staff. This information allows the behavior analyst to identify an alternative behavior (such as raising of a hand) that the person can be taught to use to access the same reinforcer (in this case, staff attention). This alternative behavior is therefore functionally equivalent to the challenging behavior. The differential reinforcement program therefore consists of withholding the reinforcer for the maladaptive behavior and making the same reinforcer available for the functionally equivalent behavior. There has been a proliferation of research describing such tactics in recent years (see Reichle & Wacker, 1993). This type of intervention is also often described as functional communication training (Carr & Durand, 1985).

An interesting example of the use of a functional analysis that incorporates the systematic examination of differential reinforcement of functionally equivalent behavior was proposed by Derby, Wacker, Sasso, Steege, Northup, Cigrand, and Asmus (1992). This assessment consists of two separate phases. In the first phase of the analysis, both the challenging behavior and an appropriate alternative behavior are assessed under analogue analysis conditions (see Figure 9.7). If the challenging behavior occurs under any of the analogue analysis conditions then this condition is replicated. In Figure 9.7, the challenging behavior occurs under the attention condition and this condition is subsequently replicated. It can be concluded from the first phase of the analysis that self-injurious behavior (SIB) is maintained by access to attention. In the second phase or contingency reversal the reinforcer (i.e., attention) is withheld for SIB and made contingent on the appropriate response. There is a dramatic increase in the appropriate response (i.e., manding) with a significant decrease in SIB. This condition is subsequently replicated. The protocol proposed by Derby et al. (1992) combines a brief assessment of the function of the maladaptive behavior with a preliminary assessment of the potential effectiveness of an intervention involving the differential reinforcement of functionally equivalent behavior.

Differential Reinforcement of Other Behavior

Differential reinforcement of other behavior (DRO) is a protocol whereby reinforcement is provided for the nonoccurrence of the target behavior over a specified interval of time. DRO is often described as *omission training* because reinforcement is delivered for omission (non-production) rather than commission (production) of the behavior (Cooper, Heron, & Heward, 1987). A DRO schedule provides reinforcement for all behaviors other than the targeted maladaptive behaviors: the focus of this procedure is thus on decreasing maladaptive behaviors, and no provision is made for increasing appropriate alternative behaviors.

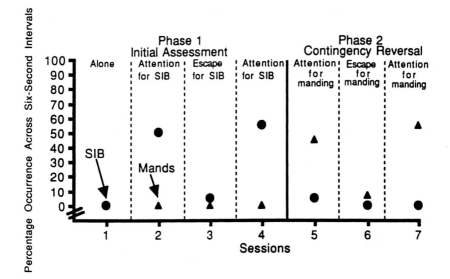

Figure 9.7   Hypothetical example of a brief functional analysis. The initial assessment identified that SIB was maintained by attention. The contingency reversal phase demonstrated that attention could be used as a reinforcer to increase appropriate responding (i.e., manding) (Derby, Wacker, Sasso, Steege, Northup, Cigrand, & Asmus, 1992).

In order to apply a DRO procedure the behavior analyst must first identify a time interval during which the behavior should not occur. It is critical to identify a time interval in which the client is currently capable of not displaying the maladaptive behavior. For example, it would be inappropriate to set the interval at 1 hour (when the requirement would be that the client must not display the behavior for 1 hour in order to access reinforcement) if the client currently displays the behavior 100 times per hour. In this example, the client would probably never access the reinforcing contingencies. The time interval must be sensitive to the current rate of responding. These intervals can be gradually and systematically increased during treatment. Second, any appropriate behavior that occurs at the end of the interval is reinforced if the target behavior was not performed. Finally, if the maladaptive behavior occurs during an interval then the interval is reset (i.e., there is a return to the beginning of the interval).

There are a large number of demonstrations of the DRO protocol in the applied literature. Many researchers describe successful applications of the procedure (e.g., Poling & Ryan, 1982; Repp, Dietz, & Speir, 1975) while others have demonstrated that the procedure did not produce reductions in maladaptive behavior (e.g., Foxx & Azrin, 1973; Meyers, 1975). More recently, researchers have begun to examine the functional properties of the DRO protocol. For example, Mazaleski, Iwata, Vollmer, Zarcone, and Smith (1993) conducted a component analysis of the reinforcement and extinction components of DRO contingencies when applied to individuals with attention-maintained self-injury. These researchers demonstrated that the active variable of a DRO was extinction and not reinforcement for clients with attention-maintained maladaptive behavior.

The results for one of the participants are presented in Figure 9.8. Phases 1 and 3 demonstrate that the behavior occurred at high rates when attention was contingent on responding. In Phase 2, a DRO schedule with music as the reinforcer for nonoccurrence of self-injury (while attention is witheld for self-injury) effectively reduced SIB. Phases 4 and 6 demonstrated that the extinction component alone (withholding attention for self-injury) produced comparable reductions in self-injury as did the DRO schedule of Phase 2. In Phase 5 the reinforcement component of the DRO schedule (music) was examined alone while attention continued to be contingent on self-injury. The results of Phase 5 demonstrate that the DRO music condition without extinction did not reduce the challenging behavior.

The results of Mazaleski et al. (1993) clearly demonstrate the continued need to examine the functional properties of DRO contingencies. It may be that in previous studies only the extinction condition embedded within the DRO schedule was effective in changing behavior.

Differential Reinforcement of Low Rates of Responding

Differential reinforcement of low rates of responding (DRL) is a protocol that provides reinforcement for decreases in the level of responding or for increases in the inter-response time (IRT) of the maladaptive behaviors (see Chapter 3 for a definition of this schedule in basic research). This is a particularly effective treatment if the overall goal is to reduce responding and not eliminate it. For example, Favell, McGimpsey, and Jones (1980) used a DRL procedure to decrease rapid eating in four individuals with severe disabilities. Inter-response times between food bites were prompted, reinforced, and systematically increased. The results of this intervention are

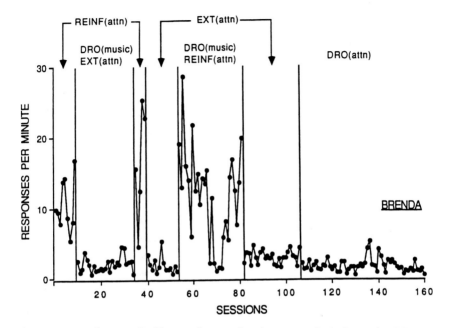

Figure 9.8   The rate of self-injury for Brenda. Phases 1 and 3 indicate that SIB was maintained by contingent attention. In phase 2 a traditional DRO treatment was implemented (music contingent on nonoccurrence of SIB and attention withheld for SIB). Phases 4 and 6 demonstrate that extinction alone (attention withheld contingent on SIB) produced similiar results to the DRO intervention. In Phase 5 the DRO music contingency remained in place while SIB continued to access attention. These results demonstrate that extinction of attention was the active treatment variable in this DRO intervention. A DRO attention condition in the final phase (attention contingent on no occurrences of SIB) successfully reduced SIB (Mazaleski, Iwata, Vollmer, Zarcone, & Smith, 1993).

presented in Figure 9.9. The frequency of eating was decreased from an average of 10 to 12 bites per 30 seconds to 3 to 4 bites per 30 seconds using this DRL protocol. The DRL protocol has a very specific use — to decrease but not eliminate behavior. Often, behaviors such as talking out, or leaving one's seat in class are appropriate, but not at high frequencies. DRL is very useful in establishing appropriate levels of such responding.

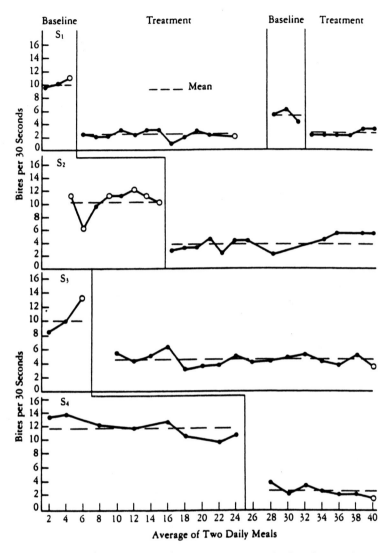

Figure 9.9   Rate of eating across four participants under baseline and treatment conditions. Open data points represent data for one meal. Solid data points represent an average for two daily meals (Favell, McGimpsey, & Jones, 1980).

Noncontingent Reinforcement

As described in Chapter 3, the noncontingent delivery of a reinforcing stimulus (NCR) can result in a rapid reduction in operant responding.

Recently, researchers have examined the use of NCR as a technique to reduce challenging behavior in applied settings. Initial results demonstrate that NCR can be an effective strategy to eliminate maladaptive behavior maintained by positive reinforcement (Hagopian, Fisher, & Legacy, 1994; Vollmer, Iwata, Zarcone, Smith, & Mazaleski, 1993) and negative reinforcement (Vollmer, Marcus, & Ringdahl, 1995). In each of these studies, a functional analysis was first conducted to identify the operant function of the maladaptive behavior. Access to the identified reinforcers was then provided independent of the behavior on a time-based schedule. This resulted in rapid and significant reductions of the maladaptive behavior. The schedule of NCR was then gradually thinned, that is, the frequency of reinforcement was gradually reduced.

In an interesting example of this work, Hagopian et al. (1994) compared the effectiveness of a dense versus lean schedule of NCR on the reduction of destructive behavior in quadruplets with developmental disabilities. The particular research question examined whether it was necessary to begin noncontingent reinforcement on a dense schedule (FT 10 s) and then fade to a lean schedule (FT 5 min), or whether treatment would be as effective using a lean schedule from the outset. The results of this investigation are presented in Figure 9.10. The intervention was introduced across the quadruplets in a multiple baseline design. Lean and dense schedules were compared using an alternating treatments design logic in the second phase of the design. The results showed that the dense schedule of NCR was more effective, at the onset, in reducing the challenging behavior (see alternating treatments phase of the design). The dense schedule was then successfully thinned from FT 10 s to FT 5 min (see final phase of the figure). These findings suggest that NCR may require a dense schedule initially, and that systematic fading can increase the effectiveness of a lean schedule.

While the findings are preliminary, this research on the use of NCR techniques provides an exciting new avenue for further applied investigations. In fact, recent findings suggest that NCR using arbitrary reinforcers (stimuli that were reinforcing to the client but did not maintain the aberrant behavior) can effectively reduce maladaptive behavior where the reinforcers for maladaptive behavior have not been identified (Fischer, Iwata, & Mazaleski, 1997). Noncontingent delivery of reinforcing stimuli would seem to be an efficient and easy to use intervention. Further research should examine whether such techniques can produce long-term reductions in challenging behavior. Additionally, research is needed to clarify the functional properties of NCR techniques.

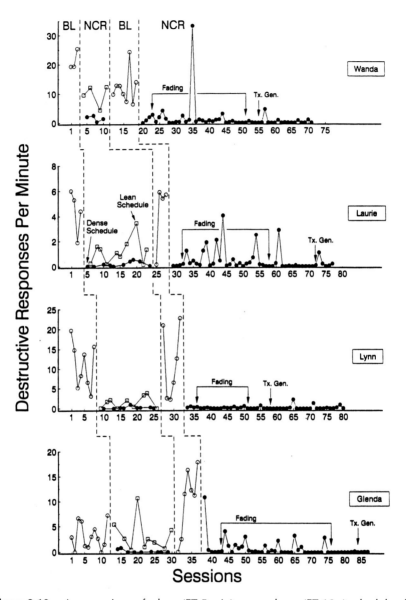

Figure 9.10 A comparison of a lean (FT 5 min) versus dense (FT 10 s) schedule of noncontingent reinforcement on destructive responses per minute with quadruplets. The dense schedule produced a more rapid reduction in the aberrant behavior and was subsequently implemented following a second baseline condition. Arrows indicate fading of the schedule and treatment generalization (Tx. Gen.) (Hagopian, Fisher, & Legacy, 1994).

9.7   ESTABLISHING NEW BEHAVIORAL REPERTOIRES

Up to this point of the chapter, strategies to increase or decrease the current frequency of responding have been discussed. As discussed in Chapter 6, behavioral strategies can also be used to establish or develop new behaviors, either specific individual skills or complex sequences of skills. In the next four sections, details of these strategies will be given. The strategies discussed in these sections of the chapter and those outlined previously are not mutually exclusive. For example, once a new behavior is performed it is important to continue to reinforce that behavior in order to increase the probability of the individual performing that behavior in the future.

This section includes a description of a number of instructional prompting strategies to establish new behavior. In the next section, the methods of removing these once the new behavior is established are described. In the following section, the use of differential reinforcement to shape new behavior will be discussed. Finally, chaining techniques, which are used to establish multiple and complex skill repertoires will be outlined.

Instructional Prompting Strategies

Prompts are antecedent cues that are used to evoke the desired response. These antecedent cues are typically supplementary stimuli that will be removed once the target behavior is performed appropriately in the presence of the natural discriminative stimuli. Prompts are of two general types. *Response prompts* are cues which describe or demonstrate the new desired response. *Stimulus prompts* are cues which highlight the natural discriminative stimuli in the environment and therefore increase the probability of correct responding. There are several types of response prompts including verbal, modeling, picture, and physical prompts.

Verbal response prompts are the most commonly and widely used instructional prompts in educational and applied settings. These prompts can be oral or written in nature. The critical feature of these prompts is that they function as supplementary cues to evoke the desired behavior. Verbal prompts are often classified as direct or indirect. An indirect verbal prompt is used to cue the person that some behavior needs to be performed, but it does not describe what the target behavior is. For example, "What do you need to do next?" is an indirect verbal prompt for it indicates that the person needs to perform but it does not indicate what the person needs to do. A direct verbal prompt specifies the behavior that the person should perform. For example, "Open your book." clearly identifies what needs to be performed. Written instructions can also be used to prompt performance. For example, Cuvo, Davis, O'Reilly, Mooney, and Crowley (1992) taught individuals with mild intellectual disabilities to use written descriptions of domestic tasks (such as cleaning household appliances) as prompts. These written descriptions of how to perform the task combined with positive and corrective feedback from the therapist following performance resulted in rapid acquisition of the targeted domestic skills. Performance remained at high levels when the written prompts were removed.

A *picture response prompt* is a visual representation of the behavior to be performed. Behaviors can be illustrated using drawings, photographs, paintings etc. Picture prompts can be used to illustrate single behaviors or many pictures can be used to ilustrate complete sequences of behaviors. Picture prompt systems have been used to teach complex daily living and vocational skills to people with intellectual disabilities. Connis (1979) used picture sequences to teach people with moderate intellectual disabilities to change work tasks independently. The workers were first taught to use photographs to sequence daily work tasks, and then to change work tasks independently throughout the working day. Similarly, Sowers, Rusch, Connis, and Cummings (1980) taught individuals with intellectual disabilities to use picture cues of clock faces to leave and return from lunch and work breaks. Johnson and Cuvo (1981) taught meal preparation skills to rehabilitation clients using picture prompt sequences.

A *modeling response prompt* involves the therapist or teacher demonstrating the desired behavior so that it can be imitated by the person. Modeling can be a very effective response prompt as it allows the therapist to show the person what is to be performed. A description of the functional properties of modeling was presented in Chapter 6. Modeling is frequently used in applied interventions to promote appropriate responding. For example, O'Reilly and Glynn (1995) used a modeling protocol to teach social skills to two students who were described as socially withdrawn. Targeted social skills were identified through consultation with the teacher and observation of the students during class. These social skills were then taught to the students on an individual basis in a room removed from the classroom. During intervention the therapist first modeled the social skills.

The participants then imitated the modeled social skills and received feedback on their performance from the therapist. This intervention produced an increase in appropriate social responding in school settings for the participants.

Physical response prompts produce correct responding by manually guiding the person through the appropriate response. Physical prompting is obviously a very intrusive way to teach somebody to respond correctly. However, in cases where the response is very difficult for the learner to perform it may be the only option. Physical prompting can consist of manually guiding the person through the entire sequence of steps of a task. For example in teaching toothbrushing to a child with severe disabilities the therapist may place his hands on top of the child's and guide the child to: open the toothpaste, reach for the toothbrush, place toothpaste on the toothbrush, replace the cap on the toothpaste etc. However, in many cases of physical prompting reported in the literature the manual guidance is only partial (for an example, see Horner & Keilitz, 1975). This form of partial physical guidance is often referred to as shadowing. When shadowing the therapist guides the student's movements by keeping his hands a few inches away from the student, and physically guiding the student only when necessary.

Stimulus prompts are additional stimuli that are used to highlight the natural discriminative stimulus or the stimulus that is to become the discriminative stimulus with training. They are used to increase the evocative effectiveness of the discriminative stimulus. Stimulus prompts can be used in conjunction with response prompts when teaching new skills to people. Several types of stimulus prompts have been used (Cooper, Heron & Heward, 1987; Snell, 1983). For example, the salient component of a compound stimulus might be artificially highlighted. When teaching cooking skills to persons with intellectual disabilities the therapist may attach a cue to the temperature dial of the oven that indicates the appropriate oven temperature for the meal. The participant need only attend to the artificial cue and not the range of temperatures on the dial when setting the oven. Another example of a stimulus cue is a point prompt. The therapist may point to the relevant stimulus during training. In teaching time a teacher may ask "What time is it?" and then point to the hour hand and minute hand on the clock.

9.8   FADING RESPONSE AND STIMULUS PROMPTS

Response and stimulus prompts are supplementary or additional instructional procedures that must eventually be removed. The goal of any instructional program is that the participant will eventually be able to perform the skills independent of these additional prompts. In other words, the natural discriminative stimuli must eventually come to control responding. Once the participant performs the new skill at an appropriate level for a predetermined period of time, the prompting conditions are then gradually faded. *Fading* is a stimulus discrimination procedure in which the discriminative stimuli for the response are gradually changed so that they become increasingly similar to the natural discriminative stimuli. In other words, fading is a gradual process by which stimulus control is transferred from the prompts to the natural stimulus in a manner that reduces the probability of error responses in the presence of the natural stimulus. Fading is therefore sometimes called errorless discrimination or errorless learning (Terrace, 1963).

Minimising error responses during instruction and fading is highly desirable for a number of reasons. First, if an incorrect response occurs it tends to be repeated and must be unlearned. This can substantially delay the overall goals of a training program. Second, incorrect responses result in corrective feedback from the therapist and the withholding of reinforcement. These conditions can result in inappropriate behaviors such as aggression on the part of the participant. A number of techniques can be used to systematically fade response and stimulus prompts. These techniques are described in the following sections.

Fading of Response Prompts

Response prompts are usually not used individually but are incorporated within a sequence of response prompts. Response prompts differ in their capacity to evoke correct responding. Physical prompts are the most effective as they virtually ensure responding. Modeling and picture prompts would be the next effective because they involve demonstrations of the behavior to be performed. Verbal prompts would be the least effective as they require the participant to be able to perform the skill when verbally requested. Response prompts can be presented in a least-to-most effective or most-to-least effective sequence when teaching new skills.

Least-to-most prompting is a prompt fading sequence that has been used to teach a large variety of skills. The participant is given the opportunity to perform a response with a minimum amount of assistance during each training trial. If the participant does not respond appropriately with minimal assistance, then more intrusive response prompts are systematically introduced. Typically, the natural discriminative stimulus for the response is presented. The participant is given a predetermined period of time (usually a number of seconds) to perform the response. If the response does not occur or the participant begins to make an incorrect response during this time period then the least intrusive response prompt is implemented (e.g., direct verbal prompt). Again, the participant is given the predetermined interval to respond correctly. If the participant does not respond or begins to respond incorrectly then the next most intrusive prompt is delivered (e.g., modeling prompt). The least intrusive prompt (e.g., verbal prompt) is almost always paired with the more intrusive prompts during instruction (e.g., physical prompt). This is done in order to pair the least intrusive prompt with correct responding and reinforcement so that it will eventually control the targeted response.

Richman, Reiss, Bauman, and Bailey (1984) used a least-to-most instructional strategy to teach menstrual care to women with moderate and severe intellectual disabilities. A series of task analyses were initially developed for menstrual care (see Table 9.1). Each step of this task analysis was taught using a least-to-most prompt sequence. The prompting hierarchy consisted of direct verbal, model, and physical guidance. For instance, a direct verbal prompt would consist of the therapist stating that particular step of the task analysis (e.g., "Pull down your underwear and sit on the toilet."). A latency of 5 seconds was used between the presentation of the natural discriminative stimulus for each step of the task analysis and the first response prompt. The authors noted that participants responded appropriately with direct verbal prompts throughout the study. Model or physical prompts were not necessary to evoke behavior. The intervention was evaluated using a multiple baseline design across participants. The results indicated that the training package was successful in teaching the skills and the women continued to perform the skills during naturally occurring menses up to five months following termination of the intervention.

Most-to-least prompt sequences employ the alternative logic to the least-to-most prompt strategy. With most-to-least prompts the most intrusive prompt

Table 9.1 *Task Analysis for Changing Underwear (Richman, Reiss, Bauman, & Bailey, 1984).*

1. Client walks into bathroom and closes the door.
2. Pulls down underwear below knees and sits on toilet.
3. Pulls up underwear and outerclothes.
4. Walks out of bathroom.
5. Obtains box containing underwear, sanitary napkin, plastic bag, and paper bag.
6. Walks into bathroom and closes door.
7. Washes complete surface of hands and fingers with soap and water so no dirt or residue remains visible on area, dries, throws paper towel in trash.
8. Brings box to stall, pulls down underwear below knees and sits on toilet.
9. Removes soiled underwear.
10. Places soiled underwear in plastic bag.
11. Wipes vaginal area at least once to remove residual blood and drops paper in toilet.
12. Puts on clean pair of underwear.
13. Pulls tab off clean sanitary napkin.
14. Disposes of strip in trashcan.
15. Fastens sticky side of sanitary napkin lengthwise in underwear and presses into place.
16. Pulls up underwear and outerclothes.
17. Flushes toilet.
18. Washes hands as in Step 7.
19. Exits bathroom putting soiled underwear in laundry bag and plastic bag in trash.
20. Places box in bedroom cabinet for storage.

is employed initially, gradually faded to the least intrusive prompt, and eventually to the natural discriminative stimulus. Many most-to-least procedures that have been reported begin with a physical prompt (Wolery & Gast, 1984). The participant is physically guided through the response sequence for a predetermined number of trials. The natural discriminative stimuli are always present during training trials. Following physical prompts the participant may be shadowed (i.e., next most intrusive response prompt) by the therapist through the response sequence. If the participant begins to err or does not respond for a predetermined time period on a particular response then the therapist can intervene with the previous prompt level (i.e., physical prompt) and complete that component of the response. Once the participant has performed the responses without error under the current prompt system for a predetermined number of trials then the next level of less intrusive prompt is initiated. This procedure continues until the participant performs the behavior under the control of the natural discriminative stimuli.

The time delay instructional protocol differs from the most-to-least and least-to-most strategies in that the instructional prompt remains the same throughout training but the delay between presentation of the natural discriminative stimulus and the response prompt is gradually increased over time. During training, a response prompt that is capable of evoking the target response is initially selected. At the beginning of training the natural discriminative stimulus and the response prompt are delivered simultaneously (zero-second delay). This gives the participant the opportunity to respond without error. This format is continued for a predetermined number of response trials. Trials are then introduced in which the prompt is delayed. This gives the participant the opportunity to respond independently in the presence of the discriminative stimulus. If the participant does not respond or begins to err during this delay then the therapist prompts the appropriate response. Finally, all correct responses are reinforced. Figure 9.11 presents a very clever representation of this instructional protocol by Grant and Evans (1994).

There are two basic time delay procedures — progressive and constant delay. In a progressive time delay protocol the delay between the discriminative stimulus and the response prompt is made longer over trials. In a constant time delay program the delay remains the same throughout instructional trials. Once the participant continues to respond correctly prior to the prompt and in the presence of the discriminative stimulus then the prompting strategy can be removed.

Halle, Baer, and Spradlin (1981) used a time delay protocol to teach language skills to students with moderate and severe developmental disabilities. Prior to the intervention the authors observed classroom activities to identify natural situations across the day where appropriate verbal requests could be taught to these children. Table 9.2 presents a list of these classroom situations identified for Experiment 1 of the study. Each of these situations identify the natural discriminative stimuli and appropriate responses within the classroom. The teachers were then taught to use a time delay protocol to teach requesting in these classroom situations. When the natural discriminative stimulus occurred the teacher attended to the student

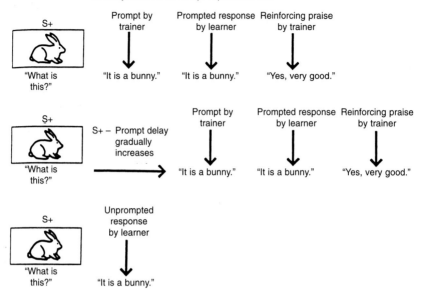

Figure 9.11 Delayed prompting. In delayed prompting at first the prompt "It is a bunny" is given immediately after the stimulus is presented. Gradually the delay is increased until the response "It is a bunny" comes to occur before the prompt is given, demonstrating transfer of stimulus control from prompt to S+ (Grant & Evans, 1994).

but did not interact for five seconds (5 seconds constant time delay). If the student made the appropriate request within the five seconds they could access the activity or item. If the student did not make the appropriate request within five seconds then the teacher modeled the request and the student imitated the request. The student then accessed the item or activity following the imitated request. This intervention was implemented in a multiple baseline design fashion across six students. The results of this study are presented in Figure 9.12. Prior to the intervention the teachers did not use the delay procedure and the students rarely engaged in any form of requesting. When the teachers were taught to use the time delay procedure there was a dramatic increase in the teachers use of the delay protocol, and in the student's use of requests.

Table 9.2 *Classroom Activities in which Language was Increased and Teaching Strategies Used (Halle, Baer, & Spradlin, 1981).*

Activities:	
Free Play.	Free play, the first activity of the day, was an unstructured time. Usually a teacher and an aide supervised the activity of four to six children. For free play, the children were taken to another room that contained games, puzzles, toys, and gross motor objects.
Snack Time.	Snacks were served in the regular classroom midway through the morning. The children were seated at two tables and the teachers and aides dispensed the snacks to the children. Usually three adults supervised about 11 children. Snack time also included a toileting routine and preparation for recess.
Lunch Time.	Lunch was served in the regular classroom at 11:30 a.m. under the same conditions that prevailed at Snack Time.

	Free Play	
Opportunity	*Baseline Conditions*	*Intervention*
Gross Motor Toys	Examples of these are scooter boards, trampolines, and very large plastic balls that children climb into. Teachers sometimes invited children to play on the gross motor toys; at other times children chose to play with them. Often when a child got in the large ball or stepped on the scooter board, the teacher spun the ball or pushed the scooter. No vocalizations were required and they rarely occurred.	As during baseline, the teacher approached the children when they were on a gross motor object. She would even put her hands on the object, but before she moved the object she delayed. Furthermore, often the teacher stopped the moving object and delayed again, waiting for a request like, "Spin" or "Push, please."

	Snack Time	
Juice	Teachers with a cup of juice in hand approached children, who were seated at the table and whose hands were raised. They dispensed this snack to the children in either of two ways: 1) by asking,	Teachers with juice in hand approached children whose hands were raised and delayed when they were in close proximity to a particular child. Anticipated responses were "Juice, please" or "I want juice."

continued

"What do you want?" and
when the children answered,
the juice was provided; or
2) by simply giving the
juice to the children with no
speech requirement.

Zip or Button	Before going out to recess, children often required assistance with zipping or buttoning their coats. The teachers provided the needed assistance with no contingency. Teachers sometimes observed the child's difficulty and at other times the teacher's attention was solicited by nonvocal means (e.g., the child approaching teacher and pointing to the zipper).	If a teacher observed a child in need of help or when a child cued a teacher, the teacher approached the child, kneeled down, and delayed. Sometimes a teacher grasped the two sides of the zipper and waited for a vocal request.
	Lunch Time	
Lunch	The lunch opportunity was the same as juice at Snack Time, except the teachers approached with an entire tray of food instead of one item.	The teachers delayed with the tray in hand waiting for a vocal initiation like "Lunch, please" or Tray, please."

Fading of Stimulus Prompts

Stimulus prompts can also be faded systematically. The goal of such procedures is to evoke the target response in the presence of the natural discriminative stimulus. In stimulus fading an exaggerated or highlighted dimension of the natural discriminative stimulus is systematically removed or included during training. In Figure 9.13 we see an example of stimulus fading in math education. In this example, the stimulus prompt is gradually faded out. Additional stimulus prompts are also often superimposed on the natural discriminative stimuli and faded during instruction. In other words,

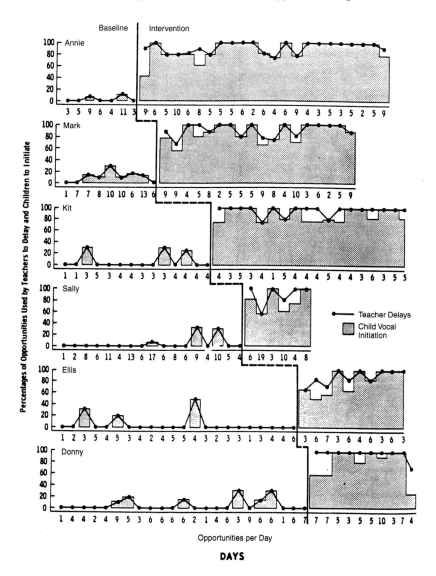

Figure 9.12   Daily percentages of opportunities used by teachers to delay and by children to initiate, before (baseline) and after (intervention) teachers programmed delays with each of the six children. Points connected by solid lines represent percentages of teacher delays; shaded areas represent percentages of child vocal initiations. Space between points and shaded area represent teacher delays during which children either did not vocalize or did not make an appropriate vocal initiation.   Numbers along abcissa represent number of daily opportunities or denominators used to calculate daily percentages (Halle, Baer, & Spradlin, 1981).

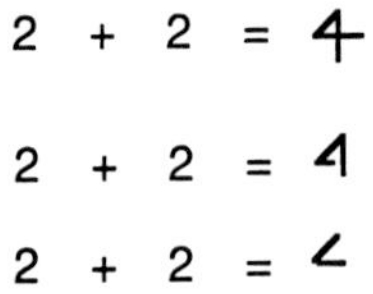

$$2 \ + \ 2 \ = \ 4$$

$$2 \ + \ 2 \ = \ 4$$

$$2 \ + \ 2 \ = \ 4$$

Figure 9.13   An example of stimulus fading in which the stimulus prompt is gradually faded out.

two specific classes of stimuli are used to prompt the target response. In one example of fading superimposed stimuli the extraneous stimuli are gradually faded out. We see an example of this in Figure 9.14.

Finally, stimulus shaping is a stimulus prompting strategy in which the topography of the stimulus is changed. Again, it is necessary to select an initial stimulus that will prompt the correct response. The shape of the

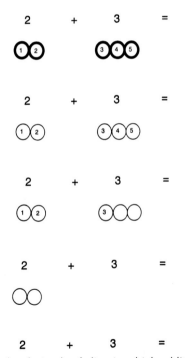

Figure 9.14   An example of stimulus fading in which additional stimulus prompts are superimposed on the natural discriminative stimuli and gradually faded during instruction.

stimulus prompt is then changed gradually so that the person continues to respond correctly. An example of stimulus shaping to teach word identification is presented in Figure 9.15.

9.9 SHAPING

Shaping involves the differential reinforcement of successive approximations to the final or goal response. As discussed in Chapter 2, this procedure is particularly valuable when the component behaviors of a target response are not currently in the repertoire of the individual. Shaping can also be used to increase a quantitative dimension of an already existing response. A shaping program is often implemented in combination with the various stimulus and response prompt strategies that have previously been outlined.

Shaping involves two basic processes. First, responses that resemble the final response, or include components of the final response, are reinforced by the therapist. Second, as responses occur that are more similar to the

Figure 9.15   An example of stimulus shaping to teach word identification.

target response these are reinforced while the original (less similar) responses are no longer reinforced. The process of reinforcing *successive approximations* to the target response while extinguishing earlier responses continues until the target response occurs. At this point in the intervention the target response alone is reinforced. Shaping is an important strategy for teaching behaviors that cannot easily be learned through the use of response and stimulus prompts alone.

Examples of shaping are common in everyday situations. For instance, when infants begin to babble this behavior is enthusiastically reinforced by parents. As time progresses the parents attend to vocalizations that more closely approximate words and now ignore babbling. Initially the tennis coach may prompt and reinforce merely getting the ball over the net with a novice. Over time the coach will eventually require appropriate stance and stroke from the student.

Shaping is a particularly effective applied strategy for developing social and language responses. For example, children with autism often do not possess rudimentary social or language skills. To develop eye contact with another person the therapist may begin by reinforcing general orientation of the child with autism towards the other person. The therapist may then reinforce facial orientation towards the other person. Eventually, the therapist will only reinforce eye contact with the other person. The final goal of the program may then be to shape eye contact over the period of an entire interaction with another person. Longer and longer periods of eye contact may therefore be reinforced. This particular example demonstrates the two uses of shaping. First, successive approximations to a final topography were shaped (i.e., general orientation, facial orientation, and finally making eye contact). Second, a quantitative dimension of the final topography was shaped (i.e, the duration of eye contact across an interaction was shaped).

In a now classic study, Isaacs, Thomas, and Goldiamond (1960) shaped verbal behavior in a person diagnosed with catatonic schizophrenia who had not spoken for nine years. Initially, any form of lip movement was reinforced by the therapist. Once this behavior was established then lip movement with sound emission was differentially reinforced. This was followed by differential reinforcement of vocalizations. Finally the patient received a reinforcer only after he verbally requested it. At this stage the patient began to converse with people. In another early example of shaping, Jackson and Wallace (1974) increased voice volume to appropriate levels for a young girl with developmental disabilities who was diagnosed as being severely withdrawn. During the intervention the girl was required to wear a microphone while speaking. Voice volume was automatically registered through the microphone. When the girl spoke at the targeted voice volume for that session she received token reinforcers which she exchanged for items following the session. The criterion voice volume for receipt of tokens was systematically increased across trials. The girl gradually increased her voice volume to normative levels. This is another example of a shaping program that was used to increase a quantitative dimension (in this case, volume) of an already existing response.

Shaping programs are sometimes difficult to develop and implement for a number of reasons. It is often difficult for the therapist to identify an initial behavior within the person's repertoire to begin the shaping process and thus move towards a new behavioral topography. The initial behavior selected should in some way be related to the terminal behavior. The previous example by Isaacs et al. (1960) clearly illustrates this. In this example lip movements were selected to begin the shaping process. Lip movements were selected because they were functionally related to the terminal response. Relatedly, the therapist should develop a clear operational definition of the target or terminal response (see Chapter 7 for guidelines on developing operational definitions of target behaviors). It is important for the therapist to know what behavior is to be shaped before selecting an initial behavior to begin the shaping process. Once the initial behavior is established, the therapist must further select a dimension of this initial target behavior that will be reinforced. The dimension to be reinforced must begin, in some way, to approximate the terminal target behavior more closely. Again, in the Isaacs et al. (1960) study, lip movements with verbalizations were then reinforced while lip movements alone were extinguished. These shaping steps to the terminal target behavior should be large enough to ensure efficient training but should not be so large as to be unattainable by the participant. If the next shaping step is too large the participant will begin to err in performance. If this occurs the therapist should re-establishing responding at an earlier step and then identify a smaller step towards the terminal target behavior for subsequent shaping. As mentioned earlier, response and stimulus prompts can be incorporated in to the shaping process in order to evoke initial behaviors to be shaped.

9.10 CHAINING

Chaining is a process whereby a series of discrete behaviors are linked together to achieve some reinforcing outcome. Many everyday tasks consist of a sequence or chain of several responses. The final response of this sequence produces some form of reinforcement and this reinforcement signals the end of the chain. Each discrete behavior in the chain acts as a conditioned reinforcer for the previous step and simultaneously acts as a discriminative stimulus for the upcoming step. (As noted in Chapter 2, a stimulus that is discriminative or predicts that responding will be reinforced also gains reinforcing value itself through pairing with a reinforcer.) For example, in brushing teeth, accessing the toothbrush and toothpaste is the first response, this acts as a discriminative stimulus for putting the toothpaste on the toothbrush, which in turn is a discriminative stimulus for brushing teeth. Brushing teeth is a discriminative stimulus for rinsing teeth, which is a discriminative stimulus for restoring the environment (i.e., putting away materials and turning off the faucet). Eventually, the stimulus-response chain ends in the desired outcome of clean teeth.

Chains can include few responses and can be accomplished over a relatively brief period of time, for example making and consuming a snack may take 30 minutes. Chains can also include a large number of responses and may be accomplished over an extended period of time. For example, the chain of behaviors involved in getting a university degree are typically accomplished over a number of years and involve such diverse behaviors as studying, attending classes, taking exams, working nights to fund university fees etc. In fact, this example could be conceptualized as a series of clusters of smaller chains (i.e., chains of behaviors are involved in studying and taking classes etc.) which are themselves chained together to form a larger chain. A chain is therefore often a valuable means by which to understand how a long series of complex responses are maintained in individuals.

The ability to identify and teach chains is an important skill for the behavior analyst. For example, when working with people with developmental disabilities, much of the effort of the behavior analyst involves developing and teaching curricula to promote independence. Daily-living skills such as grooming and meal preparation are broken down into teachable component behaviors. In other words, the first step of the teaching process is to develop a task analysis of the behaviors involved in the chain (for a description of how to develop a task analysis, see Chapter 7). The next step is to select prompting procedures and reinforcing consequences that will be used to teach each component behavior of the chain. Finally, the therapist must choose a strategy by which to link each discrete behavior together during training so that each behavior is a conditioned reinforcer for the previous response and a discriminative stimulus for the subsequent response. The strategies used to develop a behavioral chain during training include forward chaining, backward chaining and total task chaining.

In *forward chaining*, training begins with the first step of the task. Training continues on this first step until a predetermined criterion of responding is achieved. At this point the participant is then trained on the first and second steps of the chain. Once the training criterion is achieved with these two steps then the third step is included in training and so on. Each successive step trained involves cumulative practice on all previous steps. One of the advantages of forward chaining is that it involves massed practice of the earlier steps of the chain. The earlier links of a behavioral chain are often the first behaviors to begin to deteriorate following training. This phenomenon occurs because these early links are furthest removed from the reinforcement contingencies at the end of the chain.

In an example of forward chaining, Wilson, Reid, Phillips, and Burgio (1984) taught mealtime activities to four individuals with profound developmental disabilities. Mealtime activities were analyzed into three separate chains (pre-meal, meal, and post-meal), and these chains were eventually chained together. Each step of the chain was taught using physical guidance and reinforcers (edibles and praise) for correct responding. Once the participant demonstrated a step of the chain independently on two consecutive trials then the following step was added to the training sequence. Once the first chain (pre-meal skills) was mastered then the second chain (meal time) was introduced and so on. The results of this study are presented in Figure 9.16 and demonstrate that the forward chaining procedure produced maintenance of many of these skills following training.

When using a *backward chaining* procedure, the therapist begins with training the final step of the task sequence. Reinforcement is delivered once the participant performs the last step appropriately. When the participant achieves criterion responding on the final step of the task analysis then the second last step of the chain is added to the training. Once the last two steps of the chain are completed to criterion then the third last step is added to the training sequence and so on. All previously learned steps are cumulatively practiced during each training trial. Those steps of the chain

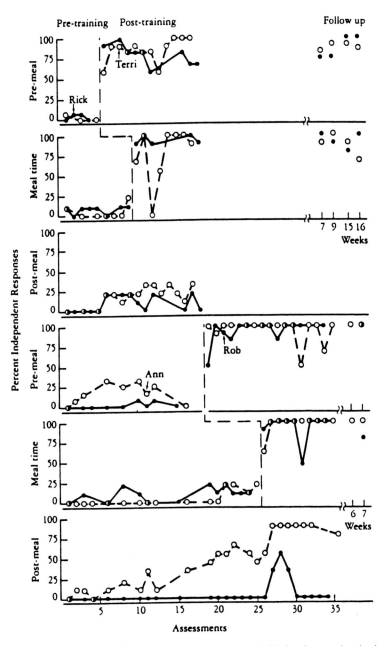

Figure 9.16 Percentage of independent mealtime skills for four individuals with profound developmental disabilities (Wilson, Reid, Phillips, & Burgio, 1984).

that are not being currently trained are completed by the therapist prior to each training trial.

Backward chaining protocols may be particularly useful for teaching skills to individuals who have difficulty maintaining extended periods of on-task behavior. Initial backward training trials are brief and end with the completion of the task. This allows the participant to escape the task and access the reinforcer almost immediately. As subsequent steps of the task are gradually added increased on-task behavior is shaped for the participant. O'Reilly (1995) used a backward chaining procedure as part of an intervention strategy to teach vocational skills to an individual with severe developmental disabilities who exhibited high rates of escape-maintained aggression. For example, when teaching floor sweeping, the therapist removed the brush and dust pan from the closet, swept the entire floor area, swept the materials into the dust pan, brought the dust pan to the trash can and emptied it. The therapist then taught the participant to complete the last step of the floor sweeping task (which was putting the sweeping materials back in to the closet) using a least-to most prompting procedure. When the participant successfully completed that step of the task he was allowed access to the reinforcer, which was to sit and listen to music for brief period of time. Once criterion was reached for the last step of the task, then the participant was taught to carry out the last two steps of the task, which were to empty the trash in to the trash can and then replace the cleaning materials. This intervention strategy resulted in increased levels of skill performance while aggression was almost totally eliminated.

With a *total task chaining* method, the participant is given the opportunity to perform each step of the task analysis during a training trial. The therapist initially selects a series of prompts and reinforcers for training. During training the task or chain is presented in the natural sequence in which the discrete behaviors are performed. Training continues until the participant is able to perform all steps of the task to a predetermined criterion. One of the major advantages of this chaining procedure is that the participant has the opportunity to practice the entire sequence of responding during each training trial. This may promote more efficient mastery of the task (Spooner, 1984). One of the disadvantages of this procedure is that training trials may be more extended than with forward or backward chaining, as the participant must perform all steps of the task during each trial. This may be particularly true during early training trials when the participant may not be competent in the majority of steps of the chain. This becomes less and less of a problem as the participant's mastery increases over training trials.

In an example of a total task presentation procedure, Zencius, Davis, and Cuvo (1990) taught complex money management skills to rehabilitation clients. Clients were taught to: write checks (to receive cash and pay bills), make deposits (coins, currency, checks, and combinations) and reconcile checking account statements. Each of these units (e.g., write checks, make deposits) were developed into task analyses. The task analysis for making deposits is presented in Table 9.3. Participants were taught the skills with modeling, written instructions, and performance feedback. Participants received instruction on the steps of at least one entire task analysis (e.g., making deposits) during a training trial. This instructional protocol resulted in rapid acquisition of these complex behavioral chains for the participants.

9.11 TOPOGRAPHICAL CHANGES IN RESPONDING DURING EXTINCTION

As described in Chapter 3, one of the fundamental properties of the extinction process is that changes occur in the topography of the response when it is placed on extinction. A number of researchers have taken

Table 9.3 *Task Analysis for Completing Deposit Slips (Zencius, Davis, & Cuvo, 1990)*

1.	Endorse
2.	Fill in name
3.	Fill in account number
4.	Fill in day, month, and year
5.	Fill in currency
6.	Fill in coin
7.	Fill in check number and amount
8.	Fill in total
9.	Subtract cash received
10.	Fill in net deposit
11.	Record date in checkbook ledger
12.	Describe in ledger
13.	Record amount under deposit
14.	Record amount under balance
15.	Add amount to balance

advantage of this to teach variability in responding to individuals with limited behavioral repertoires. For example Lalli, Zanolli, and Wohn (1994) used an intervention strategy that included extinction plus reinforcement of novel topographies to teach variability in toy play to two children with mild intellectual disabilities. Participants were taught a limited number of play behaviors with a doll, stuffed animal, and airplane. During subsequent play sessions the therapist initially praised the existing play topography and then placed that topography on extinction. Novel topographies of toy play were then reinforced during the session. Praise had been identified as a reinforcer for toy play with both children prior to the intervention. This intervention resulted in the induction of untrained topographies for both children across the different toys. The cumulative number of untrained play topographies across the toys for both children are presented in Figure 9.17.

9.12 Programming Generalization of Newly Acquired Skills

Increasing or establishing new behaviors for individuals is a small victory if these gains do not maintain following the removal of intervention or are not

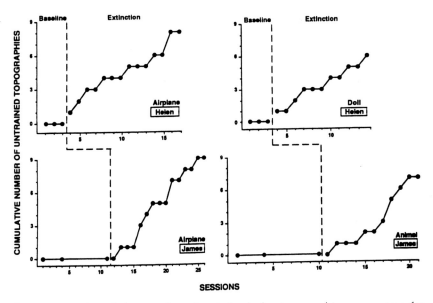

Figure 9.17   Cumulative number of untrained play topographies across toys for two children (Lalli, Zanolli, & Wohn, 1994).

performed in settings other than those settings in which they are taught. An effective behavioral intervention must therefore do more than change behavior, it must produce behavior that has generality. Baer, Wolf, and Risley (1968) describe behavior as having generality:

> ... *if it proves durable over time, if it appears in a wide variety of possible environments, or if it spreads to a wide variety of related behaviors. (p.96).*

It should be noted here that the description of generalization above differs somewhat from the definition of generalization outlined in Chapter 5. In the basic experimental paradigm, generalization can be defined as a lack of stimulus control over responding. In other words, discrimination training is an active process with generalization being no more than a demonstration of a lack of tight stimulus control. The applied definition of generalization is in some ways functionally different from the basic definition. Generalization in applied behavior analysis can be defined as:

> ... *the occurrence of relevant behavior under different, nontraining conditions (i.e., across subjects, settings, people, behaviors, and/or time) without the scheduling of the same events in those conditions as had been scheduled in the training conditions. Thus, generalization may be claimed when no extratraining manipulations are needed for extratraining changes; or may be claimed when some extra manipulations are necessary, but their cost or extent is clearly less than that of the direct intervention. Generalization will not be claimed when similar events are necessary for similar effects across conditions.* (Stokes & Baer, 1977; p. 350).

Stokes and Baer (1977) outlined a series of intervention strategies that could be incorporated into behavioral interventions to promote generalization of newly established behaviors across settings, persons, behaviors and time. These strategies for programming generalization continue to be researched and refined (Chandler, Lubeck, & Fowler, 1992; Horner, Dunlap, & Koegel, 1988). Some of these strategies include: introduction to natural maintaining contingencies; programming of common stimuli; training sufficient exemplars; and mediation of generalization.

Introduction to natural maintaining contingencies.

When selecting a behavior to teach or increase it is important to establish that this behavior will produce reinforcing consequences in the post-intervention environment. Behaviors that do not produce reinforcement outside of the intervention setting will not maintain once the intervention is removed. Baer and Wolf (1970) define the maintenance and generalization of such behaviors in terms of *trapping*. Once the behavior is established in the training setting and subsequently exposed to the natural maintaining contingencies, it becomes trapped by those natural contingencies. This strategy of programming generalization emphasizes the importance of selecting target behaviors prior to intervention that will produce reinforcement for the individual (see Chapter 7). In some instances reinforcement may currently be unavailable or dormant in the post intervention environment. In such a situation the therapist may teach the participant to recruit reinforcement in that environment when participants have performed the target behavior. For example, Stokes, Fowler, and Baer (1978) taught preschool children appropriate classroom skills such as working consistently and quietly. In addition the researchers taught the children to evaluate the quality of their work and to cue the teacher to deliver reinforcement for quality performance ("How is this work? Have I been working carefully?"). Selecting a target behavior that will result in reinforcement when the intervention is removed is of fundamental importance when developing any applied intervention program to teach new behavior.

Programming of common stimuli

Generalization to other settings is more likely to occur if salient discriminative stimuli that are present in the training setting are also present in the generalization settings. This can be accomplished by incorporating stimuli from the criterion environments (where generalization is expected to occur) in to the training environment. For example, O'Reilly and Glynn (1995) used peer confederates to train social skills to students who were diagnosed as socially withdrawn. Students were taught such classroom social skills as: to ask for help when unable to complete written exercises; to indicate to the teacher when they had completed exercises. Social skills training was conducted in a room removed from the classroom setting. Peer confederates were selected from the same classroom as the participants. These peers role-played the appropriate social skills with the participants during training. Peers were subsequently present in the classroom where participants were required to generalize the social skills. Peers therefore acted as a common stimulus between training and classroom generalization settings.

Training of sufficient exemplars

Another strategy to promote generalization of new responses is to train several examples of the response during the acquisition phase of training. For successful generalization to occur, the response topography must change as a function of changes in salient discriminative stimuli across settings (i.e., stimulus and response generalization). The therapist must therefore include a sufficient number of training examples during the training phase in order to expose the participant to the relevant response and stimulus variations that will be encountered in the natural environment. Prior to selection of training examples, the therapist must first identify those environments in which the target response will be expected to occur. The therapist must then identify the significant variations in the topography of the response that will need to be performed across these different settings. Finally, the therapist must identify those stimuli that will be discriminative for responding across the different environments. At this point the therapist can select a sub-group of teaching examples for training that sample the variety of response and stimulus variation in the natural environment. Training on this sub-group of examples should produce generalized responding to all untrained examples. This protocol for identifying the sufficient number of training examples to be used in training is described as *general case programming* (Horner, Sprague, & Wilcox, 1982). General case programming has proved to be an effective strategy for teaching generalized independent living skills such a vending machine usage to persons with severe disabilities (Sprague & Horner, 1984).

Mediation of generalization

Stokes and Baer (1977) describe the process of mediated generalization as "…….establishing a response as part of the learning that is likely to be used in other problems as well, and will constitute sufficient commonality between the original learning and the new problem to result in generalization." (p. 361). In other words, participants are taught a set of responses which are additional to the targeted skill, and these additional responses serve as discriminative stimuli to be used by participants across settings. One of the most frequently used mediation strategies is self-instructional training (Meichenbaum & Goodman, 1971). Self-instructional training typically involves teaching the participant to verbally state the required response, perform that response, and finally acknowledge to themselves that they have performed the response. These instructions can therefore act as a salient common stimulus that can be used in any generalization setting once taught in the training setting. In a recent example of self-instructional training, Hughes, Harmer, Killian, and Niarhos (1995) used a combination of multiple-exemplar training and self-instructional training to teach generalized conversational skills to high school students with developmental disabilities. Four participants were taught to initiate conversations and to respond to initiations from others. These initiations and responses were trained across multiple school settings and with multiple peers. In addition, participants were taught a series of self-instructional statements to be used during social interactions. The self-instruction protocol consisted of four statements: (a) stating the problem ("I should talk"), stating the response ("I need to look and talk"), evaluating the response ("I talked"), and self-acknowledgement ("I did a good job"). All the participants used the self-instruction steps across school settings and novel social partners. The rate of social initiations per minute across training and generalization settings under baseline, training, and maintenance conditions are presented in Figure 9.18. The results demonstrate that participants engaged in few social interactions prior to training. All participants rapidly reached the range of expected levels of social initiation in training and generalization settings once the multiple-exemplar self-instruction training package was implemented. Treatment gains were maintained for up to eleven months for two of the participants.

The strategies discussed in this section provide examples of instructional protocols that can be incorporated during training in order to maximize generalization outcomes. Techniques to promote generalization of behavior over time (i.e., fade to intermittent reinforcement schedules; use generalized conditioned reinforcers) have also been discussed in various sections throughout this chapter. Finally, it is important to note that it is probably preferable to include as many strategies as possible to promote generalization of responding during training. Research findings suggest the more generalization strategies that are included in training the greater the chances of achieving generalized responding. A move to the routine use of multiple-exemplar training would be a major improvement in behavior analysis programs.

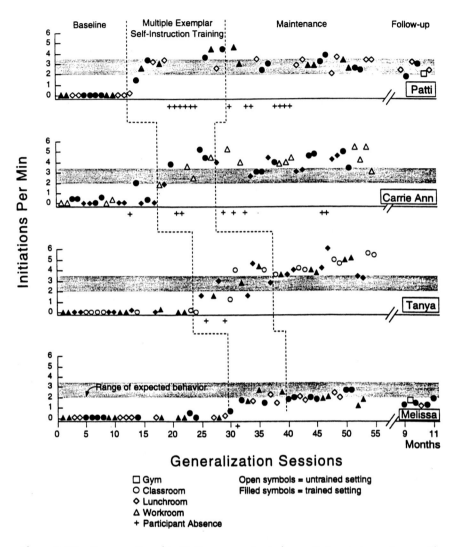

Figure 9.18 Conversational initiations per minute by participants to partners with and without disabilities across school settings. The banded areas in the graphs indicate range of expected performance based upon social comparison data (Hughes, Harmer, Killian, & Niarhos, 1995).

9.13 NEGATIVE REINFORCEMENT

Negative reinforcement is a principle of behavior that has received a significant amount of interest in the field of applied behavior analysis in recent years (Carr & Durand, 1985; Durand & Carr, 1991). Negative reinforcement is defined as an increase in the probability of responding contingent on the withdrawal, prevention, or removal of stimulation (as discussed in Chapter 5, and see Hineline, 1977; Iwata, 1987). Behaviors that prevent stimulation are typically described as avoidance behaviors as they prevent the person from coming in to contact with the stimuli. Behaviors that remove ongoing stimulation are typically described as escape behaviors as they allow the person to escape ongoing stimulation. Implied in this definition is that the potential or ongoing stimulation is aversive, and that the person engages in the behavior to avoid or escape aversive stimulation.

As discussed in Chapter 5, many everyday behaviors may be maintained by negative reinforcement. Opening an umbrella reduces the probability of getting wet. Performing the tasks required of a job reduces the probability of being fired. Brushing and getting your teeth checked regularly reduces the probability of a toothache. These examples do not preclude the possibility that positively reinforcing contingencies also exist in such situations (for example, a person may brush their teeth because they often receive positive comments from others about what beautiful teeth they have). The question as to whether a behavior is positively or negatively reinforced in any particular situation is ultimately an empirical one which functional analysis, as described in Chapter 7, may reveal.

Many aberrant behaviors such as self-injury and aggression are maintained by negative reinforcing contingencies. In a recent epidemiological analysis of the contingencies maintaining SIB in persons with developmental disabilities, Iwata et al. (1994) demonstrated that negative reinforcement was implicated for the majority of cases assessed. When negative reinforcing contingencies maintain such aberrant behavior the therapist may select to teach the person a socially appropriate alternative behavior that can access the same reinforcing contingencies. For example, if the person engages in aggression in order to escape a work task, this person may be taught to ask for a break (alternative response). In other words the person is taught a functionally equivalent appropriate behavior to access the same consequences (see the account of differential reinforcement of functionally equivalent behavior earlier in Section 9.6). The alternative appropriate response now becomes part of the same functional response class as the aberrant behavior (because both aberrant and appropriate behaviors lead to the same consequence).

When teaching alternative behaviors, it is important for the therapist to recognize that such behaviors must be more efficient than the existing aberrant behaviors for accessing the desired consequences. The alternative response must produce the desired consequence more immediately than the existing response. The alternative response must also take less effort on the part of the participant to perform than the existing response. If the alternative response is not more efficient than the existing response then the alternative response will fail to maintain over time (Horner & Day, 1991). This recent work on the treatment of negatively reinforced aberrant behavior again highlights the advantages of using pre-intervention functional analyses to identify maintaining contingencies. In these situations the maintaining contingencies can be used to increase appropriate alternative behaviors.

9.14 OVERALL SUMMARY

A summary of the wealth of strategies available to the behavior analyst to increase appropriate responding in applied settings has been outlined in this chapter. The behavior analyst is typically required to increase behavior that is already in the repertoire of an individual, or to establish new behavior for an individual. Interventions based on the principles of positive reinforcement are the most frequently used protocols. Prior to implementing an intervention based on positive reinforcement it is important to identify consequences that are of reinforcing value for a participant. Reinforcers can be identified through interview, observation, or systematically with preference and choice assessment protocol. Reinforcement programs can also be made more effective by such factors as: taking advantage of natural levels of deprivation for a reinforcer during training sessions; reinforcing immediately; using a rich schedule of reinforcement initially to establish new behaviors and then gradually thinning the schedule of reinforcement to ensure maintenance of responding; and using generalized conditioned reinforcers whenever possible.

Reinforcement strategies can also be used to decrease maladaptive behavior. These techniques are typically described as differential reinforcement strategies because selected responses or levels of responding are reinforced while other behaviors are placed on extinction. Before selecting one of these techniques it is essential to conduct a functional analysis of the maladaptive behavior. A functional analysis identifies the contingencies maintaining the maladaptive behavior. This allows the therapist to withhold the reinforcers for the maladaptive behavior and make them contingent on alternative adaptive behaviors.

Behavioral strategies can also be used to establish new behaviors for an individual. These strategies can be used to develop specific individual skills or complex sequences of skills. A variety of stimulus and response prompting strategies are typically employed to evoke the target response. These prompting strategies are systematically faded to produce responding under the control of the natural discriminative stimuli. New behaviors can also be developed or shaped through differential reinforcement of successive approximations to the targeted response. Chaining is a process whereby a complex series of discrete skills are linked together in order to achieve a reinforcing outcome. Chaining involves the teaching of a new and often complex sequence of behaviors.

Generalization of behavior does not occur automatically. It must be actively programmed during training. An applied behavioral intervention cannot be deemed successful unless it produces meaningful change outside of the intervention context for an extended period of time. Applied behavior analysts have identified several strategies that produce generalized responding for participants. As many of these techniques as possible should be incorporated in to a training program.

Many behaviors in everyday settings are maintained by negative reinforcement contingencies. Recent applied research has focused on aberrant behaviors that are maintained by such contingencies. Many of these applied intervention techniques for escape-maintained aberrant behavior take advantage of the maintaining contingencies to teach socially appropriate, functionally equivalent, escape behaviors.

CHAPTER **10**

DECREASING MALADAPTIVE BEHAVIOR IN APPLIED SETTINGS

In many applied and clinical situations the behavior analyst is faced with the task of decreasing behaviors that may be maladaptive for the client. In such situations there should of course be a very clear rationale for the need to reduce behaviors. Maladaptive behaviors may be generally defined as behaviors that result in some form of negative outcome for the person or for others. For example, a child's aggression towards other classroom students may result in physical harm to those students, or harm to the aggressive child through retaliation. The aggressive child might also be removed from the classroom setting, thereby losing access to appropriate educational opportunities. Again, the behavior analyst must conduct a rigorous assessment of the function of the behavior and establish a firm rationale for reducing such behavior prior to any intervention (see Chapter 7).

It is rare to see behavior change programs that are designed exclusively to reduce maladaptive behaviors. Typically, interventions consist of a combination of strategies designed to decrease maladaptive responding while simultaneously increasing appropriate responding. Many of these strategies were described in Chapter 9. These programs ideally consist of a three-stage process. This includes: a) a functional analysis to identify the maintaining contingencies; b) elimination of those maintaining contingencies for the aberrant behavior (through extinction); and c) presentation of the reinforcer that previously maintained the aberrant behavior, but is now contingent upon appropriate alternative behaviors (Reichle & Wacker, 1993). Such programs thus include the use of positive reinforcement to enhance appropriate behavior. However, in some situations it may simply not be possible to use this three-stage process to develop interventions to reduce maladaptive behavior. For example, in some cases a functional analysis may not be successful in revealing maintaining contingencies, and if these contingencies remain unknown then it is technically impossible to place the behavior on extinction. In such circumstances, punishment strategies may be required to achieve behavior change (Lerman, Iwata, Shore, & DeLeon, 1997). In other circumstances, although the function of the maladaptive behavior is clear, it may not be possible or desirable to replace the maladaptive behavior with alternative behaviors. For example, if a child's night time wakings are maintained by parent attention (that is, the parent enters the child's bedroom and comforts the child when crying begins or continues), then the intervention of choice may be to place the child's crying on extinction (that is, the parent should no longer enter the child's bedroom contingent upon crying). In this situation it would not be appropriate to replace the child's crying with a functionally equivalent alternative behavior.

Because functional analysis combined with positive reinforcement strategies may not be sufficient to deal with all behavioral problems, it is important that the behavior analyst be familiar with behavioral techniques that can be used to reduce maladaptive behavior. Additionally, it is essential that the behavior analyst be familiar with the basic principles of behavior from which these technologies are derived. In Chapters 3 and 5, the fundamental properties of extinction and punishment as identified in basic research were described. While both extinction and punishment result in an overall reduction in responding, there are other characteristics of responding when behavior is either punished or placed on extinction (such as the extinction burst, or the possibility of avoidance behavior following the introduction of punishment). The behavior analyst must be aware of all characteristics of these behavior reduction strategies in order to implement such strategies efficiently and effectively.

In this chapter the use of extinction and punishment procedures in applied settings will be described. Some of the general ethical issues surrounding the use of these techniques (particularly the use of consequences that may be described as aversive in treatment strategies) were reviewed in Chapter 5, and specific issues are dealt with in the present chapter. In the final chapter, these issues will be related to the human rights of individuals in treatment. Suffice it to say at this point that aversive consequences should be considered as a treatment of last resort and only administered under strict guidelines.

10.1 DECREASING BEHAVIOR USING EXTINCTION

Extinction was defined in Chapter 3 as a procedure in which the contingency between the reinforcer and response is removed. The eventual outcome of this process is a reduction of the rate of the behavior towards its operant level. Other properties of behavior during the extinction process include topographical changes in responding, extinction bursts, extinction-induced aggression, and spontaneous recovery. We noted in Chapter 9 that researchers have taken advantage of topographical changes in responding under extinction conditions to teach novel behaviors, and the other behavioral effects of extinction will be discussed in this section.

As noted in Chapter 3, extinction can be accomplished in two ways. First, the reinforcer can be removed or eliminated completely. Second, the reinforcer can be delivered but in a noncontingent manner. While both of these procedures effectively extinguish behavior there may be distinct applied advantages for using noncontingent delivery of reinforcing stimuli rather than eliminating the reinforcer entirely in many instances. This will be discussed in detail later in this section. Obviously, for extinction to be effective, the reinforcer for the maladaptive behavior must be clearly identified prior to the intervention. Recent research has identified the importance of using functional analysis methodologies to identify the operant function of behavior prior to implementing extinction, and this research will be described in Section 10.2.

Extinction Burst

An extinction burst has been defined as a transitory increase in responding almost immediately after shift to an extinction procedure when reinforcers are no longer forthcoming for that response. This effect has been reported in several applied behavior analysis studies (for example, Iwata, Pace, Kalsher, Cowdery, & Cataldo, 1990). In an early example, Neisworth and Moore (1972) trained parents to ignore the asthmatic behavior of their child. In this particular example of extinction, the reinforcer was eliminated completely. The child's asthmatic behavior, which consisted of coughing, wheezing, and gasping, usually occurred in the evenings around bedtime. During the extinction procedure, the parents did not attend to his asthmatic attacks once the boy was put to bed. Additionally, the boy received a monetary reward contingent on reductions in asthmatic behavior. The duration of coughing and wheezing was measured once the child was placed in bed. The results of the intervention are displayed in Figure 10.1. The effectiveness of this intervention was evaluated using a reversal design. It is clear from the data that there is an immediate increase in the duration of asthmatic behavior once the intervention is implemented. Asthmatic behavior then decreases dramatically under the intervention condition. A return to baseline results in an increase in asthmatic behavior and once

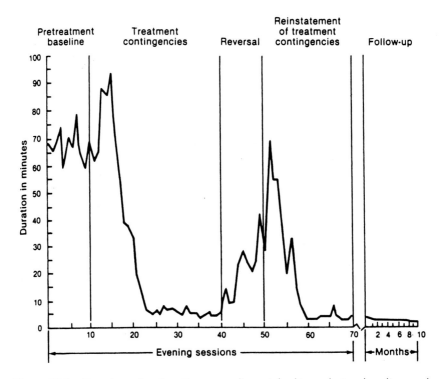

Figure 10.1 Duration of asthmatic responding at bedtime during baseline and extinction phases (Neisworth & Moore, 1972).

again we see an extinction burst when the intervention is applied for the second time. The second extinction phase also seems to demonstrate another fundamental property of extinction. In this second phase the extinction process is more rapid and contains fewer responses (see Chapter 3 for experimental studies of this effect). However, this additional interpretation of the second extinction phase must be viewed with caution, as the target behavior was not allowed to return to original baseline levels of responding in the second baseline phase. This illustrates an ethical concern often present in applied studies; in this case, considerations of the boy's health led to modification of the procedure used.

The occurrence of the extinction burst has been put forward as one of the major drawbacks for using extinction as a sole therapeutic intervention in applied contexts (see, for example, Kazdin, 1994). It may be difficult for staff or parents to tolerate an initial increase in responding no matter how benign the undesirable behavior might be. There would be obvious ethical problems with using extinction in cases where the behavior was of danger to the client or others. Additionally, parents or staff may interpret the increase in intensity of the behavior as a failure of the behavioral program and may therefore revert to reinforcing the behavior. This may in effect shape the targeted behavior into a more intense form of aberrant behavior. However, the extinction burst may not be as common as previously implied in introductory text books on applied behavior analysis (for example, Cooper, Heron, & Heward, 1987). In fact there are not large numbers of applied demonstrations of the extinction burst. Lerman and Iwata (1995) systemati- cally examined the prevalence of the extinction burst in a sample of 113 sets of extinction data. They found that increases in frequency of behavior when extinction was applied occurred in only 24% of the cases studied. In a subsequent analysis of the basic and applied research literature on extinction, Lerman and Iwata (1996) concluded that continued research is needed to directly examine the functional properties of the extinction burst.

It was noted in Chapter 3 that the extinction burst seems to be associated with one particular operation of extinction. The extinction burst seems to occur when the reinforcer is no longer available, and not under the alternative extinction operation where the contingency between the behavior and the reinforcer is broken but the reinforcer continues to be delivered in a noncontingent manner. In Chapter 9 we noted that the noncontingent delivery of reinforcing stimuli (NCR) can be an effective method to rapidly decrease aberrant behavior. During NCR interventions, reinforcement is typically delivered on a fixed-time schedule and is not influenced by the client's behavior. The formal definition of a *fixed-time schedule of reinforcement* is one in which the reinforcer is delivered after a fixed period of time, regardless of whether or not a response occurs, delivery of the reinforcer is thus not contingent on the behavior. It is instructive to compare the effects of eliminating the reinforcer for the target behavior (as demonstrated above in Neisworth & Moore, 1972) with delivering the reinforcer noncontingently. Figure 10.2 illustrates the effects of delivering attention noncontingently for self-injurious behavior that is maintained by attention (Vollmer, Iwata, Zarcone, Smith, & Mazaleski, 1993). Self-injury for Brenda consisted of banging her head on solid stationary objects and hitting her head with her fist. A functional analysis identified social attention as the maintaining contingency for self-injury. Attention was then delivered on a fixed time schedule. Self-injury was measured as number of responses per minute and NCR was evaluated using

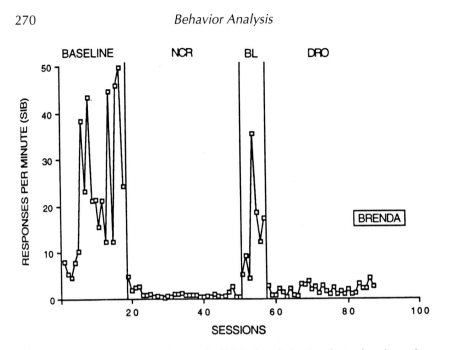

Figure 10.2 Responses per minute of self-injurious behavior during baseline when attention is delivered contingent on self-injurious behavior and during NCR intervention (phase 2 in the graph) when attention is delivered noncontingently (Vollmer, Iwata, Zarcone, Smith, & Mazaleski, 1993).

an ABAB design (with a DRO intervention implemented in the final B phase). The results of the NCR intervention demonstrate an almost immediate elimination of self-injurious behavior. No extinction burst or gradual reduction in self-injurious behavior occurred. Vollmer et al. (1993) subsequently hypothesized that NCR produces such dramatic reductions for two possible reasons. First, the contingency between responding and the reinforcer is removed (that is, extinction is in effect). Second, the person continues to have access to the reinforcer on a relatively rich (although noncontingent) schedule which may result in satiation. Noncontingent delivery of reinforcing stimuli may therefore act as a form of extinction and as an *abolishing operation*: while levels of deprivation can *establish* a stimulus as a reinforcer, or increase the power of a stimulus as a reinforcer, the opposite operation is also equally possible. Satiation with a stimulus can abolish that stimulus as a reinforcer, at least for the time being. In other words, a rich schedule of noncontingent delivery of a reinforcer may abolish that stimulus as a reinforcer, in addition to breaking the contingency between the response and the reinforcing stimulus. This provides two mechanisms by which the procedure can be effective in eliminating unwanted behavior, without creating any of the ethical problems that can arise when access to a highly-preferred reinforcer is restricted.

Gradual Reduction in Behavior and Spontaneous Recovery

The elimination of a reinforcer for a behavior often results in a gradual decrease in responding until the behavior ceases to occur. The rate of this gradual reduction in responding can be attributed to prior history of reinforcement for that response. There is ample basic research to demonstrate that intermittent schedules of reinforcement can increase resistance to extinction (Mackintosh, 1974, and see Chapter 3). However, little systematic applied research has demonstrated a functional relationship between history of conditioning and resistance to extinction (see Lerman & Iwata, 1996, for a review of relevant studies).

In applied studies, this gradual reduction in responding may be particularly problematic when the target behavior is dangerous to self and others. Additionally, many aberrant behaviors may have a long history of intermittent reinforcement prior to the application of extinction. This may result in persistence of responding under extinction conditions. In an early and often-cited example of the use of an extinction protocol with severe aberrant behavior, Lovaas and Simmons (1969) systematically removed all attention contingent upon head-banging for a child with severe disabilities. Extinction was the sole treatment used in this particular case. The child was placed alone in a room and was unobtrusively observed over an extended period of time. The authors concluded that extinction eventually occurred but only after an extensive amount of self-injury had occurred.

To allow a child to engage in such destructive behavior for extended time periods is generally agreed to be inappropriate, and this study is sometimes used as an example to caution therapists against using extinction as a sole intervention with such behavior disorders. It is important for behavior analysts to consider the results of basic and applied research which demonstrates this gradual reduction in responding during extinction under more controlled experimental conditions. This phenomenon is readily demonstrated in the laboratory, as illustrated in Chapter 3, but has rarely been systematically observed in applied settings.

Another behavioral phenomenon associated with the process of eliminating reinforcement is that of spontaneous recovery. As noted in Chapter 3, spontaneous recovery means that there is a temporary reemergence of the behavior under the extinction condition. Under experimental conditions, the recovery of responding is typically not as strong as original responding prior to the extinction program. The danger with spontaneous recovery during applied interventions is that the behavior may be unwittingly reinforced by those caregivers who are implementing the extinction program. Reinforcement during spontaneous recovery could place the behavior on an intermittent schedule of reinforcement and thus make it more difficult to eliminate.

Spontaneous recovery is clearly illustrated in an applied intervention to decrease nighttime waking in young children through extinction (France & Hudson, 1990). Nighttime waking, which occurs with approximately 20 percent of children, can cause severe disruption for parents. In this study the parents of seven children were trained to ignore nighttime wakings. Nighttime waking was operationally defined as sustained noise for more than 1 minute from the onset of sleep until an agreed upon waking time for the child the next morning. The effectiveness of the intervention was examined using a multiple baseline design across children (see Figure 10.3). The frequency of night wakings each week was plotted during baseline, intervention, and follow up assessments. These results clearly illustrate gradual decreases in the frequency of night wakings once the intervention was implemented. Additionally, there are clear instances of spontaneous recovery with all children during the intervention phase.

Extinction-Induced Aggression

One of the most frequently described side effects of placing behavior on extinction is the occurrence of extinction-induced aggression. Breaking the contingency between behavior and reinforcement seems to constitute an aversive event which results in aggression and other forms of agitated behavior (Lerman & Iwata, 1996), and there is ample evidence from experimental studies to document this effect (see Chapter 3).

The occurrence of aggression under extinction conditions is sometimes cited as one of the reasons for not recommending the use of extinction as the sole treatment in applied settings (e.g., LaVigna & Donnellan. 1986). Unfortunately, little applied research to date has documented such side effects of extinction. In fact, some studies have shown that such agitated

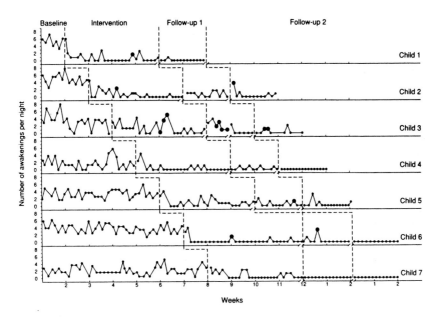

Figure 10.3 Frequency of night wakings for seven children under an extinction intervention. The large solid dots represent nights in which the infant was ill. Some level of spontaneous recovery is evident with all children (France & Hudson, 1990).

side effects may not occur in many cases where extinction is applied. For example, Iwata, Pace, Kalsher, Cowdery, and Cataldo (1990) examined the influence of extinction on self-injurious behavior that produced escape from tasks for seven individuals with developmental disabilities. Extinction consisted of not allowing participants to escape from demanding situations contingent upon self-injurious behavior; a procedure which is commonly described as *escape extinction*. Iwata et al. (1990) found that brief extinction bursts occurred, but no agitated side effects were reported.

This is not to say that extinction-induced aggression has not been reported in applied research. For example, Goh and Iwata (1994) carried out a rigorous assessment of extinction-induced aggression for a man with severe disabilities who engaged in self-injurious behavior in order to escape from demanding tasks. During the extinction condition, self-injurious behavior did not result in escape from tasks. An evaluation of the escape extinction intervention was conducted using a withdrawal design (see Figure 10.4). In the baseline phases of the design, self-injurious behavior produced escape from demanding tasks. In addition to examining self-injurious behavior under baseline and extinction conditions, the authors also examined aggression under these experimental conditions (aggression is plotted separately in Figure 10.4). This data set demonstrates some of the fundamental properties of extinction such as the extinction burst, a gradual reduction of behavior during extinction, and a more rapid extinction process during the second application of extinction. Additionally, the presence of aggression is also clearly documented when the extinction process is implemented on both occasions.

Extinction-induced aggression seems to occur occasionally when extinction is implemented as the sole intervention. The applied behavior analyst should seriously consider the implications of such a possibility when planning to implement an extinction program. Those who will implement the program must be aware and prepared for the potential occurrence of aggression. If there was a potential danger of serious aggressive outbursts (for example, when working with an adult client with a history of aggressive behavior) then the use of extinction alone may not be a practical choice of treatment.

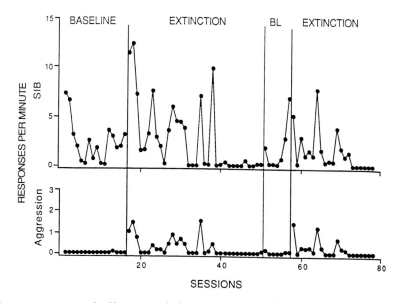

Figure 10.4 Rate of self-injurious behavior (upper panel) and aggressive responses (lower panel) for an individual under baseline and extinction intervention (Goh & Iwata, 1994).

Response Effort

It was noted in Chapter 3 that resistance to extinction can be influenced by the effortfulness of responding. If responding requires more physical effort during extinction, then extinction will occur more rapidly. While this phenomenon may have significant applied implications for enhancing the efficiency and effectiveness of interventions using extinction it has not received a significant amount of attention in the applied behavior analysis literature (Friman & Poling, 1995; Lerman & Iwata, 1996). Response effort has been systematically manipulated in several recent applied studies (Horner & Day, 1991; Shore, Iwata, DeLeon, Kahng, & Smith, 1997; Van Houten, 1993). During these studies extinction was not in effect for the target responses. However, an examination of the influence of response effort in some of these studies is instructive and may present avenues for future research involving the manipulation of effort under extinction conditions within applied contexts.

Van Houten (1993) evaluated the influence of an intervention which consisted of placing wrist weights (1.5 lbs each) on a boy who self-injured. The boy was diagnosed with severe developmental disabilities and engaged in high rates of face slapping. The effects of wrist weights on the number of self-injurious face slaps were initially evaluated using a withdrawal design (See Figure 10.5). The wrist weight condition eliminated face slapping.

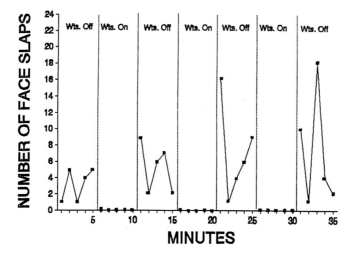

Figure 10.5   The number of face slaps per minute when wrist weights were on and when they were off (Van Houten, 1993).

Additionally, Van Houten (1993) also reported that the boy continued to engage in adaptive toy play under the wrist weight condition. Wrist weights therefore eliminated self-injurious behavior (SIB) but did not interfere with adaptive behavior for the boy. These results seem to indicate that the wrist weights eliminated hand-to-head SIB by increasing the effortfulness of responding.

Shore et al. (1997) examined the influence of response effort on reinforcer substitutability for three individuals with SIB. Functional analyses prior to the intervention indicated that SIB appeared to be maintained by automatic reinforcement for all three individuals. Following the functional analysis a preference assessment (see Chapter 9 for a description of preference assessment protocol) was conducted to identify highly preferred leisure stimuli for these individuals (i.e, vibrating massager, plastic rings, and a small plastic tube). The effortfulness of manipulating these preferred stimuli was then systematically evaluated and the results of this evaluation are presented in Figure 10.6. When the leisure materials were not available then all three individuals engaged in high levels of SIB (see baseline phase of each graph). When the participants had free access to the leisure materials (phase 2 of the graphs) then SIB was almost completely eliminated and all participants engaged in high levels of manipulation of the leisure materials (described as object manipulation in the graphs). The leisure objects were then secured by a piece of string to a work top or table. The effortfulness of responding or accessing the leisure materials (i.e., by bending over the table) was systematically examined by varying the length of string. The remaining phases of the graphs illustrate the influence of varying the length of string and thereby the effortfulness of manipulating the leisure objects. Overall, the results demonstrate that as the effortfulness of manipulating the leisure objects increased there were decreases in object manipulation with corresponding increases in SIB.

Both of these research examples demonstrate that effortfulness is a potentially important variable to examine in applied settings. These studies showed that increases in response effort could eliminate SIB (Van Houten, 1993) and result in changes in response allocation (Shore et al., 1997). To date, no study has examined the influence of changes in response effort for behavior that is placed on extinction in applied settings. If increasing the effortfulness of responding can result in a more rapid reduction of behavior when extinction is in effect then the empirical examination of such techniques in applied contexts warrant scrutiny.

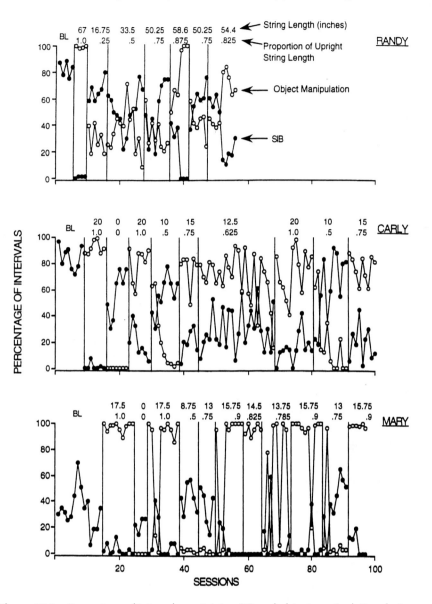

Figure 10.6   Percentage of intervals containing SIB and object manipulation during baseline (BL) and across effort (string-length) conditions for three participants. Numbers above each condition indicate length of the string attached to an object (top number) and proportion of string length while the participant was seated in an upright position (bottom number) (Shore, Iwata, DeLeon, Kahng, & Smith, 1997).

10.2 Matching Extinction Protocol to Maintaining Contingencies

For extinction to occur, the contingency between responding and reinforcement must be removed. One of the first important steps prior to implementing an extinction program is to identify what reinforcers are maintaining the targeted behavior. Functional assessment or analysis techniques should therefore be used prior to implementing an extinction program in order to identify maintaining contingencies. In fact, the extinction protocol used in a subsequent intervention will be determined by the function of the behavior to be extinguished. Many texts which discuss applied behavior analysis interventions have described the application of extinction in terms of ignoring the target behavior when it occurs (e.g., LaVigna & Donnellan, 1986). This implies that the behavior is maintained by attention from those who are doing the ignoring. We have already described several examples of extinction protocol with behavior maintained by social positive reinforcement (i.e., attention from others) and social negative reinforcement (i.e., escape from demanding instructional situations) earlier in this chapter. The extinction procedures described earlier in these studies differed depending on the functional properties of the behavior to be extinguished. For example, with behavior maintained by social positive reinforcement, the reinforcer was either removed (through ignoring occurrences of the behavior) or delivered noncontingently (on a fixed-time schedule). For behavior maintained by social negative reinforcement an escape extinction protocol was implemented whereby the individual was no longer allowed to escape from ongoing activities contingent upon the target behavior. Additionally, the contingency between the target behavior and escape can be broken by allowing the individual to escape from ongoing activities on a fixed-time schedule (Vollmer, Marcus, & Ringdahl, 1995). Extinction protocol can therefore differ dramatically depending on the maintaining contingency for the target behavior.

In fact, if the function of the target behavior is not identified prior to the intervention, the behavior analyst could unwittingly select an "extinction intervention" that may actually reinforce the behavior. For example, a student may leave his desk in order to escape instructional interactions with the teacher (i.e., the behavior is negatively reinforced by escape from tasks). The teacher typically admonishes the student when he leaves his desk at inappropriate times. The teacher might then infer that the student's inappropriate out of seat behavior is maintained by teacher attention (i.e., is positively reinforced by attention from the teacher). Under this false assumption the teacher may opt to place the behavior on extinction by ignoring out of seat behavior. In this particular situation the teacher's use of "extinction" may actually result in an increase in out of seat behavior. It would have been more appropriate for the teacher to implement an escape extinction protocol whereby the student was not allowed to escape ongoing academic activities.

In some instances of SIB with individuals with developmental disabilities the aberrant behavior may be maintained by automatic or sensory consequences. It is hypothesised that the self-injurious response directly produces the stimulation that acts as the reinforcer for responding with these individuals. Automatic reinforcement of SIB is usually concluded when levels of SIB are not sensitive to changes in social contingencies and/or SIB occurs when the individual is alone. Extinction interventions designed to eliminate behavior maintained by social positive or social negative reinforcement will have little effect on automatically reinforced responding. Extinction protocol for SIB that is automatically reinforced usually consists of techniques designed to eliminate stimulation that is directly produced by the response (Rincover, 1978). These extinction protocol are described as sensory extinction.

Iwata, Pace, Cowdery, and Miltenburger (1994) examined the influence of various extinction protocol on SIB (head hitting) that was maintained by automatic reinforcement for a boy with severe developmental disabilities. The results of this intervention are presented in Figure 10.7. A functional analysis initially demonstrated undifferentiated levels of SIB across attention, alone, play, and demand analogue analysis conditions (see the four baseline data sets in the figure). These analogue analysis results allowed for the conclusion that the behavior was maintained by automatic reinforcement. The effects of sensory extinction was then examined in the alone condition (see first leg of the graph). Sensory extinction was achieved by placing a padded seizure helmet on the boy for the entire length of the session or contingent upon episodes of SIB in a session. The sensory extinction protocol produced dramatic reductions in SIB . Next, the sensory extinction protocol were compared with an escape extinction protocol (see second leg of the design). Again sensory extinction produced reductions in SIB but escape extinction had no effect on responding. The sensory extinction protocol was then compared with planned ignoring of SIB (see third leg of the design). Ignoring SIB produced no effect whereas sensory extinction reduced SIB. These results are a rigorous demonstration of the

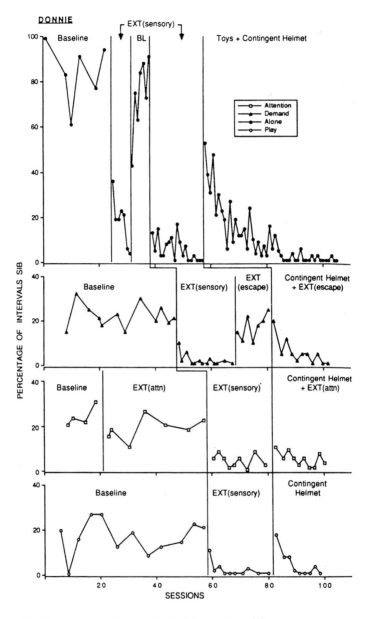

Figure 10.7 Percentage of intervals of SIB maintained by sensory consequences. Various hypothesized maintaining variables were removed (sensory extinction in panel 1, escape extinction in panel 2, and planned ignoring in panel 3 of the graph). The behavior decreased only in the sensory extinction condition (Iwata, Pace, Cowdery, & Miltenberger, 1994).

importance of matching extinction interventions to the function of the behavior. In this study the extinction strategies that were designed to eliminate behavior maintained by social negative reinforcement (i.e., escape extinction) and social positive reinforcement (i.e., ignoring) had no effect on the target behavior. The behavior only decreased under the sensory extinction (i.e., padded helmet) condition.

10.3 INTERIM SUMMARY: USING EXTINCTION IN APPLIED SETTINGS

Extinction is a process whereby the contingency between responding and reinforcement is broken. The ultimate outcome of this process is an elimination of the behavior. Extinction can be accomplished by removing the reinforcer or by delivering the reinforcer on a noncontingent basis. For extinction to be effective the behavior analyst must first identify the maintaining contingencies via a functional analysis. Extinction interventions vary depending on the function of the behavior to be extinguished. For example, behavior maintained by social positive reinforcement is placed on extinction by removing social reinforcement contingent upon performance of the behavior. Alternatively, behavior maintained by negative reinforcement is placed on extinction by eliminating escape contingent on performance of the behavior. There are many properties of the extinction process, such as extinction bursts, extinction-induced aggression, gradual reductions in behavior, and spontaneous recovery that the behavior analyst should consider prior to using extinction in an applied setting. Those who will implement the extinction program must be prepared for such issues as potential increases in the intensity of the behavior or the reemergence of the behavior at later points in time. If there is any concern that those who are targeted to implement the program may not be capable of doing so over extended periods of time, or if very rapid behavior change is required, then alternative intervention strategies should be considered.

10.4 PUNISHMENT

In Chapter 5 we outlined the basic properties of punishment as demonstrated by experimental research. In this section of the current chapter we will examine the use of punishment in applied settings. Punishment can be defined as the application or removal of a stimulus contingent on responding that decreases the probability of responding. As discussed in Chapter 5, it is important to remember that punishment is defined functionally in terms of changes in responding. Punishment in behavioral analysis is therefore very different from the way the term is used in everyday language. In everyday use punishment is typically equated with an aversive consequence for engaging or not engaging in an activity. For example, a student may be expelled from school for fighting, or a person may be fined or imprisoned for driving a car without insurance. The everyday use of the term punishment is therefore not defined in terms of its influence on responding. An aversive consequence is usually equated with causing some form of hurt or pain to the individual. In behavioral analysis a punishing stimulus does not necessarily have to cause pain. In fact, in some cases a painful stimulus can act as a reinforcer. For example, a spanking may increase and not decrease behavior. In this situation spanking would be defined as a reinforcing and not as a punishing consequence.

Painful stimuli as well as stimuli that do not cause physical discomfort can act as *punishers* in the behavioral sense and are sometimes used by behavior analysts to decrease aberrant behavior. It is important to recognize that punishment protocol should be the interventions of last resort for the behavior analyst. Punishment procedures should only be used in cases where less intrusive and positive alternatives (e.g., differential reinforcement strategies, functional equivalence training etc.) have been considered or tried and have failed to reduce the behavior. Additionally, it would be difficult to justify the use of many types of punishment techniques described below with behavior other than that which is dangerous to self or others (e.g. self-injurious or aggressive behavior). Punishment techniques should only be used in the context of an intensive intervention to increase appropriate alternative behaviors for an individual. As evidence of the importance and controversy surrounding the use of punishment techniques the National Institutes of Health (NIH) convened a consensus development conference to discuss the use of such techniques. This conference concluded that

> *"Behavior reductive procedures should be selected for their rapid effectiveness only if the exigencies of the clinical situation require such restrictive interventions and only after appropriate review. These interventions should only be used in the context of a comprehensive and individualized behavior enhancement treatment package."* (NIH, 1989, p. 13)

Today, punishment is often described as a form of default technology by behavior analysts (e.g., Iwata, 1994). In other words, punishment is the treatment of last resort and it is typically used only in cases where the function of the aberrant behavior has not been identified. In cases where a functional analysis can identify the maintaining contingencies for aberrant behavior then an intervention other than punishment may be most appropriate to eliminate the behavior. In situations where the maintaining consequences are identified the behavior analyst can withhold these consequences when aberrant behavior occurs and deliver the consequences contingent on appropriate alternative behavior. If maintaining contingencies for aberrant behavior cannot be identified through a functional analysis then it becomes impossible to withhold reinforcement contingent on aberrant responding. One treatment option may then be to override the maintaining reinforcement contingencies with a more powerful punishment contingency in order to eliminate aberrant responding. Again, punishment protocol should only be implemented in the context of a more general program to teach alternative appropriate responding to the individual.

10.5 PUNISHMENT TECHNIQUES

Punishment techniques can be divided into three general categories: The presentation of aversive events contingent on responding, which is described in this section; the removal of positive events contingent on responding, which is described in Section 10.6; and finally, there are a variety of punishment techniques that require the client to engage in activities contingent on performance of the target behavior, and these techniques are described in Section 10.7. With all these techniques, the events used can only be defined as punishers if their contingent application reduce the probability of the target behavior.

Contingent Presentation of Aversive Events

Aversive events can be divided into unconditioned or conditioned aversive events. Unconditioned aversive events are stimuli that by their nature are aversive to humans. The aversive properties of such stimuli are unconditioned or unlearned. Examples of unconditioned aversive events include electric shock, the smell of amonia, and loud noise. Conditioned aversive events are stimuli that have acquired aversive properties through pairing or association with unconditioned aversive stimuli or other conditioned aversive stimuli. For example, the verbal reprimands of a parent (e.g., "No!") to a child may become aversive through pairing with spanking or loss of privileges (such as TV time). The use of unconditioned and conditioned aversive events to reduce or eliminate maladaptive behavior has been examined by behavior analysts.

Electric shock has been used as a punishment technique in a small number of cases. The shock itself is typically of a very mild form and is delivered to the arm or leg. Shock has usually been restricted to the treatment of behaviors that are severely maladaptive or life-threatening. Alternative and less intrusive interventions have typically been tried and have failed in such cases (Linscheid, Iwata, Ricketts, Williams, & Griffin, 1990). Shock has been particularly successful in cases where life-threatening behavior is resistant to other forms of therapy. In fact shock can typically produce an almost immediate suppression of the target behavior. For example, electric shock has been found to be quite effective in treating chronic rumination or vomiting in infants (Cunningham & Linscheid, 1976; Linscheid & Cunningham, 1977). This is a life-threatening condition that can result in severe weight-loss and dangerous medical complications. Linscheid and Cunningham (1977), used electric shock to treat chronic vomiting (episodes of vomiting occurred on average over 100 times per day) in a 9-month-old child. A mild shock was applied to the child's leg at the onset of each vomiting episode. Vomiting was virtually eliminated after 3 days of treatment. Episodes of vomiting did not occur for up to 9 months following treatment.

Other unconditioned aversive stimuli have been used to treat dangerous or life-threatening behavior. Peine, Liu, Blakelock, Jenson, and Osborne (1991) examined the use of contingent water misting to reduce self-choking in an adult with severe developmental disabilities. This man engaged in self-choking to the point of syncope. Self-choking consisted of squeezing the neck region with either hand or forcefully twisting an item such as a towel or shirt around the neck. He aggressed towards staff if they attempted to redirect his behavior. The water misting procedure consisted of spraying the man in the face contingent on self-choking. A spray bottle which delivered 0.5cc of water (at room temperature) per application was used. This treatment produced rapid reduction of self-choking (see Figure 10.8). Additionally, the experimenters measured generalization of the

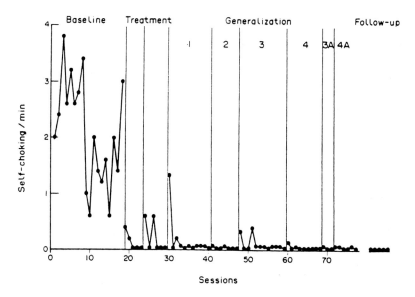

Figure 10.8 Rates of self-choking by a deaf-blind man with mental retardation before and during water mist treatment and its generalization and follow-up. The numbers in the generalization phases indicate different settings (Peine, Liu, Blakelock, Jenson, & Osborne, 1991).

treatment gains across multiple settings in the institution. As can be seen in Figure 10.8, the water misting procedure resulted in an elimination of self-choking across these settings. These treatment gains were maintained for up to 8 months as seen in the follow-up assessment phase of the figure.

One of the most frequently cited conditioned aversive stimuli used to reduce aberrant behavior is that of verbal reprimands (Kazdin, 1994). As mentioned earlier, verbal reprimands can become aversive stimuli through pairing with other conditioned or unconditioned aversive stimuli. Verbal reprimands do not necessarily act as aversive stimuli with all individuals or with the same individual in every context. In some instances verbal reprimands may act as reinforcers. For example, Iwata et al. (1994) demonstrated that contingent attention in the form of verbal reprimands can serve as a consequence that maintains aberrant behavior with many people with developmental disabilities. Whether verbal reprimands will act as reinforcing or punishing stimuli depends on the learning history of the individual.

When they do function as aversive stimuli, verbal reprimands can be an easy to implement and relatively benign way of reducing aberrant behavior.

It is important to realize that verbal reprimands, as used by behavior analysts, do not include hurtful statements or statements that ridicule. Verbal reprimands typically consist of telling an individual not to engage in a particular form of aberrant behavior. Additionally the individual is informed of the negative consequences for engaging in such behavior.

For example, Rolider and Van Houten (1984) examined the use of verbal reprimands to reduce the aggressive behavior (hitting, pinching etc.) of a 4-year-old girl towards a younger sibling (see Figure 10.9). An initial DRO procedure which consisted of positive physical attention (hugs and kisses from the mother) for every 15 minutes without aggressive behavior did not produce a reduction in aggressive behavior below the baseline assessment condition (see the figure). Finally, a DRO plus verbal reprimand intervention was implemented. The verbal reprimand condition consisted of holding the child by the shoulders, making eye contact, then telling the girl that she was hurting her sibling and that she was not to do this again. The DRO plus verbal reprimand intervention virtually eliminated aggressive behavior in the girl (see the final phase of the figure).

The individual delivering verbal reprimands is usually in close physical proximity, maintains eye contact with, and often physically holds the person being reprimanded. In fact verbal reprimands have been shown to be more

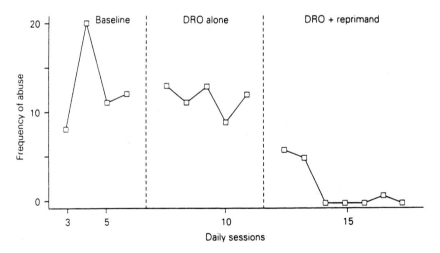

Figure 10.9   Frequency of aggressive behavior of a young girl towards her younger sibling under Baseline, DRO, and DRO plus verbal reprimand conditions. (Rolider & Van Houten, 1984).

effective in reducing behavior if they are delivered with these additional behaviors (Doleys, Wells, Hobbs, Roberts, & Cartelli, 1976; Van Houten, Nau, MacKenzie-Keating, Sameoto, & Colavecchia, 1982).

Considerations when using aversive consequences

Aversive consequences, when made contingent upon performance of aberrant behavior, can rapidly reduce that behavior. Aversive consequences can be either unconditioned (i.e., inherently aversive) or conditioned (i.e., learned) stimuli. Unconditioned aversive stimuli such as water misting or electric shock have been demonstrated to produce rapid and long lasting reductions with very severe behavior problems. When using conditioned aversive stimuli such as verbal reprimands it is important to establish that such stimuli are in fact aversive for the client concerned. Under those rare and extreme situations where aversive stimuli are selected for use they should be embedded within a more general behavioral program to increase adaptive responding in the client.

10.6 Contingent Removal of Positive Events

The removal of positive events contingent on responding can also be used to decrease maladaptive behavior. Two general techniques have typically been used by behavior analysts to remove positive events contingent on maladaptive responding. These techniques are called *time out* from positive reinforcement and *response cost*.

Time out from positive reinforcement consists of a series of protocols whereby the person is removed from all positively reinforcing events for a brief period of time. Time out can be either exclusionary or nonexclusionary. With *exclusionary time out* the person is removed from the current environment where the maladaptive behavior is occurring and placed in a barren room (usually termed a time out room) where no reinforcing items are available for a brief time period. Exclusionary time out is a particularly useful method with maladaptive behaviors such as tantrums and aggression as such behaviors can be disruptive to other individuals in the setting (for example, other students in a classroom). Once the brief time period has elapsed and the individual is observed not to be engaging in the aberrant behavior then they are allowed to return to the original activities.

The person should not be released from time out when they are engaging in the targeted maladaptive behavior. Otherwise the time out procedure may in fact reinforce or strengthen the target behavior (i.e., the person may learn to associate escape from time out with the maladaptive behavior). Brief rather than extended time periods in time out should be used. Brief periods in time out seem to be as effective as extended time out periods in reducing maladaptive behavior (Kazdin, 1994). Additionally, extended time out periods may interfere with ongoing educational or rehabilitative programming for the person.

An alternative to exclusionary time out is *non-exclusionary time out*. In non-exclusionary time out the individual remains in the setting where the aberrant behavior occurs. But the person does not have access to reinforcers in this setting for a brief period of time. Non exclusionary time out is typically a more acceptable time out procedure to professionals and parents because the person is not placed in isolation for a period of time. Additionally, the person has the opportunity to continue to observe educational activities while they are in the time out condition. One frequently cited form of non-exclusionary time out is called contingent observation. Porterfield, Herbert-Jackson, and Risley (1976) used contingent observation to reduce disruptive behaviors such as aggression and tantrums in a preschool classroom. Once targeted maladaptive behaviors occurred, staff removed the child away from toys and other children to a corner of the classroom. The child was told to remain in the corner and observe the other children playing appropriately. Staff then returned to the child after one minute and asked the child if they were ready to return to the group. If the child was not engaged in the maladaptive behavior (e.g., tantrums) and indicated that they wanted to return to the group then they were allowed to play again. This contingent observation technique was compared with a redirection intervention on disruptive behaviors in the classroom (see Figure 10.10). The redirection intervention consisted of redirecting the child's attention to another activity (such as another toy) when they engaged in disruptive behavior. The results of both of these interventions, as shown in Figure 10.10, demonstrated that contingent observation was a more effective technique in reducing overall levels of disruption and aggression for this preschool class.

In some situations non-exclusionary time out may not be the procedure of choice as some persons may attempt to escape from time out and return to ongoing activities. In such situations exclusionary time out may be considered as a back-up procedure (i.e., if a person escapes from non-

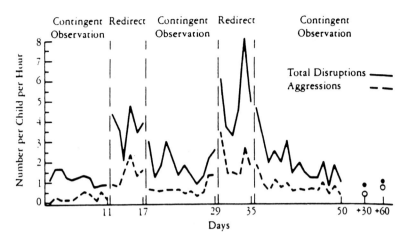

Figure 10.10 Number of disruptions and aggressive behaviors per child per hour for 50 days in a day care center with follow-up at 1 and 2 months (Porterfield, Herbert-Jackson, & Risley, 1976).

exclusionary time out then they may be placed in exclusionary time out). In order for any time out protocol to be maximally effective the person must have a rich "time in" environment. In other words the ongoing environment from which the person is removed should be highly reinforcing. The removal of reinforcers contingent on aberrant behavior to reduce that behavior can only occur if there are reinforcers in the person's environment. Again, this point highlights previous discussions in this and earlier chapters of the importance of using punishment programs only in the context of positive programming to teach adaptive skills to individuals.

In some cases, exclusionary and non-exclusionary time out will not be effective. This is particularly true for individuals whose aberrant behavior occurs independent of the social environment. For example, individuals with autism often engage in high rates of self-stimulatory behavior (e.g., hand flapping, body rocking) irrespective of the social environment. As such behavior seems to be automatically reinforced (i.e., the behavior produces its own reinforcement), time out does not remove the source of reinforcement. Rolider and Van Houten (1985) developed a form of time out technique, called movement suppression time out, which seems to be effective with such forms of automatically reinforced aberrant behavior. In one example these authors compared the effectiveness of movement suppression time out with a DRO intervention to reduce aberrant behavior in a 9-year-old boy who was diagnosed with autism. The boy engaged in arm biting which frequently broke the skin and mouthing inappropriate objects such as cloth and rocks which he sometimes swallowed. The DRO procedure consisted of reinforcing comments and hugs from his mother if he did not engage in these behaviors for 10 minutes. Movement suppression time out consisted of physically guiding the child to a corner of the room, positioning his chin against the corner of the wall with both hands behind his back and both feet together touching the wall. The child was not allowed to move for 3 minutes and was physically repositioned if he moved in any way. The results of the DRO and movement suppression time out interventions are displayed in Figure 10.11. As can be seen in the figure the DRO intervention had little effect on aberrant responding. The movement suppression procedure resulted in rapid elimination of both arm biting and mouthing. Movement suppression time out was implemented for an extended period of time (see the follow up phase of Figure 10.11) and aberrant behavior was eliminated during this period.

The effects of time out procedures may be determined by the context in which they are implemented. Under certain ongoing conditions which a person may find aversive a time out procedure may in fact reinforce

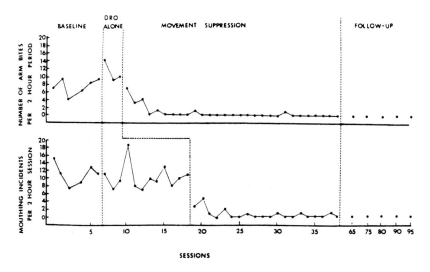

Figure 10.11 Number of arm bites (top panel) and mouthing incidents (bottom panel) under Baseline, DRO Alone, and Movement Suppression Time-Out. Follow-up observations on the target behaviors are also presented (Rolider & Van Houten, 1985).

maladaptive behavior because it allows the individual to escape from these ongoing events. Under such conditions a time out procedure will result in increases in maladaptive responding. Alternatively, during ongoing activities which the same person finds to be positive, the same time out procedure may act as a punisher. In this second condition the time out procedure will result in decreases in maladaptive responding. Haring and Kennedy (1990) demonstrated this influence of context on the effectiveness of time out protocol with a number of individuals. The effects of time out on aberrant responding under task and leisure conditions for one individual with developmental disabilities are displayed in Figure 10.12. The contextual influences on DRO protocol were also examined with this individual but will not be addressed in this discussion. The task condition involved identifying common items such as money and various foods

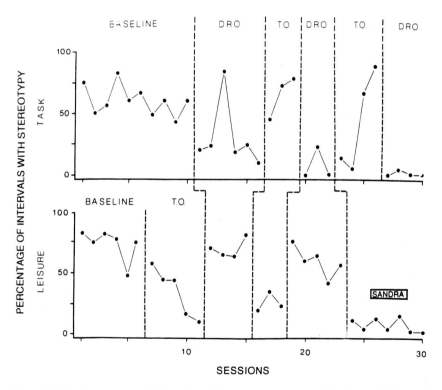

Figure 10.12 Percentage of intervals with stereotypy across Baseline, DRO, and Time-Out conditions in task (top panel) and leisure (bottom panel) contexts (Haring, & Kennedy, 1990).

during teaching trials. The leisure condition involved listening to the radio. The maladaptive behavior exhibited by this individual consisted of stereotyped responding. Time out under the task condition involved removing instruction contingent on stereotyped responding for a period of 15 seconds. Time out under the leisure condition consisted of removing the leisure items (turning the radio off) contingent on stereotyped behavior for a period of 15 seconds. The time out conditions under the task and leisure contexts were structurally identical (i.e., removal of items contingent on maladaptive behavior for 15 seconds). However, as can be seen in Figure 10.12, the time out intervention served a different function within the task and leisure contexts. Time out resulted in increases in stereotypy under the task condition and decreases in stereotypy in the leisure condition.

Response Cost

Response cost is another punishment technique which involves the removal of positive events or stimuli contingent on responding. We noted in Chapter 5 that this type of punishment can be shown to have reliable and orderly effects in experiments with adult humans. In applied contexts, response cost is a form of penalty that is imposed on the individual for engaging in a particular maladaptive behavior. This type of technique is readily recognizable to the general public (e.g., fines for late payment of domestic charges or for parking a car inappropriately etc.) and is viewed as an acceptable method to reduce maladaptive behaviors (Grant & Evans, 1994). Response cost differs from time out protocols in a number of ways. With response cost the reinforcer may be permanently withdrawn (as when somebody is fined for a traffic violation). In time out the reinforcers are withdrawn for a brief period of time. Additionally, with time out, all opportunities for reinforcement are removed for a period of time. Aside from a penalty, all other positive events continue to be available with a response cost intervention.

Response cost protocols are often used as part of a token economy system. In fact token economy systems that incorporate response cost components are more effective than either procedure if used alone (Bierman, Miller, & Stabb, 1987). Upper (1973) incorporated a response cost system as part of a token economy to increase adaptive responding of psychiatric patients in a hospital ward. Patients were fined for such behaviors as sleeping late, public undressing, and aggressive outbursts. The response cost protocol, when incorporated into the token economy system, resulted in dramatic reductions of these aberrant behaviors.

In many situations response cost procedures can be implemented alone. Rapport, Murphy and Bailey (1982) used a response cost system to decrease classroom disruption in two school children who were diagnosed with hyperactivity. For each episode of disruptive or inattentive behavior the child would lose 1 minute from their break time period. The contingent removal of time from break for disruptive behavior not only decreased aberrant behavior but also resulted in increases in academic performance.

Considerations when removing positive events

A number of behavioral techniques are designed to punish maladaptive behavior by removing positive stimuli contingent on responding. Time out from positive reinforcement describes a set of techniques which are designed to remove all positive consequences contingent on maladaptive responding for a brief period of time. Time out protocol can be exclusionary (where the person is removed from the environment) or non-exclusionary (where positive items are removed but the person remains in the environment where the maladaptive behavior occurred). Movement suppression time out is a recent technique designed to reduce maladaptive behavior such as some forms of stereotypy which are sometimes automatically reinforced. Alternatively, response cost procedures involve a penalty whereby some item (such as tokens) are permanently removed contingent on maladaptive behavior.

Overall, these procedures are more acceptable to the general public — that is they have greater social validity (see Chapter 5) — than the use of aversive consequences to reduce aberrant behavior. Time out procedures are generally effective if the person is removed from ongoing activities for a brief period of time (i.e., typically not more than several minutes). The person should not be allowed to escape from time out if they continue to engage in the aberrant behavior at the end of the time period. Instead the behavior analyst should wait until they desist in aberrant behavior and then release them from time out. If aberrant responding persists for extended time periods under time out conditions then alternative interventions should be considered. Time out is only effective as a punisher if the person is removed from activities that they find to be reinforcing. Time out may actually act as a reinforcer if the person is removed from ongoing aversive activities. Response cost procedures are often used within the context of a token economy system. Token economies which incorporate a response cost component are typically more effective than token economies which do not. Response cost procedures, when implemented alone, can also be very effective in reducing behavior.

10.7 Contingent Activity

A variety of punishment procedures employ the performance of activities contingent on maladaptive behavior. In other words the person must perform aversive activities after they engage in the targeted aberrant behavior. One of the most frequently described activity punishers is that of *overcorrection* (Foxx & Azrin, 1972; Foxx & Bechtel, 1983). Overcorrection typically consists of two components: *restitution* and *positive practice*. Initially the individual is required to restore any items in the environment that have been damaged as a result of the maladaptive behavior. For example, if an individual engaged in an aggressive outburst and overturned a chair then the individual would be required to replace the chair in its original position. The positive practice component involves repeated practice of a behavior that is an appropriate alternative to the maladaptive behavior. To continue with the overturned chair example, the individual might then be required to straighten all chairs in the room. In many situations the difference between restoring the environment and practicing appropriate alternative behaviors may be unclear. In the above example the restitution component (i.e., replacing the thrown chair) is in a sense a form of positive practice. Suffice it to say that overcorrection involves restoring the environment following the maladaptive behavior and then practicing appropriate alternative behaviors.

Merely restoring the environment (sometimes called simple correction) does not seem to act as a punisher when used without positive practice. For example, Azrin and Wesolowski (1974) compared a simple correction protocol with an overcorrection protocol to reduce theft among people with developmental disabilities in an institutional setting. In the simple correction condition the person was required to return the item that was stolen. As can be seen in Figure 10.13, this simple correction procedure did not eliminate theft in the setting. A positive practice component was then combined with the simple correction protocol. Positive practice involved purchasing an item similar to the stolen item and giving the purchased item to the victim. The simple correction procedure combined with positive practice (this is described as a theft reversal intervention in Figure 10.13)

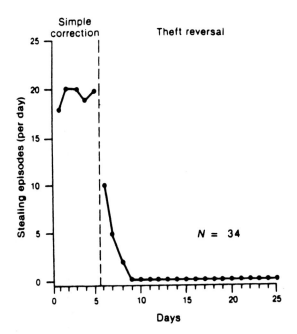

Figure 10.13 Number of stealing episodes each day for a group of 34 persons with developmental disabilities in an institutional setting. Frequent stealing occurred under the simple correction procedure (person was to return the stolen item). Stealing was eliminated in the overcorrection (theft reversal) phase (person returned the stolen item and gave the victim a further item of equal value) (Azrin & Wesolowski, 1974).

resulted in the elimination of stealing among the 34 individuals in the institutional setting. Other research has also demonstrated that restitution plus positive practice is more effective than restitution alone in reducing maladaptive behavior (e.g., Carey & Bucher, 1981).

In many cases the maladaptive behavior may not actually involve disruption or damage to the environment. For example, if a child engages in self-stimulatory behavior (such as hand flapping or body rocking) then little in the environment is altered. In such cases positive practice alone can be used. Contingent on the maladaptive behavior the child would be required to practice alternative appropriate behaviors. For example, Azrin and Powers (1975) required students who spoke out without permission in class to practice raising their hands and waiting for the teacher's permission to speak. Positive practice trials were conducted in the classroom during recess periods. The intervention markedly reduced classroom disruption with these children.

Overcorrection procedures may have some advantages over the other punishment protocol described thus far in this chapter (i.e., contingent presentation of aversive stimuli and contingent removal of positive events). The positive practice component of overcorrection protocol allows the individual to practice appropriate alternative behaviors. Overcorrection can therefore serve an educative as well as a punishing role. It also allows the therapist to focus on alternative appropriate behaviors rather than only focusing on reducing maladaptive responses. In some instances, however, overcorrection procedures may be difficult to implement. For example, if the individual is unwilling to follow through with restitution and positive practice the therapist may have to physically guide the person through the tasks. This may be particularly problematic with adults who may aggress in such situations. Also, implementing overcorrection protocol can be intensive and time consuming for the therapist. It would be difficult for a therapist to implement overcorrection protocol correctly in a situation where the therapist is simultaneously responsible for the supervision of other individuals.

Contingent exercise is another form of activity punisher that has been used to reduce maladaptive behavior. The individual is required to engage in some form of physical exercise following the targeted behavior. Contingent exercise differs from overcorrection in that the individual is not required to restore the environment nor is the individual required to practice appropriate alternative behaviors. Luce, Delquadri, and Hall (1980) used contingent exercise to reduce the aggression and disruption of two emotionally disturbed boys in a special education setting. Hitting other children was targeted for one child. The child was required to stand up and sit down on the floor 10 times contingent upon hitting another child. This brief contingent exercise markedly reduced the amount of hitting in the class (see Figure 10.14).

Considerations when using contingent activity

Activity punishers are typically described in terms of two general techniques: overcorrection and contingent exercise. With overcorrection the individual must restore any damage to the environment caused by the aberrant behavior and repeatedly practice appropriate alternative

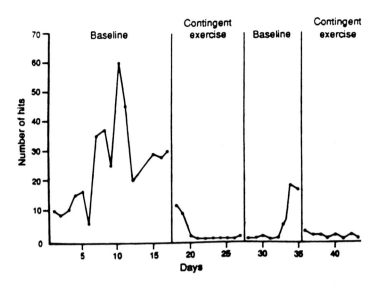

Figure 10.14 Number of hits per day during school period. During Baseline the hitting was ignored and no consequences were delivered. During the Contingent Exercise condition the child had to engage in stand up and sit down on the floor exercise contingent upon hitting (Luce, Delquadri, & Hall, 1980).

behaviors. Overcorrection is often viewed as a more acceptable punishment procedure than the contingent use of aversive stimuli because it includes an educative component (i.e., the person is required to perform appropriate alternative behaviors to the aberrant behaviors). Positive practice can be used effectively without restitution in situations where the aberrant behavior does not result in damage to the environment. Overcorrection may be difficult to implement in situations where the behavior analyst is required to supervise many individuals simultaneously. Additionally, overcorrection may not be the treatment of choice with individuals (especially adults) who are noncompliant and who may aggress to avoid such activity. Several studies have examined the use of contingent exercise as a punishment technique. While contingent exercise can reduce aberrant responding it does not include an educative component. As with overcorrection, contingent exercise may be difficult to implement when supervising groups and in cases where the individual may be noncompliant with regard to engaging in the exercise regimen.

10.8 ADVANTAGES AND DISADVANTAGES OF USING PUNISHMENT

Punishment protocol should be considered the intervention of last resort. As mentioned earlier, these techniques are best reserved for the treatment of behavior that is of danger to the person or others. Punishment is usually considered in situations where other less intrusive interventions (e.g., differential reinforcement strategies) have been tried and have failed to reduce maladaptive responding. Punishment interventions are not typically used in isolation but are combined with interventions to increase appropriate alternative behaviors. In addition to a knowledge of the various punishment techniques described in the previous sections, the behavior analyst should be aware of some of the advantages and disadvantages of using punishment protocols.

One of the major advantages of using punishment is that it can produce an almost immediate reduction or elimination of the maladaptive response. This is particularly true with unconditioned aversive stimuli such as electric shock (Linscheid, et al., 1990). In cases where unconditioned aversive stimuli are used the reduction in aberrant responding is often quite dramatic and the treatment gains generally last for extended periods of time after the intervention is removed. This effect on responding is generally true for the other types of punishment protocol described in this chapter. Aberrant behavior may however re-emerge following the removal of some punishment techniques. If punishment protocol do not produce the desired reduction in responding following several applications then alternative protocol should be considered. It is not appropriate to expose an individual to extended periods of aversive contingencies if these contingencies do not have the desired functional effect.

In addition to eliminating aberrant responding, punishment protocol may also result in positive side effects. For example, Rolider, Cummings, and Van Houten (1991) evaluated the effects of punishment on eye contact and academic performance for two individuals with developmental disabilities. Both individuals engaged in aggression and other forms of escape behavior during academic instruction. Punishment protocol used in this study included a form of restraint or movement suppression time out and contingent exercise. The effects of punishment on academic achievement and eye contact was evaluated across therapists — with one therapist delivering punishment during instructional trials while the other therapist did not. The results demonstrated greater levels of academic achievement and increased levels of eye contact during instructional trials with the therapist who delivered the punishment protocol. Matson and Taras (1989) provided an extensive review of the positive side effects which have been documented when using punishment protocol. For example, some of the positive side effects of electric shock to treat rumination have included weight gain, increased social behavior, decreased crying and tantrums, improved self-feeding, and overall increases in activity levels.

There are also several disadvantages associated with using punishment techniques in applied settings, many of which have already been alluded to in this chapter. The use of punishment techniques with humans, especially individuals with developmental disabilities who may be unable to give informed consent, has been the source of much public controversy in the last decade. Many parent support groups (e.g., The Association for Persons with Severe Handicaps) have taken stances against the use of punishment. Indeed several States in the United States have banned the use of punishment protocol in treatment. Much of this debate has been infused by a lack of understanding of the technical meaning of the term punishment in behavior analysis. Many of the position statements from non behavioral interest groups equate punishment with the more everyday usages of the term. Punishment is sometimes equated with such notions as cruelty, revenge, harm etc. While these debates may be devisive at times they do highlight the need to use punishment as a treatment of last resort, with very clear guidelines for its use, and within the context of a more general behavioral program to teach adaptive skills to the person. In the next and final chapter, we will relate these issues to the human rights of individuals in treatment.

Punishment procedures can also produce negative side effects. Many of these negative side effects have been reported with almost all types of punishment protocol. Emotional side effects include such behaviors as crying, tantrums, soiling, wetting, and general agitation. Many of these negative side effects occur when punishment protocol are first implemented and tend to decrease as the intervention is continued. It is important to note that these emotional side effects have been reported relatively infrequently in the literature. Interestingly, it is also commonly observed that in experimental studies with nonhuman animals, punishment does not persistent produce those behaviors classified as emotional.

Punishment has also been demonstrated to produce avoidance behavior in applied settings. Morris and Redd (1975) examined avoidance behavior in nursery school children. These children were supervised by men who (a) praised on-task behavior; (b) reprimanded off-task behavior; (c) praised on-task behavior and reprimanded off-task behavior; (d) ignored the behavior of the children. Children engaged in higher levels of on-task behavior with the men who reprimanded or who praised and reprimanded. When asked about which of the men they would like to play with the children chose the man who praised on-task behavior. The man who used reprimands only was ranked as the least preferred play companion. These results may highlight a more general problem with using punishment protocols in applied settings. Various neutral stimuli in an applied setting may become conditioned aversive stimuli through pairing with aversive protocols. The use of punishment with an individual could therefore result in many aspects of an environment such as a school setting becoming aversive for that individual. As we noted in Chapter 5, this would be predicted from a theoretical consideration of the effects of using aversive stimuli.

Relatedly, and as mentioned throughout this section on punishment, an individual may aggress towards the therapist in order to escape from a punishment protocol. This may be particularly problematic with adults as it may be difficult for the therapist to control aggressive outbursts while implementing a treatment. In such situations the therapist may unwittingly reinforce escape-maintained aggression if the individual is allowed to escape from treatment. Alternative treatments to punishment should obviously be considered in such situations.

When a therapist, parent, or other care provider uses punishment they are in effect providing examples of how to control another individual's behavior. Those who observe such practices can learn that such techniques can be used to control the behavior of others. The effects of what is often called modeled punishment have been extensively described in the literature (Kazdin, 1987). Children who are referred to clinicians for severe aggression usually come from homes where physical aggression is used by parents to control their children. In such home environments children learn that physical aggression is an acceptable and powerful tool for controlling the behavior of others.

It was mentioned earlier that one of the major advantages of punishment techniques is that they can produce rapid elimination of the maladaptive behavior. However, the maladaptive behavior can recover once these techniques are withdrawn. Recovery seems to occur under conditions where the behavior has not been completely eliminated during the punishment intervention. Additionally, conditioned punishers may lose their effectiveness over time which can result in a return of the target behavior to baseline levels. Such recovery following the removal of punishment may be overcome if punishment of the undesired response is embedded within a more general behavioral program to teach alternative appropriate behaviors.

10.9 OVERALL SUMMARY

The use of applied behavioral procedures based on the principles of extinction and punishment were described in this chapter. Punishment and extinction describe processes which result in a reduction or elimination of behavior. With extinction the contingency between the reinforcer and response is removed. Punishment involves the application or removal of a stimulus contingent on the performance of the target behavior. Prior to using extinction and punishment it is important that the behavior analyst establish a firm rationale for reducing targeted behaviors (see Chapter 7). The use of some of these strategies, particularly the use of aversive stimuli as punishers, should be considered the treatment of last resort and administered under strict guidelines. Typically, extinction and punishment protocols are used to eliminate aberrant behavior in the context of an intervention to increase appropriate alternative behaviors for the person.

There are certain characteristics of responding when behavior is punished or placed on extinction. For example, one can expect an initial increase in responding when a behavior is placed on extinction (i.e., an extinction burst). Additionally, behavior may re-emerge under extinction contingencies (i.e., spontaneous recovery). Punishment and extinction contingencies can also result in avoidance and aggressive behavior on the part of the client. It is important that those who administer extinction or punishment protocols be familiar with such characteristics in order to implement such protocols efficiently and effectively.

Extinction of responding can be accomplished by removing the reinforcer entirely (i.e., reinforcement is no longer available) or delivering the reinforcer noncontingently on a fixed-time schedule. In both cases the contingency between responding and reinforcement is removed. Noncontingent delivery of reinforcing stimuli has been examined relatively recently in the applied literature and seems to produce rapid reductions in responding without creating ethical problems that can arise when access to highly-preferred reinforcers is removed.

It is vital that the reinforcement contingencies are identified before any extinction protocol can be implemented. In fact an extinction protocol should be determined by the function of the behavior to be extinguished. Extinction protocols will differ depending on whether the behavior is maintained by social positive reinforcement, social negative reinforcement, or automatic reinforcement.

There are three general categories of punishment protocols. One class of punishment techniques involves the presentation of aversive stimuli contingent on the performance of the behavior targeted for reduction. These aversive stimuli can either be unconditioned (e.g., electric shock) or conditioned (e.g., verbal reprimand). A second class of punishment protocol involves the removal of positive events contingent on performance of the targeted behavior. In time out from positive reinforcement, the individual is removed from all reinforcing events for a predetermined period of time. Response cost protocols involve the permanent removal of some item or event in the form of a penalty or fine contingent on maladaptive responding. A final class of punishment techniques requires the client to engage in some form of activity contingent on the target behavior (such as overcorrection or contingent exercise).

There is much current debate about the use of punishment in therapy, particularly when it is used with individuals with developmental disabilities. Punishment is sometimes seen as being synonymous with abuse and cruelty. In behavioral analysis, however, punishment is defined functionally in terms of its influence on responding. Punishment protocols should only be used as a treatment of last resort for behavior that is dangerous to self or others.

CHAPTER 11

BEHAVIOR ANALYSIS: CURRENT STATUS AND FUTURE DIRECTIONS

This book could not have been written until recently because much of the research reported in Chapters 7 through 10 was only carried out in the 1990s, although, as we have shown, it builds on experimental research that began in the 1930s and continues to progress. In this final chapter we point to some the areas of development that we have not been able to include earlier, we consider human rights issues, and we suggest where and how some significant future developments may occur.

11.1 APPLICATIONS OF BEHAVIOR ANALYSIS TO ISSUES IN HEALTH AND MEDICINE

Basic research identifies the fundamental environmental determinants of behavior, while applied behavior analysis develops interventions which are derived from these fundamental principles to achieve meaningful change in socially significant behavior for persons in real world settings. Accordingly, the accounts in Chapters 7 through 10 of the procedures used to assess, increase, and decrease behavior in applied settings emphasized the fact that such applied procedures are derived from the basic principles of behavioral analysis that were described in Chapters 2 through 6.

It was necessary in Chapters 7 through 10 to select examples of these applied behavioral procedures that best illustrate the behavioral processes and methodologies involved. These chapters thus focused on detailed descriptions of applied behavioral techniques and the power of such techniques to change behavior, rather than describing studies on topics of social interest. In contrast, and to illustrate the potential of applied behavior analysis to embrace a broad field, this section will focus on a select number of topics of wide social concern in which behavioral principles have been systematically applied and researched. We have argued elsewhere (Leslie, 1997a), that there is no reason why applied behavior analysis should not be the "methodology of choice" across a wide area in which techniques derived from very different approaches to psychology are currently employed. This would be desirable because, when an applied behavior analysis approach is taken, the same aims of significant behavioral change

303

are set — and usually achieved — as have been evident in the many studies reviewed in this volume.

Promoting Healthy Life-styles

A significant application of applied psychology in general and applied behavior analysis in particular has been in the area of health psychology (Leslie, 1997a). One of the fundamental interests of health psychologists is the development of strategies to promote and maintain healthy life-styles. It is generally recognized that engaging in appropriate exercise and diet can reduce the probability of certain illnesses and possibly prolong healthy life (Cummings, 1986). Consequently, applied behavior analysts who work in the area of health psychology have developed interventions to increase appropriate exercise and diet.

One strand of applied behavioral research has focused on promoting healthy meal options within restaurant settings (Dubbert, Johnson, Schlundt, & Montague, 1984; Mayer, Heins, Vogel, Morrison, Lankester, & Jacobs, 1986; Wagner & Winett, 1988). For example, Wagner & Winett (1988) developed and evaluated an intervention to promote the selection of low-fat salads as an entree in one restaurant of a national fast-food chain. The intervention consisted of a series of posters with the message "Be fit & healthy; Eat a low-fat SALAD as your meal or add a side salad" and a picture of a salad. These posters were situated in proximity to where the customers placed their orders. Small "tent cards" with the same message as the poster were placed on each table in the restaurant. The intervention was conducted over an 11-week period and the effectiveness of the posters/cards was evaluated using an ABAB design. The percentages of salads sold each day were corrected for influences such as weather and customer flow. The effects of the intervention on the corrected percentage of salads sold each day are presented in Figure 11.1. Overall, the results show an increase in the purchase of low-fat salads under the prompting intervention. While effective in its own terms, this type of intervention has limitations as it stands because eating healthily in the restaurant might not generalize to other settings, such as the home. However, in Chapter 9, we discussed tactics for ensuring the generalization of new skills.

Behavioral procedures have also been successfully used to increase physical exercise. DeLuca and Holborn (1992) examined the influence of a variable ratio (VR) schedule of reinforcement on exercise behavior with six 11-year-old boys using a stationary exercise bicycle. Three of these boys

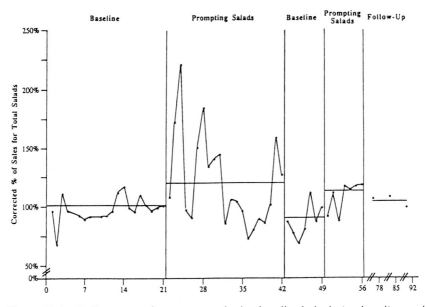

Figure 11.1 Daily corrected percentage of sales for all salads during baseline and intervention (posters etc.) in a restaurant (Wagner & Winett, 1988).

were diagnosed as obese (at least 20% above average body weight for age). Childhood obesity is a prevalent problem that can have negative physiological and psychological effects (Israel & Stolmaker, 1980; Mayer, 1970). Physical inactivity is often associated with obesity. Regular exercise is recommended in many cases as part of an intervention to control obesity. Exercise sessions, which were approximately 30 min in length, occurred each day over a 12 week period. Sets of back-up reinforcers were identified for each child (for example, comic books, model plane, puzzle). Each back-up reinforcer was assigned a number of points. The child earned points by exercising on the bicycle, and the stationary exercise bicycle was programmed to ring a bell and to illuminate a red light after a variable number of revolutions pedaled (the dependent variable being revolutions pedaled per minute). This VR schedule was gradually "thinned" during the experiment which produced marked increases in the rate of exercise for all boys. The results of the intervention on mean revolutions pedaled per minute are shown in Figure 11.2. All boys and their parents indicated that they were satisfied with the exercise program as it resulted in decreases in weight (for the obese boys) and increases in activity for all children.

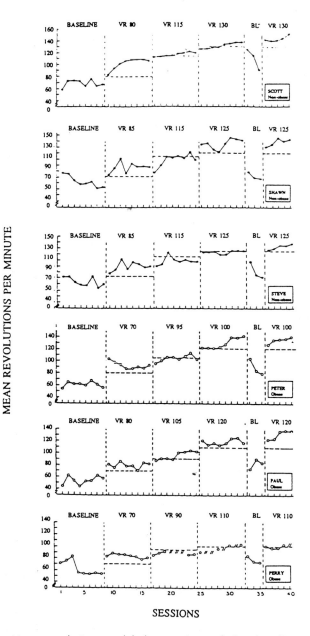

Figure 11.2 Mean revolutions pedaled per minute during baseline, VR 1 (VR range, 70 to 85), VR 2 (VR range, 90 to 115), VR 3 (VR range, 100 to 130), return to baseline, and return to VR 3 phases for obese and nonobese boys (DeLuca & Holborn, 1992).

The number of new cases of skin cancer and melanoma-related deaths rises yearly in the USA (American Cancer Society, 1990). Many of these new cases can be attributed to changes in life-style in the past thirty years which have resulted in increased sun exposure (that is, sun tanning). The incidence of such cancers could be dramatically reduced if individuals engaged in behaviors which limited direct exposure to ultraviolet radiation. These behaviors include wearing sunglasses, hats, shirts, and sunscreen. Lombard, Neubauer, Canfield, and Winett (1991) examined the effectiveness of a multicomponent behavioral intervention to increase behaviors associated with skin cancer prevention at two outdoor swimming pools. Posters and fliers were made available in the pools and these illustrated how to protect oneself against sun damage. Free sunscreen was available at the front desk of each pool. Pool attendants were required to engage in the protective behaviors (wear a hat, shirt, sunglasses etc.). A feedback poster also illustrated the percentage of adults and children who engaged in at least two protective behaviors the previous day at the pool. The overall results of this intervention demonstrated increases in the percentage of children and adults who engaged in at least two protective behaviors at poolside each day over baseline assessments.

Certain jobs or professions may expose a worker to any number of hazardous situations that may cause illness. For example, health-care workers, such as nurses, are often exposed to body fluids of patients and are thus at risk of contacting various infections such as human immunodeficiency virus (HIV). Nurses are required to engage in certain protective behaviors in order to reduce the probability of such infection (for example, wearing gloves, masks, eyewear, gowns etc.). DeVries, Burnette, and Redmon (1991) examined the effectiveness of a performance feedback intervention to increase glove wearing with emergency room nurses. Glove wearing during six high-risk situations (that is, situations where the potential for infection was quite high if protective gloves were not worn) was observed during baseline. High-risk situations included phlebotomy, giving an injection, cleaning a laceration, and inserting an intravenous catheter. The feedback intervention was implemented in a multiple baseline design across four nurses. Nurses were unaware that glove wearing was being observed during baseline. Glove wearing during high-risk situations was quite low for all four nurses (see Figure 11.3). Intervention consisted of giving feedback to the nurses regarding their glove-wearing behavior immediately after baseline and every two weeks thereafter. Feedback consisted of a request for behavior change (that is, a request to wear the

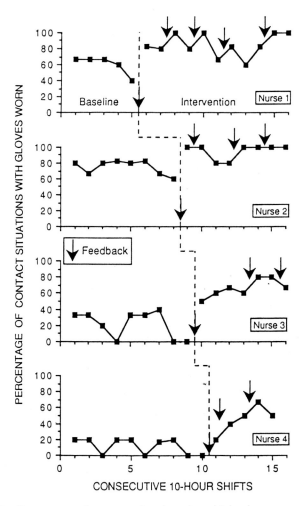

Figure 11.3 Percentage of contact situations in which gloves were worn by 4 nurses for consecutive 10-hr shifts. Arrows indicate the delivery of feedback by the infection-control nurse. (DeVries, Burnette, & Redmon, 1991).

gloves in high-risk situations) and both verbal and graphic feedback of the number of times gloves were worn during contact situations during the previous observations. Figure 11.3 demonstrates that the feedback protocol did result in increases in glove wearing. In some respects however this intervention was unsuccessful, as nurses continued not to wear gloves in many high-risk situations. In such situations an intervention should only be deemed successful if it eliminates such risk-taking behavior entirely.

These are some examples of applied behavioral research which has focused on increasing adaptive or healthy life-style behaviors in the population. In similar vein, behavioral interventions have also successfully reduced risk-taking behaviors in drivers and pedestrians (Van Houten & Nau, 1981) and increased safety belt use (Geller & Hahn, 1984). Clearly, applied behavior analysis has great potential as a behavior change strategy to promote healthier life-styles within the community at large.

Behavioral Medicine

Behavioral medicine could be best thought of as a distinct sub-discipline within the general field of health psychology. Behavioral medicine might be defined as the application of behavioral principles to treat a variety of medical disorders (Blanchard, 1992). In many respects, some of the research examples discussed in the previous section (for example, the treatment of obesity) could also be included in this section. While the distinction between behavioral applications within the field of health psychology and behavioral medicine may be somewhat blurred it is still instructive to describe behavioral techniques that are directly used to treat medical problems.

Behavioral procedures have been used to treat a variety of eating disorders including anorexia nervosa and bulimia (Garfinkel & Garner, 1982). Anorexia nervosa, which is typically found in young women but is increasingly identified in young men, involves severe reduction in food consumption. This disorder can result in significant weight loss and even death. With many of these cases, behavioral treatment is implemented within hospital settings. The client has been admitted to hospital because weight loss has reached a dangerous level and behavioral programs are designed to increase weight to an acceptable level. Typically, behavioral contracts are drawn up between the patient and therapist which make privileges contingent on consumption of daily meals and daily increases in weight throughout the program. Carr, MacDonnell, and Afnan (1989) implemented such a protocol with a 14-year-old boy who was hospitalized with anorexia nervosa. The intervention resulted in a rapid increase in weight from 29 kg to a predetermined criterion of 40 kg within 4 weeks.

Differential reinforcement procedures have been successfully used to treat chronic back pain (for example, Cairns & Pasino, 1977; Fordyce, Fowler, Lehmann, DeLateur, Sand, & Trieschmann, 1974). In these studies patients were reinforced (with social praise) by hospital staff for engaging in increased activity and exercise. Complaints and inactivity were ignored. The results of such interventions indicate that patients increase in their physical activity and report significant reductions in pain.

Behavioral techniques have also been used to teach self-performance of intrusive medical regimens for children suffering from such illnesses as diabetes, asthma, and cystic fibrosis (Lowe & Lutzker, 1979; Russo & Varni, 1982). Typically these behavioral interventions consist of developing a task analysis of the essential self-care skills. Children are then taught to perform the task analysis through various prompting strategies (see Chapter 9). Finally, these skills are maintained through reinforcement strategies such as token economies. For example, Derrickson, Neef, and Parrish (1991) taught self-care skills to four children with tracheostomies. A tracheostomy is a procedure which involves an incision into the trachea and insertion of a tube below the larynx to maintain an airway (Stool & Beebe, 1973). Some children with airway obstruction may require tracheostomy for extended time periods. A tracheostomy requires regular care and this involves the removal of secretions from the tracheostomy tube and trachea. A task analysis for tracheostomy self-care was developed initially and then the children were taught to perform the steps of the task analysis on an anatomically correct doll (simulation training) and then on themselves. The performance of the children on the doll and on themselves during baseline, following training (identified as the PT, or post training, phase in the graph), and during follow-up phases are shown in Figure 11.4. All four children performed few of the skills independently prior to training. Interestingly, during the initial post training trials (that is, following simulation training with the doll) all four children did not substantially increase their performance of self-care skills on themselves or with the doll. Remedial training during post training trials produced a rapid increase of self-care skills to criterion levels (that is, 100% correct responding on the task analysis). These positive results maintained for up to 6 weeks during follow-up assessments.

Clearly, there are many powerful demonstrations of the application of behavioral principles to treat a range of medical problems. These include chronic medical problems such as food refusal, compliance with medical treatments for such illnesses as diabetes or asthma, and teaching of self-care skills which are essential for the long-term success of some intrusive surgical procedures (as in the Derrickson et al., 1991 study above).

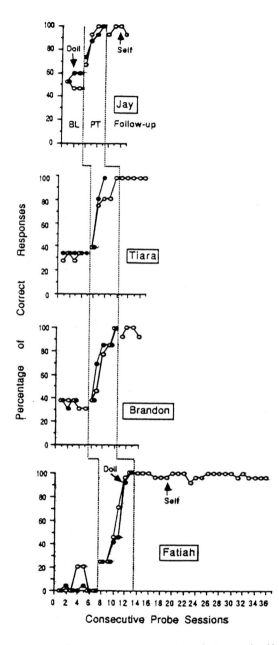

Figure 11.4 Percentage of correct responses on simulation and self-administration probes for four children who were taught self-care of tracheotomies (Derrickson, Neef & Parrish, 1991).

11.2 COMMUNITY BEHAVIOR ANALYSIS

One of the fundamental aims of applied behavior analysis is the application of behavioral principles for the amelioration of problems that are of social relevance (Baer, Wolf, & Risley, 1968/1987). Human problems can occur at the level of the individual (for example, self-injury), of the group (for example, family violence), of the community (for example, vandalism), of the state (for example, unemployment), or of the culture (for example, sexual harassment). These different levels are not mutually exclusive: any problem behavior is functionally related both to immediate, or proximal, influences and to broader, or distal, contextual influences. While applied behavior analysts have recognized the importance of designing interventions to change behavior at a community or national level they have focused in practice on the assessment and treatment of problem behaviors in the individual. Applied behavior analysts have, of course, developed powerful technologies to change the behavior of individuals and rigorous empirical methodologies to demonstrate the effectiveness of these intervention technologies. However, hard-won changes at the individual level may not be maintained over time if that person returns to a community which differentially reinforces the original problem behavior. This can be thought of as an ABA "design", where A is the community setting and B is the behavioral intervention program: we would *expect* that a return to Condition A, the community setting, should reinstate the original, unwanted, behavior.

Focusing on the individual may therefore be the least effective way to produce change at times. Indeed, targeting behavior change at the individual level may, in some cases, legitimize inappropriate or ineffective systems. For example, many individuals with mental retardation who engage in self-injury do so to escape from demand situations such as instructional tasks. The intervention of choice for self-injury maintained by escape is escape extinction (that is, in treatment the person is not allowed to escape the task contingent on self-injury). However, in a hypothetical situation where staff physically abuse the individual within the instructional situation then escape extinction should not be implemented. In such a case, stopping the physical abuse by staff, which is acting as an establishing operation for escape-maintained self-injury, would be the appropriate intervention.

The complexity of various levels of contextual influence on problem behavior is illustrated by Fawcett (1991) in his analysis of the various factors that can contribute to drug abuse:

> At the individual level, adolescents may lack the social skills to refuse drugs offered by peers or have limited alternatives for after-school activities. At the family or school level, parents and teachers may lack knowledge, skills, or other resources for monitoring youths. At a more distal level, school officials may experience punishment for reporting youths suspected of using or dealing drugs, or the school may lack financial resources to implement drug abuse prevention curricula. In the broader context, elected officials may lack information and constituent support to establish regulations for mandatory drug testing in schools or to create incentive programs or opportunities that encourage at-risk youths to stay drug-free (Fawcett, 1991; p. 625).

If applied behavior analysis is to realize its ultimate goal of successfully treating human problems then it must increasingly focus on the need to assess and intervene at systemic as well as individual levels (Baer, Wolf, & Risley, 1987). Behavior analysts have not traditionally been very effective at intervening at systemic levels of society, and there seem to be a number of reasons for this. The technical language used by behavior analysts, which is important for precision and clarity within the scientific community, may be off-putting to the general public. It was noted in Chapters 5 and 10 that there is a degree of confusion with regard to the meaning of the behavioral term "punishment", and in general the lay public equate the term "punishment" with causing harm to a person. This confusion continues to harm the public perception of the discipline. Behavior analysts can redress this problem in two ways, both by educating the public about the basic principles of behavior analysis, and by adopting more user-friendly terms to describe their profession and activities when interacting with the general public.

Other problems arise from the relationship between applied and experimental analyses of behavior. Many of the experimental designs used to evaluate the effectiveness of applied interventions require stringent forms of control, such as the systematic removal and reintroduction of the intervention, which may not be acceptable when working in community settings. A tension may sometimes occur between the need for experimental rigor and community application. Some experimental designs (such as a multiple baseline design) may be more suitable to community applications than others (such as a withdrawal design). This may explain why many behavior analysts focus their attention on research questions with populations or settings where they can have maximum control with regard to the systematic manipulation of environmental variables (such as institutionalized populations). However, it is important for behavior analysts to realize that they must succeed in doing research that is also addressed to systemic issues in wider society, and this may require modification of research designs to take account of uncontrolled variables. Scientists' behavior is itself controlled by reinforcement contingencies, and editors of academic journals may promote this type of research by suggesting that such research need not necessarily include all the rigorous empirical evaluations that would typically be required for publication (and thus reinforcement) of applied behavioral research.

Fawcett (1991) has outlined a set of 10 values to help guide action at community or systemic levels. These values are outlined in Table 11.1. Fawcett (1991) suggests that all 10 values should guide the development of any behavioral community research activity. He also outlines the expected contribution of the behavioral researcher and the community that is involved in the research project for each of the values. These values emphasize the importance of understanding applied community research as a collaborative venture between the researcher and the community. Researchers must be sensitive to community needs as they develop research projects and interventions. If behavior analysts were to adopt these values then many of the problems facing community behavior analysts (outlined earlier in the section) may be mitigated. In fact these values are helpful guidelines for all types of applied behavioral research. In Chapter 5, we introduced the concept of social validity, and the values listed in Table 11.1 operationalize social validity and demonstrate the potential benefits of collaboration to both the researcher and the community.

Behavior analysis is not without many excellent examples of behavioral applications to large scale community issues such as energy conservation, crime prevention, and business practices (see Greene, Winett, Van Houten, Geller, & Iwata, 1987). For example, Fox, Hopkins, and Anger (1987) examined the influence of a token economy system to promote safe practices of employees in two open-pit mines. The intervention was conducted over a 10-year time period and involved approximately 1000 employees in both mines during any one year of the intervention. The behaviors targeted for reduction included work-related injuries, days lost from work due to injury, and medical costs. The intervention was implemented in a multiple baseline design across the two mines.

Tokens in the form of trading stamps were given to workers at the end

Table 11.1   *Some Values Guiding Community Research and Action: Contributions from Research and Community Perspectives. (Fawcett, 1991)*

Values of community research and action	Research perspective	Community perspective
1. Researchers should form collaborative relationships with participants.	Research should be grounded in the local context.	Communities should exert some control over research that affects them.
2. Descriptive research should provide information about the variety of behavior environment relationships of importance to communities.	Research should contribute knowledge about naturally occurring events.	Research should contribute to understanding about strengths (as well as deficits) and the variety of ways that individual and community goals can be met.
3. Experimental research should provide information about the effects of environmental events on behaviors and outcomes of importance.	The effects of research interventions should be replicable, durable, and generalizable to other people and situations.	Research should help identify goals, procedures, and effects that are important and acceptable to clients.
4. The chosen setting, participants, and research measures should be appropriate to the community problem under investigation.	Applied research should use valid measures to examine real-world problems in the natural context of people actually experiencing the concerns.	Research should target all those who contribute to the problem and should leave improved valued aspects of the community.
5. The measurement system must be replicable, and measures should capture the dynamic or transactional nature of behavior-environment relationships.	Measurement systems should be replicable by typically trained researchers.	Research findings should tell the complete story, including the role that participants play in changing their environments.
6. Community interventions should be replicable and	Interventions should be replicable by those available to	Community interventions should be sustainable with local resources and should

Continued

sustainable with local resources.	implement them.	build on local capacities for addressing community concerns.
7. Community action should occur at the level of change and timing likely to optimize beneficial outcomes.	Interventions should produce the maximum desired impact.	Interventions should be targeted to optimize benefits for the community and its members.
8. Researchers should develop a capacity to disseminate effective interventions and provide support for change agents.	Interventions should be disseminated cautiously so that their continued effectiveness is assured.	Interventions should be adapted to local conditions and their use should enhance local capacities for change.
9. Results should be communicated to clients, decision makers, and the broader public.	Research findings should be submitted for peer review, and, if judged acceptable, disseminated to the broader scientific community.	Research findings should be communicated to participants and decision makers in understandable and maximally influential ways and these audiences should help assess what was valuable about the research.
10. Community research and action projects should contribute to fundamental change as well as understanding.	Community research should contribute to understanding of environmental events that affect behavior.	Community research should contribute to prevention of problems in living, capacity building, and empowerment of people of marginal status.

of each month if they were not involved in accidents. Additional stamps were given to all members of a group who were managed by a common supervisor if no member of that group had been injured in the previous month. Tokens were lost if a worker caused an accident or missed work due to a work-related injury. Tokens could be exchanged at a local store for a variety of items such as barbecue grills, bowling balls, electrical appliances etc. The intervention resulted in very positive long-term effects (see Figure 11.5). There was a substantial decrease in the number of days lost due to work-related accidents (upper panel of the figure). Additionally, the costs to the companies for work-related injuries decreased substantially (lower panel of the figure).

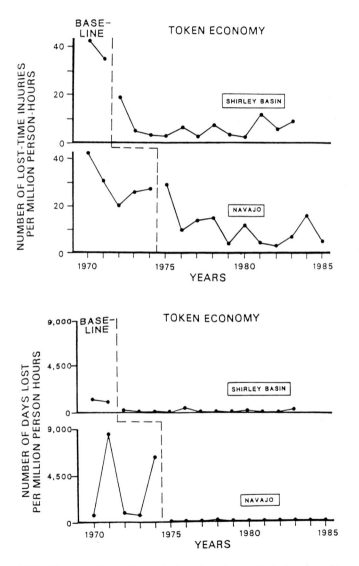

Figure 11.5 The yearly number of days lost from work (top graph) and work-related injuries (bottom graph), per million person hours worked under Baseline and Token Economy conditions in both mines (Fox, Hopkins, & Anger, 1987).

11.3 APPLICATIONS OF FURTHER PRINCIPLES OF BEHAVIOR ANALYSIS

The vast majority of applied behavioral intervention programs have relied on principles of behavior established in the laboratory (with nonhuman animals) many years ago. However, it is important that the possible applications of more-recently established, and more "advanced", principles be investigated. The relationship here is similar to that between science and technology in any discipline. In some cases, scientists pursue a particular problem because they know that there is a possible technological application for its solution — and we will return to this issue in behavior analysis later in this chapter — but more often scientists investigate problems because of their inherent interest and applications come later. Interestingly, despite the preference for funding (by governments etc.) of research of the first type, it is often research of the second type which produces really useful new applications. As examples of applications of principles additional to those described earlier, we will briefly review some applications of research on choice and concurrent schedules and of research on stimulus equivalence.

In Chapter 4 (Section 4.7), we described concurrent schedules of reinforcement. *Choice* between different responses is a general feature of operant behavior, and it can be subjected to an experimental analysis if two, or more, operants are reinforced in the same situation. This is what occurs in concurrent schedules of reinforcement. Choice can be operationally defined as the proportion of time allocated to each operant, or the relative rate of that response, and variation of the parameters of the schedules of reinforcement involved may be used as a method of discovering how those parameters affect choice. For example, if the rate of reinforcement for Response R1 doubles, how is the time allocated to, or the rate of, that response changed?

In 1961, Herrnstein proposed the matching law. This states that the time allocated to an activity is proportional to the rate of reinforcement of that activity relative to other current sources of reinforcement. A great deal of subsequent research has been directed at testing this law under varying conditions, and the occurrence of some systematic deviations from the predictions of Herrnstein's simple formula led Baum (1974) to propose the generalized matching law :

$$\frac{R_1}{R_2} = b \, \frac{Rf_1{}^a}{Rf_2}$$

where R stands for the response rate, Rf stands for the reinforcement rate, and the subscripts 1 and 2 stand for the two response alternatives. This is a "power law" and the shape of the function is determined by whether the parameter a is less than 1.0, or greater than 1.0; when it equals 1.0 a linear relationships exists, which is what Herrnstein originally proposed. These three types of function are illustrated in Figure 11.6. If *a* is more than 1.0, greater changes in responding occur as the ratio of reinforcement rates varies, and this is called *overmatching* because it indicates a high sensitivity to changes in the rate of reinforcement. Correspondingly, if a is less than 1.0, this is called *undermatching*. If *b* is less than 1.0 then *bias* towards the second response alternative, R_2, is shown. This is also illustrated in Figure 11.7.

The generalized matching law represents a promising start towards being able to incorporate some aspects of real-world complexity into laboratory analyses of operant behavior, and real-world applications have also been investigated. For example, Beardsley and McDowell (1992) carried out a study with college students where, during conversation, verbal praise was used as a reinforcer for eye-contact. Reinforcement was administered at five different rates on VI schedules in different phases of the experiment. The results in Figure 11.7 show a good fit to Herrnstein's matching law (indicated by the curves which are hyperbolic functions) for each individual and for the group median performance.

A concurrent VI VI schedule of monetary reinforcement for completion of math tasks was used by Mace, Neef, Shade, and Mauro (1994) with teenagers with behavior disorders. During each experimental session, a

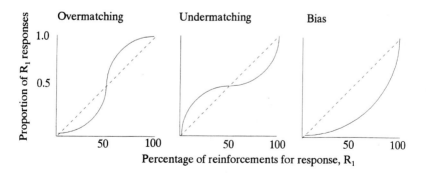

Figure 11.6   The percentage of R1 responses as a function of the percentage of reinforcements for that response alternative. The diagonal line indicates Herrnstein's matching law. Three types of deviation from this can be described by the generalized matching law. Details are given in the text.

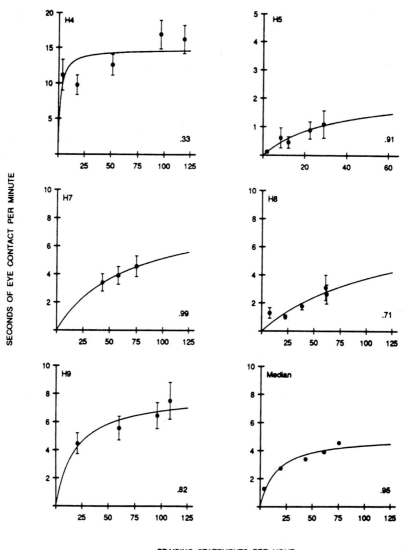

Figure 11.7   Amount of eye contact as a function of rate of social reinforcement (Beardsley & McDowell, 1992). Details are given in the text.

participant was offered a series of choices between two piles of distinctively marked math-problem cards, which were placed directly in front of them. The participant worked through as many problems as they wished and, according to the pile (left or right) from which the problems were selected, the experimenter provided reinforcement for correct problem completion with nickels on the VI schedule appropriate for that task. Typical results for an individual participant are shown in Figure 11.8. In the first condition experienced, VI 20 sec VI 240 sec, Matt allocates nearly all his time and responding to the much "richer" schedule (VI 20 sec) as would be predicted from the matching law. Later transitions to other schedule combinations, however, did not always produce immediate shifts in preference until additional procedures (which encouraged some shifting to the less reinforced schedule) were used. Eventual performance on all schedule combinations showed a good fit to the generalized matching law.

These studies provide encouraging demonstrations of the continuing power of extrapolations from experiments done in the laboratory with maximal control of variables and, usually, with nonhuman experimental participants, to real-world human conditions. Additionally, all sorts of

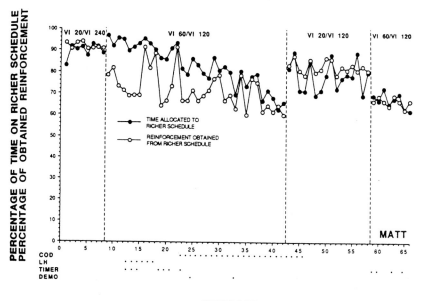

SESSIONS

Figure 11.8 Percentage of time that one experimental participant, Matt, allocated to performing arithmetic problems on the richer reinforcement schedule (Mace, Neef, Shade, & Mauro, 1994). Marks at foot of graph indicate sessions on which additional procedures were used. Details are given in the text.

applied issues can be investigated with variants of these techniques. Recent studies have used choice procedures to look at reinforcer preference assessments, to compare reinforcer effects, and to analyze and improve clinical interventions (see Fisher & Mazur, 1997, for a review).

Chapter 4 (Section 4.10) gave an account of stimulus equivalence classes, and indicated their probable importance for a general account of human learning. "Preverbal" children do not generally show the capacity for stimulus equivalence class formation that is characteristic of older children and adults, and this suggests that stimulus equivalence class formation and verbal abilities are intimately related. (The nature of this relationship is not yet established; see Horne & Lowe, 1999, and Barnes, Healy, & Hayes, 1999, for a vigorous debate about this issue.) As suggested in Chapter 6 (Section 6.8), it may be a capacity to form stimulus equivalence classes that distinguishes human psychology from that of other species. This possibility has, of course, stimulated research designed to *disprove* this hypothesis by demonstrating equivalence in nonhuman species. (A strength of the scientific method in general is that scientists may be highly motivated to complete difficult sets of experiments because they disagree with someone else's claim that the experiments "won't work".)

A number of such experiments has either demonstrated some, but not all, aspects of stimulus equivalence, or the training procedure has been modified (for example, by including appetitive or aversive stimuli as members of stimulus classes, or by training specific response patterns to various sample stimuli). A recent study with pigeons sought to demonstrate transitivity (one of the essential requirements of stimulus equivalence class formation) using a procedure that avoided the methodological shortcomings of a number of earlier studies (Kuno, Kitadate, & Iwamoto, 1994). Aspects of the training and testing procedure are shown in Figure 11.9. Following A-B and B-C matching-to-sample training (in a manner that closely resembled that described in Chapter 4 for humans, with the obvious differences that the stimuli were presented on pecking keys, the responses were pecks directed at one of three wall-mounted keys, and the reinforcer for "correct" responses was food presentation), A-C transitivity tests were carried out. For example, the pigeons would have been reinforced in an earlier phase of the experiment for pecking A1 (circle) followed by pecking B1 (triangle), and on separate trials they would have been reinforced for pecking B1 (triangle) followed by pecking C1 (red). On some trials in the transitivity test, the sample stimulus would now be A1 (circle), and a correct sequence, indicating transitivity, would be to peck this and then to peck C1 (red),

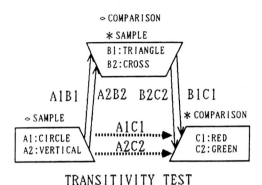

TRANSITIVITY TEST

Figure 11.9   Pigeons trained to match A1 to B1 and A2 to B2, and to match B1 to C1 and B2 to C2, were tested for transitivity by presenting A1 or A2 as sample stimuli and C1 and C2 as comparison stimuli (Kuno, Kitadate, & Iwamoto, 1994).

which would be presented as a comparison along with the C2 stimulus. Kuno et al. found that two of their four pigeons showed a tendency to select the "correct" stimuli (in that they were "right" more often than would have been predicted by chance alone), but these birds still only made around 60% "correct" responses.

We might tentatively conclude that at this stage rigorous experiments have shown only a weak tendency towards stimulus equivalence class formation in nonhuman species, while it is a behavioral process which has striking behavioral effects in verbally-competent humans. (This conclusion is "tentative" because, as we have seen on a number of occasions, the history of research in behavioral analysis is one where apparent differences between species often turn out, following further research, to be gaps that can be bridged with careful and extensive training.) What about humans who are less verbally competent, such as those with developmental delays? Recall that Sidman (for example, 1971, 1990) originally devised equivalence training procedures to facilitate reading development in just this group, and more recent experimental findings with equivalence have in turn been applied with such individuals.

An example of this is provided by the study of Kennedy, Itkonen, and Lindquist (1994). Experimental studies with verbally competent adults (for example, Fields, Adams, Verhave, & Newman, 1990) have shown that following A-B, B-C, C-D, D-E training, for example, with matching-to-sample procedures (again, see Chapter 4 for an explanation of the terminology used), that some relationships may require more training to emerge than others. For example, B-A matching is liable to emerge before C-A matching, which may in turn emerge before E-A matching (although all these relationships, and many others, would be expected to occur once a stimulus equivalence class was established, see Chapter 4). This is called the *inter-nodal distance effect*.

Table 11.2 shows the stimuli used by Kennedy et al. with young adults with moderate learning disabilities. Following sight-word training, to establish accurate labeling of all the words, matching-to-sample training was carried out to establish A-B, B-C, and C-D links within each of the four classes, meats, dairy products, cereals, and vegetables. A pattern of results was obtained resembling those from the Fields et al. study. That is, symmetrical relations (e.g., B-A) were established more quickly than transitive relations with one node (e.g., C-A) which were established more quickly than those involving two nodes (e.g., D-A). Amongst other implications, these findings can aid the construction of effective training materials for important educational tasks.

11.4 ETHICAL GUIDELINES FOR THE USE OF BEHAVIORAL TREATMENT

Applied behavioral scientists have amassed a wealth of data which demonstrates the effectiveness of behavioral procedures to increase appropriate behavior and decrease inappropriate behavior. These techniques have been used in a variety of applied settings (including the community, the clinic, and education) and with many populations (including the developmentally disabled, mentally ill, preschoolers, parents, etc.). However, those who advocate the use of applied behavioral

Table 11.2 *Stimulus Classes (1 through 4) and Stimuli (A through D) Used(Kennedy, Itkonen, & Lindquist, 1994).*

	Food group			
	Meats	*Dairy products*	*Grains/cereals*	*Vegetables/fruits*
	(1)	(2)	(3)	(4)
A	bacon	cream	toast	onion
B	salami	yogurt	muffin	potato
C	flank	gouda	cookie	garlic
D	liver	butter	donut	squash

techniques have not been without their critics (see Walsh, 1997). It was noted in earlier sections of this book (see Chapters 5 and 10) that punishment procedures in particular have been misconstrued by some audiences. In fact, some individuals have gone so far as to describe behavior analysis and those who practice behavior analysis as evil and controlling (McGee, Menolascino, Hobbs, & Menousek, 1987). Such conclusions are based in part on misinformation about applied behavior analysis, in part on a small number of cases of abuse, and in part on ideological objections to all scientific accounts of human behavior (see Leslie, 1997b, for a review of these issues). Nonetheless, this only strengthens the need for behavior analysts to explain how and why their practices are ethical.

While no professional group can exert total control over the practices of each individual member, applied behavior analysts have developed a set of guidelines designed to guide their professional practices (Van Houten, Axelrod, Bailey, Favell, Foxx, Iwata, & Lovaas, 1988). These guidelines for the practice of applied behavior analysis are described as a set of six fundamental rights of the client. Each of these rights are summarized below.

An individual has a right to a therapeutic environment

Individuals have a right to appropriate living standards within the environment where treatment is applied. The individual should have access to leisure activities and materials. The social environment should be pleasant and the person should have frequent opportunities for social interactions with others. Activities should be age-appropriate and of educative value. Minimal restrictions should be placed on the preferred activities of the person. The safety and protection of the individual should be considered at all times.

An individual has a right to services whose overriding goal is personal welfare

The goal of any behavioral intervention is to develop functional skills which promote greater independence for the individual. The individual or legal guardian should therefore be actively involved in selecting target behaviors, intervention protocol, and identifying goals of treatment. *Peer review* and *human rights committees* are also important and should be involved in the treatment selection and program evaluation process. Peer review committees should be composed of experts in the field of behavior analysis and can provide feedback on the clinical efficacy of the intervention protocol. Human rights committees, comprised of parents, advocates, and consumers examine the acceptability of the program in terms of basic human rights.

An individual has a right to treatment by a competent behavior analyst

Persons who develop and supervise behavioral programs should be trained to the highest standard. This should include doctoral level training in behavior analysis and practicum training under qualified supervision. Individuals who deliver treatment should be properly trained in the methods of intervention. Qualified behavior analysts should monitor those who deliver treatment.

An individual has a right to programs that teach functional skills

Every individual has a right to full participation in every aspect of community life. The goals of intervention should not be based on a priori assumptions of an individuals potential or limitations. Interventions may be of three general types. Individuals may be taught new skills to access preferred stimuli. Individuals can also be taught skills to reduce or avoid unpleasant stimuli. Finally, certain behaviors may need to be eliminated as they may act as barriers to inclusion in society.

An individual has a right to behavioral assessment and ongoing evaluation

The selection of any behavior-change strategy should be based on an assessment of the environmental determinants of that behavior. This includes the assessment of antecedents and consequences. Assessment should involve interview of the individual and significant others when necessary. This should be followed by observation of the individual in the criterion environment (that is, contexts where the behavior will be targeted for increase or decrease). Once the intervention is implemented it should be continuously evaluated. Continuous evaluation allows the behavior analyst to determine if the treatment is effective and to modify the intervention if it is not achieving the desired objectives.

An individual has a right to the most effective treatment procedures available

Treatments that have been scientifically validated should only be selected for use. Exposure of individuals to restrictive treatments (for example, some punishment protocols — see Chapter 10) is unacceptable unless these treatments are essential to produce clinically significant behavior change. Alternatively, exposure to less restrictive interventions may be equally unacceptable if they produce gradual change with behavior that may be of immediate danger to the individual or other individuals in that person's environment.

People who practice applied behavior analysis are fundamentally interested in improving the lives of the people they work with and of society in general. The guidelines outlined above make this very clear. There will be individuals in any discipline, who, from time to time, will violate such guidelines. These individuals should not be allowed to practice behavior analysis. It is important not to generalize the inappropriate practices of a few to an entire discipline.

As mentioned at several earlier stages, it is punishment protocols which most often raise ethical concerns within and concerning behavior analysis. Several of these statements of rights are relevant to the use of punishment. As also stated in earlier discussion and supported by these statements of rights, it is scarcely conceivable that the use of punishment on its own can be justified. However, the requirements to maintain personal welfare as an overriding goal and to provide the most effective treatment available, may mean that it is sometimes appropriate within a program that also teaches functional skills.

Because behavior analysis is an emerging rather than an established profession, issues of professional competence are of current concern. Whereas, for example, the role "clinical psychologist" is well-established and defined by specified training and experience in many countries, these developments have no yet taken place for "behavior analysts"; it is not established, for example, whether all behavior analysts will have initial training to graduate level in psychology or not, as some other backgrounds are certainly appropriate. However, the behavior analysis community is highly committed to specification of behavioral objectives, including those of training for themselves, and there is currently active debate on these matters. It is to be hoped that international standards and availability of common training are rapidly established.

11.5 THE RELATIONSHIP BETWEEN BASIC AND APPLIED BEHAVIOR ANALYSIS

In Chapter 1 (Section 1.10) the relationship between the experimental analysis of behavior and applied behavior analysis was examined. Because this topic is of great importance for the future development of the whole field of behavior analysis it will be discussed again in this chapter. It is now over thirty years since applied behavior analysis identified itself as a separate sub-discipline within behavior analysis (Baer, Wolf, & Risley, 1968). As originally conceptualized, applied behavior analysis was to busy itself with the application of the basic principles of learning to problems of social significance. In the first position paper which outlined the basic tenets of the applied field, Baer et al. (1968), drew a clear distinction between the activities of behavioral scientists who discover basic functional relations and those who apply such principles to ameliorate society's current problems. In some ways therefore, the original conceptualization of the relationship between the basic and applied dimensions of the science was a linear one. The basic scientist identified the fundamental properties of behavior and the applied scientist then developed interventions based on such principles.

Whatever the relationship between the basic and applied behavioral sciences there was certainly an enormous amount of development in applied behavior analysis during its first decade (roughly the 1970s). Behavioral techniques were applied to increasingly diverse topics of social interest (see Section 11.1 of this chapter), and problems that had been resistant to other forms of therapy (for example, self-injury of individuals with developmental disabilities) seemed capable of being successfully treated using behavioral methods (for example, Lovaas & Simmons, 1969). However, within a decade of its inception applied behavior analysis was being criticized as not fulfilling many of its objectives. Holland (1978) proclaimed that behavior analysis had become divorced from the parent science of behaviorism. Some suggested that basic research addressed topics that had no potential real-world applications (Cullen, 1981). Alternatively, other scientists saw the divergence between basic and applied research agendas as inevitable (Baer, 1981). According to Baer (1981), the fundamental principles of behavior had already been discovered (that is, reinforcement, punishment etc.) and the task of the applied scientist was to examine such principles in applied settings. By the 1980s behavior analysis was clearly two separate sub-disciplines with little cross-fertilization. For example, very few behavioral scientists published findings in both basic and applied journals. This trend continued through the 1990s.

Does this "separate development" matter? We think it does, and so do others as there have been calls for more integration of basic and applied research periodically during the last 20 years (Deitz, 1978; Michael, 1980; Mace, 1994a; Wacker, 1999), and in recent years the impetus for this integration seems to be greater (see Mace, 1994a in particular). We will briefly consider the costs of separation, and then go on to the possible benefits of greater integration and how that might be achieved.

We have been able to point to many successes for applied behavioral analysis, but current technology is not yet capable of treating many complex human phenomena. One could say that this is simply because there has not been time to develop it, but we have noted earlier that there was a long period when there seemed to be no progress on applications to complex human behavior. As recently as 1994, Mace (1994a) notes that the majority of applied technology is derived from the law of effect, and thus not much influenced by developments in the experimental analysis of behavior at all (as the discovery of the law of effect preceded Skinner's experimental analysis of behavior). That situation has now begun to change radically (see Leslie & Blackman, 1999, for many advances in application to complex human phenomena), but damage was done in the interim. In some respects, applied behavior analysis waned in popularity through apparent lack of progess on the "big issues" in human behavior and there was also continuing controversy about the use of aversive techniques which was out of all proportion to their use. Another negative factor, and one affecting the availability of funds for research and new developments as well as the general popularity or esteem of applied behavior analysis, was the tendency towards a narrow focus on individuals with developmental delay and behavior disorders at the expense of wider social and community issues. This arose not directly from a separation from the experimental analysis of behavior itself, but more from a preoccupation with continuing to work in those areas where techniques had already been successfully applied. In a similar vein, Hayes (1991) claims that applied researchers have focused on the examination of behavior modification techniques per se with little attention paid to basic research issues.

This disconnection of the basic and applied fields can also have negative effects on the basic research tradition. Many basic researchers are content to examine fundamental properties of behavior that may not have any direct relevance to human problems (Mace, 1994a). Such a position is academically defensible and may lead eventually to useful but unpredicted applications as mentioned earlier, but it may not garner public support in the form of research grants and other financial incentives. This in turn could produce an erosion of academic positions at universities and may negatively influence graduate applications to such research programs. More importantly, behavior analysis may simply lose the opportunity to address many of the issues to which it could potentailly make a contribution (Leslie, 1997a).

Mace (1994a) summarises some of the costs of separation and suggests some of the potential benefits of integration:

> ....the basic and applied sectors of our field have evolved toward greater separation during the past 30 years; this separation, to some extent, has been to the detriment of both areas. Behavioral technologies have been founded on only the rudimentary principles of behavior. Further, because applied behavior analysts have little connection to the basic literature, basic findings with potential to improve behavioral technologies are unlikely to be recognized and stimulate new technologies. Basic research, on the other hand, has been generally insulated from the applied agenda and has given greater emphasis to the specification and testing of behavioral laws without due consideration to their relevance to human affairs. As a result, opportunities to collaborate on the solution of important social problems and to demonstrate the tangible value of basic behavioral research to the culture have been missed (Mace, 1994a; p. 532).

Mace (1994a) also provides some concrete suggestions for establishing collaborative research relationships between the basic and applied research communities (also see Chapter 1). He models this potential relationship on the medical model of basic biomedical research which is designed to produce effective medical procedures. First, basic research could develop animal models of intractable human problems (that is, behaviors that are sometimes resistant to current applied technologies; for example, some forms of self-injury in individuals with developmental disabilities). In such laboratory analogues historical influences could be systematically manipulated. Potential independent variables (potential applied treatments) could also be systematically investigated. If robust results are eventually demonstrated with nonhuman subjects then these functional relationships could be examined with humans under laboratory conditions. This second phase of the experimental continuum is to examine whether similar functional relationships are demonstrable with humans under similar laboratory conditions. The final stage of the process is the application of the technology to deal with real human problems in applied settings. This model has potential for producing collaborative research as it is quite successful in the medical and other natural science fields. If the relationship between basic and applied behavior analysis was in some way similar to basic research and therapy in the medical professions then basic research could profit by increased financial support etc. Many lay people can see the need to conduct research to find cures for such illnesses as HIV and cancer and will probably fund such research. Basic and applied behavior analysis could possibly achieve such a symbiotic relationship and public perception in the future

Behavior analysts are now actively attempting to overcome this separation of basic and applied research interests. Wacker (1999) has urged activity in what he calls "bridge research". Bridge research can take several possible forms but fundamentally a bridge research project produces findings that can influence both basic and applied research programs. For example, a basic research question could be examined with human participants in a non-laboratory setting. While many aspects of experimental rigor might be sacrificed with such an experimental preparation the results might produce general interest across basic and applied research communities. Future systematic replications could eventually substantiate the findings of such a bridge study. One of the fundamental properties of bridge research is that it breaks the mold of the basic and applied research traditions. Wacker (1999) notes that if such research is to develop, then the editorial practices of many of the major journals in the field will have to change to support this novel research agenda.

11.6 SUMMARY

This final chapter extends the account of behavior analysis provided earlier in several ways. Applications to health and medicine are reviewed, both because of their inherent importance, and because they illustrate that the techniques shown to be effective in earlier chapters can be applied more widely. Healthy life-styles, through selection of low-fat meals, increases in physical exercise, or avoidance of risk of skin cancer or exposure to HIV infection, have been shown to be reliably enhanced with behavioral techniques, and medical problems, such as anorexia nervosa, chronic back pain, and management of self-care following tracheostomy, have been successfully treated. These types of examples of applied behavior analysis show that there is huge potential in areas traditionally regarded as the province of medicine, and they also demonstrate that even when there is clearly a biological or organic origin of a problem, behavioral intervention may nonetheless be appropriate and effective.

Consideration of applications to community issues throws light on to some assumptions that have underpinned the applications discussed throughout the rest of this volume. It has generally been presumed that the focus of attention, and treatment or intervention, will be the individual, but we must also examine the social or systemic level of analysis. Elimination of a drug abuse problem, for example, may require more attention to the situation and contingencies that prevail in the school or on the street than to the behavior of individual drug users. Alternatively, self-injurious behavior within a residential care setting may be maintained by escape from physical abuse by staff, and it is the latter that would require attention rather than the behavior of individual clients. For behavior analysis to develop further, the need to address the systemic as well as the individual level of analysis must assume a high priority. Additionally, the techniques of behavior analysis must be adapted to make them usable in less well-controlled contexts, and the language in which behavior analysis is presented to a wider public must be simplified.

Applications of behavioral analysis have, until recently, drawn on a limited number of well-established principles. However, more complex processes can be shown to be effective in real-world contexts. The matching law, for example, which has been extensively studied in the laboratory has also been demonstrated to predict behavior in naturalistic human situations — such as one where eye-contact was "unknowingly" reinforced with verbal praise — and in application to educational issues with people with developmental delay. Stimulus equivalence classes, which have been the subject of much recent laboratory research, also have important applications. Sidman's pioneering studies were concerned with the development of reading skills in those who do not readily learn to read, and recent discoveries about equivalence classes have application to the construction of effective strategies for teaching reading.

It has been evident at several points in this volume that ethical issues are raised by behavioral interventions, as indeed they are by all attempts to influence the behavior of others. The behavior-analysis community is aware of these issues, particularly because behavior analysis has often been criticized by others who are not necessarily very well informed about behavioral principles, and has generated a set of ethical guidelines. These guidelines concern the right of an individual to a therapeutic environment, the right to services aimed at enhancing personal welfare, the right to treatment by a competent behavior analyst, the right to a program that teaches functional skills, the right to assessment and ongoing evaluation, and the right to the most effective treatment procedures available. As with any ethical code, these guidelines will not resolve every issue, but they do provide an articulated framework within which judgements can be made.

The relationship between the experimental analysis of behavior and applied behavior analysis is of great importance to the future of both sub-disciplines. Although they have "grown apart", there is now much concern to sustain the interface between and, in particular, to foster bridge studies that make an impact on both the experimental analysis of behavior and applied behavior analysis. This would make behavioral research more akin to medical research in its organization, and more likely to generate the wider understanding and use which it richly deserves.

REFERENCES

Allen, K.D., Loiben, T., Allen, S.J., and Stanley, R.T. (1992). Dentist-implemented contingent escape for management of disruptive child behavior. *Journal of Applied Behavior Analysis, 25*, 629–636.

Allen, L.D., and Iwata, B.A. (1980). Reinforcing exercise maintenance: Using existing high-rate activities. *Behavior Modification, 4*, 337–354.

Allison, J. (1993). Response deprivation, reinforcement, and economics. *Journal of the Experimental Analysis of Behavior, 60*, 129–140.

Allison, J., and Timberlake, W. (1974). Instrumental and contingent saccharin licking in rats: Response deprivation and reinforcement. *Learning and Motivation, 5*, 231–247.

American Cancer Society. (1990). *Cancer facts & figures, 1990.*

Anrep, G.V. (1920). Pitch discrimination in the dog. *Journal of Physiology, 53*, 367–385.

Antonitis, J.J. (1951). Response variability in the white rat during conditioning, extinction and reconditioning. *Journal of Experimental Psychology, 42*, 273–281.

Axelrod, S. (1987). Functional and structural analysis of behavior: Approaches leading to reduced use of punishment procedures? *Research in Developmental Disabilities, 8*, 165–178.

Ayllon, T., and Azrin, N.H. (1965). The measurement and reinforcement of behavior of psychotics. *Journal of the Experimental Analysis of Behavior, 8*, 357–383.

Ayllon, T., and Azrin, N.H. (1968). *The token economy.* New York: Appleton-Century-Crofts.

Azrin, N.H., and Holz, W.C. (1966). Punishment. In W.K. Honig (Ed.), *Operant behavior: Areas of research and application.* New York: Appleton-Century-Crofts.

Azrin, N.H., Hutchinson, R.R., and Hake, D.F. (1966). Extinction-induced aggression. *Journal of the Experimental Analysis of Behavior, 9*, 191–204.

Azrin, N.H., and Powers, M.A. (1975). Eliminating classroom disturbances of emotionally disturbed children by positive practice procedures. *Behavior Therapy, 6*, 525–534.

Azrin, N.H., and Wesolowski, M.D. (1974). Theft reversal: An overcorrection procedure for eliminating stealing by retarded persons. *Journal of Applied Behavior Analysis, 7*, 577–581.

Baer, D.M. (1981). A flight of behavior analysis. *The Behavior Analyst, 4*, 85–91.

Baer, D.M. (1977). Perhaps it would be better not to know everything. *Journal of Applied Behavior Analysis, 10*, 167–172.

Baer, D.M., Peterson, R., and Sherman, J. (1967). The development of imitation by reinforcing behavioral similarity to a model. *Journal of the Experimental Analysis of Behavior, 10*, 405–416.

Baer, D.M., and Wolf, M.M. (1970). The entry into natural communities of reinforcement, In R. Ulrich, T. Stachnik, and J. Mabry (Eds.), *Control of human behavior* (Vol. 2, pp. 319–324). Glenview, IL: Scott, Foresman.

Baer, D.M., Wolf, M.M., and Risley, T.R. (1968). Some current dimensions of applied behavior analysis. *Journal of Applied Behavior Analysis, 1*, 91–97.

Baer, D.M., Wolf, M.M., and Risley, T.R. (1987). Some still-current dimensions of applied behavior analysis. *Journal of Applied Behavior Analysis, 20*, 313–328.

Bandura, A. (1965). Influence of model's reinforcement contingencies on the acquisition of imitative responses. *Journal of Personality and Social Psychology, 1*, 589–595.

Bandura, A. (1969). *Principles of behavior modification.* New York: Holt, Rinehart and Winston.

Bandura, A., and Barab, P. (1973). Processes governing disinhibitory effects through symbolic modeling. *Journal of Abnormal Psychology, 82*, 1–9.

Barlow, D.H., and Hersen, M. (1984). *Single-case experimental designs: Strategies for studying behavior change* (2nd ed.). New York: Pergamon Press.

Barnes, D., and Keenan, M. (1993). Concurrent activities and instructed human fixed-interval performance. *Journal of the Experimental Analysis of Behavior, 59*, 501–520.

Barnes, D., Healy, O., and Hayes, S.C. (1999). Relational frame theory and the relational evaluation procedure: Approaching human language as derived relational responding. In J.C. Leslie and D. Blackman (Eds.), *Issues in experimental and applied analyses of human behavior* Reno: Context Press.

Barry, J.J., and Harrison, J.M. (1957). Relations between stimulus intensity and strength of escape responding. *Psychological Reports, 3*, 3–8.

Bates, P., Renzaglia, A., and Clees, T. (1980) Improving the work performance of severely/profoundly retarded young adults: The use of the changing criterion procedural design. *Education and Training of the Mentally Retarded, 15*, 95–104.

Baum, W.M. (1974). On two types of deviation from the matching law: bias and undermatching. *Journal of the Experimental Analysis of Behavior, 22*, 231–242.

Baum, W.M. (1994). *Understanding behaviorism: Science, behavior, and culture*. New York; HarperCollins.

Beardsley, S.D., and McDowell, J.J. (1992). Application of Herrnstein hyperbola to time allocation of naturalistic human-behavior maintained by naturalistic social-reinforcement. *Journal of the Experimental Analysis of Behavior, 52*, 177–185.

Bentall, R.P., Lowe, C.F., and Beasty, A. (1985). The role of verbal behavior in human learning. *Journal of the Experimental Analysis of Behavior, 43*, 165–183.

Bhatt, R.S., Wasserman, E.A., Reynolds, W.F. jr., and Krauss, K.S. (1988). Conceptual behavior in pigeons: Categorisation of both familiar and novel examples from four classes of natural and artificial stimuli. *Journal of Experimental Psychology: Animal Behavior Processes, 14*, 219–234.

Bierman, K.L., Miller, C.L., and Stabb, S.D. (1987). Improving the social behavior and peer acceptance of rejected boys: Effects of social skill training with instructions and prohibitions. *Journal of Consulting and Clinical Psychology, 55*, 194–200.

Bijou, S.W, Peterson, R.F., and Ault, M.H. (1968). A method to integrate descriptive and experimental field studies at the level of data and empirical concepts. *Journal of Applied Behavior Analysis, 1*, 175–191.

Blampied, N.H., and Kahan, E. (1992). Acceptability of alternative punishments: A community survey. *Behavior Modification, 16*, 400–413.

Blanchard, E.B. (Ed.). (1992). Special issue: Behavioral medicine: An update for the 1990s. *Journal of Consulting and Clinical Psychology, 60*, 491–463.

Bolles, R.C. (1970). Species-specific defense reactions and avoidance learning. *Psychological Review, 77*, 32–48.

Boring, E.G. (1929). *A history of experimental psychology*. New York: The Century Company.

Bradshaw, C.M., Szabadi, E., and Bevan, P. (1977). Effects of punishment on human variable-interval performance. *Journal of the Experimental Analysis of Behavior, 27*, 275–280.

Brigham, T.A., Meier, S.M., and Goodner, V. (1995). Increasing designated driving with a program of prompts and incentives. *Journal of Applied Behavior Analysis, 28*, 83–84.

Bruner, J.S., Goodnow, J.J., and Austin, G. (1956). *A study of thinking*. New York: Wiley.

Bullock, D.H., and Smith, W.C. (1953). An effect of repeated conditioning-extinction upon operant strength. *Journal of Experimental Psychology, 46*, 349–352.

Cairns, D., and Pasino, J.A. (1977). Comparison of verbal reinforcement and feedback in the operant treatment of disability due to chronic low back pain. *Behavior Therapy, 8*, 621–630.

Capehart, J., Viney, W., and Hulicka, I.M. (1958). The effect of effort upon extinction. *Journal of Comparative and Physiological Psychology*, **51**, 507–507.

Carey, R.G., and Bucher, B.B. (1981). Identifying the educative and suppressive effects of positive practice and restitutional overcorrection. *Journal of Applied Behavior Analysis*, **14**, 71–80.

Carr, A., MacDonnell, D., and Afnan, S., (1989). Anorexia nervosa: The treatment of a male case with combined behavioural and family therapy. *Journal of Family Therapy*, **11**, 335–351.

Carr, E.G. (1994). Emerging themes in the functional analysis of problem behavior. *Journal of Applied Behavior Analysis*, **27**, 393–399. *Journal of Family Therapy*, **11**,335–351.

Carr, E.G., and Durand, V.M. (1985). Reducing behavior problems through functional communication training. *Journal of Applied Behavior Analysis*, **18**, 111–126.

Carr, E.G., Newsom, C.D., and Binkoff, J.A. (1980). Escape as a factor in the aggressive behavior in two retarded children. *Journal of Applied Behavior Analysis*, **13**, 101–117.

Carr, E.G., and Smith, C.E. (1995). Biological setting events for self-injury. *Mental Retardation and Developmental Disabilities Research Reviews*, **1**, 94–98.

Catania A.C. Concurrent operants. In W.K. Honig (Ed.), *Operant behavior: Areas of research and application*. New York: Appleton-Century-Crofts, 1966.

Catania, A.C., Matthews, B.A., and Shimoff, E. (1990). Properties of rule-governed behaviour and their implications. In D.E. Blackman and H. Lejeune (Eds.), *Behaviour analysis in theory and practice*. Hillsdale, New Jersey: Erlbaum.

Chandler, L.K., Lubeck, R.C., and Fowler, S.A. (1992). Generalization and maintenance of preschool children's social skills: A critical review and analysis. *Journal of Applied Behavior Analysis*, **25**, 415–428.

Chomsky, N. (1959). A review of Skinner's Verbal Behavior. *Language*, **35**, 26–58.

Cone, J.D. (1987). *Behavioral assessment with children and adolescents: A clinical approach*. New York: Wiley.

Connis, R. (1979). The effects of sequential pictorial cues, self-recording and praise on the job task sequencing of retarded adults. *Journal of Applied Behavior Analysis*, **12**, 355–361.

Cook, T.D., and Campbell, D.T. (Eds.) (1979). *Quasi-experimentation: Design and analysis issues for field settings*. Chicago: Rand-McNally.

Cooper, J.O., Heron, T.E., and Heward, W.L. (1987). *Applied behavior analysis*. Columbus, OH: Charles E. Merrill.

Crosbie, J. (1993). The effects of response cost and response restriction on a multiple-response repertoire with humans. *Journal of the Experimental Analysis of Behavior*, **59**, 173–192.

Cullen, C. (1981). The flight to the laboratory. *The Behavior Analyst*, **4**, 81–83.

Cummings, C. (1986). A review of the impact of nutrition on health and profits and a discussion of successful program elements. *American Journal of Health Promotion*, **1**, 14–22.

Cunningham, C.E., and Linscheid, T.R. (1976). Elimination of chronic infant rumination by electric shock. *Behavior Therapy*, **7**, 231–234.

Cuvo, A.J. (1979). Multiple-baseline design in instructional research: Pitfalls of measurement and procedural advantages. *American Journal of Mental Deficiency*, **11**, 345–355.

Cuvo, A.J., Davis, P.K., O'Reilly, M.F., Mooney, B.M., and Crowley, R. (1992). Promoting stimulus control with textual prompts and performance feedback for persons with mild disabilities. *Journal of Applied Behavior Analysis*, **25**, 477–489.

Cuvo, A.J., Leaf, R.B., and Borakove, L.S. (1978). Training janitorial skills to the mentally retarded: Acquisition, generalization, and maintenance. *Journal of Applied Behavior Analysis*, **11**,345–355.

Darwin, C.R. (1873). *The expression of the emotions in man and animals*. London: Murray.

Deitz, S.M. (1978). Current status of applied behavior analysis: Science versus technology. *American Psychologist*, **33**, 805–814.

Deitz, S.M., Repp, A.C., and Deitz, D.E.D. (1976). Reducing inappropriate classroom behavior of retarded students through three procedures of differential reinforcement. *Journal of Mental Deficiency Research,* **20**, 155–170.

DeLuca, R.V., and Holborn, S.W. (1992). Effects of a variable-ratio reinforcement schedule with changing criteria on exercise in obese and nonobese boys. *Journal of Applied Behavior Analysis,* **25**, 671–679.

deLissovoy, V. (1964). Head banging in early childhood: Review of empirical studies. *Pediatric Digest,* **6**, 49–55.

Dennis, I., Hampton, J.A, and Lea, S.E.G. (1973). New problem in concept formation. *Nature* (London), **243**, 101–102.

Derby, K.M., Wacker, D.P., Sasso, G., Steege, M., Northup, J., Cigrand, K., and Asmus, J. (1992). Brief functional assessment techniques to evaluate aberrant behavior in an outpatient setting: A summary of 79 cases. *Journal of Applied Behavior Analysis,* **25**, 713–721.

Derrickson, J.G., Neef, N., and Parrish, J.M. (1991). Teaching self-administration of suctioning to children with tracheostomies. *Journal of Applied Behavior Analysis,* **24**, 563–570.

DeVries, J.E., Burnette, M.M., and Redmon, W.K. (1991). Aids prevention: Improving nurses' compliance with glove wearing through performance feedback. *Journal of Applied Behavior Analysis,* **24**, 705–711.

Dinsmoor, J.A., and Winograd, E. (1958). Shock intensity in variable interval escape schedules. *Journal of the Experimental Analysis of Behavior,* **1**, 145–148.

Doleys, D.M., Wells, K.C., Hobbs, S.A., Roberts, M.W., and Cartelli, L.M. (1976). The effects of social punishment on noncompliance: A comparison of time out and positive practice. *Journal of Applied Behavior Analysis,* **9**, 471–482.

Dubbert, P.M., Johnson, W. G., Schlundt, D.G., and Montague, N.W. (1984). The influence of caloric information on cafateria food choices. *Journal of Applied Behavior Analysis,* **17**, 82–85.

Dugdale, N., and Lowe, C.F. (1990). Naming and stimulus equivalence. In D.E. Blackman and H. Lejeune (Eds.), *Behaviour analysis in theory and practice: contributions and controversies.* Hove, Sussex: Lawrence Erlbaum.

Dunham, P.J. (1971). Punishment: Method and theory. *Psychological Review,* **78**, 58–70.

Dunlap, G., Kern–Dunlap, L., Clarke, S., and Robbins, F. R. (1991). Functional assessment, curricular revision, and severe behavior problems. *Journal of Applied Behavior Analysis,* **24**, 387–397.

Durand, V.M. (1990). *Severe behavior problems: A functional communication training approach.* New York: Guilford Press.

Durand, V.M., and Carr, E.G. (1991). Functional communication training to reduce challenging behavior: Maintenance and application in new settings. *Journal of Applied Behavior Analysis,* **24**, 251–264.

Durand, V.M., and Carr, E.G. (1987). Social influences on self-stimulatory behavior: Analysis and treatment application. *Journal of Applied Behavior Analysis,* **20**, 119–132.

Eisenberger, R., Karpman, M., and Trattner, J. (1967). What is the necessary and sufficient condition for reinforcement in the contingency situation? *Journal of Experimental Psychology,* **74**, 342–350.

Estes, W.K. (1944). An experimental study of punishment. *Psychological Monographs,* **57**, (Whole No. 263).

Estes, W.K., and Skinner, B.F. (1941). Some quantitative properties of anxiety. *Journal of Experimental Psychology,* **29**, 390–400.

Fantino, E. (1977). Conditioned reinforcement: Choice and information. In W.K. Honig and J.E.R. Staddon (Eds.), *Handbook of operant behavior.* Englewood Cliffs, New Jersey: Prentice Hall.

Favell, J.E., McGimpsey, J.F., and Jones M.L. (1980). Rapid eating in the retarded: Reduction by nonaversive procedures. *Behavior Modification, 4*, 481–492.

Fawcett, S.B. (1991). Some values guiding community research and action. *Journal of Applied Behavior Analysis, 24*, 621–636.

Fearing, F. (1930). *Reflex action: A study in the history of physiological psychology.* Baltimore: Williams and Wilkins.

Ferster, C.B., and Skinner, B.F. (1957). *Schedules of reinforcement.* New York: Appleton-Century-Crofts.

Fields, L., and Verhave, T. (1987). The structure of equivalence classes. *Journal of the Experimental Analysis of Behavior, 48*, 317–332.

Fields, L., Adams, B.J., Verhave, T., and Newman, S. (1990). The effects of nodality on the formation of equivalence classes. *Journal of the Experimental Analysis of Behavior, 53*, 345–358.

Fischer, S.M., Iwata, B.A., and Mazaleski, J.L. (1997). Noncontingent delivery of arbitrary reinforcers as treatment for self-injurious behavior. *Journal of Applied Behavior Analysis, 30*, 239–249.

Fisher, W.W., and Mazur, J.E. (1997). Basic and applied research on choice responding. *Journal of Applied Behavior Analysis, 30*, 387–410.

Fisher, W.W., Piazza, C.C., Bowman, L.G., Hagopian, L.P., Owens, J.C., and Slevin, I. (1992). A comparison of two approaches for identifying reinforcers for persons with severe and profound disabilities. *Journal of Applied Behavior Analysis, 25*, 491–498.

Fordyce, W.E., Fowler, R.S., Lehmann, J.F., DeLateur, B.J., Sand, P.L., and Trieschmann, R.B. (1974). Operant conditioning in the treatment of chronic pain. *Archives of Physical Medicine and Rehabilitation, 54*, 399–408.

Foster-Johnson, L., Ferro, J., and Dunlap, G. (1994). Preferred curricular activities and reduced problem behaviors in students with intellectual disabilties. *Journal of Applied Behavior Analysis, 27*, 493–504.

Fox, D.K., Hopkins, B.L., and Anger, W.K. (1987). The long-term effects of a token economy on safety performance in open-pit mining. *Journal of Applied Behavior Analysis, 20*, 215–224.

Foxx, R.M., and Azrin, N.H. (1972). Restitution: A method for eliminating aggressive-disruptive behavior of retarded and brain damaged patients. *Behaviour Research and Therapy, 10*, 15–27.

Foxx, R.M., and Azrin, N.H. (1973). *Toilet training the retarded: A rapid program for day and nighttime independent toileting.* Champaign, IL: Research Press.

Foxx, R.M., and Bechtel, D.R. (1983). Overcorrection: A review and analysis. In S. Axelrod and J. Apsche (Eds.), *The effects of punishment on human behavior* (pp.133–220). New York: Academic Press.

France, K.G., and Hudson, S.M. (1990). Behavior management of infant sleep disturbance. *Journal of Applied Behavior Analysis, 23*, 91–98.

Frick, F.S., and Miller, G.A. (1951). A statistical description of operant conditioning. *American Journal of Psychology, 64*, 20–36.

Friman, P.C., Finney, J.W., Glasscock, S.T., Weigel, J.W., and Christophersen, E.R. (1986). Testicular self-examination: Validation of a training strategy for early cancer detection. *Journal of Applied Behavior Analysis, 19*, 87–92.

Friman, P.C., Hayes, S.C., and Wilson, K.G. (1998). Why behavior analysts should study emotion: The example of anxiety. *Journal of Applied Behavior Analysis, 31*, 137–156.

Friman, P.C., and Poling, A. (1995). Making life easier with effort: Basic findings and applied research on response effort. *Journal of Applied Behavior Analysis, 28*, 583–590.

Friman, P.C., and Vollmer, D. (1995). Successful use of nocturnal urine alarm for diurnal enuresis. *Journal of Applied Behavior Analysis, 28*, 89–90.

Garcia, J., and Koelling, R.A. (1966). Relation of cue to consequence In avoidance learning. *Pychonomic Science,* **4**, 123–124.

Garfinkel, P., and Garner, D. (1982). *Anorexia nervosa: A multidemsional perspective.* New York: Brunner/Mazel.

Gaylord-Ross, R.J., Haring, T.G., Breen, C., and Pitts-Conway, V. (1984). The training and generalization of social interaction skills with autistic youth. *Journal of Applied Behavior Analysis,* **17**, 229–247.

Geller, E.S., Hahn, H.A. (1984). Promoting safety belt use at industrial sites: An effective program for blue collar employees. *Professional Psychology: Research and Practice,* **15**, 553–564.

Gladstone, E.W., and Cooley, J. (1975). Behavioral similarity as a reinforcer for preschool children. *Journal of the Experimental Analysis of Behavior,* **23**, 357–368.

Goh, H., and Iwata, B.A. (1994). Behavioral persistence and variability during extinction of self-injury maintained by escape. *Journal of Applied Behavior Analysis,* **21**, 173–174.

Goldstein, A.P., and Krasner, L. (1987). *Modern applied psychology.* New York: Pergamon.

Gormezano, I., Schneiderman, N., Deaux, E.B., and Fuentes, I. (1962). Nictitating membrane: Classical conditioning and extinction in the albino rabbit. *Science,* **138**, 33–34.

Grant, L., and Evans, A. (1994). *Principles of behavior analysis.* New York: HarperCollins.

Gray, J.A. (1975). *Elements of a two-process theory of learning.* London: Academic Press.

Greene, B.F., Winett, R.A., Van Houten, R., Geller, E.S., and Iwata, B.A. (1987). *Behavior analysis in the community: 1968–1986 from the Journal of Applied Behavior Analysis.* Lawrence, Kansas: Society for the Experimental Analysis of Behavior, Inc.

Guthrie, E.R., and Horton, G.P. (1946). *Cats in a puzzle box.* New York: Rinehart.

Guttman, N. (1956). The pigeon, the spectrum and other complexities. Psychological Reports, **2**, 449–460.

Guttman, N., and Kalish, H.I. (1956). Discriminability and stimulus generalization. *Journal of Experimental Psychology,* **51**, 79–88.

Hagopian, L.P., Fisher, W.P., and Legacy, S.M. (1994). Schedule effects of noncontingent reinforcement on attention-maintained destructive behavior in identical quadruplets. *Journal of Applied Behavior Analysis,* **27**, 37–325.

Hailman, J.P. (1969). Spectral pecking preferences in gull chicks. *Journal of Comparative and Physiological Psychology,* **67**, 465–467.

Hall, R.V., Lund, D., and Jackson, D. (1968). Effects of teacher attention on study behavior. *Journal of Applied Behavioral Analysis,* **1**, 1–12.

Halle, J.W., Baer, D.M., and Spradlin, J.E. (1981). Teacher's generalized use of delay as a stimulus control procedure to increase language use in handicapped children. *Journal of Applied Behavior Analysis,* **14**, 389–409.

Halle, P.A., De Boynson-Bardies, B., and Vihman, M.M. (1991). Beginnings of prosodic organisation: intonation and duration of disyllables produced by Japanese and French infants. *Language and Speech,* **34**, 299–318.

Halliday, S., and Leslie, J.C. (1986). A longitudinal study of the development of mother-child interaction. *British Journal of Developmental Psychology,* **4**, 211–222.

Haring, T.G., and Kennedy, C.H. (1990). Contextual control of problem behavior in students with severe disabilities. *Journal of Applied Behavior Analysis,* **23**, 235–243.

Harlow, H.F. (1949). The formation of learning sets. (1949). *Psychological Review,* **56**, 51–65.

Hawkins, R.P., and Dobes, R.W. (1975). Behavioral definitions in applied behavior analysis: Explicit or implicit. In B.C. Etzel, J.M. LeBlanc, and D.M. Baer (Eds.), *New developments in behavioral research: Theory, methods, and applications: In honor of Sidney W. Bijou.* Hillsdale, NJ: Erlbaum.

Hayes, S.C. (1991). The limits of technological talk. *Journal of Applied Behavior Analysis,* **24**, 417–420.

Hayes, S.C., and Hayes, L.J. (1992). Verbal relations and the evolution of behavioral analysis. *American Psychologist, 47*, 1385–1392.

Hearst, E. (1961). Resistance-to-extinction functions in the single organism. *Journal of the Experimental Analysis of Behavior, 4*, 133–144.

Hearst, E., Besley, S., and Farthing, G.W. (1970). Inhibition and the stimulus control of operant behavior. *Journal of the Experimental Analysis of Behavior, 14*, 373–409.

Hefferline, R.F., and Keenan, B. (1963). Amplitude-induction gradient of a small-scale (covert) operant. *Journal of the Experimental Analysis of Behavior, 6*, 307–315.

Herman, L.M., and Arbeit, W.R. (1973). Stimulus control and auditory discrimination learning sets in the bottlenose dolphin. *Journal of the Experimental Analysis of Behavior, 19*, 379–394.

Herman, R.L., and Azrin, N.H. (1964). Punishment by noise in an alternative response situation. *Journal of the Experimental Analysis of Behavior, 7*, 185–188.

Herrnstein, R.J. (1961). Relative and absolute strength of response as a function of frequency of reinforcement. *Journal of the Experimental Analysis of Behavior, 4*, 267–272.

Higgins-Hains, A., and Baer, D.M. (1989). Interaction effects in multielement designs: Inevitable, desirable, and ignorable. *Journal of Applied Behavior Analysis, 22*, 57–69.

Hineline, P.H. (1977). Negative reinforcement and avoidance. In W.K. Honig and J.E.R. Staddon (Eds.), *Handbook of operant behavior* (pp 364–414). Englewood Cliffs, NJ: Prentice-Hall.

Hoffman, H.S., and Fleshler, M. (1962). The course of emotionality in the development of avoidance. *Journal of Experimental Psychology, 64*, 288–294.

Holland, J.G. (1978). Behaviorism: Part of the problem or part of the solution? *Journal of Applied Behavior Analysis, 11*, 163–174.

Honig, W.K., and Slivka, R.M. (1964). Stimulus generalization of the effects of punishment. *Journal of the Experimental Analysis of Behavior, 7*, 21–25.

Horne, P. and Lowe, C.F. (1999). Putting the naming account to the test: Preview of an experimental program. In J.C. Leslie and D. Blackman (Eds.), *Issues in experimental and applied analyses of human behavior.* Reno: Context Press.

Horner, R.D., and Keilitz, I. (1975). Training mentally retarded adolescents to brush their teeth. *Journal of Applied Behavior Analysis, 8*, 301–309.

Horner, R.H., and Day, H.M. (1991). The effects of response efficiency on functionally equivalent competing behaviors. *Journal of Applied Behavior Analysis, 24*, 719–732.

Horner, R.H., Dunlap, G., and Koegel, R.L. (Eds.), (1988). *Generalization and maintenance: Lift-style changes in applied settings.* Baltimore: Paul H. Brookes.

Horner, R.H., Sprague, J.R., and Wilcox, B. (1982). Constructing general case programs for community activities. In B. Wilcox and T. Bellamy (Eds.), *Design of high school for severely handicapped students.* Baltimore: Paul H. Brookes.

Howie, P.M., and Woods, C.L. (1982). Token reinforemenet during the instatement and shaping of fluency in the treatmenet of stuttering. *Journal of Applied Behavior Analysis, 15*, 55–64.

Hughes, C., Harmer, M.L., Killian, D.J., and Niarhos, F. (1995). The effects of multiple-exemplar self-instructional training on high school students' generalized conversational interactions. *Journal of Applied Behavior Analysis, 28*, 201–218.

Hull, C.L. (1943). *Principles of behavior.* New York: Appleton-Century-Crofts.

Hunt. H.F, and Brady, J.V. (1951). Some effects of electro-convulsive shock on a conditioned emotional response ("anxiety"). *Journal of Comparative and Physiological Psychology, 44*, 88–98.

Hunt, H.F., and Otis, L.S. (1953). Conditioned and unconditioned emotional defecation in the rat. *Journal of Comparative and Physiological Psychology, 46*, 378–382.

Isaacs, C.D., Thomas, I., and Goldiamond, I. (1960). Application of operant conditioning to reinstate verbal behavior in psychotics. *Journal of Speech and Hearing Disorders, 25*, 8–12.

Israel, A.C., and Stolmaker, L. (1980). Behavioral treatment of obesity in children and adolescents. In M. Hersen, R.M. Eisler, and P.M. Miller (Eds.), *Progress in behavior modification*. New York: Academic Press.

Iwata, B.A. (1987). Negative reinforcement in applied behavior analysis: An emerging technology. *Journal of Applied Behavior Analysis,* **20**, 361–378.

Iwata, B.A. (1994). Functional analysis methodology: Some closing comments. *Journal of Applied Behavior Analysis,* **27**, 413–418.

Iwata, B.A., Dorsey, M.F., Slifer, K.J., Bauman, K.E., Richman, G.S. (1982). Toward a functional analysis of self-injury. *Analysis and Intervention in Developmental Disabilities,* **2**, 3–20. (Reprinted in *Journal of Applied Behavior Analysis* (1994), **27**, 197–209.)

Iwata, B.A., Pace, G.M., Cowdery, G.E., and Miltenberger, R.G. (1994). What makes extinction work: An analysis of procedural form and function. *Journal of Applied Behavior Analysis,* **27**, 131–144.

Iwata, B.A., Pace, G.M., Dorsey, M.F., Zarcone, J.R., Vollmer, T.R., Smith, R.G., Rodgers, T. A., Lerman, D.C., Shore, B.A., Mazaleski, J.L., Goh, H. Cowdery, G.E., Kalsher, M.J., McCosh, K.C., and Willis, K.D. (1994). The functions of self-injurious behavior: An experimental-epidemiological analysis. *Journal of Applied Behavior Analysis,* **27**, 215–240.

Iwata, B.A., Pace, G.M., Kalsher, M.J., Cowdery, G.E., and Cataldo, M.F. (1990). Experimental analysis and extinction of self-injurious escape behavior. *Journal of Applied Behavior Analysis,* **23**, 11–27.

Iwata, B.A, Vollmer, T.R., and Zarcone, J.R. (1990). The experimental (functional) analysis of behavior disorders: Methodology, applications, and limitations. In A.C. Repp and N.N. Singh (Eds.), *Prespectives on the use of nonaversive and aversive interventions for persons with developmental disabilities* (pp. 301–330). Sycamore, Ill: Sycamore Publishing Company.

Jackson, D.A., and Wallace, R.F. (1974). The modification and generalization of voice loudness in a 15-year-old retarded girl. *Journal of Applied Behavior Analysis,* **7**, 461–471.

Jackson, N.C., and Mathews, M.R. (1995). Using public feedback to increase contributions to a multipurpose senior center. *Journal of Applied Behavior Analysis,* **28**, 449–455.

Jason, L.A., and Liotta, R.F. (1982). Reduction of cigarette smoking in a university cafeteria. *Journal of Applied Behavior Analysis,* **15**, 573–577.

Johnson, B.F., and Cuvo, A.J. (1981). Teaching mentally retarded adults to cook. *Behavior Modification,* **5**, 187–202.

Kamin, L.J. (1957). The effects of termination of the CS and avoidance of the US on avoidance learning: An extension. *Canadian Journal of Psychology,* **11**, 48–56.

Kamin, L.J. (1968). Attention-like processes in classical conditioning. In M.R. Jones (Ed.), *Miami symposium on the prediction of behavior: Aversive stimuli.* Coral Gables, Florida: University of Miami Press.

Kazdin, A.E. (1980). Acceptability of alternative treatments for deviant child behavior. *Journal of Applied Behavioral Analysis,* **13**, 259–273.

Kazdin, A.E. (1982). *Single-case research designs: Methods for clinical and applied settings.* New York: Oxford University Press.

Kazdin, A.E. (1987). *Conduct disorder in childhood and adolescence.* Newbury Park, CA: Sage.

Kazdin, A.E. (1994). *Behavior modification in applied settings.* Fifth edition. Pacific Grove, California: Brooks/Cole.

Kazdin, A.E., and Polster R. (1973) Intermittent token reinforcement and response maintenance in extinction. *Behavior Therapy,* **4**, 386–391.

Keller, F.S., and Schoenfeld, W.N. (1950). Principles of psychology. New York: Appleton-Century–Crofts.

Kennedy, C.H., Itkonen, T., and Lindquist, K. (1994). Nodality effects during equivalence class formation: An extension to sight-word reading and concept development. *Journal of Applied Behavior Analysis, 27*, 673–683,

Kennedy, C.H., and Meyer, K. (1996). Sleep deprivation, allergy symptoms, and negatively reinforced challenging behavior. *Journal of Applied Behavior Analysis, 29*, 133–135.

Kennedy, C.H., and Souza, G. (1995). Functional analysis and treatment of eye poking. *Journal of Applied Behavior Analysis, 28*, 27–37.

Kern, L., Wacker, D.P., Mace, F.C., Falk, G.D., Dunlap, G., and Kromrey, J.D. (1995). Improving the peer interactions of students with emotional and behavioral disorders through self-evaluation procedures: A component analysis and group application. *Journal of Applied Behavior Analysis, 28*, 47–59.

Kuno, H., Kitadate, T., and Iwamoto, T. (1994). Formation of transitivity in conditional matching to sample by pigeons. *Journal of the Experimental Analysis of Behavior, 62*, 399–408.

Lagomarcino, A., Reid, D.H., Ivancic, M.T., and Faw, G.D. (1984). Leisure-dance instruction for severely and profoundly retarded persons: Teaching an intermediate community-living skill. *Journal of Applied Behavior Analysis, 17*, 71–84.

Lalli, J.S., Zanolli, K., and Wohn, T. (1994). Using extinction to promote response variability in toy play. *Journal of Applied Behavior Analysis, 27*, 735–736.

LaVigna, G.D., and Donnellan, A. (1986). *Alternatives to punishment: Solving behavior problems with non-aversive strategies.* New York: Irvington.

Lea, S.E.G., and Harrison, S.N. (1978). Discrimination of polymorphous concepts by pigeons. *Quarterly Journal of Experimental Psychology, 1978, 30*, 521–537.

Lea, S.E.G., Tarpy, R.M., and Webley, P. (1987). *The individual in the economy.* Cambridge: Cambridge University Press.

Lennox, D.B., and Miltenberger, R.G. (1989). Conducting a functional assessment of problem behavior in applied settings. *Journal of the Association for Persons with Severe Handicaps, 14*, 304–311.

Lerman, D.C., and Iwata, B.A. (1993). Descriptive and experimental analyses of variables maintaining self-injurious behavior. *Journal of Applied Behavior Analysis, 26*, 293–319.

Lerman, D.C., and Iwata, B.A. (1996). Developing a technology for the use of operant extinction in clinical settings: An examination of basic and applied research. *Journal of Applied Behavior Analysis, 29*, 345–382.

Lerman, D.C., and Iwata, B.A. (1995). Prevalence of the extinction burst and its attenuation during treatment. *Journal of Applied Behavior Analysis, 28*, 93–94.

Lerman, D.C., Iwata, B.A., Shore, B.A., and DeLeon, I.G. (1997). Effects of intermittent punishment on self-injurious behavior: An evaluation of schedule thinning. *Journal of Applied Behavior Analysis, 30*, 187–201.

Leslie, J.C. (1993). The kraken wakes: Behaviourism in the twenty-first century. *Irish Journal of Psychology, 14*, 219–232.

Leslie, J.C. (1996). *Principles of behavioral analysis.* Amsterdam: Harwood Academic.

Leslie, J.C. (1997a). Applied psychology from the standpoint of behavioural analysis. In K. Dillenburger, M.F. O'Reilly, and M. Keenan (Eds.), *Advances in behaviour analysis.* Dublin: University College Dublin Press.

Leslie, J.C. (1997b). Ethical implicatons of behavior modification: Historical and current issues. *Psychological Record, 47*, 637–648.

Leslie, J.C., and Blackman, D. (Eds.) (1999). *Issues in experimental and applied analyses of human behavior.* Reno: Context Press.

Lindsley, O.R. (1956). Operant conditioning methods applied to research in chronic schizophrenics. *Psychiatric Research Reports, 5*, 118–139.

Lindsley, O.R. (1960). Characteristics of the behavior of chronic psychotics as revealed by free-operant conditioning methods. *Diseases of the Nervous System* (Monograph Supplement 21), 66–78.

Linscheid, T.R., and Cunningham, C.E. (1977). A controlled demonstration of the effectiveness of electric shock in the elimination of chronic infant rumination. *Journal of Applied Behavior Analysis*, **10**, 500.

Linscheid, T.R., Iwata, B.A., Ricketts, R.W., Williams, D.E., and Griffin, J.C. (1990). Clinical evaluation of the self-injurious behavior inhibiting system (SIBIS). *Journal of Applied Behavior Analysis*, **23**, 53–78.

Lombard, D., Neubauer, T.E., Canfield, D., and Wiinett, R.A. (1991). Behavioral community intervention to reduce the risk of skin cancer. *Journal of Applied Behavior Analysis*, **24**, 677–686.

Lovaas, O.I., and Schreibman, L. (1971). Stimulus overselectivity of autistic children in a two stimulus situaton. *Behaviour Research and Therapy*, **9**, 305–310.

Lovaas, O.I., and Simmons, J.Q. (1969). Manipulation of self-destruction in three retarded children. *Journal of Applied Behavior Analysis*, **2**, 143–157.

Lowe, K., and Lutzker, J.R. (1979). Increasing compliance to a medical regimen with a juvenile diabetic. *Behavior Therapy*, **10**, 57–64.

Luce, S.C., Delquadri, J., and Hall, R.V. (1980). Contingent exercise: A mild but powerful procedure for suppressing inappropriate verbal and aggressive behavior. *Journal of Applied Behavior Analysis*, **13**, 583–594.

Mace, F.C. (1994a). Basic research needed for stimulating the development of behavioral technologies. *Journal of the Experimental Analysis of Behavior*, **61**, 529–550.

Mace, F.C. (1994b). The significance and future of functional analysis methodologies. *Journal of Applied Behavior Analysis*, **27**, 385–392.

Mace, F.C., and Knight, D. (1986). Functional analysis and treatment of severe pica. *Journal of Applied Behavior Analysis*, **19**, 411–416.

Mace, F.C., Neef, N.A., Shade, D., and Mauro, B.C. (1994). Limited matching on concurrent-schedule reinforcement of academic behavior. *Journal of Applied Behavior Analysis*, **27**, 585–596.

Mackintosh, N.J. (1974). *Psychology of animal learning*. London: Academic Press.

Mackintosh, N.J. (1977). Stimulus control: Attention factors. In W.K. Honig and J.E.R. Staddon (Eds.), *Handbook of operant behavior*. Englewood Cliffs, N.J.: Prentice-Hall.

Mackintosh, N.J. (1997). Has the wheel turned full circle? Fifty years of learning theory, 1946–1996. *Quarterly Journal of Experimental Psychology*, **50A**, 879–898.

Matson, J.L., and Taras, M.E. (1989) A 20-year review of punishment and alternative methods to treat problem behaviors in developmentally disabled persons. *Research in Developmental Disabilities*, **10**, 85–104.

Mayer, J. (1970). Some aspects of the problem of regulating food intake and obesity. *International Psychiatry Clinics*, **7**, 225–234.

Mayer, J.A., Heins, J.M., Vogel, J.M., Morrison, D.C., Lankester, L.V., and Jacobs, A.L. (1986). Promoting low-fat entree choices in public cafaterias. *Journal of Applied Behavior Analysis*, **19**, 397–402.

Mazaleski, J.L., Iwata, B.A., Vollmer, T.R., Zarcone, J.R., and Smith, R.G. (1993). Analysis of the reinforcement and extinction components in DRO contingencies with self-injury. *Journal of Applied Behavior Analysis*, **26**, 143–156.

Mazur, J.E. (1997). Choice, delay, probability, and conditioned reinforcement. *Animal Learning and Behavior*, **25**, 131–147.

McGee, J.J., Menolascino, F.J., Hobbs, D.C., and Menousek, P.E. (1987). *Gentle teaching: A nonaversive approach for helping persons with mental retardation.* New York: Human Sciences Press.

Meichenbaum, D., and Goodman, J. (1971). The developmental control of operant motor responding by verbal operants. *Journal of Experimental Child Psychology, 7*, 553–565.

Meyers, D.V. (1975). Extinction, DRO, and response cost for eliminating self-injurious behavior: A case study. *Behavior Research and Therapy, 13*, 189–191.

Michael, J. (1974). Statistical inference for individual organism research: Mixed blessing or curse. *Journal of Applied Behavior Analysis, 7*, 647–653.

Michael, J.L. (1980). Flight from behavior analysis. *The Behavior Analyst, 3*, 1–24.

Michael, J. (1982). Distinguishing between discriminative and motivational functions of stimuli. *Journal of the Experimental Analysis of Behavior, 37*, 149–155.

Michael, J. (1993). Establishing operations. *The Behavior Analyst, 16*, 191–206.

Millenson, J.R., and Hurwitz, H.M.B. (1961). Some temporal and sequential properties of behavior during conditioning and extinction. *Journal of the Experimental Analysis of Behavior, 4*, 97–105.

Millenson, J.R., and Leslie, J.C. (1974). The conditioned emotional response (CER) as a baseline for the study of anti-anxiety drugs. *Neuropharmacology, 13*, 1–9.

Morris, E.K., and Redd, W.H. (1975). Children's performance and social preference for positive, negative, and mixed adult-child interactions. *Child Development, 46*, 525–531.

Mowrer, O.H., and Jones, H.M. (1943). Extinction and behavior variability as functions of effortfulness of task. *Journal of Experimental Psychology, 33*, 369–386.

Muenzinger, K.F., and Fletcher, F.M. (1936). Motivation in learning. VI. Escape from electric shock compared with hungerfood tension in the visual discrimination habit. *Journal of Comparative Psychology, 22*, 79–91.

Nation, J.R., and Woods, P. (1978). Persistence: The role of partial reinforcement in psychotherapy. *Journal of Experimental Psychology: General, 109*, 175–207.

National Institutes of Health Consensus Development Conference Statement (1989). *Treatment of destructive behaviors in persons with developmental disabilities.* Bethesda, MD: NICHD.

Neisworth, J.T., and Moore, F. (1972). Operant treatment of asthmatic responding with the parent as therapist. *Behavior Therapy, 3*, 95–99.

Northup, S., Wacker, D., Sasso, G., Steege, M., Cigrand, K., Cook, J., and DeRaad, A. (1991). A brief functional analysis of aggressive and alternative behavior in an outclinic setting. *Journal of Applied Behavior Analysis, 24*, 509–522.

O'Donoghue, D., and O'Reilly, M.F. (1996). *Assessment of chronic self-injury in an adult with dual diagnosis.* Unpublished manuscript. Department of Psychology, University College Dublin.

Oliver, C. (1995). Annotation: Self-injurious behaviour in children with learning disabilities: Recent advances in assessment and intervention. *Journal of Child Psychology and Psychiatry, 30*, 909–927.

O'Neill, R., Horner, R., Albin, R., Storey, K., and Sprague, J. (1990). *Functional analysis: A practical assessment guide.* Sycamore, Illinois: Sycamore Publishing Company.

O'Reilly, M.F. (1995). Functional analysis and treatment of escape-maintained aggression correlated with sleep deprivation. *Journal of Applied Behavior Analysis, 28*, 225–226.

O'Reilly, M.F. (1996). Assessment and treatment of episodic self-injury: A case study. *Research in Developmental Disabilities, 17*, 349–361.

O'Reilly, M.F., and Cuvo, A.J. (1989). Teaching self-treatment of cold symptoms to an anoxic brain injured adult. *Behavioral Residential Treatment, 4*, 359–375.

O'Reilly, M.F. and Glynn, D. (1995). Using a problem-solving approach to teach social skills to students with mild intellectual disabilities. *Education and Training in Mental Retardation and Developmental Disabilities, 30*, 187–198.

O'Reilly, M.F., Green, G., and Braunling–McMorrow, D. (1990). Self-administered written prompts to teach home accident prevention skills to adults with brain injuries. *Journal of Applied Behavior Analysis, 23*, 431–446.

O'Reilly, M.F., O'Kane, N., Byrne, P., and Lancioni, G. (1996). Increasing the predictability of theraputic interactions for a client with acquired brain injury: An analysis of the effect on verbal abuse. *Irish Journal of Psychology, 17*, 258–268.

Osgood, C.E. (1953). *Method and theory in experimental psychology.* New York: Oxford University Press.

Pace, G.M., Ivancic, M.T., Edwards, G.L., Iwata, B.A., and Page, T.J. (1985). Assessment of stimulus preference and reinforcer value with profoundly retarded individuals. *Journal of Applied Behavior Analysis, 18*, 249–255.

Paclawskyj, T.R., and Vollmer, T.R. (1995). Reinforcer assessment for children with developmental disabilities and visual impairments. *Journal of Applied Behavior Analysis, 28*, 219–224.

Pavlov, I.P. (1927). *Conditioned reflexes.* London: Oxford University Press.

Pavlov, I.P. (1928). *Lectures on conditioned reflexes.* New York: international Publishers.

Pearce, J.M., Redhead, E.S., and Aydin, A.(1997). Partial reinforcement in appetitive Pavlovian conditioning with rats. *Quarterly Journal of Experimental Psychology, 50B*, 273–294.

Peine, H.A., Liu, L., Blakelock, H., Jenson, W.R., and Osborne, J.G. (1991). The use of contingent water misting in the treatment of self-choking. *Journal of Behavior Therapy and Experimental Psychiatry, 22*, 225–231.

Perin, C.T. (1942). Behavior potentiality as a joint function of the amount of training and the degree of hunger at the time of extinction. *Journal of Experimental Psychology, 30*, 93–113.

Poling, A. and Ryan, C. (1982). Differential-reinforcement-of-other-behavior schedules: Theraputic applications. *Behavior Modification, 6*, 3–21.

Porterfield, J.K., Herbert-Jackson, E., and Risley, T.R. (1976). Contingent observation: An effective and acceptable procedure for reducing disruptive behavior of young children in a group setting. *Journal of Applied Behavior Analysis, 9*, 55–64.

Premack, D. (1962). Reversibility of the reinforcement relation. *Science, 136*, 255–257.

Pyles, D.A.M., and Bailey, J.S. (1990). Diagnosing severe behavior problems. In A.C. Repp and N.N. Singh (Eds.), *Prespectives on the use of nonaversive and aversive interventions for persons with developmental disabilities* (pp.381–401). Sycamore, Ill: Sycamore Publishing Company.

Rapport, M.D., Murphy, H.A., and Bailey, J.S. (1982). Ritalin versus response cost in the control of hyperactive children: A within-subject comparison. *Journal of Applied Behavior Analysis, 15*, 205–216.

Rasing, E.J., and Duker, P.C. (1992). Effects of a multifaceted training procedure on the acquisition and generalization of social behaviors in language-disabled deaf children. *Journal of Applied Behavior Analysis, 25*, 723–734.

Repp, A.C., Deitz, S.M., and Speir, N.C. (1975). Reducing stereotypic responding of retarded persons through the differential reinforcement of other behaviors. *American Journal of Mental Deficiency, 80*, 51–56.

Reichle, J., and Wacker, D.P. (1993). *Communicative alternatives to challenging behavior: Intergrating functional assessment and intervention strategies.* Baltimore: Paul Brookes.

Rescorla, R.A. (1968). Probability of shock in the presence and absence of CS in fear conditioning. *Journal of Comparative and Physiological Psychology, 66*, 1–5.

Rescorla, R.A. (1988). Pavlovian conditoning: It's not what you think it is. *American Psychologist,* **43**, 151–160.

Rescorla, R.A., and Wagner, A.R. (1972). A theory of Pavlovian conditioning: variations in the effectiveness of reinforcement and nonreinforcement. In A.H. Black and W.F. Prokasy (Eds.), *Classical conditioning II: Current research and theory.* New York: Appleton-Century-Crofts.

Rheingold, H.L., Gewirtz, J.L., and Ross, H.W. (1959). Social conditioning of vocalizations in the infant. *Journal of Comparative and Physiological Psychology,* **52**, 68–73.

Richman, G.S., Reiss, M.L., Bauman, K.E., and Bailey, J.S. (1984). Teaching menstrual care to mentally retarded women; Acquisition, generalization, and maintenance. *Journal of Applied Behavior Analysis,* **17**, 441–451.

Rincover, M. (1978). Sensory extinction: A procedure for eliminating self-stimulatory behavior in psychotic children. *Journal of Abnormal Child Pychology,* **6**, 299–310.

Ringdahl, J.E., Vollmer, T.R., Marcus, B.A., and Roane, H.S. (1997). An analogue evaluation of environmental enrichment: The role of stimulus preference. *Journal of Applied Behavior Analysis,* **30**, 203–216.

Rolider, A., Cummings, A., and Van Houten, R. (1991). Side effects of theraputic punishment on academic performance and eye contact. *Journal of Applied Behavior Analysis,* **24**, 763–773.

Rolider, A., and Van Houten, R. (1984). The effects of DRO alone and DRO plus reprimands on the undesirable behavior of three children in home settings. *Education and Treatment of Children,* **7**, 17–31.

Rolider, A., and Van Houten, R. (1985). Movement suppression time-out for undesirable behavior in psychotic and severely developmentally delayed children. *Journal of Applied Behavior Analysis,* **18**, 275–288.

Routh, D.K. (1969). Conditioning of vocal response differentiation in infants. *Developmental Psychology,* **1**, 219–226.

Russo, D.C., and Varni, J.W. (Eds.). (1982). *Behavior pediatrics: Research and practice.* New York: Plenum.

Sasso, G.M., and Reimers, T. (1988). Assessing the functional properties of behavior: Implications and applications for the classroom. *Focus on Autistic Behavior,* **3**, 1–15.

Seligman, M.E.P. (1970). On the generality of the laws of learning. *Psychological Review,* **71**, 406–418

Shore, B.A., Iwata, B.A., DeLeon, I.G., Kahng, S., and Smith, R.G. (1997). An analysis of reinforcer substitutability using object manipulation and self-injury as competing responses. *Journal of Applied Behavior Analysis,* **30**, 21–41.

Sidman, M. (1953). Two temporal parameters of maintenance of avoidance behavior by the white rat. *Journal of Comparative and Physiological Psychology,* **46**, 253–261.

Sidman, M. (1960). *Tactics of scientific research.* New York: Basic Books.

Sidman, M. (1966). Avoidance behavior. In W.K. Honig (Ed.), *Operant behavior, areas of research and application.* New York: Appleton-Century-Crofts.

Sidman, M. (1971). Reading and auditory-visual equivalences. *Journal of Speech and Hearing Research,* **14**, 5–13.

Sidman, M. (1986). Functional analysis of emergent verbal classes. In T. Thompson and M.D. Zeiler (Eds.), *Analysis and integration of verbal units.* Hillsdale, New Jersey: Lawrence Erlbaum.

Sidman, M. (1990). Equivalence relations: Where do they come from? In D.E. Blackman and H. Lejeune (Eds.), *Behaviour analysis in theory and practice: contributions and controversies.* Hove, Sussex: Lawrence Erlbaum.

Skinner, B.F. (1935). The generic nature of the concepts of stimulus and response. *Journal of General Psychology,* **12**, 40–65.

Skinner, B.F. (1938). *The behavior of organisms.* New York: Appleton-Century-Crofts.

Skinner, B.F. (1953). *Science and human behavior.* New York: Macmillan.

Skinner, B.F. (1956). A case history in scientific method. *American Psychologist,* **11**, 221–233.

Skinner, B.F. (1957). *Verbal behavior.* New York: Appleton-Century-Crofts.

Skinner, B.F. (1969). *Contingencies of reinforcement: A theoretical analysis.* Englewood Cliffs, New Jersey: Prentice-Hall.

Slifer, K.J., Ivancic, M.T., Parrish, J.M., Page, T.J., and Burgio, L.D. (1986). Assessment and treatment of multiple behavior problems exhibited by a profoundly retarded adolescent. *Journal of Behavior Therapy and Experimental Psychiatry,* **17**, 203–213.

Smith, R.G., Iwata, B.A., and Shore, B.A. (1995). Effects of subject- versus experimenter-selected reinforcers on the behavior of individuals with profound developmental disabilities. *Journal of Applied Behavior Analysis,* **28**, 61–71.

Snell, M.E. (Ed.) (1983). *Systematic instruction of the moderately and severely handicapped* (2nd ed.). Columbus, OH: Charles E. Merrill.

Sowers, J., Rusch, F.R., Connis, R.T., and Cummings, L. (1980). Teaching mentally retarded adults to time manage in a vocational setting. *Journal of Applied Behavior Analysis,* **13**, 119–128.

Spencer, H. (1878). *The principles of psychology.* New York: D. Appleton.

Spooner, F. (1984). Comparisons of backward chaining and total task presentation in training severely handicapped persons. *Education and Training of the Mentally Handicapped,* **19**, 15–22.

Sprague, J.R., and Horner, R.H. (1984). The effects of single instance, multiple instance, and general case training on generalized vending machine use by moderately and severely handicapped students. *Journal of Applied Behavior Analysis,* **17**, 273–278.

Stark, L.J., Knapp, L.G., Bowen, A.M., Powers, S.W., Jelalian, E., Evans, S., Passero, M.A., Mulvihill, M.M., and Hovell, M. (1993). Increasing calorie consumption in children with cystic fibrosis: Replication with 2–year follow-up. *Journal of Applied Behavior Analysis,* **26**, 335–350.

Stokes, T.F., and Baer, D.M. (1977). An implicit technology of generalization. *Journal of Applied Behavior Analysis,* **10**, 349–367.

Stokes, T.F., Fowler, S.A., and Baer, D.M. (1978). Training preschool children to recruit natural communities of reinforcement. *Journal of Applied Behavior Analysis,* **11**, 285–303.

Stool, S.E., and Beebe, J.K. (1973). Tracheostomy in infants and children. *Current Problems in Pediatrics,* **3**, 3–33.

Sturmey, P., Carlsen, A., Crisp, A.G., and Newton, J.T. (1988). A functional analysis of multiple aberrant responses: A refinement and extension of Iwata et al's (1982) methodology. *Journal of Mental Deficiency Research,* **32**, 31–46.

Sulzer-Azaroff, B., and Meyer, G.R. (1977). *Applying behavior analysis procedures with children and youth.* New York: Holt, Rinehart, and Winston.

Tawney, J., and Gast, D. (1984). *Single subject research in special education.* Columbus, OH: Charles E. Merrill.

Taylor, B.A., and Harris, S.L. (1995). Teaching children with autism to seek information: Acquisition of novel information and generalization of responding. *Journal of Applied Behavior Analysis,* **28**, 3–14.

Taylor, I., and O'Reilly, M.F. (1997). Toward a functional analysis of private verbal self-regulation. *Journal of Applied Behavior Analysis,* **30**, 43–58.

Taylor, I., O'Reilly, M.F., and Lancioni, G. (1996). An evaluation of an ongoing consultation model to train teachers to treat challenging behavior. *International Journal of Disability, Development and Education,* **43**, 203–218.

Terrace, H.S. (1963). Errorless transfer of a discrimination across two continua. *Journal of the Experimental Analysis of Behavior,* **6**, 223–232.

Thorndike, E.L. (1898). Animal intelligence. *Psychological Review Monograph Supplement*, No.8.

Thorndike, E.L. (1911). *Animal intelligence: Experimental studies*. New York: Macmillan.

Tierney, K.J., and Smith, H.V. (1988). The effect of different combinations of continuous and partial reinforcement on response persistence in mentally handicapped children. *Behavioural Psychotherapy*, **16**, 23–37.

Touchette, P.E., MacDonald, R.F., and Langer, S.N. (1985). A scatterplot for identifying stimulus control of problem behavior. *Journal of Applied Behavior Analysis*, **18**, 343–351.

Toulmin, S., and Goodfield, J. (1962). *The architecture of matter*. New York: Harper and Row.

Tustin, R.D. (1995). The effects of advance notice of activity transitions on stereotypic behavior. *Journal of Applied Behavior Analysis*, **28**, 91–92.

Ulrich, R.E. (1967). Pain-aggression. In G.A. Kimble (Ed.), *Foundations of conditioning and learning*. New York: Appleton-Century-Crofts.

Upper, D. (1973). A "ticket" system for reducing ward rule violations on a token economy program. *Journal of Behavior Therapy and Experimental Psychiatry*, **4**, 137–140.

Van Houten, R. (1993). The use of wrist weights to reduce self-injury maintained by sensory reinforcement. *Journal of Applied Behavior Analysis*, **26**, 197–203.

Van Houten, R., Axelrod, S., Bailey, J.S., Favell, J.E., Foxx, R.M., Iwata, B.A., and Lovaas, O.I. (1988). The right to effective behavioral treatment. *Journal of Applied Behavior Analysis*, **21**, 381–384.

Van Houten, R. and Nau, P.A. (1981). A comparison of the effects of posted feedback and increased police surveillance on highway speeding. *Journal of Applied Behavior Analysis*, **14**, 261–271.

Van Houten, R., Nau, P.A., MacKenzie-Keating, S.E., Sameoto, D., and Colavecchia, B. (1982). An analysis of some variables influencing the effectiveness of reprimands. *Journal of Applied Behavior Analysis*, **15**, 65–83.

Van Houten, R., and Rudolph, R. (1972). The development of stimulus control with and without a lighted key. *Journal of the Experimental Analysis of Behavior*, **18**, 217–222.

Verhave, T. (1959). Avoidance responding as a function of simultaneous and equal changes in two temporal parameters. *Journal of the Experimental Analysis of Behavior*, 1959, **2**, 185–190.

Vollmer, T.R. and Iwata, B.A. (1991). Establishing operations and reinforcement effects. *Journal of Applied Behavior Analysis*, **24**, 279–291.

Vollmer, T.R., Iwata, B.A., Zarcone, J.R., Smith, R.G., and Mazaleski, J.L. (1993). The role of attention in the treatment of attention-maintained self-injurious behavior: Noncontingent reinforcement (NCR) and differential reinforcement of other behavior (DRO). *Journal of Applied Behavior Analysis*, **26**, 9–26.

Vollmer, T.R., Marcus, B.A., and Ringdahl, J.E. (1995). Noncontingent escape as treatment for self-injurious behavior maintained by negative reinforcement. *Journal of Applied Behavior Analysis*, **28**, 15–26.

Wacker, D. (1999). Building a bridge between research in experimental and applied behavior analysis. In J.C. Leslie and D. Blackman (Eds), *Issues in experimental and applied analyses of human behavior*. Reno: Context Press.

Wagner, J.L., and Winett, R.A. (1988). Promoting one low-fat, high-fiber selection in a fast-food restaurant. *Journal of Applied Behavior Analysis*, **21**, 179–185.

Walsh, P. (1997). Bye-bye behaviour modification. In K. Dillenburger, M.F. O'Reilly, and M. Keenan (Eds.), *Advances in behaviour analysis*. Dublin: University College Dublin Press.

Warren, J.M. (1965). Primate learning in comparative perspective. In A.M. Schrier, H.F. Harlow and F. Stollnitz (Eds.) Behavior of nonhuman primates. New York: Academic Press, pp. 249–281.

Watson, J.B. (1913). Psychology as the behaviorist views it. *Psychological Review,* **20**, 158–177.

Watson, J.B. (1914). *Behavior: an introduction to comparative psychology.* New York: Holt.

Watson, J.B. (1930). *Behaviorism.* Revised Edition. Chicago: University of Chicago Press.

Williams, J.B. (1938). Resistance to extinction as a function of the number of reinforcements. *Journal of Experimental Psychology,* **23**, 506–522.

Wilson, P.G., Reid, D.H., Phillips, J.F., and Burgio, L.D. (1984). Normalization of institutional mealtimes for profoundly retarded persons: Effects and noneffects of teaching family-style dining. *Journal of Applied Behavior Analysis,* **17**, 189–201.

Wolery, M., and Gast, D.L. (1984). *Effective and efficient procedures for the transfer of stimulus control.* Unpublished manuscript, University of Kentucky, U.S.A.

Zener, K. (1937). The significance of behavior accompanying conditioned salivary secretion for theories of the conditioned response. *American Journal of Rsychology,* **50**, 384–403.

Zencius, A.H., Davis, P.K., and Cuvo, A.J. (1990). A personalized system of instruction for teaching checking account skills to adults with mild disabilities. *Journal of Applied Behavior Analysis,* **23**, 245–252.

AUTHOR INDEX

351

SUBJECT INDEX